THE SHIFT

THE SHIFT

WAR DIARY

Air-defense missile officer war diary: a day-by-day life
in a deadly "cat and mouse" game of air-defense combat
crew and attacking aircraft

Lieutenant Colonel Djordje Aničić

with

Mike (Mihajlo) Mihajlović & Mihailo Zoranov

MSM

THE SHIFT
War Diary
First published in Serbia 2009
First English language publication published in Canada in 2022 by
MSM publishing @ Slobodno Nebo Srbije
http://www.slobodnonebo.org.rs

Belgrade - Perth - Toronto

Copyright © Djordje Aničić

ISBN 978-1-7753953-3-1
The right of Djordje Aničić to be identified as Author of this work has been asserted by them in accordance with the Copyright, Designs and Patents Act 1988.

A CIP catalogue record for this book is available
from the Library of Canada.

Typeset & design by Mike (Mihajlo) Mihajlović, Canada.

Translation by Mike (Mihajlo) Mihajlović & Mihailo Zoranov

Printed and bound by Amazon.

Preface

In the history of warfare, there are many diaries written by ordinary infantrymen to military commanders, however, there is no book published in the English language covering the diary of a missile officer in the air-defense unit during wartime. This book is an attempt to correct that gap and bring to the reader first-hand experience of life in the missile battery with all that comes with it. The intention is to try to put the reader into the missile operator's shoes but not only in the missile guidance station but throughout the whole daily life on and off duty.

The book is based on the original war diary by Lieutenant Colonel Djordje Aničić, deputy commander of the 3rd missile battalion, which he wrote on daily basis during the NATO aggression on the Federal Republic of Yugoslavia - the last war of the 20th century. The diary covers every single day as well as an additional explanation that helps the reader to understand the overall situation in the society, military organization, roles of individual members, and enlighten the events which fell into obscurity and are still covered with some kind of mystery.

The author doesn't spare himself and the superior command and bitterly criticizes some of their decisions and the people involved, for example, drunkness in the Brigade Operation Center and orders to the crew to execute ridiculous tasks or avoiding the duties during the ,hottest' hours when the enemy airplanes are about the attack the battalion position. While other members of his shift and other teams tried to use any time off to catch some rest, the author spent considerable time taking meticulous notes about each day's events, conversations, and sometimes funny stuff as well as bitter ones.

There are plenty of names involved and going through the diary the reader gets familiar with some of them. The diary is also illustrated with original wartime photos. As a base, some of the material explaining the functions of the missile unit is borrowed from the book ,Shooting Down the Stealth Fighter' by the same authors.

We, the authors, hope that this book will allow a reader to dive into one unknown segment of warfare and help to understand how the life of an air defense missile unit and its members looks like.

Foreword

"The Shift" - war diary of Lieutenant Colonel Djordje S. Aničić

In defense of life and truth

"Only ignorant and unreasonable people can think that the past is dead and separated from the present by an impenetrable wall forever." The truth is, on the contrary, that everything that man thought, felt, and did was inextricably woven into what we think, feel and do today. To bring the light of scientific truth into the events of the past is to serve the present. "

Ivo Andrić (Yugoslav Nobel Prize Winner for Literature)

War diaries, memoirs, and autobiographies have always been important testimonies of the past for understanding and illuminating a time. War diaries are very important for national history, literature, but also always current and interesting for readers.

National literature and history would be impoverished if diaries or memoirs were taken away from them. And while imagination is allowed in literary works that describe wartime, war diaries are immediate and personal. The charm of diary writing is precisely in the truth of the narration. Narrations in war diaries are human, emotional, concise, and direct, which is the basic feature of a diary entry. For all the diaries, regardless of whether they were written by soldiers or officers, it is common that the historical event is viewed from the inside, from the position of the participants, and in real-time. I must emphasize that all war diaries are written by heart. Everything in them is a consequence of personal observation, experience, feelings, honestly to the end.

The focus of the war diary of Lieutenant Colonel Đorđe Aničić is his desire to preserve his memory and tear it from oblivion and hand over the truth to the future. The author expresses great love that the ordinary people, the members of the 3rd Air Defense Missile Battalion felt towards their homeland in the days of the NATO aggression against the Federal Republic of Yugoslavia (FRY) in 1999 besides all hardship they encountered. Reading the pages of the diary, we admire the courage and skill of the heroes born of necessity, to defend the skies of Serbia, to save their own and the lives entrusted to them.

The author does not spare the critics firstly himself than the people around him including the sharp critics of the military chain of command and the superiors which some decisions were made in a completely ignorant, sometimes alcohol-intoxicated manner.

The writer of the war diary is Lieutenant Colonel Djordje Aničić, a man with rich life and military experience. Lieutenant Colonel Aničić is one of the Serbian heroes who, in 1999, directly participated in the downing of the "Stealth" (often presented as an invisible for radar) American F-117A bomber. In this diary, he talks excitingly, truthfully, and comprehensively about the conflict between the missile technology from the 1960s, the Russian S-125 Neva (SA-6) missile system, and NATO stealth technology, during the NATO bombing of the FRY. But this is not just the story about one event, rather a comprehensive story of the life of the missileers and the relationships inside the unit and the unit with the upper echelons of the military hierarchy and bureaucracy as well as the presentation of the complex situation in society.

The book "The Shift", which is in front of the readers, whose publication has been delayed for a long time, arose from the need of the author to openly oppose the entries in it, as he says, F-117A, belongs to the missile team and not to the individual or individuals.

The war diary covers the period from Wednesday (24 March 1999) to Sunday (20 June 1999). The day-by-day activities of the 3rd Air Defense Missile Battalion during the NATO aggression on the Federal Republic of Yugoslavia are presented. From the first day of the bombing, NATO bombers and cruise missiles were opposed by the Yugoslav Air Force and Air Defense. During the NATO bombing of the FRY, on 27 March 1999, by the action of the 3rd Battalion S-125 Neva-M missile system, the pride of NATO, the American tactical bomber F-117A, was overthrown. "Night Hawk" had his wing bent. The Yugoslav Army is the first and only one in the world to officially shoot down a plane of this type and break the myth of its "invisibility". The downing of the "invisible" is inscribed in history textbooks.

The diary was written and published to preserve and defend the truth about the downing of the "Stealth". Reading the pages of the diary, readers understand all the challenges and complexity of the events faced by professional soldiers, but also have the personal experience of a missile crew member, duties, fears, expectations, and thoughts - live and fight another day. A methodical approach gives special value to diary entries.

Lieutenant Colonel Đorđe Aničić's war diary is a defense of the truth and represents an important source for reading events from the time of the NATO aggression in 1999. With its content, it provides us with a personal experience and an inside picture of the actions and operations during the NATO aggression. The events of the war from the point of view of the immediate participant are included, thus completing the mosaic of that important period of Serbian history. The book "Shift" should be read carefully, in order to understand and preserve the truth, to affirm the culture of remembrance, to understand courage and patriotism in the difficult and dramatic days of NATO aggression.

Bringing the light of truth into the events of the past from the time of the NATO aggression, the war diary "Smena" of Lieutenant Colonel Đorđe Aničić, serving the present and the future, teaches the truth to be remembered.

Due to all the above, I am very pleased to recommend to all future readers the war diary of Lieutenant Colonel Djordje Aničić.

24 March 2021

Vladica Tošić, MA

Historian and politicologist

Recension

Serbia's war with NATO was the first combined air-cosmic war in history because the system of waging and controlling war was in the cosmos. Our adaptive air defence addressed a very complex task in which the key was the experience from Iraq, which applied to the 3rd missile battalion.

In 78 days of the war, NATO Air Force conducted 38,004 combat missions over the FRY and used 23,614 air-launched weapons, weighing 6,303 tonnes (the explosive power of 3 nuclear bombs dropped on Hiroshima and Nagasaki) and 736 TOMAHAWK cruise missiles. 1,055 aircraft were engaged, out of which 700 US aircraft were used.

In the first two days, two massive strikes were carried out, lasting more than three hours each.

The efficiency of the Air Defense (AD) system by the world's expert analysis was 0.5%. Many aircraft were hit, but only 2 planes were shot down and fell in the FRY territory (F-117 A and F-16 CG), for which there is material evidence, and there are a lot of intelligence reports confirming that many more were damaged or crashed landed in the neighboring countries. The most important feature of the PVO system is its continuous functioning during all days of the war. Characteristics of the AD system and operators are:

- The courage, persistence, and stamina of the unit members.
- Proper leadership of the combat units, as a high level of operatioal and tactical composition training.
- The high combat readiness of the regiment, brigade, and battalions in the AD system, proven during the peacetime training and live-fire exercises in Russia.
- Implementation of a large number of completely new tactical and technical procedures in combat activities.
- Excellent field camouflage measures. Quick manoeuvre and changing fire positions.

One such unit was the 3rd battalion.

NEVA missiles have a range of 25km and the ability to fire at an altitude of up to 18km. NATO formations flew the most missions at altitudes of 5-10 km. However, only proper use of the system had confirmed hits, which is described in the book.

The battalion has implemented 5 completely new tactical and technical procedures in AD. The main creator of these actions was Djordje Aničić, who imposed them and as a result, planes were hit and downed.

- The use of radar radiation imitators to protect the unit during combat operations.

- Shortening the radiation time to less than 30sec in targeting, due to the use of Anti-Radar missiles by opponents (the 3rd battalion was targetted 22 times by these missiles, but not once was it hit or had any casualties. Protecting the guidance station with logs.

- Quick maneuver and possession of a large number of fire positions (22 times).

- Minimal engineering arrangement of fire positions to prevent unmasking.

S -125 M NEVA is the best AD missile system in recent history, which on the battlefield won over the most modern NATO aircraft from the late 20th century. The injustice was experienced by Djordje Aničić, the author of this book, even if he was one of the most deserving of the achieved results of the 3rd AD battalion. In his official notebook, Djordje wrote his war diary in addition to the many obligations he had during the war. I read the material cover to cover with great interest and relived 78 days of war with NATO, which raised my adrenaline a lot. I have known the author for decades as an officer with great moral values and an exceptional connoisseur of missile technique. Therefore, Without hesitation, I accepted to be an expert reviewer of the war diary. I highly recommend it to readers because it faithfully reflected the events of that difficult time.

Belgrade
09/24/2021

Colonel Veselin Pavlović

450th Missile Regiment commander

Table of content

The Author Lieutenant Collonel Djordje Aničić

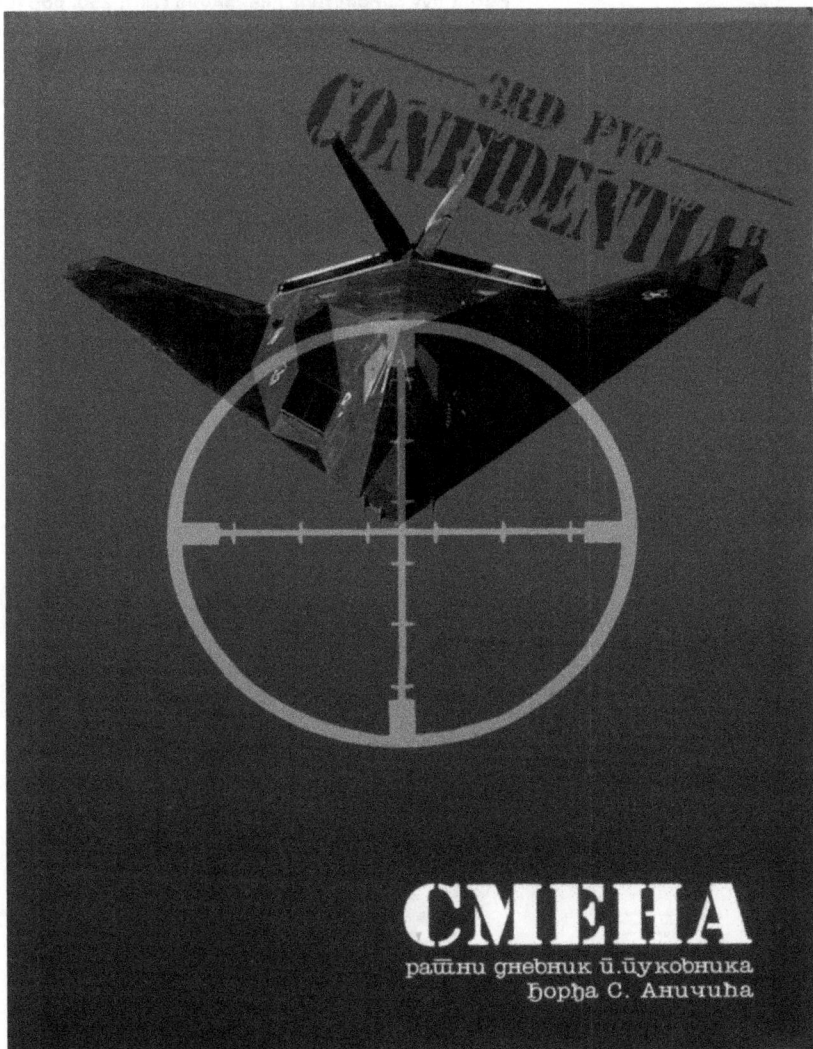

The Shift - first edition in the Serbian language (2009)

3rd Battalion combat path

(Нева) од 24. 03. до 10. 06. 1999 године
125 М1 «Нева») в период 24.03.-10.06.1999
) combat path from March 24 to June 10, 1999.

Табела уништених циљева
Таблица уничтоженных целей.
Table of destroyed targets

	1 - Шимановци Simanovci	6 - Карловчић Karlovčić	17 - Бечмен (2) Bečmen
Ватрени положај Огневая позиция Launching position	1 - Шимановци Simanovci	6 - Карловчић Karlovčić	17 - Бечмен (2) Bečmen
Датум и време Дата и время Date and time	27. 03. 1999. 20. 42'	02. 05. 1999. 02. 08'	20. 05. 1999. 06. 13'
Уништен цил. Уничтоженная цель Destroyed target	F 117A, Locheed AV-HO-806	F 16CG, Locheed Martin (General Dynamics) AV-555-19	B-2A, Spirit, Northrop
Азимут Azimuth β	270'	515'	180'
Даљина Дальность Du Distance	12 km	12 km	13 km
Висина Высота Нc Altitude	8 km	7 km	7 km
Брзина Скорость Vc Speed	200 m/s	300 m/s	200 m/s
Периметар Периметр Pc Perimeter	16 km	7 km	4.5 km
Уништен са Уничтожена с помощью Destroyed with	1 ракетом 1-ой ракеты 1 rocket	1 ракетом 1-ой ракеты 1 rocket	2 ракете 2 ракет 2 rockets

Датум поседања и напуштања ватрених положаја
Даты занятия и оставления огневых позиций
Dates of taking up and leaving the launching positions

3. Ракетни дивизион
3. Зенитный ракетный дивизион
3. Missile batalion

број номер number	подиција позиција position	поседата занятие taking up	напуштање оставление leaving
		datum, дата, date	
0	Јаково вп Jakovo ур	до 24. 03.	24. 03.
1	Шимановци Simanovci	24. 03.	27. 03.
2	Прхово 1 Prhovo 1	27. 03.	31. 03.
3	Огар 1 Ogar 1	31. 03.	04. 04.
4	Прхово 2 Prhovo 2	04. 04.	07. 04.
5	Попинци Popinci	07. 04.	11. 04.
6	Карловчић 1 Karlovčić 1	11. 04.	16. 04.
7	Деч 1 Deč 1	16. 04.	19. 04.
8	Бечмен 1 Bečmen 1	19. 04.	23. 04.
9	Петровчић 1 Petrovčić 1	23. 04.	25. 04.
10	Огар 2 Ogar 2	25. 04.	29. 04.
11	Петровчић 2 Petrovčić 2	29. 04.	30. 04.
12	Карловчић 2 Karlovčić 2	30. 04.	02. 05.
13	Дечаи виноград Dečki vinogradi	02. 05.	03. 05.
14	Мољавеиi Mihaljevci	03. 05.	10. 05.
15	Карловчић 3 Karlovčić 3	10. 05.	12. 05.
16	Соко салаш Soko Salaš	12. 05.	16. 05.
17	Бечмен 2 Bečmen 2	16. 05.	20. 05.
18	Ашања Ašanja	20. 05.	25. 05.
19	Карловчић 4 Karlovčić 4	25. 05.	31. 05.
20	Бољевци Boljevci	31. 05.	06. 06.
21	Деч 2 Deč 2	06. 06.	06. 06.
22	Сибач Sibač	06. 06.	04. 07.
23	Јаково касарна Jakovo kasarna	04. 07.	од 04. 07.

Аутори карте, Авторы карты, Authors of the map:
пуковник Ђорђе Аничић, подполковник Джордже Аничич, Beograd colonel Đorđe Aničić;
др Борис Вакањац, др Борис Вакањац, Dr Boris Vakanjac;
Растерска основа, Растровая основа, Raster basis:
SAS.Planet Release.151111-OpenStreetMap contributers CC-BY-SA
rendering OpenTopoMap.org, Map OSM Boundary (mapsurfer.net)
Рецензенти: др Саша Миланович и др Владица Ристић
Рецензенты: др Саша Миланович и др Владица Ристич
Reviewers: Dr Saša Milanović and Dr Vladica Ristić
Грб, Герб, : Немања Јовановић, Вук Миљуш
Coat of arms: Nemanja Jovanović, Vuk Miljuš
-2016-

Djordje (Sava) Aničić was born in 1958 in the village of Jazak, municipality of Irig, in the foothills of the Serbian mountain of Fruska Gora in the northern Serbian province of Vojvodina. He finished elementary school in Vrdnik and high school (mathematical department) in Aleksinac and Ruma. After high school he enrolled into the Air Force technical academy, air defence branch. After graduation, he started his first commission as a Sub-Lieutenant in Skopje (now in Macedonia) and later in Belgrade, serving in SA-3 air defence missile units. During his service he passed through all the duties in the missile battalion from platoon commander to battalion executive officer. On a few occasions he went to the former USSR for combat and live missile launching.

At the beginning of the NATO air campaign he was 3rd Battalion deputy commander with the rank of Lieutenant Colonel. He was one of the two commanders of the combat crew which downed F-117A on 27 March 1999. He holds the record for the officer with the most combat hours in the entire Yugoslav air defence.

After the war, during the reorganization of the Yugoslav military and the dismantling of the 3rd Battalion, he was demoted, despite being decorated by the president personally. His criticisms of the military establishment were drastically sanctioned after the war.

After spending less than a year in the lower rank, he was sent to the military academy to teach 'missile unit tactics'. He was retired on his own request in 2002 after a bitter struggle with the military establishment. After retiring he decided to publish the missile battalion diary which he kept day-by-day during the entire war in the form of book with the title 'Smena'. The book was published in the Serbian language in 2009. In it he disclosed all aspects of the combat both positive and negative, military organization, function and command structure. He contributes to the few Internet portals and often participates in TV documentaries and shows. He is also a member of the 3rd Battalion defence veteran's organization slobodnonebo.org.rs. he is also the coauthor of the book 'Shooting Down the Stealth Fighter'.

Introduction

The 3rd Battalion was one of eight active battalions under the command of the 250th Missile Brigade. It consisted of command, command and control platoon, technical battery, missile launchers battery, and support platoons. Battalion command consisted of commander, Lieutenant Colonel Dani Zoltan; deputy commander and executive officer (XO) Lieutenant Colonel Djordje Aničić; commander's aid for logistics Major Boško Dotlić; commander's aid for techniques and equipment, Major Boris Stoimenov; to mention few. In total, the battalion was around 200-men strong. In wartime, It comprised of a mix of reserve and regular personnel.

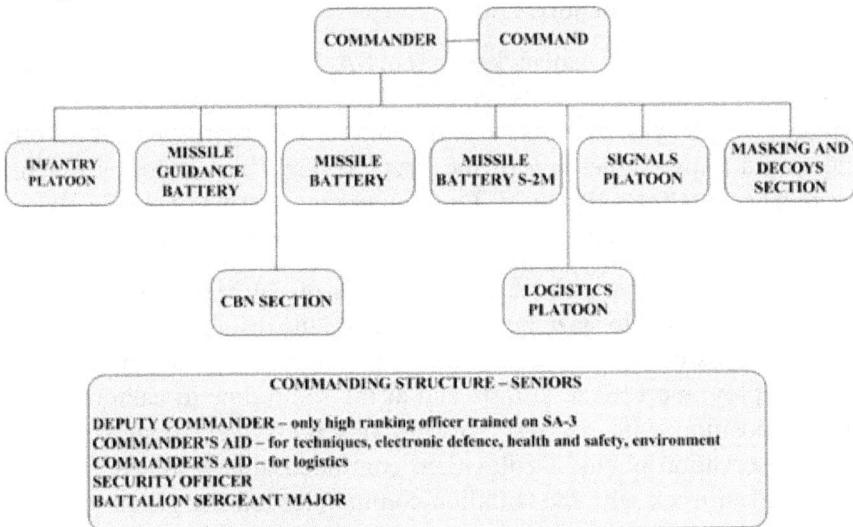

COMMANDER — COMMAND

INFANTRY PLATOON | MISSILE GUIDANCE BATTERY | MISSILE BATTERY | MISSILE BATTERY S-2M | SIGNALS PLATOON | MASKING AND DECOYS SECTION

CBN SECTION

LOGISTICS PLATOON

COMMANDING STRUCTURE – SENIORS

DEPUTY COMMANDER – only high ranking officer trained on SA-3
COMMANDER'S AID – for techniques, electronic defence, health and safety, environment
COMMANDER'S AID – for logistics
SECURITY OFFICER
BATTALION SERGEANT MAJOR

3rd Battalion organizational structure.

Command and control platoon's main role was to provide control over the other units and link with the brigade command. Technical battery responsibility was to provide technical support to the fire control center, radars, launchers and power supply for all equipment. Missile battery included four launchers with four missiles each, sixteen in total. The responsibility of the missile battery was to provide warehousing, transport, preparation for combat and installation on the launchers. The battery consisted of two platoons; each platoon was responsible for two launchers. Third battalion also had an automotive section with the trucks and support vehicles.

In the months before the NATO attack, 3rd Battalion was not in good shape. According to some of the parameters, it was the lowest ranking battalion in 250th Brigade, as of August 1998. The biggest problem was in equipment readiness. There were malfunctions in both missile channels and the target channel. The battalion was simply not combatworthy. Command structure changes were initiated, and the battalion got an infusion of 'fresh blood'. The existing commander, Lieutenant Colonel Dani, remained in his position, but new senior officers arrived. The new command initiated intensive training activities, which included extensive simulator training, combat crew coordination, procedures for different scenarios, etc, and by February 1999 the crews were brought to an acceptable state of 'war readiness'. Much of burden of this peacetime transformation fell onto the XO, who was the only senior officer trained and experienced on the SA-3 system. Besides the regulars, the reserves were also trained. Key to the training was personnel motivation. More detailed description of SA-3 system is given in the Appendix.

Lieutenant Colonel Aničić knew the SA-3 system like 'the back of his hand'. The only junior officer with SA-3 training was 2nd Lieutenant Crnobrnja, who was battalion security officer during the war. The other officers did know something of the SA-3 system, but as not as much as Aničić. The battalion relied on NCOs for operation and maintenance. Brigade command had SA-3 trained officers but they were not part of the battalion.

Third Battalion was in a state of readiness on 24 March when at 11:00 the order was issued to start the transition from the primary combat position (peacetime positions) to reserve combat position at Šimanovci. The order was to deploy one vehicle at time and at the same time to camouflage the primary position with decoys. Forward observers were deployed to the visual observation points. Deployment continued almost all afternoon. At 19:00 the last truck with the battalion commander left the primary position towing the last launcher ramp.

Base camp in the vicinity of Šimanovci was at the local community farm where most of the unit was based including the transportation section and maintenance. Before the war it was used as temporary lodgings for seasonal workers. The firing position was actually reserve SA-2 position. It was built as per the older system requirements, which were not very well suited for the SA-3 system. The firing positions had all power and communication cables preinstalled and the unit need basically only to 'plug in' the equipment. In the years before the war there were an intention to modify the location to suit SA-3, including the concrete bunker, but it was never finalized. The position

4

was well known to NATO mission planners. It was distinctive and highly visible in the flat terrain. Battalion HQ reasoned that because the position was so obvious the enemy would assume it was unmanned and not attack it, so they deployed in that position; curious logic perhaps, but that was HQ's gamble.

At 19:30 the combat readiness alarm was issued at the command of the Brigade. The primary position was in the meantime evacuated with just a few soldiers left there. 20:06 was the exact time the first missile hit the primary position. The first detonation was followed with a second one at 20:15, then the third at 20:20. The primary combat position was obliterated. In the meantime, all vehicles and ramps were relocated to the secondary position.

How Missile Battalion Works

Through this book the certain terminology will be repeated over and over again. The following is a brief explanation what are the main duties in the combat shift and what are the sequencies of work that the crew take to engage and hopefully down the target.

Roles and duties in an SA-3 missile battalion are defined and regulated through the operation and service manuals issued by the Ministry of Defence and Air Defence branch of the armed forces. It is essentially based on Soviet military doctrine with some minor local modifications. The subjects of these manuals are not much different from those of their western counterparts: combat service, organization, system equipment, communication, safety, etc.

To have a fully trained and functional missile system combat crew, years of training and exercising are necessary. For example, for an officer direct from military academy, to be fully familiar with every component of the system, a minimum of five years on the designated system is necessary. For a commander, ten years work on the system is a necessary minimum. As we saw previously, only Lieutenant Colonel Aničić had such experience. Other officers were trained for other systems but still had some experience on SA-3, thanks to intensive pre-war training and exercises on the AKKORD simulation and training system.

In peacetime conditions, in the missile battalions classified as 'A formations', there are always two combat crews fully trained in the following:

AKKORD – specially designed realistic combat simulator cabin (an identical copy of a UNK station) for simulation of different combat scenarios);

- Training with own air force during tactical exercises and combined tactical training, and

- Unit deployment from primary to reserve fire positions.

Typically the first combat crew includes the most experienced and trained staff. They consist of four officers, two NCOs and two enlisted servicemen. The peacetime formation of the combat crew consists of: shift commander - unit commander as a shift commander; the deputy commander (XO) who is the deputy shift commander; the missile battery commander (on the missile preparation station); missile guidance officer; manual tracking NCO on F1; and manual tracking NCO on F2. The two enlisted servicemen manned the manual plotting table and fire control plan as well as the shift register. The roles of each member of the crew will be explained in detail later.

In some peacetime exercises, depending on the location of the P-18 surveillance radar, and to reduce the number of people engaged, it was possible to consolidate the duty of the shift commander and the deputy commander in one role. In war conditions this was not acceptable, nor did SA-3 combat procedures allow it. Some of the missile battalions acted in this way with a reduced combat crew consisting of three officers, two NCOs and no enlisted men. One reason why this happened was that there were some 'older cadres' trained on SA-2 systems in which the manuals and rules of engagement did not consider the position of a deputy shift commander. We will solve this dilemma when we come to the consideration of the duties of the shift commander and the deputy shift commander. The designers of the SA-3 system established the formation position and role for the deputy shift commander to achieve the optimal number of combat crew. War conditions require a completely different arrangement. NATO aviation was active around the clock, which required continuous standby and rotation of people and equipment in combat readiness No. 1 and 2. Equipment was sometimes ON twenty-two hours a day. This required two shifts who, rotated every six or eight hours, were under enormous psychological and physical strain.

In the 3rd battalion, the first combat crew was commanded by Lieutenant Colonel Dani, the second crew was commanded by Battalion XO Lieutenant Colonel Aničić.

To save one life in the event of a missile strike on the station, one of the enlisted serviceman positions – fire control plan and register – was eliminated. That position was taken by a serviceman who controlled the manual plotting board. The manual plotting board was used only in the initial period of the war until NATO degraded the airborne surveillance and guidance system (VOJIN). The data about the situation in the air received from them had a few minutes delay which meant that it was basically useless by the time it was received in the battalion command center. In those few minutes, the situation could change drastically. The brigade commander insisted at the beginning of the war that the station and all its subordinate units must be manned continually and to report what they saw to the plotting board. This mistrust irritated the combat service. Very soon after the battalions got hit by the HARM missiles or laser guided bombs from the SEAD groups, this practice was terminated. Soon after that the other enlisted positions in the power generation station and P-18 radar were eliminated too. Since then, up to the end of the war, the fire control station was manned by only four officers and two NCOs. The power supply station and P-18 radar were not manned during combat engagement, but the operators were very close in case their presence in the station was necessary. This reorganization and reduction of people exposed to enemy fire reduced casualties in some battalions.

The 3rd Battalion has an impressive war record: during the 78 days of combat, the unit changed combat position 22 times. Its engineering section built eleven new combat positions. It was targeted by 23 anti-radiation missiles, remains of which were found. It is possible that it was targeted more but missile fragments were not found. Not a single missile ever hit any object and not a single battalion member was killed or injured. It is the only unit in the 250th Brigade with this record. It made two confirmed kills: one F-117A and one F-16CG which crashed in Serbian territory. During the night of 19/20 May a very large aerial target was hit, and although there is no material evidence that it crashed in Serbian territory, there is much to indicate that it was a large aircraft. At the time, the only three large aircraft used in the bombing of Yugoslavia were B-2, B-1B and B-52.

Applying the rules and manuals of engagement, with some field innovations and modifications at the insistence of the battalion XO, the combat roles of every crew member were clearly defined and not a single time did the battalion lose the connection with brigade command, properly informing them about the situation in the designated area. They never unnecessarily exposed themselves to the enemy and also were always aware of the positions of their own airplanes in the designated airspace and in the vicinity of Batajnica military airport and Surčin civilian airport.

As we have seen, the battalion has three stages of readiness.

Readiness No. 1 means that all equipment is powered and at least two missiles are in position ready for launch. The missile station and other equipment is tested for functionality. The shift commander then reports that the battalion is at full readiness with two guidance channels and in combat readiness with two, six, eight or more missiles. All communication goes through landlines.

Missiles in firing positions can be held in the following positions:

- Transport position on PR-14 vehicles
- Loading position
- Duty position - on the 5P-73 launching ramp
- Combat position on the launching ramp

In the combat position to transfer the missile from 'stand by' to readiness for launch an interval of at least 30 seconds is necessary. Command transfer is executed from the UNK with the button switch. In this regime, the maximum duration for the missile to be ready for launch is 25 minutes, after which the system automatically turns it off. There is an embedded system restriction that the missile must be 20 minutes in 'off' mode before it can be transferred again to the 30 second regime. One cycle of missile preparation includes 25 minutes in 'ready for launch' position and 20 min in 'off' position. After that the cycle starts again. There is the possibility that in case of emergency the missile can be turned on in the launch position; that is regulated in the manuals.

Readiness No.2 means that the crew are in combat positions; the equipment is powered but the manual switches are in the 'off' position; the temperature of the oil and coolant must be kept higher than 37°C.

Readiness No. 3 means that the crew is in base camp with 15 minutes readiness. That means that the crew must be ready to get into position, test equipment functionality and report that it is in readiness for combat within 15 minutes.

'Ready for launch' is when the brigade assigns the target to the battalion or, in the case of the sudden appearance of a target in the assigned sector, that missiles are ready for launch. It is basically the same as readiness No. 1 except that in this case at least four missiles are ready for immediate launch on two different launchers. Missiles are turned onto readiness No. 1 at 3-5 seconds intervals about thirty seconds before the functionality checking of the station is finished.

'Rapid readiness for launch' from readiness No. 2 is executed in the same way as readiness No. 1 with the exception that the functionality of the station is performed until the fire control radar is turned 'on' at high voltage which then turns 'off' the functionality check. The fire control radar then immediately starts to search for the target.

Because there is a timeframe restriction for how long missiles can be in 'ready to launch' mode, it is crucial for the commander to determine when and how missile readiness is distributed. The last thing that the commander wants is to have a target inside the engagement envelope but no ready missiles on the launchers. The 'golden rule' is not to put the missile into launching readiness unless the target is within the engagement zone.

Combat Crew - The Shift

The role of every member of the combat crew is crucial and every member has a predetermined role. The positions are as follows:

- Combat shift commander – Fire Control Officer
- Deputy combat shift commander – Deputy Fire Control Officer
- Battery commander
- Missile guidance officer
- Manual tracking operator on F1
- Manual tracking operator on F2
- Manual plotting board operator
- Fire control plotting board operator and shift clerk

Every workplace has a determined role and not all positions are engaged at the same time. Commands and reports overlap and for a well-trained and synchronized crew that is not a problem. The goal is that within 25-27 seconds the aerial target must be engaged and downed otherwise the unit can be targetted with anti-radiation missiles.

Missile system operators positions (front to back) – manual tracking operator, missile guidance officer, battery commander, manual plotting operator.
(Source: Bojan Dimitrijević, Jovica Draganić - 250. raketna brigada PVO)

Combat Shift Commander

The working position of the shift commander is in front of the detached

P-18 radar screen (VIKO) which is on his right-hand side (Figure 8-28). His workplace is about 32 cm higher than the other crew members' work stations. This allows the shift commander to have an unobstructed view to the rest of the cabin, excluding the position of the manual tracking operator on F1. Behind the commanders back there are electronic blocks that control the missile launchers. The commander's position is intentionally designed this way so that the deputy shift commander also has an clear view of the detached P-18 radar screen. The rules direct that at least the battalion commander, battalion deputy commander (XO) and missile battery commander must be fully trained on the SA-3 system. The 3rd Battalion had two trained crew commanders – the battalion commander and the XO. The missile battery commander was not fully trained as a crew commander. As the battalion commander was often absent because of other obligations, the battalion logistics officer was trained for the duties of the shift commander. He was not checked by the brigade command, but he was fully trained and with a lot of experience on SA-2. He was partially familiar with SA-3.

The combat shift commander must command as per the directives of the combat procedures manuals and fire control manuals which includes:

VIKO - surveillance radar screen. Typical positions of the fire control officer (shift commander) and deputy shift commander are in front of this screen. In some station it is located deeper in the station while in the 3rd battalion it was located right at the entrance.

- Control of airspace through the detached surveillance radar

11

(VIKO) screen from the P-18 radar

- Issues orders for target search, starts and stops the search in the designated sector taking into consideration time durations critical for operation

- Issues orders for tracking the designated target; issues order to launch missiles; determines missile guidance methods, numbers of missiles, launch methods, warhead activations

- Keeps communication link with upper command

Combat Shift Deputy Commander

His work place is beside the shift commander on his left-hand side, right at the side entrance, directly facing the VIKO screen. He has an unobstructed clear and ergonomic view of the screen. Some of his defined roles include:

- Together with the crew commander controls the airspace through the VIKO screen; marks the potential target and assigns priorities using charts and nomograms (diagram representing relations between three or more variable quantities by means of a number of scales)

- Determines the primary target

- Commands the interior battalions' units - communications, guards, P-18 surveillance radar, power supply, radar emission imitator etc.

Battery Commander

The battery commander sits at the missile preparation station. The distance from this position to the shift commander's place is about 2 meters towards the middle of the command van and is the furthest officer position from the commander and deputy commander. In the first combat shift, that duty was performed by the battery commander and in the second shift it was the first missile battery platoon commander. His duties include:

- Follows orders issued by the commander or deputy commander

- Turns on and off high voltage at the fire control radar transmitter

- Turns on and off the fire control radar ('antenna-equivalent' switch),

- Commands/instructs the missile guidance officer to the assigned azimuth and angle to get target acquisition radar beam at the same point the surveillance radar detected the target. Commands may include left, right, up or down. Under his instruction the missile guidance officer, turning his azimuth and angle wheels, can scan the designated aerial sector on two levels.

- Determines possibilities for target engagement based on the circular indicator PKO (Figure 8-30)
- Determines which missile launcher will be used
- Prepares launchers
- Commands the missile section

The deputy commander and the missile battery commander are two different functions. They do not have the same duties.

Battery commander position with screen and command console.

When the command 'Azimuth 210, search!' is issued, the battery commander, looking at his UK-31 screen, starts to guide the missile guidance officer to turn the UNV antennas to the commanded azimuth (in this case azimuth 210). The commands may be right, left, up or down depending on which azimuth he directed his fire control radar. The exact position of the UNV the battery commander can determine based on the instrument scale located beneath the UK-31 screen or by the reading directly from the screen in front of him. If the position was azimuth 180 and he needed to direct to azimuth 210, the command is 'RIGHT, RIGHT!' As the missile guiding officer moves his wheels to the right, on the battery commander's UK-31 screen the line which starts from the middle of the screen (zero radiation emission line, in other words, emitter, missile battery) and ending at the periphery, shows movement from 180 to 210. When the antenna movement reaches 5-10 degrees before azimuth 210, the battery commander turns the switch 'ANTENNA-EQUIVALENT' to 'ANTENNA' and at that moment high frequency energy is radiated into space. He then reports to the shift commander: 'ANTENNA!'

With this action, the fire control radar is emitting into space and starts illuminating the area where the target is.

The battery commander continues to guide the missile guiding officer 'RIGHT, RIGHT' searching for the target up to azimuth 220. If the target is not acquired, he commands 'STOP, LEFT' until azimuth 200 is reached. That mean plus or minus 10 degrees left and right from the azimuth ordered by the shift commander.

If by any chance the target is not acquired in one sweep, he then commands the guidance officer 'UP!' which means sweeping the space at the same azimuth but at a different altitude. An experienced missile guiding officer will know how to sweep the area with 3-5 wheel turns even without commands in the shortest possible high frequency emission time. Every time the battery commander sees on his screen the line pass over the target and there is a blip he must warn the guidance officer with: 'YOU HAVE TARGET!' An experienced battery commander will do that routinely. Sub-Lieutenant Nikolic, fresh from the academy, was not experienced.

If high frequency radiation is emitted for too long there is a real danger that the position of the radar may be detected and an anti-radiation missile launched.

Missile Guiding (Guidance) Officer

The missile guidance officer is positioned on the left-hand side of the battery commander. His duties include:

- During combat engagement acts as per commands issued by the shift commander and battery commander
- In passive regime performs the controls of the designated sector
- Transfers the UNK station into the combat regime
- Acts as ordered by the battery commander searching for the target turning the two wheels on azimuth and angle (elevation) 3-5 clicks left-right or up-down,
- Reports to the shift commander on the detected and acquired target
- Tracks the target distance
- Commands the manual operators on F1 and F2 in manual tracking mode.
- Performs the missile launch. Reports target acquisition, guidance and hit or miss
- Assesses the results

In the first combat shift this duty was performed by the assigned missile guidance officer. In the second shift this position was assigned to the commander of the transmission platoon from the missile guidance battery.

Behind the missile guidance officer there is an empty space where it is only possible to stand during the combat engagement. This space during peacetime training was often used by the senior officers of the brigade or military control bodies during assessments and evaluations.

The missile guidance officer acts as ordered by the battery commander and his main task is to 'overlap' the target on his two UK-32 screens. The goal is to get the target into the cross of the horizontal and vertical markers. Experience and practice play a great role and can save vital seconds. The crew commander must stop the search if it is taking too long. If the commander doesn't do it then the deputy commander must issue that order. In short, time management is essential for survival.

The SA-3 system requires simultaneous manipulation of the three metal wheels (Figure 8-31). Hand coordination and speed are key. Captain Muminovic was not experienced at working with the three wheels at the same time: azimuth, elevation and distance – and it took him longer to acquire the target. We saw that he had acquired the target by the third attempt and at that time he was able to track it.

By the clicking of the wheels, the commander may determine the situation. Manual tracking operators on their screens also see the target. When the

Missile guidance officer position with screen and command console.

guiding officer pushes the wheels for himself and commands 'TRACK MANUALLY!' he transfers the tracking to the manual tracking operators who then track the target. Although the operator on F2 can acquire the target on his screen, the guidance officer can transfer tracking if he has it.

On the block UK-62 in front of the guiding officer the lights 'RS F1' and

Tthe look of the screens during the missile approach to the target.

'RS F2' are illuminated.

Manual Tracking Operator F1

This NCO position is right behind the missile guidance operator. It is located in a 'cavity' off the central passage in a very tight space. In the first shift it

Manual tracking operator Fi screen and controls.

was the system operator who was also tracking operator from the missile guidance battery. In the second shift it was the system operator (Figure 8-33). His duties include:

- Manually tracking the target as ordered by the missile guidance officer

- Reports to the missile guidance officer on tracking conditions

Manual Tracking Operator F2

This position is located beside the shift and deputy shift commander. On his right-hand side is the missile guidance officer. With a half turn he can see the VIKO screen.

His duties include:

Manual tracking operator F2 station. At the top of the picture is a TV screen for visual optical tracking in passive mode.

- Assess the optical visibility on the television optical system (VPU-44)

- Manually track the target as ordered by the missile guidance officer

- Report to the missile guidance officer on tracking conditions.

When the missile guiding officer switch the tracking to the manual operators, on their stations the switch "Peredacha na RS", which is original Russian designation and mean "Manual tracking transfer" is illuminated on the blocks UK-68. Both F1 and F2 operators must push the button "VKL RS" to activate the manual tracking (Figure 8-34, Figure 8-35).

Turning their wheels their vertical markers must be positioned over the target centre. With this, they established the conditions for the missiles launch.

Manual Plotting Board Operator

This is an enlisted position. He is positioned a few meters from the shift commander, behind the 1.5 x 1.5 m transparent Plexiglas plotting board. His working position takes almost the whole width of the station. His main duty includes:

Plot the aerial situation as per information received from the VO-JIN service or as per information received from the battalion's own surveillance radar (P-18). Information is plotted in mirror so that the shift commander can see it in normal view.

A challenge of this position is that the enlisted man must be capable of writing numbers in mirror writing. When the shift commander sees the board and the target is within the engagement zone he may order the target to be engaged. By modern standards, this manual plotting board is obsolete and no modern air defence missile system now uses it.

Fighting Sequences

Once the surveillance radar from the brigade detects the target and assigns it to the battalion or the battalion detects the target with their own surveillance and tracking radar, either under direction from the brigade post or independently, the shift commander issues the order to the battery commander to search with the engagement and fire control radar in the direction of the target and its estimated height. That is the meaning of command 'Azimuth (such and such)...Search.' At that moment, the engagement and fire control radar is turned on and high frequency energy emits into the space in the direction of the target. The target is illuminated with that energy. At the same time as the energy illuminates the target, the receiver at the target may detect that it is 'caught', and typically the audio signal accompanied with a flashing light informs the pilot that he is 'in the radar sight'. Energy can also be detected by other airplanes in the vicinity.

Typical Soviet-style combat engagement rules and manuals require that

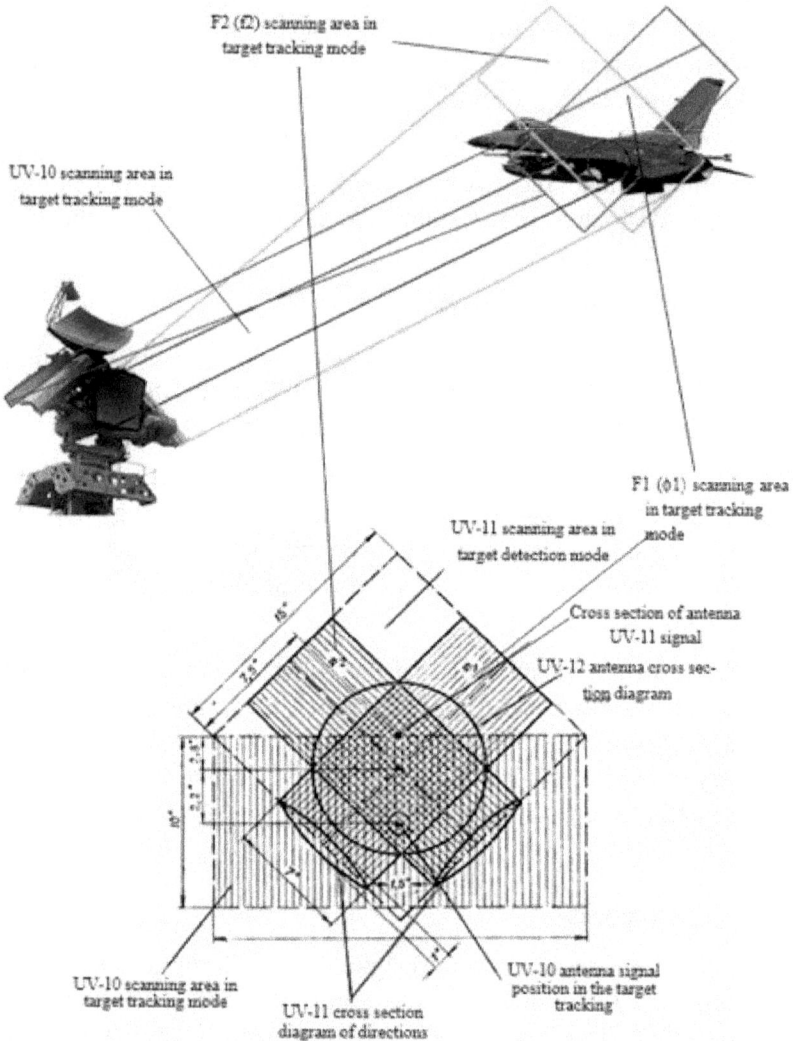

F2 (f2) scanning area in target tracking mode

UV-10 scanning area in target tracking mode

F1 (φ1) scanning area in target tracking mode

UV-11 scanning area in target detection mode

Cross section of antenna UV-11 signal

UV-12 antenna cross section diagram

UV-10 scanning area in target tracking mode

UV-11 cross section diagram of directions

UV-10 antenna signal position in the target tracking

Fire control radar SNR-125 emission zones and interlocking diagram.

the engagement of the target shall be at the furthest zone of destruction. The disadvantage of this is that the whole procedure extends, the target has a greater chance of knowing it is being tracked, and it can then perform counter-missile maneuvers thus lowering the chance of a hit. Also, if the target is equipped with anti-radiation missiles such as HARM it can shoot at the radar. The speed of an anti-radiation missile may be higher than the speed of the SAM missile, so there is probability that the radar will be hit before the guided missile reaches the aircraft.

Because of this, it was a wise tactical decision of the crew to let the target get deeper into the destruction zone. For example, if the effective range of NEVA is 25 km, the optimal distance for probable destruction is half that, 12-13 km. The high frequency energy emission of the engagement and fire control radar is for only a limited period of time, 5-6 seconds, which reduces the time for an anti-radiation missile to acquire and hit the radar. The Low Blow is designed to acquire targets using only bearing and range inputs from an external 2D acquisition radar, such as a P-12/18 Spoon Rest or P-15M Squat Eye. Third Battalion has only P-18 radar. When acquiring an aerial target, the Low Blow radar head is rotated to the target bearing and the UV-10 antenna scanning feed engages to produce a pencil beam 1° wide swept in elevation.

During target acquisition, the pencil beam of the UV-10 antenna scans a 10° sector vertically. The maximum range for target detection is 80 km. During target tracking, the pencil beam of the UV-10 antenna illuminates the target and measures its range. The two wide-beam UV-11 antennas receive the target, and angle of missiles (F1, F2). The maximum range for target tracking is 50 km. Two main range modes can be selected: 80 km and 40 km. In 80 km mode, only half of the electromagnetic impulses are sent, as they have to travel twice the range compared to 40 km mode.

Once the target is acquired the Low Blow is switched into tracking mode, using the UV-10 antenna to transmit, the UV-12 to receive for ranging, and the scanning UV-11 chevron receiver antennas for angle tracking. The radar head is mechanically steered in azimuth and elevation to maintain track.

Russian doctrine in the presence of heavy jamming was often to cease emitting and use the scanning receiver to effect angle tracking of the jammer, acquire the target with the TV telescope, and perform a range unknown missile shot against the jammer in CLOS mode.

Due to the addition of a clutter canceler and analogue MTI circuits, the Low Blow has significantly better clutter rejection performance than the earlier Fan Song radar used in SA-2. Low altitude capability is cited as low as 20 meters.

The command 'Equivalent' is to turn off the high frequency energy emission, but not to turn off the radar. This means the system keeps the equivalent load but the energy is redirected and effectively 'encapsulated' into the system and turned into heat. The heat generated means that there is still some energy emission which could be detected by an anti-radiation missile. The command 'Get the high down' means that the high voltage is turned off but the emitter is still working in normal mode but there is no high energy emission. It is the role of battery commander to work on this on his UV-61 station.

Manual operators on F1 and F2 guide the missile on F1 and F2 levels. In search and guiding regime there are two standard levels - azimuth and elevation. When the command to start manual tracking is issued, this is done on levels F1 and F2. They are positioned at 90° relative to each other and 45° related to the surface.

The radar imitator starts emitting a few seconds before the fire control radar, on the same frequencies, and continues to do so during the entire fire sequence. It is turned off few seconds after the fire control radar is turned off or in the 'equivalent' mode. This provides additional protection for the UNK because an anti-radiation missile may pick up the emission from the imitator and divert from the UNK.

The disadvantage at that time was that the radar imitator crew needed to manually turn the imitator to the designated azimuth as per order from the UNK. It would be way better if the movement of the imitator was synchronized with the movements of the radar antenna. At that time the battalion had to make the best of what was available.

What is of the crucial importance for any missile unit is the power supply. All is useless without power. The SA-3 system is supplied with 200 kW from two diesel generators. During combat, both generators are connected in parallel providing dual supply as fail-safe.

Immediately After Engagement

Immediately after the crew observed the hit and disintegration of the aircraft, the engagement and fire control radar was turned off. Standard procedure calls for immediate evacuation of the existing position and relocation to the previously chosen alternative. UNV S-125 engagement and fire control radar and tracking surveillance P-18 radar does not have any ability to recognize what kind of airplane is in the air. It is just a blip on a radar screen and for the missile crew it is a target. No exact shape can be determined, no type, just the size because of the reflection. For the crew, that was the target that was tracked, engaged and destroyed according to the rules of combat engagement.

March 1999

The war is imminent… Tension is in the air…

Today we are moving out. We are off combat readiness at 11:00. Somber atmosphere… "Million" things to do, and waiting the first bombs to fall… most likely tonight, as the dark fell…

What we have to do immediately is to:

- Prepare for march with two launch ramps. March with individual vehicles, immediately after transitionig the assets from the combat to marching configuration.
- Prepare everything for manning a reserve combat position in the region of village of Šimanovci.
- Pack things - everyone on their level and by basic units.
- At the place of key assets, after their withdrawal, set up dummy assets.
- Distribute to commanders the list of all reservists per unit.
- Use a decontamination water tank as a drinking water tank at the new firing location.
- Organise theguard - consult the commanders of the basic units.

Major Milorad Roksandić, the missile battery commander, will order an officer for the guard duties and a young conscripts for two guards and handlers for guard dogs. The security guard should be organized by observers. A total of seven people.

- Bus driver Lukić to transport the troops to a new position.
- Bring the typewriter to the operation office. Take the computer later.
- Also, carry warnings related to danger assessments and instructions from the mobilization room.
- Determine the duty officer and his assistant in the camproom and take the daily command, as well as the command and reporting keys for the second quarter and the worksheet for the month of April.
- Keep the Operational Diary on predefined issues.

At 12.15, the visual observation stations (VOSt) in the responsible sector need to be engaged, said Colonel Dragan Stanković, the 250th Air Defense Missile Brigade HQ chief.

By pre-defined plans and technical means, Sergeant Zoran Tepavac went with the necessary people to the task. This crew consisted of:

Željko Jaćić, sergeant, an NCO in the missile battery,

Predrag Manić, a soldier from the reserve,

Sasa Civrić, a soldier from the reserve,

Davor Crepuljar, a soldier from the reserve,
Dejan Mitrović, a soldier from the reserve.

At 16:25, I called the brigade mobilization department and asked what to do with the mobilization documentation. Sergeant Goran Mihajlović responded and after consulting with the officer in charge of the mobilization station said that we carry with us what we need, and to lock the rest in the safe box in the mobilization room.

We waited long for Sergeant Tepavac to report. He set the airspace visual observers to two locations. Lieutenant Colonel Dani, our battalion commander, and Sub-Lieutenant Darko Nikolić left the combat position around 19:00. Their vehicle, with the assets, was the last one to leave the site. They towed the missile launcher ramp.

About 19:30 from the Brigade Command was announced: "Airborne danger!" I am reporting this to the commander of the guard, sergeant Miroslav Denčev, who remained at the combat position with seven other soldiers. I explained to him what he should do. By his voice, I felt that he was worried and afraid (who wouldn't be when the war is imminent?).

At 20:05, Major Boris Stiomenov, assistant commander for the engineering support (battalion engineer), Radisav Jović and Slavko Varga, left the barracks. Major Boško Dotlić, assistant commander for the logistics, Warrant Officer Mića Mijalković, the supply officer and I, with the officers and soldiers from the logistics unit, remained waiting for Tepavac to return from the road.

At 20:06, the first detonation was heard from the first combat position direction on the road village Jakovo - vilage Boljevci. We run from the Jakovo barracks building and observed in the direction of the position. We did not see the glare, but we felt the intense shaking of the ground.... That was it... War broke out!...

The engineering support section consisted of Vukosav Žugić, Senior Sergeant Milan Barvalac, master mechanic Milenko Golubović and private Maljković, moved towards the reserve combat position Šimanovci around 20:15.

The FAP truck broke down at the beginning of the pig farm, on the outskirts of Jakovo. Here we left Žugić and mechanics Golubović to repair it. At this moment there was a powerful and glittering detonation at the combat position. Another detonation erupted at the instance of our turn to the road to Bečmen. It was clear that the aggression started and that we were the target of the first attack. We were concerned for our people on guard duty, who remained at the combat position.

Thursday, March 25

The equipment was placed on the reserve combat position in Šimanovci. I had the task of setting up the rear echelon units at the agricultural farm in Šimanovci and ensuring the placement of vehicles in hangars and accommodation for the people. Then I took the people of the lightweight, man-portable, shoulder fired, low altitude, air-defence system (MANPAD) "Strela – 2M [1]" unit intended for Prhovo, placed it there and explained to the people their duties. I wrote down the telephone number for the communication with them. We have only one cell phone in battalion and radio communications are prone to jamming and "ear dropping" so good old wired phone line works the best for us.

The 3rd battalion peace-time position pre-strike (left) and post-strike (right). All equipment was relocated prior the attack.

Upon returning from Prhovo, I went to the combat position in Šimanovci, where the unit was transitioning the equipment under the illumination of vehicles headlights. I didn't like that because we are in war and exposed to any kind of observation. Immediately I ordered the commanders to turn off the headlights on the vehicles and transition their equipment under the illumination of the flashlights. The rumbling sound of remote detonations was reaching to us and we saw blazes in the distance – they bombed the Batajnica military air base and airport. Airplanes flew very high above us. The equipment was transitioned into the combat position. During the work on autonomous self-checks for correct operation of the missile equipment, Senior Sergeant Dragan Matić, the system operator and in the combat duty the operator of manual tracking and guidance, burst into the missile guidance cabin yelling; "Djole, the Tomahawks are pounding again." I ordered the crew to leave the cabin and get away from the equipment. I had in mind that the transition was done under the headlights and that we were probably detected and about to be attacked because we took the position they were aware of. They struck the primary positions, and there is no reason why not struck the reserve one. We were yet to do the orientation of the launching ramps and radar, to load the missiles and to establish a communication with the brigade command. The ramps and radar were transitioned into the combat configuration at around 04:00.

Lieutenant Colonel Dragovan Matijević, my classmate from the Military Academy, 250th Missile Brigade Assistant Commandant for information and moral, together with Lieutenant Colonel Drago Stojacić, also from the brigade command, have visited our primary combat position on their way back

1   NATO code name "SA-7b Grail", missile 9M32, Russian project name 9K32 *Strela-2*

from Progar. They visited the 5th Missile Battalion, under the command of Lieutenant Colonel Miroslav Noskov, which had moved into the region of the village of Progar. They could not enter our previous position because it was locked. The area was burning. There was increasing anxiety for the seven people who remained on guard duty, wondering if they were still alive. In the meantime, Lieutenant Colonel Zoltan Dani, our battalion commander, Lieutenant Boro Crnobrnja, battalion security officer, Sergeant 1st class, Dejan Tiosavljević, system operator, and Captain 1st Class Senad Muminović, the 1st platoon commander and missile guidance officer, went to the combat position in Jakovo. There, they found two destroyed missile warehouses with about 80 missiles. At the center of the combat position (the location of the fire control radar, as we call UNV), a crater about 5 meters wide and about 3 meters deep, of strictly cylindrical shape, was found. Damage to the bunker for the missile-launching cabin was minimal. Everything pointed to the laser marker and that the position was hit by a laser-guided bomb. The men, seven of them from the guard unit, were found in the shelter No. 2. towards the missile station's bunker. They were scared but unharmed. They felt as if they were sacrificed. The building for the guard and combat shift crew remained in place, but the windows were broken, and the door frame of the sleeping room for the commander of the duty combat shift was knocked out. TV was not damaged. The guard dog, Efa, who was on the guard next to the missile storage, remained alive, only visibly scared. There was electricity in the building, even at the point for the guards loading and unloading weapons. Not a single neon lamp was damaged.

What was left of the 5V27D missiles warehouse. The amount of destruction is huge. For the size comparison and the concrete thickness Senior Sergeant Matić (standing), is 190 cm tall.

Decoy SNR-125 (Low Blow) radar destroyed during the first attack on 24 March 1999.

About fifteen minutes after the arrival of our officers at the combat position at the exit from Jakovo village, Colonel Dragan Stanković (250th Brigade Chief of Staff) arrived with Lieutenant Colonel Drago Orić and a soldier driver. Stanković ordered Dani to continue the transitioning when he returns to Šimanovci. Only two people were left in the combat position now – sergeant Denčev and Milić, soldier from the reserve.

We tried all day to establish a civilian connection at the command post in the UNK cabin, because there was no other communication with the superior command. Danny's mobile phone worked on and off. The equipment was camouflaged, vehicles sheltered in a safe place, and people provided with accommodation.

That night, around 20:30, the owner of the Arkom hardware store from Šimanovci, Zoran Armuš, provided us with the Belgrade area code civilian telephone number. He used his Belgrade connection, in a very simple and "no brainer" manner, "God, where do we live and what we do?" I wondered. "Who else in this country is thinking about the defense and how?"

Around 20:00, at the battalion command post in Šimanovci (in the UNK missile guidance cabin), Lieutenant General Ljubisa Veličković (who had been demoted from the position of the Commander of the Air Force) arrived accompanied by Colonel Vukosavljević, a former commander of the 250th Missile Brigade, now an officer in the Air Force Command responsible for missile defense issues. Dani tried to give him a proper report, but he acted totally unsoldierly. He seemed to be very angry. He arrived in "Mercedes", wearing a pilot jacket and some sweatshirt below, and ordinary pants. He was very lightly dressed for the circumstances. He asked us why we were

29

not working and not destroying the airplanes. Do we know how many airplanes flew over? We told him that we had just established communication with the Brigade and that we did not know the situation in the air. We tried to explain to him that we can't act independently and just keep our radars on until we get a different order. He does not have a clue about the nature of our business. I recalled that on one of the meetings he said that in the event of war, he would command the aviation from the fighter airplane and he would be able to find the missile operators at the Zeleni Venac (well known fruit and vegetable market) in Belgrade. I came to ask him what the aviation is waiting for and what is he doing among us now. Did his pilots return from Kopaonik[2] and whether they sufficiently rested[3]. They give importance to themselves in peace times and entertain the people on air shows, and when the war comes, then all eyes are turned onto the Air Defense. And they were trained, as we were, primarily for the war. Veličković was not liked by the people, that could be seen from everything. As if we were guilty of war and the unobstructed roaming of NATO aviation towards the targeted objects. Colonel Vukosavljević justified us, saying that we should not work without the permission of the Brigade. They moved to the "Mercedes" and went to try to find the command post of the 250th Brigade.

We got Readiness No.1 (the assets switched on, people are on the working stations and everything is ready for the combat) and Dani with his shift stayed manned the equipment, and I went to the camp with the another shift. We drove our TAM 150 truck without the lights turned on, until we arrived at the road Šimanovci - Prhovo. Just before we were about to get onto the road, the car came in and headed towards our position. I left TAM to see who that was. They were General Veličković and Colonel Vukosavljević in their "Mercedes" again. He asked me where we are going. I told him that we are going to the camp, and that Dani, with one shift, had stayed on the equipment. I felt and was sure that he was not quite clear where to look for the Brigade. They returned to call again from our phone, because they did not find the command post of the 250th Brigade nor its commander Colonel Miroslav Lazović. They lit the lights on the "Mercedes" and went towards the combat position. Did the general think that he was demasking us using his headlights to illuminate the road to our position?! He was not cold at all in his car – as the Mercedes is well heated.

Upon arriving at the camp, we listened to the news and saw and heard of many objects being targeted and destroyed. Practically, we did not know about the explosions and the effects of their destruction. The theory is one thing, and the practice is completely different. It's a war, and that's a skill. This kind of warfare has to be learnt, and in this respect, we were greenhorns, aware of our huge technical inferiority. Increasing anguish just seems to be seeping into the people.

---

2   A prominent mountain ski resort, and relatively expensive for ordinary people.

3   Air force pilots' roster included two weeks mandatory high-altitude recreational leave every six months

At 02:00, as the combat shift commander, I took my shift to the command post on the combat position to replace Dani and his shift. I was more tired than before, deprived of sleep, dirty and war inexperienced. The only thing that was occupying my mind was the realisation that we must be quick, very careful and tactically wise while trying to do something. It was a matter of seconds and a lot of knowledge concentrated in that short time. In less than 30 seconds of the synchronous operation of the six officers and NCOs in the shift, it was required to shoot down the plane without being hit by an anti-radar missile. Practically, we needed to halve the firing cycle time, relative to that stipulated in the Instructions for Combat Work and Procedures that we used in the peacetime. This was the cat and the mouse game. It was crucial that everyone did his part of the job. Teamwork was the only way. Everyone was dealing with his own thoughts and feelings. I remembered Danka, my partner after breakup of my marriage and divorce. I missed her. She loves me and cares for me. What was the day of the war? We counted aloud. From the Wednesday morning, to that day, we had slept only a few hours. My job was miserable. I studied to wear boots... I had not washed my face yet, I felt the stench of my sweat, my legs were in the water. My boots were brand new, and yet they stench of sweet. There was mud between my toes. Time was passing and I, the combat shift commander, like in some kind of trance, observe the uniform rotation of the surveillance radar screen time-base. The brigade operation center command was encouraging us with the news that Lieutenant Colonel Bacetić, the battalion commander from Mladenovac with his shift, had downed a plane. At the crack of dawn, we started working to make operational the imitator of the radar radiation emission. We had cables for about 500 meters from the centre of the combat position. That cable length was insufficient to put the imitator as far away from the command post as the higher command envisaged. Fuck the military which did not have a cable, and you have to fight against the whole NATO pact...

I ordered the commander of the signals platoon, reserve Lieutenant Miodrag Stojanović, to go to the village of Kupinovo, to the forest farm, and to provide at any cost at least 50 acacia logs, 4.5-5.0 meters long and 30-45 centimeters in diameter. The trunks must be raw [4]. They provide ideal protection against "HARMs" – anti-radar missiles. We would pile the trunks around the command post (missile guidance station) van and thus protect the people during combat work. This was my idea and initiative. The tree trunks were not stipulated in the brigade's asset base. No one in the brigade had ever applied them.

The combat shifts changed every 8 hours. Dani will be with his shift from 10:00 to 18:00. My shift will replace them again from 18:00 to 24:00 hours. After that, we will change every 6 hours. After my shift had finished, I was in the camp at 10.30. I got a message on the pager to urgently contact Major Srbislav Popović, an officer from the brigade command. From the farm (Agricultural Cooperative or Economy) I could only call a civilian line, and

---

4   Freshly cut trees are moist, therefore not brittle. Ideal for absorbing tungsten alloy fragments from HARMs.

they were overwhelmed. I had been trying for a long time from the farm and then from "Termomont" in Šimanovci, where they had three civilian lines, and I barely managed to get the number. Colonel Lazović, 250th brigade commandant, told me with a very excited voice that two "Mirages" (French fighter jets) are coming to our combat position and to inform the people to immediately leave the missile guidance station. I found a "Lada Niva" SUV and drove off to the combat position to inform Dani and people of the danger. Upon arriving at the position, I found the station empty, and Dani with his shift had pulled out the telephone line along the irrigation channel, where they sat about a hundred metres away from the station and watched the planes. I was surprised they were there, not manning the command post. I did not comment. I, and my combat crew, have never left the command post without order. I was relieved, but I took a lot of risk. The plane flew about 500 meters above the combat position and was clearly visible. We did not have SA-7 MANPAD on the combat position, as I had previously ordered. All SA-7 systems formed a circle around us, about 10-15 kilometers away. That was the first thing I had learnt in this war. We must have a point air-defense for the close protection of the combat position, regardless of the fact that these SA-7 systems were sent to the forward approaches. The original role of SA-7 systems was to safeguard transition of the combat assets from combat to marching configurations, and vice versa; since the units are most vulnerable then and unable to defend themselves. We suspected that the airplane had photographed our position and that we would be certainly targeted tonight.

It turned out later, as a miracle, that the plane did not notice the disposition of our combat assets on the field. Perhaps, he thought it was a dummy combat position. We were scared. The guidance station van became the place of expectation and anxieties.

Everything was camouflaged. My role in the combat shift is to be a fire control commander and to determine the target that we are going to engage and order the crew to bring their equipment to get the firing solution before I can issue an order to launch the missiles. During the NATO attack, two of our MIGs 29 took off and went to Tuzla direction, flying on azimuth 270[5]. The brigade operation centre command warned us not to engage them. We continually correlated the azimuth and distance so that there was no mistake. It was always very complicated to coordinate actions of fighter jets and missile defense units. A top-trained crew would let through own fighter jets into their zone of engagement and engage the hostile ones. I followed them. The crew had been wondering how it was possible that they were ours, when they went to Tuzla (Bosnia). At 70-80 km from us, the airplanes disappeared from our screen. Back, At the Brigade command center, we trust only Colonel Lazović, Colonel Stanković and Major Popović. The work of others (some of them are charlatans) in the brigade command was putting us

5   Mike Mihajlović: That morning was nice and sunny. I was at my position in Zrenjanin speaking with two of my guys when suddenly I heard approaching jet engines. In a second, I saw two double-tailed jet flying toward me and I recognized MiG-29. I yielded to my guys "Ours!" They flew barely 60-70 meters from us while changing direction. I could clearly see the pilot's white helmets through the canopy.

in danger: they did not have the slightest self-initiative in their work or clue, and they went by the book to a tee.

Saturday, March 27

Daily "routine" has been established. Combat shifts changes are regular - in 6 hours intervals. I was in the shift until 12:00. After my return to the resting area, I was called up by the courier from the brigade headquarters with the verbal orders to go to the three pre-determined decoy locations and perform the radar imitator emissions in the period from 14:00 until 20:00.

The order reads: "Radiate from the local road and after that return the radar emission imitator to the base (firing) position for your own needs. The command expected the radiation would be recorded by NATO electronic re-connaissance airplanes flying over Hungary, Romania and Bosnia and Herzegovina and that their strike forces would enter tonight into the zone of our battalion, which would ambush them."

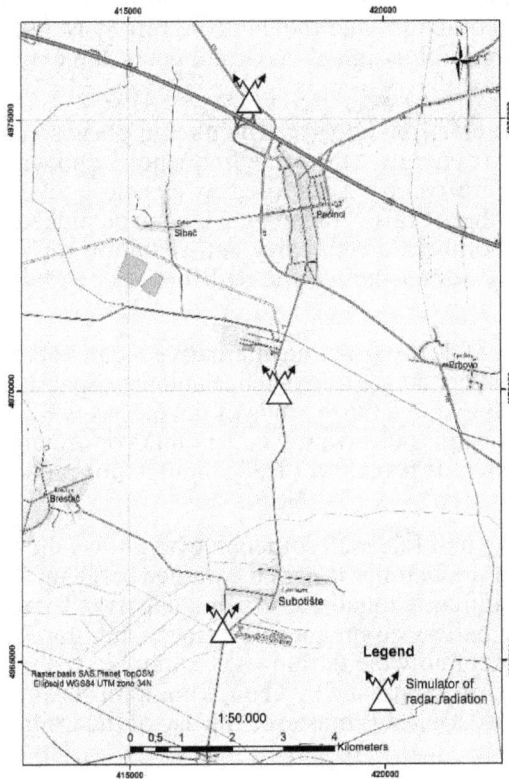

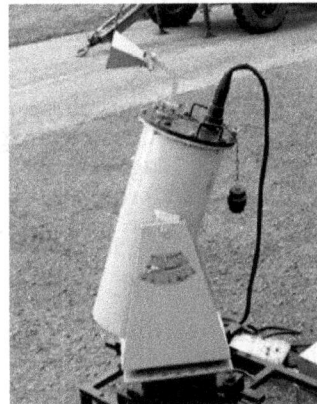

Three position of the radar emission imitator (left) and the actual imitator (top). The idea was to radiate and attract NATO EW assets and possibly organize an ambush.

The idea of the brigade HQ was to use radar emission imitator to simulate the work of tracking and engagement radar. Brigade HQ was sure that NATO ELINT airplanes will pick up emissions and plot the approximate locations. Moving from one location to another and emitting simulated radar emission in the 20 minutes intervals may create the false pictures that there are more tracking radars around thus meaning presence of other missile batteries as well. NATO will record all positions and if the decoys work as planned, the area will be plotted as a SAM sites. Mission planners will plot the locations and they will be implemented into the aircrew's flight computers as potentially dangerous zones thus to be avoided. As the real battalion was in complete radio and radar emission silence, the hope was that it will wait in ambush for unsuspected airplane to appear in the zone of engagement while avoiding false SAM areas.

The plan was to use location No. 1 Subotište and perform 20 minutes emissions on azimuth 270, then move to the location No. 2, Pećinci and perform the same task on azimuth 270 for the same time, then relocate to the location No. 3, Dobrinci and perform the emission on azimuth 230. The task shall be executed by 20:00 than the radar imitator will be positioned in the proximity of the battalion and use as a decoy. I, as a deputy commander and battalion XO, was also scheduled to take the combat shift at 18:00, so the timeframe was tight to perform all assigned tasks and get to the combat position on time to take over the shift.

Radar emission imitator is an electronic device which main purpose is to generate and emit electromagnetic energy at the same frequencies and wavelengths as an engagement and fire control radar used in missile guidance. There is a great probability that these "false" radar signals may be picked up by ELINT aircraft and fighter-bombers which carry anti-radiation missiles such as HARM. The decoy may attract the missile and force her to fly off from the real radar

It is obvious that the emission of decoy from the alternative location created the desired effect. NATO was very aware of existence and the capabilities of Yugoslav decoys. Above all, they have those kinds of devices as well, but they couldn't determine are those emissions from the real radars or imitators. If the emissions are not scheduled as a pattern of 20 minutes but random, they may appear more realistic.

The task was very responsible, and I needed someone who knows the terrain. I was thinking who to send. In October last year I trained sergeant Igor Radivojević to work with the imitator together with his superior Captain Golubović, the missile guidance battery commander. I cannot send Igor Radivojević alone because he does not know the terrain and Golubović is now in the combat shift as the deputy shift commander. Then, I am a bit unsure to which extent the second sergeant Jović has mastered the use of the imitator. So, I was the only candidate.

I told Popović that I know the area, and that my ex wife is from Pećinci. "Then you go with the imitator crew," he said. I agreed with him. I told Dani who was in the shift on the combat position that I would take away the imitator from the position and that I would be probably late for my shift. I was ordered to go out with driver Lukić and operator of the imitator Radivojević:

"I will return around 20:00 and will tell you everything then". I informed Major Stoimenov, deputy shift/fire control officer in my combat shift, that I was leaving to carry out the assignment ordered by the brigade HQ and taking the imitator with me; I will be late for the shift, and to ensure that the afternoon shift timely departs to the combat position. After taking the imitator away from the combat position we went to do our assignment.

When we got there, I decided from the map on the exact places of radar radiation. I visited once all three locations with Lukić and Radivojević. At each location we unloaded the device and portable generator from the vehicle, rolled out the power supply cable and radiated on the given azimuth. After finishing the work there, we loaded the equipment back into the vehicle and repeated it on the next location. We visited the locations from the given order Subotište-Pećinci-Dobrinci. Rare car drivers, who were passing by, curiously watched us, and quickly moved away. After Dobrinci, I was convinced of the Radivojević's correct work, and on the way back to the first location, I got out in Pećinci to try to buy flashlights (torches) and batteries (inserts, cartridges) for them from Luki, the owner of the chain of stores in the villages of Pećinci. Lukić and Radivojević still have the enough time to visit all three locations once again. We ran out of the batteries the previous night, while transitioning the assets. If you need to transition the combat assets, buy the batteries, very simple. It has always been the case; the officers have been buying them themselves. He gave me 15 batteries of 4.5 volts and did not have any flashlights. He would try to get it. I signed up the invoice. The invoice, at this time!? We are fighting, and he thinks how to refund the money. Why is this more my war than his? He needed the signed invoice as a proof for the Municipality Crisis and Civil Defense Headquarters.

We arrived at the camp at the Economy around 19.30 and had a lunch and dinner at the same time. Around 20:00, the siren sounded airborne danger for the village. At 20.30 we arrived at the combat position: I will replace Dani as the shift commander, and Lukić with the Sergeant Radivojević will set up the imitator. For the first time that night I brought to the combat position the commander of the signals platoon, second Lieutenant Miodrag Stojanović from the reserve[6].

We split up at the intersection within the position and I approached the missile guidance station. I heard the familiar noise of generators and operation of the station. Lit by the moonlight, missiles are visible on the launch ramps. The missiles are ready to launch. The ramp does not move. There is no sudden or uniform movement, which is a sure sign that the combat work is not in progress.

In the meantime, at 18:00 my combat crew took their evening shift and because I was absent, Lieutenant Colonel Dani continued his previous shift as a commander until my return. Major Boris Stoimenov took over the position of the deputy combat crew commander with the new crew. The combat readiness was No.3, which is the lowest one, usually when there are no activities in the air. The crew is in 15-minute readiness. During the previ-

---

6   Officers who are not in the active duty during peacetime are deemed to be in "reserve". During wartime soldiers are mobilized and officers are "called in from the reserve".

ous shift, it was informed that there is a problem with P-18 radar receiver because there was no any picture on the screen below 60-70 km. After the conversation with the commander, Major Stoimenov, who was also battalion technical officer, went to the radar van and together with the radar crew tried to fix the problem. There was an issue between parameters of signal and cluster. Major Stoimenov reported to the commander that the repair may last about 90 minutes. Sergeant Ljubenković and Major Stoimenov worked on equipment adjustment without turning on high voltage and radar emission. After the repair, Major Stoimenov requested from Lieutenant Colonel Dani to turn on P-18 for the final adjustment and tune-up. He was back in UNK at 19:20 and reported to Dani that the radar is ready, but that receiver also needs to be adjusted. Because the probable attack has been expected from the west, radar antenna was positioned on azimuth 90^0 and emission was turned on. After the final tune-up the high voltage was turned off.

Situation was quiet and nothing was on the radar screens. In the first few days' air raid alarm usually sounded around 20:00. That was the local time where NATO airplanes were approaching designated targets and were picked up by surveillance radars and visual observation pickets.

Lieutenant Colonel Dani got the information from the brigade command to put the crew into the read- iness No. 1 around 19:35. Missile guidance station (StVR in the local terminology) and radar P-18 are turned on and the crew performed the final parameters control and check-up. In the Combat readiness No. 1, the crew is ready to engage the target on momentary basis.

Combat procedure requires that the crew is in constant communication with the brigade command center. Position of the commander is in the front of the P-18 screen (VIKO) (see the schematics for the precise location of the combat positions in the UNK van). Beside him, sits deputy commander and both can see the radar screen. Every turn on radar screen (sweep with the time base) show that there are airplanes in the air…but they were far away.

UNK of S-125M is very cramped space; with the comfort of the crew was the last worry regarding to ergonomics. Chairs are all but comfortable; humming noise from all electrical equipment is a bit loud; not effective air-conditioning, just to move the stall air, odour of uniforms, muddy boots and unwashed bodies…all in all, not really pleasant working space and environment. In that space, six officers, NCOs and enlisted man performed their tasks.

Missile battalion combat crew is a team… every member of that team plays his role, and all roles are critical. If any member of the team does not perform his duty, that mean the whole team fail…and in the war circumstances, that often mean that the complete or partial team may be eliminated, together with their combat station.

The life of combat crew during the engagement is measured in seconds. That is how much is necessary to fulfill the mission or die trying to do that. In ordinary life seconds does not mean much, but for the missile operators that is the crucial difference are they going to bring down their target or be shredded into pieces by anti-radiation missile or laser bomb.

On the evening of 27 March, the crew consisted of Lieutenant Colonel

Dani Zoltan, commander, responsible for all performing in UNK; Lieutenant Colonel Djordje Aničić, battalion deputy commander and XO and assigned shift commander arrived at 20:30, responsible for all activities out of UNK such as power supply, radar, communication, signals etc.; Major Boris Stoimenov, until the arrival of Lieutenant Colonel Aničić deputy shift commander; Captain I class, Senad Muminović, fire control officer; Sub- Lieutenant. Darko Nikolić, battery commander; Senior Sergeant Dragan Matić, manual tracking operator on F2; Sergeant Dejan Tiosavljević, manual tracking operator on F1; private Davor Blozić, clerk and manual plotting board operator. Beside the combat crew in UNK, detached truck with power source pack unit (Senior Sergeant Djordje Maletić and private Sead Ljajić) and P-18 early warning and surveillance radar station (Sergeant Vladimir Ljubenković and private Vladimir Radovanović) also played a critical role.

Missile guidance station SNR-125-M1: It is a cramped noisy space, filled with equipment and indicators. Combat shift perform its duty in this space.

What was unusual this evening, and something that will never repeat again in the combat situation, was that in the moment of engagement, there were two commanders in the UNK. Combat rules of engagement and procedures allows only one commander but in the war circumstances it may be different.

I climbed up the metal steps and opened the side door of the missile guidance station van. I stepped in. The deputy shift commander Boris Stoimenov was sitting at the very entrance to the station. The headphones with a micro-phone for communication with subordinate units and HQ were on his head. Dani, the shift commander, was taking a nap with his back leaned against the blocks for control of the launch ramps, sideways from the surveillance radar screen. Major Stoimenov raised and moved behind the fire control officer so that I can take the sit (as a senior officer and his shift commander). I took over the headset with the microphone which is used to be in direct contact with the brigade operation center. Technically, as I entered the UNK, Dani is still the shift commander and keeping over the position with my shift which came earlier. Lieutenant Colonel Dani is about to leave after we exchange thoughts and information of the day reflecting activities in the battalion and the individual tasks. Lieutenant Colonel Dani is still sitting in the shift commanders place until formal duty handover and I set at the deputy commander's chair. When Lieutenant Colonel Dani leave in a few minutes, Major Stoimenov will take the position of the deputy commander. It was routine procedure that the previous and new shift commanders exchange information in the duty handover. There was no formal military reporting to each other, rather was more conversation.

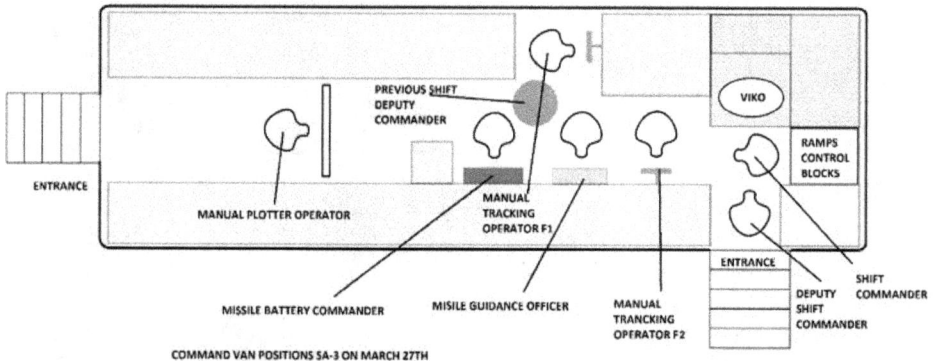

COMMAND VAN POSITIONS SA-3 ON MARCH 27TH

3rd battalion missile guidance station layout with the individual worksta-tions during the engagement on 27 March. This layout is slightly different (designs vary from model to model, but the roles of the operators are the same).

While discussing the afternoon situation and performed tasks, I faced P-18 screen directly and clearly saw what is going on the radar screen. The time base of the surveillance rotated at a uniform speed. There were no targets in the nearby airspace. I saw some far away at various azimuths. The reminder of the combat crew, the four officers and the note-taker [7], were at their work-stations. They were assigned to my shift and my combat crew. Lieutenant Colonel Dani is turned sidewise and not facing the screen this time. P-18 radar screen on VIKO showed that there are airplanes in the air...but still out of range on different azimuths, somewhere in vicinity of Belgrade. Radar imitator that I brought back from the field was not yet connected.

---

7   The main role of the note taker was to record the combat conversations and instructions for post-event analysis; including mapping the area where the target was hit, disappeared and/or crashed, in order to guide the search teams.

While exchanging thoughts of the day about the situation in the unit and performed tasks, suddenly the surveillance radar showed three blips at azimuth 195, distance 23 km. I followed three more sweeps when I saw that one target got 17-18 km from the radar. The operator of the surveillance radar P-18, Sergeant Ljubenković reported via intercom that we have the target. Obviously, we were following the same situation in the airspace. I told Dani about the blip on the radar screen.

"Dani, this guy is going toward us."

P-18 radar screens when the target was first observed, azimuth 195, azimuth 210, and azimuth 230 (left to right)

Dani quickly opened his eyes and looked at the screen. The next sweep showed that the blip was now 14-15 km away...approaching...After two more radar sweeps Lieutenant Colonel Dani ordered:

"Azimuth - 210... Search!"

Sub-Lieutenant Nikolić, the battery commander, started to turn control wheels on his UK-31 plan position indicator and the start zone (part of UK60 station) in attempt to guide the missile guidance officer by azimuth and elevation:

"To the left...to the left stop!...right...up...up...up, stop! "Antenna!"...

At this moment the fire control radar is turned on.

The cat and mouse game started...Whoever is faster and more agile – wins!

Battery commander guided the fire control officer to the target. Captain Muminović, fire control officer on his UK-32 station (indicator of guidance and manual tracking by range, which is part of UK-30 station), franticly turned three wheels at the same time trying to find a target... The "metallic" sound of the wheels the missile guidance officer pushed away and his brief contact with the panel showed that he had been trying hard to overlap the target with the cross mark of the two markers. His first attempt was not successful and on his two screens he was not able to see and marked up the target and handover to the manual tracking operators. The target had high angular velocity, maneuvering, and that may the reason why the operators were not able to start tracking. The fire control radar emission seemed too long. What battery commander thought was that the target most likely got the warning signal in his cockpit that he is illuminated by the engagement and fire control radar.

The cumulative time since the target was detected, fire solution acquired, firing command issued, missile launched and target intercepted must be 25-27 seconds maximum. Anything longer and the station will be hit by anti-radiation missile. That was the time AGM-88 HARM need to fly from the launching airplane to the radar.

The tension was in the air...

As the fire-control radar emission was 10 s long I ordered very loudly:

"Stop search - Equivalent!"

Sub-Lieutenant. Nikolić didn't hear that command or he might be confused because two combat shift commanders issuing the orders. I ordered much louder:

"Get – the – High - down!!!" and Sub-Lieutenant Nikolić immediately turned it off:

"High - off!"

Few seconds later - the next attempt...Lieutenant Colonel Dani ordered:

"Azimuth – 230 - Search!"

The guiding station was saturated with the humming noises from the electrical equipment and clicking of the switches and wheels and loud commands. This time guiding officer was able to see the target on both screens. Metal wheels clicked...Captain Muminović pushed the wheels hard forward to get the target in the crosshair of his two markers but after few attempts he was not able to put the target in the intersection of the horizontal and vertical markers. When the target is in crosshair of both markers, he can transfer to the manual tracking operators on F1 and F2. The second attempt was when the target was approximately 14 km away.

Again, radar emission was a way to long and I commanded:

"Stop searching - Equivalent!!!"

Sub-Lieutenant Nikolić responded promptly: "Equivalent!"

Few seconds later, Lieutenant Colonel Dani ordered: "Azimuth – 240 - Search!"

The third attempt on target was when it was 12 km away.

A couple of seconds later, guidance officer found the target and it was clear that the target is maneuvering. The Clicking of the wheels and again the target is escaping...emission was 5- 6 seconds and I told to Dani:

"Dani, be careful, we don't want them to screw us"

The reason for this concern was that airplanes may use decoys, in some case towed decoys which represent large reflective surface that can confuse the radar operators and mask the real target.

It happened during the first Gulf War that Iraqi crews had the decoy target on their radar screens, locked their firing parameters just to be hit by an anti-radiation missile fired from the side by one of the fighter-bombers equipped with HARMs.

I was about to issue an order to stop search again because the search time is too long, when the operator for the manual tracking on F2, Senior Sergeant Matić vigorously turning his wheels in attempt to get the target in the center of his crosshair on his screen. Sergeant Matić yield:

"Give it to me! Give it to me!...I have him!!!"

Senior Sergeant Dragan Matić, the crew member that "caught" the stealth in his crosshair at the F2 manual guidance operator station.

At that moment Captain Muminović pushed his wheel forward and handed over the target to the manual tracking operators.

"Track manually!"

Sergeant Matić locked the target on F2 crosshair on his UK-33 screen... and that was it...he got him!

The second operator on the manual tracking on F1, Sergeant Tiosavljević, got the target on his screen markers as well. The screen reflection was very big. The target is "caught" and both manual tracking operators have it on their screens.

Captain Muminović reported that the station has stable tracking, the target is in approaching path...distance to target 13 km. Both F1 and F2 operators reported that they have stabile target tracking. All parameters for the firing solutions were achieved.

"Station tracking target, target in approach...distance 13 km!"

Operators reported: "F1 manual tracking on!" "F2 manual tracking on!"

The battery commander didn't report target engagement probability, but Lieutenant Colonel Dani still commanded:

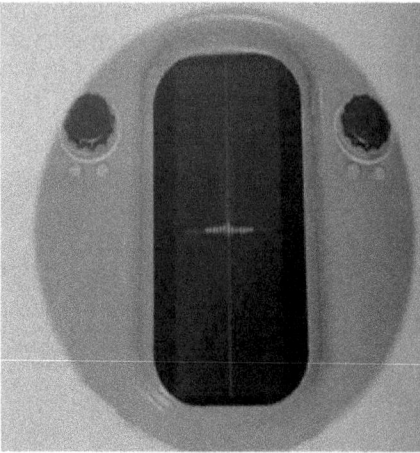

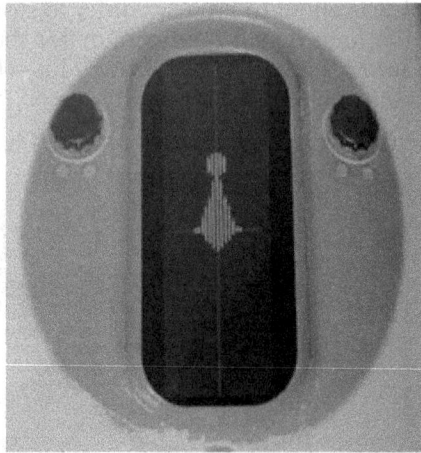

Manual tracking operator on F2 screen showing F-117A (left); missile in the moment of explosion by the target (right).

"Destroy the target! Three-point method!... "Launch!!!"...

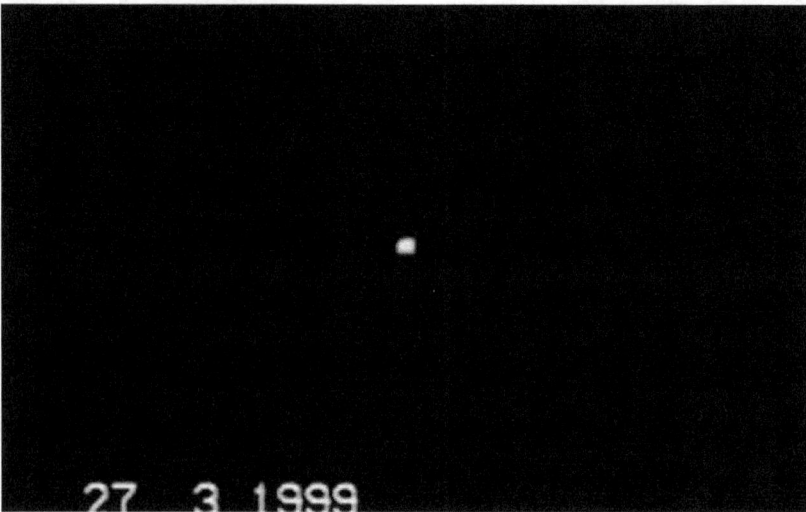

A still from the only video of 27 March launch. The missile is approaching the target.

Captain Muminović pushed the start button and the first missile engine started and the missile blasted off from the launcher. The muffled explosion. The booster motor of the first missile roared.

"First missile launched - first missile tracking! (both F1 and F2 operators manually guide the first missile).

After 5 seconds the second missile blasted too. The noise of launching was so loud that everybody in the surrounding area, including the base camp heard it. Gravel beneath the launchers was blown with the rocket engine

42

blast and hit the UNK van like shrapnel.

"Second missile launched - second missile not tracking!!!"

As both F1 and F2 operators reported stable manual guiding for the first missile the second missile didn't acquire the target and the tracking was lost. The first missile was 5-6 second in flight and 10 more seconds to the interception point. F1 operator reported that the target has large RCS[8].

I rose from my seat and looked over the manual tracking operator shoulder:

"How come it didn't catch the target?!! Why?!!"

The first missile was on the stable trajectory to the target but the second one lost the contact with the station and continued on the ballistic trajectory, away from the target. Something went wrong with the channel.

The crew looked the last few kilometers before the missile reach the target…Than the large flash blips on the missile guiding officer's screen. The missile reached the target at 20:42…Target destroyed… The interception was at 8.000 m altitude. The target was acquired at 6.000 m. Obviously, the pilot saw the launching or has been warned that he was illuminated by the fire control radar and tried to perform anti-missile maneuver but once locked, there was no chance that he can avoid hit.

The whole operation lasted about 23 seconds. We found later that upon the impact on the ground, the wreckage caught fire and the fuselage is destroyed but the left wing and the canopy stayed almost intact.

After that, panic was in the air – a target was nowhere to be seen, suddenly all targets disappeared [9]. At the command post of the 250th brigade Major Janko Aleksić, an officer from the engineering department, asked me to dictate to him the list of names of the combat crew who carried out the engagement. How to report to the superior command? Due to the circumstances both shift commanders of were in the command post, Dani and I, and both commanders were commanding the combat crew during the downing of the plane. It was my combat shift that fired. I dictated to Aleksić the composition of the combat crew that carried out the engagement, in the order as we were sitting in the command post, and as required by the Instructions for Combat Work and according to the pre-defined workstations.

Because I was sitting at the deputy commanders chair, I did put myself in that role, regardless of the fact that I had commenced my combat shift as the shift commander at the moment I entered into the guidance station. The following combat crew carried out the engagement:

Lieutenant Colonel Zoltan Dani, shift commander,

Lieutenant Colonel Đorđe Aničić, deputy shift commander,

Captain Senad Muminović, missile guidance officer,

---

8   RCS – radar Cross Section.

9   All operations intended for that day were immediately halted and search for the pilot begun.

Sergeant Dejan Tiosavljević, manual tracking operator on F1,

Senior Sergeant Dragan Matić, manual tracking operator on F2,

Sub-Lieutenant Darko Nikolić, missile guidance battery commander,

Private Davor Bložić, note taker and manual plotter operator.

F-117A Nighthawk after missile hit - left wing was almost torn off.

Major Boris Stoimenov, who was deputy shift commander in my combat shift, was also present in the guidance station. He was standing behind the missile guidance officer, the workstation of the battery commander from the moment I entered the station, i.e. from 20.30 to 20.42. He did not participate in the combat work.

Standing left to right: Sergeant Dejan Tiosavljević, Senior Sergeant Dragan Matić, Lieutent Colonel Zoltan Dani, Lieutenent Colonel Djordje Aničić, Major Boris Stoimenov.

Kneeling left to right: Sub-Lieutenant Darko Nikolić, Sergeant Djordje Maletić, Captain Senad Muminović, Sergean. Vladimir Ljubenković.

Also, present on the combat position, on the other combat assets and in the guard were:

Sargent Đorđe Maletić and private Sead Ljajić, on the power supply van;

Senior Sargent Vladimir Ljubenković and private Vladimir Radovanović on the surveillance radar P-18;

Sub-Lieutenant Miodrag Stojanović and a private on the signals control post;

Lieutenant Igor Radivojević and Senior Sergeant Radisav Jović on the imitator of the radar radiation.

Dani commanded only "Launch", and I now, according to the Instructions for Combat Procedures, I also have to report on the other launch parameters that were not commanded during the launch: the guidance method, the way of launching, the number of missiles used, the missile warhead activation method, and, as per the Muminović's announcement, the basic target destruction parameters[10].

10   The crew assumed the worst-case scenario of a highly maneuverable fighter jet airplane and pre-set the relevant selections accordingly in order to "be quicker than HARM missiles". This was not "by the book", hence the officer felt uncomfortable on what to report to the superior command (also knowing that many of them "do by the book to a tee").

45

F-117A engagement indicators – speed, distance, altitude.

"Congratulations legends!", we heard from Colonel Aleksić. Just after ten minutes, Colonel Dragan Stanković, the 250th brigade chief of the staff, also asked for the list. I dictated it all again. Private Davor Bložić, the note taker of the combat operations, wrote the "history" in the journal of combat operations. Joy in the van. We congratulated to each other and we were hugging each other. "We will be the strongest battalion in the brigade. We will have two colonels", said Dani, while we congratulated each other. 30 minutes after the launch, the brigade command post ordered: "Preparation for march." I told the camp to send the drivers with their vehicles and people. The combat equipment should be moved to the next combat position as soon as possible, in the region of Prhovo village. While waiting for the vehicles and people from the camp, the combat crew transitioned the assets from combat to marching configuration. I was exhausted. I had not slept for two days and a night. I told Dani that I was going to the camp to sleep, because I was not needed for the transition. I was going to the Economy. In the camp, Major Boško Dotlić, commanders aid for the logistics, said that he had heard the start of the first rocket and ran outside of the "office". He personally saw everything. The missile entering into the clouds, he heard the explosion and saw a huge fireball falling. It appeared to him that the second missile hit he target too. I doubt it, as there was no take up – the instant in time from when the operators began to guide the flight of the missile. I knew that it went along the ballistic curve trajectory and plunged somewhere in Srem plow field. The plane wreckage fell into the region of village of Buđanovci. The relocation of the assets was very fast. In about two hours, the assets were transitioned from the combat to the marching configuration and relocated to the new combat position in the region of village of Prhovo. The people of the surrounding villages were enthusiastic. Everyone watched us with the great respect. I thought again about Danka. She would probably be proud when she found out what we had done that night.

In the camp at the Economy around 22.00, the news on the radio station Studio B was heard that we downed the F-117A, the "Stealth" technology aircraft, the pride of the NATO pact and of the Air Force of United States of America. The people were in a frenzy of celebration. The airplane that was the backbone of American Air Force strike capability for the next century. The public was in shock, so was the Pentagon and Washington. During the night, the pilot was rescued. The rescue team consisted of three helicopters, two MH-53 and one MH-60 with the special forces. Sub-Lieutenant Darko Nikolić, a member of the combat crew, was awarded the Order of Courage medal from the president Slobodan Milošević, and the commandant of the Air Defence, general Spasoje Smiljanić, promoted him to the rank of Lieutenant. He completed the Military Academy a year and a half before. What a great start for the young officer. It was good that the list of the completed shift had not been announced, and everyone knew that if we were not adequately rewarded and awarded, it would be a great fraud afflicted on the people and Yugoslavian Army. Euphoria and morale in the unit had significantly increased. The attention had been relaxed, and so was the tension. There were no cramps anymore. Our belief that something could be done has returned. [11]

F-117A wreck in the Srem mud – the wing was in relatively good shape. The rest is burned.

---

11   Mike Mihajlović: on that night I took my position in the command center around 18:00. One of my tasks was to track NATO combat groups. From the northern direction, for them it was optimal to refuel over Hungary, wait for their time than push south, skimming the Yugoslavia & Romania border. We couldn't engage them even if detected because technically we will shoot into the foreign airspace. My calculations based on the takeoff time from Aviano, from which I have information as soon as they took off, through the flight over Slovenia and Hungary showed that we can expect the "first guests" around 20:15-20:30. Everything was based on the optimal speed. This information I forwarded to the upper command but knowing that

The F-117A canopy. A pilot other than the one whose name was written on the canopy piloted the plane that night.

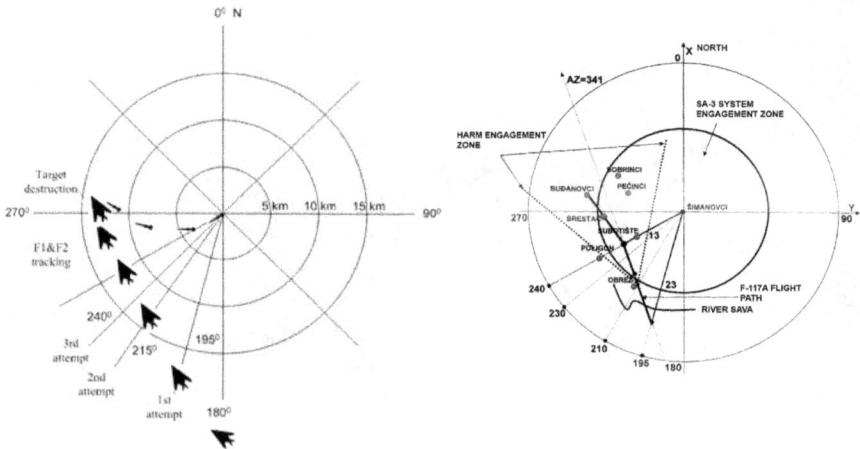

F-117A horizontal engagement diagram (left) and parametric analysis (right)

while it goes through the inert chain of command and somebody to make decision and inform the units, most likely the pilots will be already in their beds back home. Too bad that we didn't have the direct link to the designated missile battalions. At least, we cooperate with the radio-amateurs and they were able (even during the intense jamming) to pass the information as much as they can. It was almost by the book that they will try to hit us with the stealth jets under the intense escort and jam-

F-117A became a souvenir place. Locals and many others picked up parts as memorabilia.

Sunday, March 28

After sunrise I called Danka. She was very happy to hear from me. I did not know if she knew that we were the ones who shot down the plane. This was the breaking news on all radio and TV stations in our country and around the world. We manned the new combat position in the village of Prhovo. After the dark fell last night, Sub-Lieutenant Stojanović (the commander of the signals platoon) and people from the logistics support platoon returned from the forest farm in Kupinovo and brought 54 or 56 acacia tree trunks, 30-40 cm thick and 4-5 meters long to protect the missile guidance station/command post van and the crew at the combat position. He professionally executed my command.

I met Zoran Armuš who had returned from abroad and opened a building material store in Šimanovci. He helped us a lot to pile up the trunks around the combat assets. A few nights ago, he had also provided us, through his mate, a secure communication link to our superior command - the command of the 250th brigade. The government issued a decree that all state and private resources could be used for the purposes of the Yugoslav Military.

Kovačević, the deputy commander of the Pećinci police district, brought parts of the downed aircraft in the morning. Everyone was calling out congratulating us, and when they came to the unit, they all hugged us. We learnt that Lieutenant Colonel Stevan Djević, commandant of the missile battalion from Batajnica, missed the target. They launched missiles by using the thermal imaging camera. During the missile start, the operators of manual track-

ming but even under these circumstances we can still make some surprises which actually happened.

49

ing were blinded by a cloud of dust that covered the thermal vision screens and tracking failed. Some of the NATO pilots were terribly afraid, and they had no motive.

We found out what had been ailing us since a few nights ago. Both of our MIG-29 had been shot down. That was why they had disappeared from our surveillance radar. One pilot died, and the other one managed to eject over Bosnia. He fell near his village. Were they our first victims? Glory to the heroes.

The combat equipment was transitioned in the combat configuration. The surveillance radar was defective. We had requested from the Operational Center of the Brigade command to send us help. The operator of the surveillance radar, Sergeant Vladimir Ljubenković, was utterly exhausted - he worked in two combat shifts in a row over and over again. The shifts were changing each other, only he had no shift. He had been eating and sleeping in the radar truck. I doubt that he would be able to fix the malfunction of the radar while so exhausted. The missile guidance station had been running hours unnecessarily because I did not have a picture from the surveillance radar. The people were worked hard unnecessarily. That was how we went about our business. No one had the balls to say: "Rest time for the people and combat assets, fix the malfunction and then go on." The command (operations center) ordered us to radiate in a particular sector with the radar emission imitator and with the fire control antenna. I would have revealed my location while I would have not been able to defend myself because I did not have a radar image. That was madness and someone's great stupidity. Allegedly that was the tactics - the imitation of the launch. "And if they went after me, then what?" I asked them "They would not, they were afraid," they replied to me. "Fuck there are always been fools, here, on the ground and up in the air," I thought. We worked according to our plan and the shift arrangement. During the break between the two shifts Armuš and I went to the Municipality of Pećinci to meet with the mayor. The fuel distribution had stopped at the pump. They could only serve the priority vehicles and individuals who had the approval of the Municipality Crisis HQ. Zoran Armuš was allocated a quantity of 200 liters of diesel fuel and 50 liters of gasoline per month. The man uses his own machinery (trucks, loader for tree trunks, cars). He was allowed to purchase fuel for his money - without a refund. Even that was good, I just thought that he should get the fuel for free, not buy it. Well, administration – the hardest one to work with.

The crew was resting when not in the shift unless there were some obligations in the base unit. I was so exhausted that I could hardly to fall asleep. Warrant Officer Zoran Ristić, came to repair the surveillance radar. There was rarely time for me, as the deputy commandant, to take a break. I allocated to basic units the reservists who arrived and reported to me, wrote reports to the mobilization section and superior command, resolved the ongoing management issues of the unit, permanent stand-by duty for the combat crew shifts, and many other things. My son, Vladimir, was living with my ex mother-in-law in Pećinci. I fought the war in the territory of the Pećinci municipality, and I had not seen him yet. I met his friend and neighbour from childhood Aca Rogulić, who told me that Vlada went to Belgrade today. That evening I talked with Danka. She told me that Vladimir is with her.

Only then, after many days day I spoke with my son.

I was consuming one pill of "Renisan" medication daily for my duodenum ulcer. It reduced cramps in my stomach and tension. I was lying to Danka that I was fine, in order to calm her down. I was in no pain, as I was regularity taking the medication. Perhaps I should have stopped taking it. I was running out of cigarettes. Today I was worried that I often changed cigarettes - I smoked one brand today, and tomorrow the another one, whatever was available.

Monday, March 29

The on-call duty is perpetual. Our shifts change every 6 hours. We are on every night from 00:00 to 06:00 and then we have 6 hours of rest, of which I really sleep for only two or three hours, and then again on duty. Dragovan Matijević, my classmate, brought me a part of the downed airplane as a souvenir. He also told me that he had left with a gypsy named Ručko from Buđanovci (village) a part of the F-117A wing that was 3 meters long and the exhaust cooling system unit as a war trophy. During the break, I cannot concentrate on the TV or the newspapers. I discussed with Muminović why we had only acquired the target in the third attempt. Senad is not experienced on this system. In future, our lower elevation target acquisition threshold will be set just above the vertical effective range of anti-aircraft guns "Praga"[12] and "Bofors"[13], and man portable air-defense (MANPAD) systems "Strela"[14] and "Igla"[15]. We measured this height by turning the wheel of the elevation angle at missile guidance officer's workstation. "Remember the value. It is zero for you. Pass it on to Janković, the other missile guidance officer. This way, the search time should be significantly reduced".

I decided to visit Danka's parents. They fled from Banija[16] and now they settled in Karlovčić. They were known as "the Kurds", as the refugees called each other among themselves. I knew that they were upset. Milan, Danka's father was ill – his kidney stones had started moving, her mother Nada was

---

12   The M53/59 Praga is a Czechoslovak self-propelled anti-aircraft gun developed in the late 1950s. It consists of a heavily modified V3S six-wheel drive truck chassis, armed with a twin 30 mm anti-aircraft automatic cannon.

13   The Bofors 40 mm gun, often referred to simply as the Bofors gun, is anti-aircraft automatic cannon designed in the 1930s by the Swedish arms manufacturer AB Bofors. In 1970's Zastava Arms (Serbia) acquired from Bofors license to produce L/70 version together with laser-computer group. Ammunition is locally produced in Sloboda Čačak.

14   The 9K32 Strela ("arrow") NATO reporting name SA-7 Grail.

15   The 9K38 Igla ("needle") NATO reporting nameSA-18 Grouse.

16   Banija or Bosanska Krajina - A geographical region in central Croatia, between the Sava, Una, and Kupa rivers. The main towns in the region include Petrinja, Glina, Kostajnica and Dvor.The area suffered during the breakup of Yugoslavia in the 1990s, with much of the Serb majority population fleeing during the hostilities and never returning.

holding on. I took a decent shower and felt refreshed. For the meal I ate soup and fried eggs and talked to them. In our conversation, I gave them some hope. I gave to Milan a sample of the downed airplane for safekeeping, until I framed it after the war, if I'm stile alive.

Thoughts were flashing through my mind. We may have slowed down or turned the wheel of history by downing the F-117A. They were attacking like a pack of mad dogs - bombing, destroying and killing. I was sorry that the pilot of the fallen aircraft was not caught, that the helicopters were not downed, and that the rescue team was not eliminated. Images of the destruction of civilian objects should have been broadcasted by CNN, if they are still independent, for America to see what their sons and daughters doing to others. Let everyone see what is happening to a sovereign country. This craziness will have to end some day. During the day Lieutenant Bora Crnobrnja, battalion security officer, arrived. He covered two missile battalions: ours and Noskov's. He said that the Lieutenant Colonel Miroslav Noskov's battalion shot down an airplane and that Dejan Jovanović, sergeant under contract with Noskov, shot one "tomahawk" with a "SA-7". They were fired upon. His equipment was damaged - the target acquisition radar. Fortunately, nobody was hurt. Bora said that they were screwed by Lieutenant Colonel Luka Trgovčević, operative at the command of the 250th brigade.

Tuesday, March 30

The combat crew wrote a funny song about Nikolić:

A very personal ID of the Sub-Lieutenant

Name and surname: Darko Nikolić Nevsky[17],

ID: F-117A, missile guidance station van S-125M,

Hobby: Black sheep shearing,

Favorite bird: Nighthawk,

Nickname: Stealth,

Favorite novel: "Eagles Fly Early" (and fall even earlier),

Favorite zodiac sign: Black Ram (Aries),

External Debt: US$ 900,000,000

Favorite TV series: "The Invisible Man (1984)",

Favorite toy: 5V27D (missile model),

In love with: Virgin NATO,

Favorite Movie: Rocky I, II, III, IV and V

The favorite time of the day: 20:42 hours,

---

17   Nevsky means "of Neva" (river) and a name for S-125 (SA-6) Goa missile system.

Favorite folk verses: "Ay rocket rocke-take-take-ta",

Favorite writer: Slobodan Raketić.

Favorite rock lyrics: "Airplane, I will break your wings".

Tonight, a "gyrocopter" floated above us. Zoran Tepavac, Senior Sergeant, shot at it with a sniper, but we do not know what happened to it. We should be leaving this position tonight. Local people guarded and fed us. I did not know when or who had brought roast meat, cakes, gibanica[18], but there was a feast at the camp when I returned from my shift. Many things flew through my head and I lost my appetite. The village of Šimanovci and its surrounding area had marked its place in the history of warfare. The locals were thanking us for the fight in their own way.

One of the pictures that circulated in world mass media was the "jubilant aunties" dancing on the F-117A wing. People were simply happy that the aircraft that was considered invisible was downed.

Primakov, Ivanov and Sergeyev[19] arrived in Belgrade. They talked for 6 hours with President Milošević. All missile units had been ordered not to engage or be active while their airplane was landing at the Belgrade's Airport. After their plane landed, the temporary halt order was lifted. In the air defense jargon - we opened our zone of protection in order to allow their airplane to land and then we closed it again for all air-traffic.

---

18   Gibanica is a traditional pastry dish popular all over the Balkans. It is usually made with cottage cheese and eggs.

19   Russian leaders: The Prime Minister Yevgeny Primakov, accompanied by Foreign Minister Igor Ivanov and Defense Minister Igor Sergeyev.

Local Roma people were very interested in the F-117A wreck, trying to sell it as scrap metal, however, the plane was made with a lot of composite material which is useless in their business. Some of them used parts to cover outhouses and pig stays. After the war, a lot of scrap parts were later purchased by the Chinese team.

Wednesday, March 31

My shift ended at 06.00. I was sleepy. During the changeover, I told Dani that we radiated few times from the target acquisition radar searching for the cruise missiles, as ordered by the Operational Center. That was madness (one of many) they requested from us. We took life-threatening risk without any practical chance to detect and destroy "Tomahawk" cruse missile. In theory, the chance existed, however very short radiation time reduced this possibility to almost zero and we practically open our position for NATO electronic surveillance. Dani with his shift manned the combat position, and my shift set off to the camp. At 07:30. I received a message from Dani on the pager: "Djole [20], bring your suitcases, we are going on a trip!"

I was asleep and my head was empty. I said loudly to Major Dotlić: "What does this mean?", and I gave him the pager. He did not get it either, shrugged his shoulders and shook his head. I laughed and ordered alarm for the battalion and drivers bring vehicles to the combat position. We arrived at 08:10 immediately commenced transition of the equipment from the combat to marching configuration. Once again, my shift would have a sleepless night followed by the day's effort to relocate the equipment, and then we would re-commence combat operations as the night fell. I did not know for how

---

20   Djole is a nickname for Djorđe.

long the unit would be able to last at this pace. Did anyone think of resting the crews? One of the enemy objectives was to exhaust us. Tired crews make mistakes, and in the war these mistakes were paid by the loss of equipment and lives. By 09:45 we connected all trailers to the trucks and off we go. Wow, I was amazed how quick it was. From the stationary system, with the possibility of relocation, we made a mobile system; motivated people relocated it to the new combat position in the blink of an eye.

Yesterday, I gave to Armuš my sketch of the "table" that we needed to quickly transition the target acquisition radar from the combat to marching configuration. He brought it with him this morning. He must have made it last night from his own material. What an incredible man, that Armuš. We left in two columns towards the village of Subotište. It was foggy and the weather was helping us. It camouflaged our movement. We waited there for a new combat position to be selected. In the afternoon, we were going to individually relocate and transition assets from the marching to combat configuration and connect them in a combat ready system.

Dani and the commanders of missile guidance battery, Captain Golubović, and the missile battery, Major Roksandić, went for the reconnaissance. The rest of the people and I stayed in the bus waiting for their return. I was too tired, napping, but the arrival of Major Vlada Krsmanović from the Brigade Operation Section, at 11:55 completely woke me up. We were ordered to go to the region of village of Ogar; start relocation and transition of the assets at 12:00 and be combat ready by 19:00. No way, I immediately told Krsmanović. When Dani and the commanders returned from the reconnaissance, it was concluded that the access road to the new combat position need to be prepared, so that the unit could set up the lea [21] in the Ogar area. A vehicle, gravel and stone must be found. Dani and I discussed on how we can do it. He went back to manage it, and I returned my people to the camp in Šimanovci for lunch.

At 15:30 we headed back and after returning to Subotište, I released 1 to 2 vehicles every five minutes. Dani was waiting in Ogar. I left with the last vehicle. We manned the position, and by 20:30 we were ready for action. During the relocation and transition, Dani and I organised cover for vehicles and accommodation for people at the Economy. After returning to the combat position, I decided where to locate the radar emission imitator, and locations for MANPAD systems SA-7. My shift remained on duty until 24:00 hours, because the officers persuaded us that they would not be non-stop on duty after midnight: hardly anyone could fall asleep before midnight, and from midnight until the morning we were on the combat duty. There was always something to do during daytime, so my combat shift was exhausted. Dani's shift was due at 24:00. At 23:35 I changed the command signals codes, which, after a lot of peripeteia, Major Dotlić delivered to me. Around 23:50 I went out of the van and saw that the combat position was illuminated. A civilian truck driver had brought a full trailer of a stone to fill in the road. I thought he was crazy and asked him if he had been a conscript in the army, and did he know what the camouflage was?!

---

21   lea is land used for a few years for pasture or for growing hay, then plowed over and replaced by another crop.

At 00:05, we went into Readiness No.1 - preparedness for combat operations. We had a problem with the surveillance radar. The Operational Center was constantly calling and asking when it will be fixed. In the end, I was so pissed off that I had to say that I would report them as soon as it was repaired and not to call me. They were weird about it.

April 1999

Captain Darko Rašković, from the Brigade Operation Centre command post, requested us to search targets located 30 km away by using the fire control and target tracking radar. I told him, "You are crazy, that is out of question. What is the purpose of locating targets at the distance much longer than my range? I would be revealing my location, without being able to shoot at it. I called Dani at 00:30 and asked him where his shift was. He said they were coming soon. The surveillance radar was repaired around 01:00 and Corporal Ristić, who was assisting, left the combat position. Vacuum tubes in the delay loop in block 27 were replaced with the new ones. It was finally repaired. I reported it to the higher command at the Operations Centre by using the signals codes. Dani came at 01:50. The people in my shift were pissed off. They shortened our rest time for more than 2 hours, and we will lose some time travelling to the camp. "In the morning we will not come at 06.00, but at 08.00". That was our unanimous decision. "If they do not respect us as mates, then we will not have respect for them. "The culmination was when they forgot to bring drinking water, so Sergeant Volf , operator of manual tracking, returned to the camp to bring it. We had to remain at the combat position until he returned because their crew was short of an officer. We left the combat position in a TAM 150, which was not taken off last night. In the morning at 05:50, Dani woke me up to bring my shift and replace them. I refused, so we had an argument. "When did you come to us last night?" I asked him. He called again around 07:00 to tell me to wake up people. He must have understood what he had done and what kind of frustration he had caused. I always came in time, and he did not. When my shift came to the combat position around 08:00, he asked me if I had anything personal against him. I replied that I did not, but it was not fair that someone was carrying more weight than another. "If you are a commandant, that does not mean you can do what you want. Why you were late last night? "I asked him. He was silent.

The higher command ordered us not to use MANPAD systems from 08:25 to 09:00. I told this to the commander of the SA-7 missile battery, reserve Captain Cvetić, and to inform his subordinate units, which were located in 4-5 different locations around us. In the event of an attack on our combat position, the combat crews at the missile guidance van, surveillance radar and power distribution van had no weapons and ammunition. I ordered Captain Golubović, commander of the missile guidance battery, to provide ammunition for automatic rifles in the combat position. Bags with magazines and rifles were to be distributed by vans. The crew at the radar emission imitator had already been armed.

Representatives of the Russian Duma came on a state visit.

Last night they destroyed the old bridge in Novi Sad, between Petro-varadin and Novi Sad. Rugova[22] said in a conversation with Milošević in Belgrade that the bombing should have been stopped and that the meeting should have been held at the negotiating table. During the changeover of shifts, Dani's shift had left us with a defective system for the selection of moving targets, so Senior Sergeant Milan Panić, the operator of that system, had to adjust it.

Armuš came around 09:30 with a civilian Đurđević, who worked on an excavator, to manually install the acacia tree trunks and protect the guidance station van. The antenna should have been directed towards Belgrade in order to provide another communication line with the Brigade Operation Centre. Senior Sergeant Saša Bugarin, from the missile battery, took ZIL transloader truck and went to the village of Zuce to Lieutenant Colonel Petar Dubaić, the commandant of the missile technical battalion (he supplied the missile battalions with the missiles), to give us two missiles to replace the ones we had launched. He should have also filled in our compressed air bottles needed for operation of the target acquisition and fire control radar. He brought back the missiles, but he forgot to fill in the bottles. He went back in a TAM 150. I was angry at him because he did not think that his forgetfulness threatened our combat readiness. The generators on the combat position were re-fueled. I asked Armuš to, together with our mechanic Binke Golubović, inspect the cooling system of the "ZIL" transloader truck that remained in the hangar in Šimanovci, because of unexpectedly high coolant temperature. This vehicle was very important to us because it towed the missile guidance station van.

At 11:30 Danka sent me a message to the pager to contact her. She watched the TV and saw Colonel Miroslav Lazović, the 250th Brigade commandant, at the Military Medical Academy (MMA). She knew him. She was asking me why Lazović was laying "broken" in the (Orthopedic Surgery Wing of) MMA. I told her that he had not been injured in combat operations, but that he had a traffic accident the other day after the bombing, when he went to Sremčica. I just could not understand why the Commandant of the Brigade, as tired as we all were, sat down and drove off himself in an "Opel" car! I saw it as a classic misuse of office. There is assigned and dedicated soldier-driver position in our military formation - the brigade commandant driver, who has no other duties other than to be rested to drive the commander. He drove at high speed, flew off the road and severely injured himself. The car was destroyed. Fuck the car, it was more important he was recovering well. Danka told me that our neighbour Trišić was mobilized.

Two days ago, I ordered Major Dotlić to report back to the military mobilization service and check who responded to the mobilization notice, and who did not; to call them and to request mobilization of soldiers for the infantry platoon and for the chemical, biological and radiological section (CBR).

Stress cause me to smoke a lot. I was smoking local cigarettes branded "Best" – it was good, and it was still available. Before the war I smoked

---

22   Ibrahim Rugova – Albanian leader from Kosovo and Metohija province of Serbia. Did not support achieving political goals by military means, hence did not have support of interventionist foreign powers.

"Winston S-100" brand. Dani told me once that I should not be smoking "Winston" brand because they are western - American cigarettes. Who knows who and where they were made. Captain Muminović replied to him that German marks (Deutche Mark) were also theirs, and yet that everyone was collecting, respecting, and saving them.

In the period from 14.00 to 16.00, when my shift rested, my classmate and roommate from the Academy, Lieutenant Colonel Stojanče Tomić, security officer from the Corps HQ, led by general Bane Petrović, Lieutenant Bora Crnobrnja and Senior Sergeant Crepuljar came to the camp. At the Academy, my second roommate and I called Stojanče "Dad". He used to say, "My sons, where are you?" I still called him "Dad" now. He asked me how things are going and if there are any problems. I told him about the nonsense in the course of our combat work, overtiredness and exhaustions of crews, unnecessary radar emissions on cruise missiles, helicopters, and unmanned aerial vehicles. "Take care, my classmate, do not talk on mobile phone from the combat position because they can register the conversations," he warned me.

Major Dotlić brought the roasted pig that locals sent to us from Šimanovci. Good for morale, though…

Senior Sergeant Mića Mijalković, the NCO in charge of receiving and dressing up mobilized reservists, brought six reservists to deploy. I still did not have enough people in key batteries. For this reason, I deployed them to the missile guidance battery and a missile battery. I would re-deploy them later to units by their specialty. The volunteer, Sub-Lieutenant Nenad Belović from Obrenovac showed up. He had been deployed earlier to our battalion and got used to our unit. I sent him back because he was a reserve military officer of the missile battalion from Obrenovac, according to the new war schedule. "Stay at home and wait for a notice from your unit, so that you do not get in trouble with the law." He listened to me.

Friday, April 02

I had been on duty on the combat position Ogar, from 06:00 to 12:00. Until 10:00 we were in combat readiness No.2 (people manning their combat assets, equipment not switched on), and after that in readiness No. 1 (people manning their combat assets, equipment switched on and ready for combat operations).

Between 11:30 and 12:00, helicopters appeared on azimuths of 270° to 300°. Lieutenant Colonel Boro Samardžić, assistant-commandant for the equipment, from the operational center of the brigade communicated that helicopters were visually observed in Sremska Mitrovica. I ordered readiness to the missile battery SA-7 (MANPAD). At one turn of the surveillance radar markers, I thought that I had a target at a distance of 8 km. I ordered the target acquisition radar to search for it. We searched for about 10-12 seconds. We could not identify helicopters among the clutter of permanent reflections from stationary objects. Dani and his shift timely replaced us at 12:00. At 12:25, they were ordered from the brigade command post, probably by a mistake, to switch to readiness No.3 (the assets are shut down and people are on the standby, 15-minute combat readiness). This means people have 15 minutes to arrive and man their stations, turn them on, check for correct operation of the missile guidance station and report back that they are combat ready). A part of Dani's shift went to the camp. He walked off from the combat position, so I was not sure where he was, with someone in the village or going to the camp? At 12:50 they received readiness No.2 (people manning their combat assets, equipment not switched on) order. Only Senior Sergeant Radivojević and Captain Golubović were in the camp at that time. There were not enough officers from his shift to go back and man the missile guidance station van, surveillance radar, power supplies and radar emission imitator; the MANPAD crews and signals platoon were combat ready at their designated locations. We were almost caught with our pants down. That was Dani's "smart" decision. The available officers must man the combat shift, so the bus left the camp at 12:55.

I was so tired and had slept until 15:30, when I was woken up to go to the combat position, together with Captain Muminović, Senior Sergeant Tiosavljević and now, Lieutenant Nikolić. We expected a visit from "the highest command," the command of the air force and air defence. At 16:00 we set in "Lada Niva" and went to the combat position. General Slavko Biga, Chief of Staff of the Air Force and Air Defense Corps led the delegation. The representatives of the Russian State Duma arrived, led by Lieutenant General, Major General, designer and director of the Missile Systems Institute. A representative of Belarus was present as well. They admired us and said that we were for the Guinness World Records 1999 book, because we shoot the fourth-generation airplane armed with the second-generation system. Their delegation and generals arrived before our delegation. So far, no official from the superior command had lined up the combat crew and officially congratulated them. Colonel Vukosavljević, former commandant of the brigade, was also with them. Dani got a wristwatch from the Russians. They promised to send us the S-300 system[23] tomorrow, and maybe a "little bit after tomorrow" meaning never, I thought to myself.

They said that only God was above Yeltsin. Their politicians drink a lot and Russia had lost its primacy in the world. Serbia was also fighting for Russia. They were short and had huge Russian military officers' caps on their heads. Dani handed over a part of the plane to one Russian. I stood on the side and saw that particular moment. I did not understand why he did it. At around 18.00 they went to the camp to see the wing of the stealth airplane, so my shift remained at the combat position, on combat duty, until 24.00. Again, there was no break for my shift. A soldier from the reserve Mikica Petrović and Lieutenant Boro Crnobrnja came to the combat position for Mikica to see me and to congratulate for downing the aircraft. Mikica told me they watched our shooting. He was thrilled. He told me that Corporal Saša Šabanović, had worked on a "Kraz" crane to transition the target acquisition radar to Progar. Before they got out, they were shot at. During their third run away from the "Kraz" towards the shelter, he turned towards the missile, which he saw in the air and asked, "Why are you shooting at me again, you

---

23   S-300 (NATO reporting name *SA-10 Grumble*) is a potent long-range surface-to-air missile system.

fucking fuck?!!!"

Boro promised that he would bring us 10 cigarettes each, which was our daily ration, from the Monitoring and Information Centre in the "13th May" suburb. Well, better something than nothing. A sole trader made juices, sparkling and spring water for the army and police; he would bring some too.

Around 17.00 mechanics from the workshop arrived to repair on the Maletić's diesel aggregate. Today I found out that instead of the two 5V27D missiles we fired, we got 5V27U model as replacement. "They must be joking or there are no other missiles." The former had been modified to much better engage maneuvering targets and escaping aeroplanes. So, we will only fire on the incoming airplanes, and if it undertakes an evasive maneuver or tries to escape, then it would be unlikely that a 5V27U missile would kill it. This was madness! It was raining.

Around 19:00 I called Danka. She was depressed. I did not like when she was depressed. This condition often dominates her behavior. She said that my sister, who lived and worked in Trieste (Italy), did not call me. Her younger daughter Bojana operated her tonsils. I guess that she was ok. Today was Good Friday for Catholics.

At 21:15 we were ordered to the Readiness No.1, all equipment switched on. US President Clinton said there would be actions during their Easter. In Kosovo, near the Macedonian border, two US non-commissioned officers and one US reconnaissance soldier, based in the Federal Republic of Germany, were arrested - they were shown on the media. The US Congress insisted they should be given the status of prisoners of war and should be treated according to the Geneva Convention. They admitted, therefore, they were at war, which meant they were aggressors. One day they should be tried in the court of law. But who is going to put that evil force on trial? The world and European public are upset. Major Stiomenov, Senior Sergeant Tiosavljević and Captain Muminović discussed international relationship in the van. As if Muminović repented for not listening to his wife to demobilize when transferred from Obrenovac to Jakovo. He emphasised the quality of life in the West, relative to that here. I knew that tiredness made people say what was not usually thought of. Or it made their real personality to show out. Well, try them under pressure and you'll of what kind of "material" they were made... I did not participate in the discussion. The euphoria regarding the "stealth" (we call him "invisible") was slowly fading. Yesterday, the women from the village were literally drowning the army with cakes. Bora Crnobrnja told me that Lieutenant Colonel Noskov, with his battalion, was near me in the village of Ašanja.

The brigade assigned one "Kub" (K12, SA-6 Gainful) mobile missile battery to us. They were located in Bogatić, near us. "Kub" is a more mobile and newer missile system than "Neva". It is part of the Army Air Defense, while we are part of the Air Force and Air Defense Corps. The commander was Lieutenant Sreten Cvetković, while Captain Dušan Žarković and Lieutenant Colonel Bane Milosavljević were assigned to help him. They were located 20 km away. The chain of command will go through us, and as if they were subordinated to the 3rd battalion.

Mechanic Binke Golubović and Senior Sergeant Žugić brought another part of the downed airplane today. Were we really the legends, apparently most respected by the people? That was the most important thing. It was good for the reputation of the army among the people.

My ulcer was hurting me. Was the pain caused by the weather or because of mixing different brands of cigarettes? Today, Senior Sergeant Mića Mijalković brought and dressed up six reservists. At 24:00, I drove "Niva" back to the camp. I squashed the middle finger of my right hand while closing the door. The pain was intense. I hope I did not break it. Next week, if I do not forget, I should go to the dentist because I have a medication in my teeth. Was the Military Medical Center (MMC) open and was my dentist Milica Stojanović still there? Just before the war, she put the medication.

Danka told me she had bought a box with 20 packets of "Partner" cigarette brand. I told her not to buy it for me anymore. I had to send her some money. I received an advance of 250 dinars. It was time to sleep. At 06:00 I should be going again on duty on the combat position. Today Armush brought 10 liters of distilled water for our power generating units. He was a great guy. He respected me a lot. He also brought coffee in the thermos for the shift crew.

Saturday, April 03

Last night, 44 years after the Second World War, Belgrade was bombed again. The State Government Building Complex and the Interior Ministry Headquarters were hit with eight cruise missiles. We did not know if there were any casualties. One cruise missile exploded just 30 meters away from the Maternity Ward of the Belgrade University Medical Centre and broke all windows. It was a big shock for young women and babies. NATO is really a fascist organisation. The other day a few new generals were promoted. There seemed to be some turmoil at the top. Colonel Stojanče Tomić, my "classmate", told me that some individuals from the political elite had been bringing their own cars into the shelters, in addition to their families. They are protecting their "hard earned assets". People at the Air Force and Air Defence Corps Operations Center were pissed off because they had no radar images to observe combat operations. Long range surveillance radars are almost all taken out. Their radar did not work. Unbelievable, if that was true. If I'm in charge, I would send them, one at a time, to our units. Here, they would have something to see on the radar screen. I wanted to see if they would still need the images or they would be happy to be alive and safe in the bunker. During the exchange of shifts at 06.00, Dani told me that a helicopter had being flying in the Kupinovo village area and that I should watch the space. He said: "Do not radiate, because you would not be able to find it." I absolutely agreed with him. We had earlier agreed on that.

Yesterday, Lieutenant Crnobrnja told Vukosavljević that he found parts of the "Tomahawk" cruise missile in the village of Progar, and that Lieutenant Colonel Gojko Vučic found an unexploded one. It was more likely that these were "HARMs" - anti-radar missiles. Bora said that Lieutenant Colonel Noskov was lucky during the explosion, because the large shrapnel pierced the van above his head and went out to the other side. Despite one door being open, the burst, pressure and compression blew out the second door on the van. Yesterday afternoon Sergeant Ljubenković had a shower in the house of hairdresser Milanka. She greeted me. I reprimanded her husband the other night when he brought the gravel to the combat position while driving his truck with the lights turned on. Yesterday, while we were waiting for the Russian delegation, each officer was given a fake name (Nome de Guerre). We godfathered[24] each other. The greatest burst of laughter came after I baptized Dragan Matić as Taško Načić[25]. I was Anđelko Đorđević. We made jokes and one-liners. We did not baptize Senior Sergeant Sedlak and Mijalković.

Anti-aircraft fire over Belgrade. Surreal scene of the Europe at the end of the 20th century.

We should send out thanks to Pošarac, the superintendent of the "Telecom" maintenance crew from the Pećinci mail office, for helping us with the phone line. Danka was concerned for her father. He worried what would happen if he had to have a kidney surgery. There was no one to look after our families, as it was during the war in Bosnia. They were destined to look after themselves; those who had money, and those who did not.

No one was talking about our salaries, whether they were credited into our accounts of if someone received cash "in their hands", so that we can send some money to the family at home. At 07.00 the Operations Center ordered us to go to Readiness No.2. Sergei Baburin from the Russian State Duma said in Belgrade, after visiting the bombed sites, Russia will not remain aside. The slopes of Fruška Gora mountain were also bombed. What about Vrdnik, my birthplace? It was nestled in the beautiful valley in the

---

24   It is a custom that the godfather names the child at the Christening (typically, the name given is the one parents had chosen)

25   Taško Načić – the famous actor. Their very similar body build, and appearance caused laughter.

65

foothill of the southern slopes.

Milošević and Rugova said that a political solution must be found. The Shiptars[26] realized they were pawns in the American hands. They definitely gave up the war option because the KLA (the so-called Kosovo Liberation Army) was badly beaten in Kosovo and Metohija, the media reported yesterday. The analysts reported that the annual production capacity of the US military industry was 100 cruise missiles. The same analysts estimated that 300 - 400 cruise missiles had been fired on us so far, if we can really trust the media.

The radiator on one generator set leaked coolant, while the oil leaked from the flywheel on the other. The system for selection of moving targets [27] was still defective. Dani did not report it to the Operations Center. We heard again detonations 8 kilometres away from us. They came from the direction of Nikinci - they were trying to do something there. Danni's crew did not know that yesterday, so they radiated searching for targets. Obviously, they did not communicate with the local army Operations Center. The commander of the signals platoon, Lieutenant Stojanović, checked for the correct operation of all available internal and external communication lines.

At 08:43, we were ordered to go to Readiness No.1. At 09:00, I notified Major Janko Aleksić about leaks in the generators, and that we had received two 5V27U missiles, instead of the requested 5V27D missiles.

A few hours later, the brigade workshop team came to repair the power units. They were unable to fix the radiator leak. They sent the Senior Sergeant Jurković to try to sort out the power unit that leaks oil. He was an outstanding officer and expert, who had worked with me in the missile guidance station.

Lieutenant Colonel Dragovan Matijević and journalist Branko Kopunović from the "Vojska" journal, came to the unit. They interviewed Lieutenant Nikolić and me and took pictures of us. I sent 300 dinars to Danka, via Matijević.

Major Roksandić, the missile battery commander, and Lieutenant Nikolić checked if the launch ramps are leveled correctly.

At 21:30 hours the "locators"[28] appeared on the night sky. They showed up as bright spots that changed colors several times. There were at least three or four of them. Dani called me to the combat position - he thought

26   Shiptar or Shqiptar is an Albanian language ethnonym, by which Albanians call themselves. In 1990s, in order to simplify their exclusive claim for the land (Serbian province of Kosovo and Metohija, inhabited by multiple ethnic groups), they started calling themselves "Kosovars". According to the same "script", and at the same time Muslims, in the former Yugoslavian Republic of Bosnia and Hercegovina, renamed themselves to "Bosniaks".

27   This system eases target acquisition and tracking by removing images of the stationary objects (hills, forests, etc.) from the radar screens. Images of the moving objects only (airplanes, helicopters, etc.) show up on the radar screens.

28   In general, devices dropped from the airplanes. Sometimes they were meteorological sensor and sometimes markers.

these were gyrocopters. At 21:40, the bowl of the fuel filter on the power unit of the surveillance radar raptured. We transferred power supply to the other unit. At 23:10 I was notified that the second power unit on the surveillance radar failed. I reported it to Colonel Srba Blagojević at the Operations Center. He angrily replied: "Djole, I'll fucking kill you! How come it blow just now? "There are no targets in the air. You exaggerate," I told him. We all call him "Locator No. 2[29]" because he is an alcoholic. I will tell him to get the fuck off the first time I see him in person. I told him, "As far as the power unit was concerned, we will try to solve the problem. I did not screw it. Do you know what the equipment failure means?!" I never comprehended how someone who was known to drink alcohol excessively, off and on duty, could be appointed to the role where he decided about people and their lives. How the heck we know that he is sober and there is no hangover?! Someone should be held to account for it, instead of abusing the subordinate units and their commanders.

At 23:38, he asked me to turn on the target acquisition radar in the sector from 350 to 0 degrees. He wanted me to look for a helicopter in the Sava River region. The riverbed was not in our zone of responsibility. I refused. Yesterday, we searched in that direction for 10 – 12 seconds with the target acquisition radar, and there was no way we could find anything. Srba then told me, "Go home then!" Colonel Stanković took over the radio and ordered us to search the sector by radiating electromagnetic energy from the antenna. Nobody trusted you, and vanities were marveling. Permanent reflections from stationary objects were so strong that the missile guidance officer could not see anything. I fictitiously commanded it to the crew. This order was a big joke. The helicopter would not fly high enough above the riverbed for me to see it. The helicopter and "Tomahawk" would fly very low above the riverbed following the curvature. Otherwise, they would not need a river. Where are the army air defense units if we are requested to seek targets at the lowest possible altitudes? At what altitude helicopters fly? They could use all their weapons to shoot down helicopters, yet they chose to use us. Our role was to shoot at other targets. Which other word could describe it, other than bashing. Sometimes I'm asking myself do those guys in the Ops know they are doing.

Sunday, April 04

I was on duty from 06:00 to 12:00. At 09:30 we received the signal: "out of readiness" and immediately began transitioning combat assets into the marching configuration. Dani's after midnight shift noticed two targets on the surveillance radar. One was a group target[30] 15 km away, another was just 8 km away. They turned tracking radar two or three times seeking for

---

29   Locator (Serbian: "Lokator") is a derogatory term for an alcoholic. Derived from the verb "lokati", which means "excessively drinking". It is a similar for "locator" - military term for a device used to mark the location of the target.

30   Group target is the radar screen image of a group of airplanes flying in the close proximity of each other.

the target, but they did not find it. It was necessary to sit down together and consider why. Senior Sergeant Ljubenković, operator of the surveillance radar P-18, saw them clearly on his radar screen, while Major Dotlić and Captain Golubović, located at the missile guidance station van, said that the target was very small, as big as a ball-pen point. Was it possible that the cable losses were so high? As soon as possible we should send another officer to assist Ljubenković.

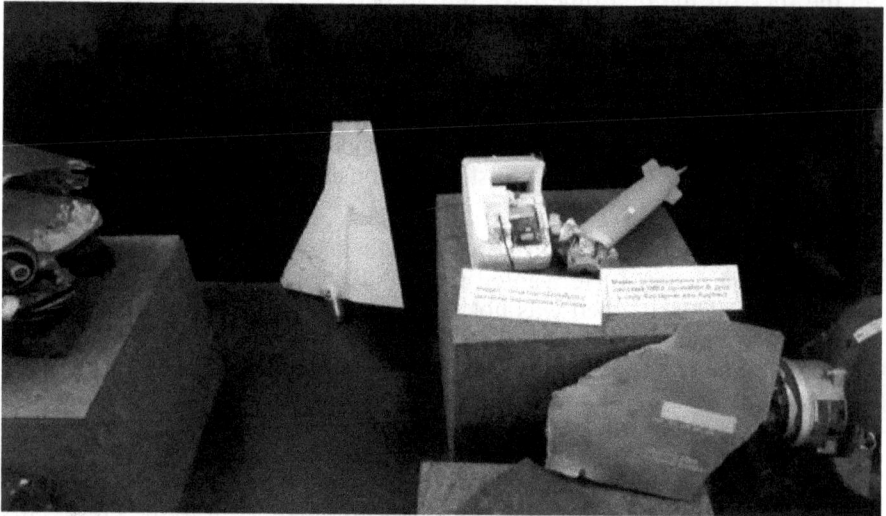

"Locator" packed into the styrofoam box (middle section of the photo) and towed decoy right beside.

Dani sent Major Dotlić, commander's aid for logistics, to the after-midnight shift to replace him as the shift commander. Danni's behaviour recently changed. Yesterday on my way to shower, Žika, the manager of the cooperative farm, told me that Dani had told him that he was promoted to the rank of colonel few days ago. That was it! Hence the behavioral change. He told that news to the man he had met for the first time a few days ago and has been hiding it from his closest associates. What was the reason?! It was not by chance or maybe it was?! People believed that he was Biga's man - protege. Probably general Biga told him that when the Russians visited us.

During transition of the target acquisition radar, the operators Tiosavljević and Volf had disconnected all power cables, but not the command transmitter cable. They inclined the pole, the swivel started to break, and the cable was damaged. Senior Sergeant Tiosavljević with two or three soldiers should go to Jakovo to bring the spare cable. Major Dotlić with driver Lukić went in the "Lada Niva" to Lieutenant Colonel Đević to try to salvage anything useful from his equipment and bring the part with which the cable was connected to. Major Janko Aleksić from the brigade, announced that he would come to the unit to inspect the damage. After I returned from the combat position the local police visited us. They talked about the procedures to be followed after shooting down the aircraft, how best to protect the unit location, and the searching of the terrain by the local hunters to collect whatever they tossed and scattered in the fields [31]. Upon returning to the camp, around 11:30 hours, I found two bags of a new underwear on the bed. The locals raised funds and bought the underwear for the army. Žika's younger daughter led the action. They received us exceptionally well. Vehicles and combat equipment individually left Šimanovci for the predetermined location in the village of Subotište (the Cooperative farm), as soon as it was transitioned into the marching formation. This morning Dani went into reconnaissance for a suitable site and had not returned yet.

Senior Sergeant Milan Barvalac brought the army's ration of cigarettes for the previous six days - three packs per person.

I talked to Danka. Last night they bombarded the Block 70 suburb, the district heating plant or the fuel tanks next to the plant. "It was terrible," she told me. "Whoever did not open windows or balcony doors, the glass shattered."

Lieutenant Crnobrnja told me that Dotlić should contact Terzić from payroll regarding payment of daily allowances for the officers from March 24 to March 31. Dotlić was away with Lieutenant Colonel Đević, so I gave the Terzić's phone number to Kosta, courier, to give it to Dotlić so he can call Terzić when he returned to the command post.

A volunteer Jovica Jovičin from Ruma reported to the unit. Dani wrote a confirmation letter that we needed Jovica and told him to go to the Sremska Mitrovica Military Department, that is, to its Outpost in Ruma, since he was not assigned yet, and we needed him.

This morning around 06:30 Dani called me and told me to tell Colonel Stanković that a locator was found near us. Stanković asked Dani to contact him. I transferred him to Dani. They probably had a conversation.

I sent a pager message to Pošarac to come to Ogar and pick up the cables. Živan Jovanović from Buđanovci saw the shooting and the fall of the of the missile parts. Someone from the missile battery should be sent there to record the number of the missile. "The missile is almost intact", Dani told me when he returned from the reconnaissance around 12:15. On his way back, he met Major Popović from the 250th brigade. The verbal order was issued: "We are returning to the village of Prhovo." I ordered the commander of the missile guidance battery to analyze the behavior of individuals and eliminate mistakes caused by the human factor.

By 20:00 we completed transition into combat configuration on the new combat position in the village of Prhovo. Dani's shift remained on duty until 24:00. All combat assets were fully operational. Major Popović and Captain

---

31   Such things as a land target position-indicating radio-beacon station (LT-PiRBS). The basic purpose of this system is to electronically tag the enemy target. Its radio signal is picked up by missiles and guided bombs, and used in the terminal phase of their flight to pin-point it to the target. During the 1999 war, NATO used special forces and humanitarian workers from Non-Government Organizations (NGOs) to manually put them and mark for destruction the critical infrastructure, for example bridges and other key civilian, government and military facilities.

Vučković were respectively assigned to the neighbouring surveillance radars P-15 and P-12, operated by the command platoon. They verbally communicated to us the airspace situation on their radar screens, just in case our surveillance radar P-18 did not work. They reported over 50 – 60 cruise missiles. This made no sense. It seemed to me that every noise on the screen was interpreted as a cruise missile.

P-18 surveilance radar. A common radar attached to SA-3 battery. This metric wave radar is capable to detect any stealth airplane for at least 40 km. Remote screen VIKO is installed in the missile guidance station.

Monday, April 05

My shift was on duty from 00:00 to 08:00. At 01:00, Stanković ordered us to power up the system and put the voltage on high on the transmitter antenna and be prepared, because cruise missiles had been launched. Around 02:00 a very massive air attack began. We returned to the same position, and Dani's shift radiated for about 45 seconds on cruise missiles and helicopters. They did not find anything. When would our superiors from the brigade command realize that it is very hard to detect targets at the lower limit of the system's ability, and that it is very hard to lock-on a target flying less than 100 meters altitude above the ground? What the army anti-aircraft artillery was doing? The have "Pragas", "Bofors" and "Strelas" located along the trajectory of the likely cruise missiles paths, along the river valleys, main

70

highway, railway lines, etc? Dani told me that he also had an argument with Stanković about it. NATO aviation knew roughly our location, so at one time there were about 10 targets at various azimuth at distances from 20 to 22 km which was just outside of our effective range. They were hunting for us. We reacted calmly. We waited for someone to enter into our 20 km zone of destruction. They were probing us like a fish nibbling the bait and waited for us to reveal our location – by turning on our fire control radar. Further away, at distances 30-35 km, there was another "ring" of the aircraft flying around. Our launch ramps were constantly under "hot start" readiness and there was a danger of being left without a missile[32]. In one situation, the radar emission imitator helped us a lot and drove off two aircrafts, while we were focused on two other aircrafts. Then, another aircraft entered into our zone from the opposite direction to 16 km away from us and, as we were turning our antennas towards him, he quickly escaped before we were able to lock-on him. They were detected at altitudes of 5 to 8 km. Our surveillance also reported that, at the same time, 5 to 6 airplanes crossed over at high altitudes. My attention was directed to the airplane approaching us, and I was unable to simultaneously cover other targets at different altitudes. The S-125M Neva system was designed to lock-on a single target and at anytime it can be a dozen preying on us from different directions. The situation was extremely serious and difficult. There was a deafening silence in the station. Being aware of the situation I was in, Colonel Stanković ordered that if they tried to enter again, I should pick one and shoot at it, without waiting for confirmation from the missile guidance officer and operators of manual tracking that they had taken it up [33]. On three or four occasions that night, we radiated for about 10 seconds in order to discover the target, but we did not succeed. That night shift should be remembered for the enormous workload on the crew. Around 04:00 communication with the brigade command center was lost. It was an extremely strong high-pitched noise, as if the phone was constantly ringing without any interruption. I found out that my classmate Djordjević had shot at around 02:30. 20-30 minutes after that the pressure subsided and they left. Crnobrnja told me that around 09:00, when he came to see me in the Šimanovci camp. He also told me that Djokic had been hit, and that he had three people injured and that Tepavac (not the guy with the same name in our unit) was killed. I did not know the man, and it looked like he was the first officer of the 250th brigade who was killed on duty. Glory to the hero! It could have been my shift that was hit instead of his. Thanks God for keeping us unharmed.

---

32   For three reasons: 1 - the hot start preparation is of limited duration (25 minutes), and it takes time to cool it down (20 minutes) before it can be prepared for launch again; 2 - two missiles are simultaneously "warmed up" on each launch ramp; 3 - this risk does not exist when all four missiles are on a ramp, as the two pairs are alternating in the hot start preparation and cooling down states.

33   The tactical maneuver of the last resort to the effect of "shoot with no clear target" aimed at scaring the enemy aviation to run-away by tricking them to go into an evasive maneuver, because the airspace situation was too difficult for the air-defense unit to manage. The visual impact of the launch of the two missiles, clearly seen from the airspace, is the psychological agent. The missile cost was about $85,000 each.

About 07:00 I talked to Colonel Pauljević, who came to the aid to brigade. I told him to convey to the demagogues at the brigade command center that I would no longer radiate and look for helicopters and cruise missiles. They should find ways to engage the army to be more proactive and to cover the incoming approaches with "Strela", "Igla", "Bofors" and other mall caliber weapons. They should find a way to "light-up" all possible approaches of the incoming cruise missiles, both in the depths and in heights. They should spread across all available anti-aircraft artillery and other assets and let us fight with the aviation. They are all demagogues, who thought they knew everything. Let them come here, man the workstations and let them radiate and work as they can and know how to fight. No one from the brigade command volunteered to join to any of the combat battalions and fight along them, where it was firing and dying. Lieutenant Colonel Gojko Vučić was the only officer who went to the unit of his classmate Lieutenant Colonel Noskov.

At about 16:30, Pera Banga, a friend who resigned from the military and who lived in Prhovo, came to the combat position. His parents were there - he called me to visit him and that he would cook a goulash in the clay pot. I thanked him and said that it was not feasible under the current circumstances. Goulash in the clay pot will be delicious, though... but we have to wage a war.

I talked to Danka. She was calm this time. We were used to war. I was glad she was not panicking any more. She changed the building where she worked. She worked every other day. I was eager to have a coffee with her. I lost weight. I noticed from the holes on my belt.

Around 17:00 the police came in and asked me to assign an officer to go with them and examine the missile, which was found near the Mihaljevci village, half-length buried into the ground. I sent them to Dani in Šimanovci, to send someone from the missile battery. I was in the shift tonight from 18:00 to 24:00.

Lieutenant Colonels Bajić, Koman and Major Stančić came around 17:30 to mount a thermal imagining camera to the target acquisition radar, which could "see" for an hour and a half after sunset and for the same period before sunrise. They explained to us to shoot with the aperture fully open [34] because of the flash of light if we launch. The officers praised me with the words: "Bravo man, you became the legend. You fucked up all their sales to Saudi Arabia, they had a pre-contract for the delivery of 40 Nighthawks [35]."I asked Bajić, if he could, to put pressure for the urgent completion of the remote control upgrade of the radar emission imitator. The quick upgrade was very important, as it would speed up its operation and could save lives. The remote control would enable the operator, officer, to remain in the trench all the time. Currently, when ordered to change the azimuth of radar emission imitator, the officer must leave the trench, run to the device, manually turn it to the new azimuth, run back into the trench and then radiate. The trench was located about a hundred meters away from the device. It was a rather primitive operation!? Was there a more adequate expression to describe it?

---

34   With the low aperture number, say f/2, for initial wide-angle view.
35   F-117 Nighthawks, were marketed as an invisible and undetectable stealth tactical bomber aircrafts (before 27 March 1999).

And it could have been even more automated: synchronized rotation of the radar imitator as the missile guidance officer turns the target acquisition radar. This should be very simple and cheap. There had been no investments in the army for years. Everyone wants success now. With what? With a sling shot?! And on top of all that officers from our superior command acted as if they did not know how and in what way we had been working.

Lieutenant Crnobrnja told us that he heard that the Captain, Tepavac from Obrenovac battalion was killed because the blocks in the missile guidance station van were not firmly fixed. When the anti radar missile hit the target acquisition radar, the detonation blasted the block from the housing and killed him. Senior Sergeant Zdenko Volf, checked and tightened everything in our guidance station.

At all times four missiles should be on the launch ramp, due to the missiles' reset times whilst on the ramp. Otherwise, it may occur that there is no launch ready missile on the launcher ramp. I did not think that the missile battery commander, Roksandić had thought about that.

At 19:25 hours, Crnobrnja stopped a civilian person - Teodor Rajić from Rakovica, who was jogging. Rajić was a high-performance athlete who represented Yugoslavia in karate and won few medals for us.

Bajić finished installing the camera, set it up and focused until 19:50. The field of view was solid.

In the period from 20:00 to 24:00 we were in Readiness No. 1, practically to the end of the shift.

I watched on the surveillance radar the orgy of NATO aviation over Novi Sad. I remembered my beloved city. I remembered last summer having a coffee with Danka in the beautiful pedestrian oasis. But then, an airplane appeared at a distance of 22 km. It did not enter our engagement zone. Everything was ready. The missiles were prepared. Adrenaline was pumping, but our heartbeats were regular. They have got the nerves of steel. Captain Muminović, missile guidance officer and Senior Sergeant Tiosavljević admitted that they have had big cramps the previous night. Tiosavljević told me that when he had looked at my screen and saw how many targets were around us, he got sick and turned his head away towards his screen and did not dare to look again at my screen again. Tepavac told me that an aircraft had just flew over in our vicinity. I did not see it on my radar screen.

After yesterday, when I told to Colonel Pauljević that we would not be fucked anymore by anybody form the brigade HQ and that we would not be looking for cruise missiles and helicopters with our target acquisition and fire control radar SNR-125, the situation improved. They realized that it was crazy, or impossible, to discover and successfully engage a very low flying target.

Upon arrival to his shift, Dani told me that he had dreamt soldier Kosta was waking him up, and he told him that I volunteered to stay on the combat position for another shift. He continued to sleep. When the soldier came again and said that all the officers and soldiers were on the bus and waited only for him, he jolted and jumped out of bed as if he was scalded with hot liquid or steam. For this reason, the shift was 10 minutes late. I did not take it to heart, I knew that all of us are exhausted.

Last night Senior Sergeant Ilija Vučković experienced an intense electronic interference and active noise interference at the surveillance radar, while working for the brigade command. He had been providing us the airspace situation data under very difficult conditions.

Senior Sergeant Slavko Varga replaced Ljubenković on our surveillance radar and fitted very well into the role. He did everything as I had ordered him.

I felt that the crew looked at me with great respect and trust. They precisely executed every command. They are aware that we are a team and that only a highly trained and well-rehearsed team can do something and survive. It is weird that the men remained calm in these exceptional situations, and that there was no fear, and how much everything was focused on cold-blooded decision-making.

Tuesday, April 06

Every day is a win. An officer said that he thought that it would be fucking shitty tonight from 00:00 to 06:00. I was not worried. Major Dotlić and Senior Sergeant Bugarian visited us. They went to the village of Mihaljevce to look at the booster, the first stage of the missile, and to bring it back. We will compare the serial numbers to check if it was part of our missile. I ordered Major Stoimenov, the battalion engineer, to power up the surveillance radar P – 18 from the missile guidance station van generator. The generator on the surveillance radar could then be switched off, which would save fuel.

Lieutenant Nikolić called home and gave our phone number to his father so he can call him. It was customary that we call our relatives, not the other way round. The telephone lines would be "red hot" otherwise. I brought this to his attention. I watched mother nature wake up. Wonderful morning. The "džanarika"[36] plums blossomed. How nice Spring is.

Fuck the war and the stupidities of this world.

Danka works today. I did not know her phone number. I will call her in the afternoon. She was much calmer after she heard me. I understood her and I wanted to see her. Thirteen days of war. Sargeant Maletić has a reservist assigned to his power supply equipment, a nice boy, Slaviša Pavlović. "If the war goes on for another month, Slaviša would be screwed. "Everyone was laughing at their workstations.

In the "Novosti" newspaper I saw Tepavac's death notice. We were all sorry.

---

36   Džanarika – is a wild cherry tree. Its status is more of a weed than a fruit, probably because of ease of its germination. Its thick shade makes it suitable for landscaping. For many urban kids dzanarika is the first contact with a fruit on the tree.

Danka told me yesterday that she had not received her fuel vouchers. I was angry. I will call Kovačević in the local police station and fix it. I knew she was worried about her old parents. They think that e and my guys saving the face of this country and brought glory to it. I slapped NATO in the face and the whole world saw it, yet our administration system had not solved the procurement of fuel vouchers. I was disappointed at the indifference regarding the care for our families.

At 11:30, Stoimenov reported that they had transferred the power supply of the surveillance radar to the distribution switchboard of the command post van. The launch ramp to the west direction[37] was topped-up with 2 additional missiles, so now we have plenty[38] of missiles and the utilization[39] of the missile battery was now at 75%.[40]

Kovačević called me from the police station in Pećinci and said he would bring me a 40 litres fuel voucher for Danka, just in case.

I went for the reconnaissance for the potential new combat sites in the village of Karlovčić and found one that was very nice and easy to set up. After that I found an engineering unit. The commander is Lieutenant Colonel Nikola Stanisavljević. We visited site and I explained to him in detail and drew a sketch on how to engineers can prepare it and construct earthwork berms.

Later I visited Milan and Nada, Danka's father and mother, whose house is located on the outskirts of the village. Finally, I had a bath and slept for an hour or an hour and a half. Nada was happy. In their house I also met a retired Colonel Sima. He hugged me and congratulated for my achievement.

Tonight I'm in a shift from 00:00 to 06:00.

When passing through Deč, the sky was burning from marker ammunition rounds of 20/3 mm anti-aircraft artillery cannons. They probably shot at cruise missiles. The second tie belt on my left boot snapped, and now left boot was a bit loose.

Today, Colonel Stanković visited our unit, so Dani and his shift were 45 minutes late. Dani told me that he had asked him why I had been nervous. Dani answered him: "How can you not be, I am nervous too when you give us stupid orders!" Today I found out, if that was true, how Djokić's Obrenovac battalion was hit. They discovered a pair of planes at 30 kilometers apart and switched to the tracking radar with an emission interval of 6-10 seconds, and someone on the side hit them with an anti-radar missile. Waging the war "by-the-book" was not good. The enemy was certainly aware of our training manuals and capabilities of our weapon systems.

---

37   The unit started the war with just two launching ramps. Each ramp could accommodate 4 missiles.

38   For the first time during the war on the combat position Prhovo the unit had 6 missiles loaded.

39   Utilization of the missile battery (in the air-defense jargon) – is the ratio of the number of loaded missiles and the maximum number of missiles that can be loaded on the available ramps.

40   The unit had 6 missiles loaded (6 out of 8 is 75%). Before that, the unit had only four missiles loaded, two on each ramp, so the utilization was 50%.

Seleznev[41] was visiting Yugoslavia today.

I was in the shift from 00:00 to 08:00 hours.

Novi Sad was bombed during my shift. Colonel Pauljević was at the brigade command post in the Operations Center. He gave us a sector of responsibility and it was pleasurable working with him. After the shift I tried to rest and bit. At 10:15, Dani called me and said we are moving. I told the Senior Sergeant Žugić, the commander of the camp in Šimanovci, to send drivers with vehicles to pick the equipment and private Lukić, a driver, to pick up the troops. They came very quickly. The shift crew was in place and we began transitioning equipment into the marching configuration, when the order came from the brigade command to immediately get into the Radiness No.1. The battery commander Golubović asked them how to turn back into the combat configuration when we had already started transitioning. Blagojević (the drinker) replied: "Okay, you should have started at 10:15, immediately after you were ordered to relocate." It was obvious the order was not communicated to the shift crew until the vehicles that I sent from Šimanovci arrived.

The transition was completed very quickly, at 12:15. Dani was still scouting for the new position.

Senior Sergeant Jović packed the radar emission imitator (IRR) and Sergeant Volf drove the vehicle with the device.

From "Termomont" in Šimanovci I took 14 m of cable, with a male and female socket and handed it to the battery commander, Captain Golubović. They needed an extension cable.

During the transition, Lieutenant Colonel Noskov with his battalion was on the Readiness No.1 and guarded us. Crnobrnja came and we talked in the car. He said he would get a flack jacket. We needed at least 10 pieces per battalion, for the people on the combat position. I looked forward to it, but since I did not sleep the last day and night, and I will not sleep again all day today, I felt that my head was in chaos.

Major Stoimenov and Armuš went to the woods to collect another 50 tree trunks.

We were going to the village of Popince. This was our fifth relocation since the war started.

Doctor Djukić, the battalion medical doctor, reminded me that tomorrow I should go to the dentist in Pećinci.

Fuel workshop - FAP truck broke down. We need to provide another vehicle. Everyday something happen... well, it is not boring at all to be mis-

---

41   Gennadiy Nikolayevich Seleznyov was a Russian politician, the Chairman of the State Duma.

sileers in the war.

By 19:10 we completed transition to the combat configuration, which I reported to the Operational Center. In the meantime, we were masking and protecting the missile guidance station van and the power distribution switchboard van with the tree trunks. Sergeant Volf carried out the works. I admired him working professionally on "Kraz" vehicle crane.

Major Roksandić arranged the launch ramps at an angle of 60° at the new combat position. That was not good. The reservist soldiers objected when I interrupted the works, one reservist said to Roksandić: "Congratulations Major, you really know your job well." I told them that everyone could make a mistake, that it is human to make mistakes and that the major is exhausted. It was better to correct the error now than when someone lose his head. They looked at me and agreed with me and drove the launch ramp where I ordered it. A problem arose during the mounting of the camera monitor because the cable had no connectors, so the picture was lost.

When I reported it to Blagojević at the Operations Center that we set up the combat position in Popinci, he expressed admiration: "Is it possible, Djole, that you have finished? Congratulations." He finally reacted with understanding, unlike the other day. I went to Šimanovci to order courier Kosta to set up the camp room for the command. I had beans for dinner... no, wait... that was for lunch... Whatever... This was only the second or third time that I ate on time and with the others. Major Dotlić brought our daily allowances while we were transitioning the equipment. This allowance raised the morale of the soldiers and officers.

At 20:00 we went to Readiness No. 1. Regular duty... The equipment was working again, our eyes were tied to the radar turning time base. How long will it be? The sky was clear until 23:30, then I noticed six airplanes. Their azimuths ranged from 30 to 350 degrees. They were far away, so not a danger for us. As if they were probing for our air defense sites and looking where are missile units are located. This was a relatively quiet night compared to the last one. We heard on the news that the General Staff Headquarters building was hit by "Tomahawks." No formal confirmation of that action yet. When I took the water bottle, I did not notice that it was open, and the water spilt a lot. I wetted everything - trousers, blouse, underwear. It was a cold night, so I ordered a soldier to turn on the heater.

The NATO meeting was held in Brussels. They acknowledged huge losses in aviation, and Crnobrnja called me and said that he got information that they would diversify combat operations by deploying helicopters with special forces. At that moment, I thought that people on the combat position were unprotected during combat operations and that we had to take measures regarding this issue. Some 36 planes were downed or damaged so far. I set up one SA-7 (Strela 2M) MANPAD section on the highway overpass. Lieutenant Stojanović and his signal platoon provided excellent communications. I watched my shift. Captain Muminović, the missile guidance officer; Sergeant Volf operator of manual tracking on F1; Senior Sergeant Tiosavljević operator of manual tracking on F2; behind my back, deputy shift commander, Major Stoimenov; commander of the missile battery, newly promoted Lieutenant, Nikolić, and; private Davor Bložić, note-taker.

Senior Sergeant Maletić and soldier-reservist Slaviša Pavlović were on the power generation unit. Ljubenković was on the surveillance radar. Lovely guys and good soldiers. They were having a nap. I allowed it. We finished the shift last night, transitioned and relocated to the new position and are in the shift again. During a check for the correct operation of the missile guidance station van, it was found out that the amplydine[42] that controls vertical movement of the target acquisition radar was not working. The fault was repaired by Stoimenov, Muminović and Tiosavljević, while the others went to the camp to rest.

The logistics support did not do its job in the camp. I was angry. This must be resolved in the morning. The accommodation had to be arranged and furnished before the shift crew returned to the camp. It was unacceptable that the combat crew had no place to sleep.

Thursday, April 08

Major Boris Stoimenov woke me up at 07:00. He wanted us to go to the village post office before our shift commenced to send the allowances we had received yesterday to his wife. The post office was closed. Some local people explained to us where we can find the postman. He has a private grocery store, where Boris gave him the address and money. He wanted to eat burek[43] and yoghurt. He loved yoghurt very much. There was none to buy in Popinci. We went back to the camp. Stoimenov led our shift, went to the combat position, and Dani's shift crew returned to the camp without him. Dani stayed on the combat position as my replacement, having known about my dental appointment. He must have forgotten our agreement yesterday that Boris would take up my role too, until I return from the dentist. I went to the combat position and there we confirmed that Boris would replace me, and agreed to improve logistics in the camp: after duty, the shift crew must return toa well-arranged camp and do not have to worry about where they would sleep. This required the action of Senior Sergeant Sedlak. I returned Dani to the camp and went to Dr. Djukić to find out the details of my dental appointment he had arranged earlier. I had to take out a drug from my upper right-hand fifth tooth that was put in there to kill[44] my nerve. He was having breakfast when I came to the house he resided in. There was ham, boiled eggs and cheese. The hosts did not want to have breakfast without me. I joined them out of courtesy.

---

42   An amplidyne is an electromechanical amplifier invented prior to World War II to amplify low power control signals to control powerful electric motors (tens of kilowatts). It consists of an electric motor driving a DC generator. Its applications include to aim the antiaircraft missile artillery radar or naval gun to a target, or to control processes in steelworks. Amplidynes are now obsolete technology, replaced by modern power semiconductor electronic devices, such as MOSFETs and IGBTs.

43   Burek is a traditional pastry dish popular all over the Balkans where it is considered as fast food, so you can try it on nearly every corner in bakeries, pastry shops or burek shops, but you must never forget – the yogurt with it.

44   To devitalize the pulp which has the nerve tissue of that tooth.

I left Pećinci and went to the shoe-repairer Cveja to fix the buckle on my left boot and my gun holster, which was completely ripped. He did not have a buckle, and instead, put one gray and one white metal plate. He said, "to protect you against spells", as a joke. I went to the local police station to meet Kovačević to arrange for Danka's vouchers. I provided her vouchers for 20 liters of petrol. While we were having a coffee, they were looking to find me a new pair of boots. They did not have my size.

I went to the medical centre to visit the dentist. While on the staircase I felt the vibration of the pager. The message was from Danka. She asked me if I had received her message yesterday. "No", I replied. "How come?" She wondered. I contacted Danka after my appointment and told her that I had a job to do in Karlovčić and that I would visit her parents. There were plenty of beautiful places in the village. The soil was sloppy with salt marshes and uncultivated. I visited her parents. Milan hugged me. Some guy was chopping firewood for him. They packed sausages, smoked pork shoulder ham and eggs for soldiers. Nada prepared lunch. It was a pleasant feeling, at least for a moment, to feel the domestic atmosphere for several hours and try to forget about the ongoing war. We had a coffee. The flower pots were taken out of the house onto the terrace[45]. The living room doors were wide open. There was not enough time for longer conversations. I had a shower and tried to relax, but that was far from real relaxation. It was the relaxation of the body, but not that of the mind. They were also getting used to the war conditions of life. I fell asleep, relaxed and clean, after removing the dirt accumulated in the last few days. After 15-16 days of war and sleeping in lairs and dirt, this was "bingo". I may have been a bit confused as if it was strange. My life and my time now went the other way: in the direction of survival and subsistence. I told them about Muminović's daughter. Senad told to Dule Lupulov that he, as the missile guidance officer, had launched the missile that shot down the F-117A, and Dule passed it on to Senad's wife. The woman said that to their daughter and son. When he phoned home, his daughter asked him: "Is it true what the mom says?" He answered her that there was some truth in it. "If that's true, Dad, I'm proud of you to the moon and back," said his daughter. She was only 11-12 years old. I remembered my son. Was he proud of me? Pera Banga told me a few days ago in Prhovo that my neighbor Novica, who lives across my ex-father-in-law, would bring my son Vlada to Prhovo to see me. He did not come. I secretly hoped he did not know or did not receive the message. I might be wrong, or I just did not want to believe otherwise. Perhaps the truth was something else. I was about to go towards a new uncertainty and sleepless night. The unrest was creeping up into my body and soul. It was happening every evening and every night. God how long was the night. Milan told me that the whole Srem[46] was talking about some Aničić. The officers were trusted and highly regarded. They were highly knowledgeable and respected. Why we did not have more modern weapons? Before we parted, I left 550 dinars for Danka if she come. I also left Milan parts from the F-117A to share with their friends and with whomever they wanted to. He was proud of this, and all those to whom he

45   It is a custom in rural and semi-rural areas to take sensitive plants inside the house during winter, usually lemons and Mediterranean flowers. These non-native plants cannot survive the snow and outside sub-zero temperatures.

46   Srem is the name of the region.

gave a piece were highly honoured.

I sat in the car and arrived at 19.00 at the Popinci camp. Dani was sleeping, and Major Dotlić replaced him in the shift; after Dani called him to come from Ogar. We talked about what we did today. He took Golub and Roksandić to Šimanovci for lunch. They didn't pay. The owner did not want to charge them. In the evening, after half an hour, the President of the Local Municipality Slobodan (Boban) Petrović and Radovan Babić came. They brought two (apparently air dropped) leaflets[47] with different contents. I had the originals in my wallet. They were printed on the same machine and had different document identification (ID) numbers at the bottom[48]. I did not write their content, because there was no time[49]. The debate was about how they were thrown out and from what. How best to organise the village to search the terrain?[50] The hunters are overloaded. The ladder in the church was damaged[51]. "Make a new one," I told them. It looked as if we were not burdened. They were unorganized and were dealing with themselves. I told them that there was a saying in my village: "you are making a chapel from that thing." They laughed, but they understood the message very clearly. They discussed the mentality of the people of Srem. They were right. Sremac[52] was proud and hot headed.

It started to rain, and thunder roared. I received a pager message to call Danka. I could not call her now. If time allows, I will call back later or in the morning. Danka told me that she had told Ljuba and Djole[53] in Vrdnik that we shot down the airplane. Both first cried from the happiness that I was in the crew and commanded the shooting of the airplane, and then celebrated with their friends and neighbours. I could only imagine how that news spread among the residents of Vrdnik.

I laid down to sleep, as I will be in the shift tonight from 00:00 to 06:00 but could not fall asleep and a thousand spined thoughts on my mind. About life, status, my future... I now understand the pre-war horoscope for Nataša, Danka's daughter, Danka and me. I was told that I would live a long time if

---

47   The leaflets were written in the Serbian Cyrillic script on a glossy paper.

48   The document IDs were probably intended for the field operatives who could not understand them.

49   These largely followed key messages intended for domestic audience in the NATO and NATO-friendly countries. As such, they caused quite unintended reaction of the bombed population, homogenizing it against the aggressor.

50   Searching around the combat position for any enemy radio locator that would reveal the (approximate) location of the division (combing of the terrain as in search for forensic evidence near the crime-scene). The radio locator(s) could have been placed overnight or by a daytime passer-by.

51   A typical Serbian church has the adjacent bell tower that dominates the landscape. A hunter or local resident would climb up on the top of the bell tower and monitor all access roads to the village, whenever it was possible. They provided additional security for the battalion, they knew each other and signaled us each time they spotted an approaching outsider.

52   Sremac is a resident of the Srem region.

53   Ljuba and Djole are good friends.

I survived the age of 42. In a few days, I will be 41 and I will enter the 42nd year of my life. That gave me a shiver. I always carried a church calendar in my pocket, which Djordje, my namesake from Ogar, gave me to keep me safe. In it there was Trojeručica[54,55]. In October, Danka gave me a consecrated cross of teak wood and placed it around the door to keep me safe. I was exhausted, random thoughts were flashing through my mind. Somehow, I fell asleep and it seemed to me that I just closed my eyes when the courier Kosta woke me up with a double size, mid-strength, coffee. It was time to prepare for the shift. Just before my departure Dani returned from the bar. I could smell alcohol. He said he drank two or three beers. Colonel Ivanović, called Munja[56], from the Corps Air Defense, came to visit us. Together with the crew from my shift, I left for the combat position in the Lada-Niva, and then into the missile guidance station van, into the air stillness and the hum and the buzz of the equipment working monotonously. Maybe Danka was right when she said: "Well, you are all deaf." I did not get the underwear yet which she had sent to me via Matijević, my classmate. Dotlić left to Ogar in the Lada Niva and at 00:03, we were ordered to go into Readiness No. 1, until the morning. There were no targets in our zone. During the whole night we saw only a few airplanes north of us at the distances 45 km and further away. Around 01:00, Colonel Ivanović and Dani arrived in the station. He was with us until 02:30. He told us that our two "Kub" (SA-6) system missile batteries were hit. He liked the idea that we strapped the tree-trunks around the missile guidance station van. I learned from Major Stoimenov that he liked to drink. I didn't know him but realised that he knew about me. Around 03:00 thunder started and one lighting struck somewhere on the combat position. There was a lot of bare metal equipment all around. Immediately before the lightning strikes, the lamps on the intercom turned on from the induction, which was followed by the lightning strike. Senior Sergeant Jović, from the radar emission imitator, wanted to leave the position and go into the vehicle. "How can I get you if I need you?" "Not at all." "Well, then you cannot go. Stay where you are. You can save our lives." He was not happy. At the combat position in Šimanovci, he was afraid to be at the signals control centre, which was located at the combat position. He wanted to go to the imitator. Now he did not like that either. He now wanted to go back to the signals control centre, because the center was now located much further away from the center of the combat position. Apparently, he had difficulty in controlling his fear.

At about 05:00 I heard the news. They heavily bombarded Belgrade, Kragujevac, Jagodina, Valjevo, etc. Danka told me that she had seen on TV

---

54   *Bogorodica Trojeručica* meaning *"Three-handed Theotokos"*) or simply *Trojeručica* (*Three-handed*) is a famous wonderworking icon in the Serbian Orthodox monastery of Hilandar on Mount Athos, Greece. It is the most important icon of the Serbian Orthodox Church.

55   It depicts Theotokos (Virgin Mary) with young Jesusin the *hodegetria* position: holding the Child Jesus at her side while pointing to Him as the source of salvation for humankind. The Virgin's head usually inclines towards the Child, who raises his hand in a blessing gesture. In the Western Churches this type of icon is sometimes called *Our Lady of the Way*

56   Munja means the "lighting bolt".

a short news report about the three American soldiers that were captured in Kosovo: the news said that they were good kids and students; their parents and their nation were worried about them. Whose children are we? Was the nation worried about us? They were disgusting and filled me with abhorrence. And, our children were crying in the bone-chilling cold of the cellars, sharing their space with mice and rats. How would this affect our children and how would they grow up? Indeed, this period was evoking the darkest thoughts and wishes in people.

Friday April 09

The replacement shift came at 08:00 and my shift went back to the camp. Senior Sargent Djordje Maletić's house was just 7-8 km away from the combat position, near Golubinci. He asked me to give him a lift home, to have a cup of coffee there and have breakfast. How could I refuse? We are friends. I was tired, but I went. I saw an old adobe house[57], his mother, an old woman, I think she was one and a half meter tall, Djole's wife and son. His elderly mother was good-natured. They were very happy to see us. His son name is Saša and I jokingly told him: "Come on, uncle Djole will give you a lolly." Everybody laughed, and so am I while I'm writing this in my diary. Today is Good Friday. I was not a fussy eater when visiting other people's homes and I had fried eggs, salami, and homemade sausages. After the breakfast, I returned to Popinci and Djole remained at home. Someone will give him a lift. I was very tired and laid to sleep and slept until 14:00. Mika Stojanović, commander of the signals platoon, made a coffee. While I was sleeping, Danka's second message came in. I told her to calm down and not to worry. I promised her that I would message her whenever I can, so she would know that I'm alive. She replied that when all this ended, she would never quarrel; she missed me and the peacetime. "I miss my pension," I added.

It was Todor's birthday today. Nataša gave him a present: a piece of the stealth foil from the plane[58]. She said that she would not buy him any other present for his birthday, and that no one would ever give him such a gift in his life. Todor's father was thrilled and said he would frame it for safe keeping; he was a retired Colonel with a professional habit of collecting war memorabilia.

They sent us a fish soup for lunch from Ogar. We received the best possible welcome here; they really took the best care of us. The soup was good, but it was full of bones. I remembered how Danka always sieved fish soup. At 15:50 I went to the combat position. Dani told me that the commandant of the Air Defense Corps, general Bane Petrović, would come to visit us around 16:30. This morning around 07:50, Crnobrnja called me to tell me

57   The building is built from sun-dried mud-bricks, rendered with mud plaster and painted white inside and outside. Mud is usually mixed with sawdust (or straw, and/or sand).

58   The stealth skin of the downed F-117A stealth airplane, dark colored, about 1mm thick. Namely, it was easier to peel-off the skin, than to cut it together with the solid piece of the airplane frame or wing to which it was glued.

that Noskov, with his battalion, was ordered to cross to the North side of the Danube River and go to the Pančevo region[59], instead of going to Bečmen as was planned earlier. He told me that nothing was clear to him now, nor did he know how to transport the column of vehicles through Belgrade[60]. Everyone would see it! He seemed to be worried and frightened for Noskov. He told me he did not know his status yet, whether he would go with Noskov or he would stay with us. So far, we have always been in front of Noskov[61], which probably suited him. I noticed that he was not indifferent anymore, after Noskov was ordered to relocate to the region defended only by Lieutenant Colonel Mijović with his battalion.

Dani told me he was going to the camp to shave, and then he would return to the front "checkpoint" on the combat position to greet the general. It looked as if I did not know how to report to the general. "Nobody will take away your glory," I thought, "because even you cannot take it away from us. That downing of the stealth fighter was a team effort, the team shot, not the sole individual action." Let him do it, as he wanted. He had completely immersed himself in some other, higher, role and function. From our perspective, he had been exploiting the success of the whole team for himself. This was clearly noticeable from a few days ago. My intuition, his actions and behaviour that disregarded the collective indicated that I'm right. The command post van was fully operational when we arrived, and the crew was in Readiness No. 1 – also known as 'on-the-active-duty regime'.

I am sitting in front of the van while writing this. I laughed at Miki Stojanović today - he said: "The Command has cars, and I procured myself a bike." Lieutenant Nikolić asked me for permission to go to the surveillance radar, because some local girls had brought bags, to see what they had brought. I let him go, and after 15-20 minutes he returned with a bag full of popcorn. He said: "Tomorrow will be pancakes; today popcorn, because today is a fasting day." I recalled Colonel Ivanović "Munja" and his stories: "During the explosion of an anti-radar missile targeting a Kub[62] antiaircraft system, two officers died. One was in the cabin with a shirt on, the other in a blouse. The third one had a windproof jacket on him, and he survived. Apparently, the windproof fabric stopped the shrapnel from the HARM missile." Madness. I had said many times so far "There is no death without judgement day." I often remember my late mother and father. For a long time I had not been at the cemetery. I would go as soon as I can, to light up the candles and ask them to keep me safe. I knew that both loved me a lot in their

---

59   To strengthen, probably, air-defenses on the incoming approaches of the enemy aviation.

60   In 1999, there was only one bridge in Belgrade across the Danube River. After the war ended, the Chinese government built the 2nd bridge and gifted it to the Serbian people.

61   Facing first the incoming enemy aviation on its way out of the war theatre, before they 'cross' the border and escape.

62   The 2K12 *"Kub"* (NATO reporting name: SA-6 "Gainful") mobile surface-to-air missile system is a Soviet low to medium-level air defence system designed to protect ground forces from air attack. Relative to S-125 Neva system the 3rd battalion had the Kub was the next generation air defence system.

own ways. Mother, after all this, would be very proud of me.

Before our shift began, Maletić brought home made cherry pies to the camp. He also brought one box to the combat position. Major Stoimenov asked Dani to go home to Smederevo. He did not allow him. Stoimenov got confused. He did not win the argument. I was nibbling pumpkin seeds.

I noticed that night duty was wearing me off without a chew. I chewed my chewing gum and probably all my fear, anxiety and uneasiness shifted into my teeth, relieving my body and mind. Maybe it was just illusory, but I knew that I felt better and safer, and I felt as if I was spreading my confidence to the people. At 18:55 I got a pager message from Dani. He was in Pećinci with Kovačević from the local police department. At 19:00 we went into Readiness No. 2. The newspapers reported a recent NATO media statement that, according to the latest information, 32 to 36 planes had been lost or damaged. Serbia is a small country and if any airplane had a chance to fly over any border, they will do that just not to crash on our territory. The material damage was huge. The Dutch and Norwegian pilots refused to fly. NATO had lost over 88 soldiers and officers (probably some special forces with Albanian terrorists), and some 1,500 soldiers in Macedonia threw their guns and deserted to Greece and Bulgaria. Is this true, I don't know but I hope it is. Seleznyev announced that Yeltsin and Lukashenko agreed for Yugoslavia to form the alliance of Russia and Belarus. The Albanians[63,64,65,] tried to get into the territory of Yugoslavia at the Košare border post[66] on the Yugoslavia – Albanian border. That was a serious international incident[67,68,69]. The attack

---

63   In February 1998, the USA State Department removed the Kosovo Liberation Army (KLA from the Terrorism List.

64   The para-military forces NATO trained in Albania included: about 1,500 KLA members; foreign Muslim jihad volunteers (better known as Al-Qaeda at the time) with the aim of fighting for Islam (as mujahideen) and helping their co-religionists in Kosovo and Metohija; and veteran Bosnian mujahideen.

65   In October 1998, an annual international Islamic conference in Pakistan formally characterized the Kosovo Liberation Army's struggle as 'jihad'.

66   Located in the Metohija region on the slopes of the Prokletije Mountains, near town of Djakovica and the famous medieval Serbian Orthodox monastery Dečani.

67   The forceful attack surprised the Yugoslav Army (as the NATO land attack was expected from Macedonia, where NATO troops were amassed) and the KLA seized the Košare border post, but failed to penetrate deeper into Kosovo and Metohija, which was the main goal of the attack. Until 9 April 1999 NATO did not bomb Košare, but did bomb other positions on the Yugoslavia-Albanian border.

68   The military objective of the KLA, NATO and the Albanian army was to penetrate Metohija and engage the Yugoslavia Army forces, hidden and well masked at the time, in the open fight in which the technological advantage of NATO aviation would prevail.

69   At that time, there were just over 100 members of the Yugoslav Army's order units. Due to fierce air attacks and diversions of the KLA, more help could not have arrived at once.

was broken, just like many times before[70,71,72,73]. I heard it on the news at 18:00. I did not watch TV and I did not read newspapers regularly, so I was largely disconnected from the outside world and events reported in the media[74]. I did not see the images of destruction, which was probably better for all of us who were sitting in the missile guidance station van in the meadow. Dani informed me that general Bane Petrović was in a hurry and that he did not have enough time to visit the combat position and my shift. I was sitting and thinking: "The injustice was done to the people who were not listed as members of the combat crew that shot down the airplane: soldier Davor Bložić, notetaker, soldier for liaison with external radar stations, Major Boris Stoimenov, my deputy shift commander, the crew of the power supply section, and the one of the surveillance radar, the signals platoon.

At 19:25 hours, Readiness No. 1 was ordered via a civilian telephone line. After about 3 to 4 minutes I reported back that the order had been executed. Blagojević asked me to signal him the message, as he apparently did not understand me. "You are a douche bag," I thought, "We should minimally use the communication lines to understand each other, preferably without using the official signals code in effect." His mind was shackled in some rigid peacetime military jargons. It looked like he had not adapted to the wartime conditions yet. On the first occasion/when the first opportunity arises, and I knew that this moment would come, I will tell him to "go and fuck yourself," because he had long been annoying me. Changes in his mood toward the subordinate crews were drastic. The people from the unit called him the "alcoholic". Boris Samardžic had the same nickname, but quite nice personality when under the influence.

It just came to my mind, Danka told me yesterday that it had been reported that three pilots had flown over us and that one of them could not dump the bombs, turned the plane around and landed at the Sarajevo airport. The other two acted out. I did not know which country the first pilot was from; but

70   After the fall of the border post, there was an increase of hundreds of members of the Yugoslav Army from infantry and special units, so that the front line was stabilized on 19th April and there were no major movements until the end of the war. The territory captured was only four kilometers wide and a few hundred to one thousand meters deep.

71   At the height of the battle, the army of Yugoslavia had about 1,200 soldiers, and the KLA, with volunteers and Albanian units of five to six thousand. The KLA forces waged shifts, while the Yugoslav soldiers had no rest.

72   Awareness that if the Košare front line falls, much more serious clashes with the KLA and NATO would ensue, with an uncertain outcome, had kept morale at a high level. The Yugoslav Army often went into attacks in the icy rain, cold, fog, and snow, one meter deep, and defended every position until the last moment - which further affected the fall of morale in the enemy.

73   The Yugoslav Army had 108 dead, while the KLA had more than 200 plus unknown number of mujahedeen.

74   Foreign mujahideen were required to leave the Balkans under the terms of the 1995 Dayton Agreement, but many stayed; some were even granted citizenship. In 1995, veterans of the Bosnian mujahideen established the Active Islamic Youth, regarded the most dangerous of the Islamist groups in Bosnia and Herzegovina.

probably his conscience did not allow him to carry out the aggression. I was thinking about the other night when Captain Raščanin ordered us to radiate at the targets located 30 kilometers away with our target acquisition radar. Djokić followed that order and lost one man, perhaps two, as well as some equipment. It seemed to me that the order was often a cover for stupidity.

At 20:50 Stoimenov and Tiosavljević tried to turn on the camera but something was wrong, and it did not work. We turned it off at 21:00. Tiosavljević made notes, saying: "Reading the notes will help me later to recall where and how I spent my youth. While everyone was napping in their chairs around 22:30, I was thinking: "After the war starts, rarely any combat rule is valid anymore. Each potential enemy uses the rules and searches for holes in them in order to eliminate us. Djokić was screwed because he followed the rules by the book. He strictly followed the rule to radiate for 6-10 seconds and then to stop for 6-10 seconds. He radiated at a target, which was 30 kilometers away, far from the engagement zone. We did the opposite: we waited for the target to enter into the launch zone before we radiated, and therefore its anti-missile maneuver failed, although he tried to carry it out. The angular velocities were large. From the great excitement and short work time, the missile guidance officer Muminović did not read the parameters of the target (the coordinates and altitude at instant of destruction and where it fell down/disappeared from the radar screen). These parameters will remain a secret for the reminder of history."... or maybe not... Lieutenant Colonel Krume Jovanovski, the 250th brigade head of signals, kept insisting on using the radio communications. That was unacceptable for us. In Iraq, Coalition forces intercepted radio communications - they did not interfere with them, so they detected the location of the command positions and those of the missile batteries and then selectively destroyed them. The same would occur to us if we used the "Jaguar"[75]device for communication. For God's sake, they made it, they coded it and they will decode it. We were in standby from 16:00 until 24:00. It looked like command had forgotten about us. I did not call them. "How reliable is this equipment?" I wondered. I knocked on wood for a good luck. That equipment was our big friend. About 22:00 Stanković called, asking for Dani. I gave him Dani's phone number. This was our third night here, in this position. We were likely to leave this position tomorrow or the day after tomorrow, and not return to it. We had once returned to the same position, and that was the trap we naively fell into in Prhovo. That was the longest night of my life. After the action of my classmate Djordjević, and our tactical maneuvers, they left us alone. Earlier tonight the launch of cruise missiles from Novi Sad direction to Belgrade was announced. We still did not know any of the effects. I learned from Crnobrnja that Vučković had psychically "jumped out of the rail"; so did Lieutenant Colonel Mijović, who recovered after we launched the missile on the plane and returned to duty. Vučković has not returned yet. A few nights ago, he warned me about

---

75   The "Jaguar" radio communication device was intended for secure communication with the higher command. The messages were encrypted and then sent. The 3rd division did not trust the device, hence did not use it; assuming the enemy could listen the conversation if they capture its radiofrequency wave as powerful airborne computers could probably decode it in real time. These are typically located on AWACS planes (Airborne Warning and Control System) or RC-135.

50-60 incoming cruise missiles. It looked like these missiles are a dime a dozen, so they could easily throw them away.

At 22:40 Blagojević called me and asked if I had brought the encrypted maps with me. "I think I did not. I need to look at Ogar. The safety box was near Dotlić. We will check it tomorrow. I asked him if there is anything in the airspace, since our surveillance radar was turned off. He replied there was nothing near us at the moment. "They can choose the target, any time and place," I thought. "They should go back home and be good parents there, and not villains and murderers here. The first casualty of the war is the truth. The peoples of the aggressor countries do not know what is really happening here."

The other day Danka told me that my son-in-law Victor and his mate Pajče, who live in Trieste, Italy, wanted to come. They wanted to prevent attacks on Vrdnik; as if I did not want to, but I had nothing to defend it with. Vrdnik was too far away. They expressed their patriotism from the distance, and that did not cost anything. The other day I spoke with Suzana Tomić, my sister's godmother. She told me that she had watered flowers in the house, everything was fine and Vrdnik was not targeted. The phone in the camp was busy all the time. There was no way that, if needed, one could urgently inform someone about something. It seemed as if they all relaxed. The tension fell. It can be good, but it can cost us dearly too. Carelessness slows down one's reflexes and thoughts. My niece (sister's daughter) Bojana had an operation on her tonsils and was probably recovering well after the surgery. I did not congratulate her older sister Sandra a happy 17th birthday. We were in a war... I was thinking how a person really could not appreciate what he has until lose it; then you see how much you need it, miss it and want it greatly. We had peace, but people were greatly dissatisfied. Everyone counted on the dissatisfaction, even NATO. They screwed up. Yet, we were far more aware and insightful than they could have anticipated. Fuck the ruling class. They were a passing category. We must not lose our freedom and the state. We must not be servants to anyone, like our neighbouring countries. The price that we are still paying is high, but it was worth it. I remember talking to Todor, Nataša's former boyfriend. He could not kill anyone, even if his life was threatened. He would rather give them what they were looking for. Now, I would like to talk to him about this topic again. The clock was approaching 23:00 hours, and I will listen to the news soon. I felt like eating something sweet, so I asked soldier Bložić for Maletić's box with cakes.

In Belgrade, the first war game between Partizan and AEK[76] was played yesterday, which was deliberately interrupted in the 60th minute, when spectators with the Yugoslav and Greek flag ran on the field. Solzhenitsyn[77] said that at the turn of the 21st century, the law of the jungle and the international banditism ruled the world, headed by NATO.

---

76   AEK Athens Football Club also known as AEK FC, is a Greek football club based in Nea Filadelfeia, a suburb of Athens, Greece.

77   Aleksandr Isayevich Solzhenitsyn was a Russian novelist, dissident, dramatist, historian and political activist. 1970 Literature Nobel Prize winner. Became disillusioned and critical of the capitalism in the West. Returned to Russia in 1994; in 1997 became a member of the Russian Academy of Sciences.

At about 23:30 we were suddenly attacked from several directions. Six planes were waiting, circling around us about 50-60 kilometers away, while three or four pairs attacked us. One came to 15 kilometers from the azimuth 180-190 degrees when I ordered to engage him. As soon as we illuminated him with a fire control radar, he immediately carried out an evasive maneuver and left the 22 km zone at the azimuth 240 degrees. Stanković from the brigade command post communicated this direction to Lieutenant Colonel Djević, but he could not find it on their radar screens. Then they asked me to tell them what I saw in the airspace. Were they seeking help or checking on me? How did they think that I could command the combat actions of my shift crew while reporting to them what I see on my radar screens? The chaotic situation perplexed me. I felt no anger, just bewilderment. I was very calm.

Saturday April 10

I woke up at 07:00. Lieutenant Colonel Nikola Stanisavljević from engineering logistics called me to request food for his 35 people to be brought to the next combat position in Karlovčić at about 10:00, as they had completed only 70% of the earth works. I passed on that food delivery request to Dani to organise it after his shift ends at 08:00, as I was preparing to go to my shift from 08:00 to 16:00. When we exchanged the shift duties, he told me, "Well done my friend, you drove them all away so there was nothing left for me." I found all the equipment was switched off. Last night, general Bane Petrović came to officially promote Dani to the rank of Colonel. I was in my shift. He did not mention his promotion to me, who was his deputy and executive officer (XO)! He had known that since the day general Biga came with the Russian delegation. Žika was right. This explains the change in his behavior! We all congratulated him. It was the 13th day since the downing of the "invisible" stealth plane. "We are next on the promotion schedule, I just do not know when," I thought. Last night they destroyed the TV communication tower at Goleš[78].

Armuš called around 08:30 to talk to Senior Sergeant Žugić or mechanic Golubović about some parts for the FAP truck, which he had been repairing. Lieutenant Colonel Drago Stojačić from the brigade command requested to meet Dani at 15:00 at the "Šarić" restaurant on the "Ibar River" highway. Colonel Stanković ordered us to provide food for 35 people for Stanisavljević (engineers) in Karlovčić, nine people for Vučković in Deč and eight people for Lieutenant Colonel Bajić in Progar. At 10:50 Dani called from Stanisavljević. I told him about the meeting and that Major Dotlić has to deliver food for an additional 52-53 men to Progar, Deč and Karlovčić. Around 10:30, Senior Sergeant Slavko Varga brought fuel to the combat position. I told him to send someone from the workshop to repair the faulty aggregate for the radar emission imitator.

About 11:50 a target appeared suddenly in the engagement zone at a dis-

---

78   Overlooking Mehmed Paša Sokolović Bridge in Višegrad (UNESCO heritage) across the Drina River.

tance of 5 km and on azimuth 210 degrees. At the same time radio amateurs[79,80,81,82,83,84] reported two targets coming from the direction of Sremska Mitrovica, at a distance of 30 km at the azimuth of 300 degrees. We tried to use a camera to visually pinpoint them, but we couldn't find anything. We could not see through the low laying clouds. Who knows what they saw[85,86]. We sparingly radiated from the surveillance radar: radiating for one 'circle' of the antenna rotation, then not for the next two or three circles, and so on. Our objective was to limit the time of radar radiation, as a precaution against anti-radar missiles. Private Radovanović manned the surveillance radar, while Sergeant Ljubenković rested. Blagojević called me and said some-

---

79   Radio amateurs have their own radio stations at home. Their equipment is used to communicate with other radio amateurs.

80   By international agreement, radio amateurs are allocated a range of frequencies or "bands". Some of these bands are more suitable for relatively short-range communication (say across town) whereas others are suited to world-wide communication.

81   Radio communication is the most reliable communication, particularly during emergencies when mobile networks fail and batteries run-out. Since 1924, the Serbian radio amateurs helped in many crisis situations.

82   They rose to prominence in 1999 during NATO bombing of Yugoslavia, providing an invaluable 24 hours a day service during all 78 days of war to the state and people. Thousands of radio amateurs carried out airspace surveillance and gathered information from the field; communicated information on the arrival of the bomber aircrafts, cruise missile attack corridors, reported on the explosions and damage, and directed rescue services to the injured. They also transmitted over 30,000 humanitarian messages reconnecting separated families, particularly those on Kosovo and Metohija.

83   Radio amateurs from the world and Europe, ordinary people who believed it was not right for the world's greatest powers to bomb Serbia, also helped them (including many from Republika Srpska, who had been bombed) by sending certain information by radio waves or telephone. For example, on take-off of bomber aircrafts from the NATO Aviano Air Base near Venezia, Italy, and from the US Ramstein Air Base near Kaiserslautern, Germany, and often, what their targets were.

84   It was difficult to establish these radio communications due to deliberate interference and jamming not only from hostile radio amateurs, but also from the intelligence agencies in Bosnia, Croatia and Hungary.

85   They were organized in tens of local (town, city, shire, etc.) and regional "Emergency Warning Centre" networks, which re-transmitted relevant information (with more powerful transmitters) to the public, often announcing air raids. The hidden and camouflaged military units passively listened to these public announcements, which eliminated the need to use their own transmitters and potentially reveal their location(s).

86   The information radio amateurs provided was generally of little use for the autonomous missile air-defense battery crews due to the one to two minutes intrinsic communication delay, as the future location of a typical high-speed maneuvering fighter aircraft cannot be interpolated by a straight line over that time interval; particularly in the geographically confined Serbian airspace.

thing like: "Djole, where have you been legend?". "This time he took a more positive attitude" I thought. Major Dotlić called to tell me that he would come at 16:00 instead of Dani who need to go to a meeting. Maletić told me: "Eh, how good it would have been if we had knocked down that bastard last night..." A sudden load change on the aggregate told me that something had occurred. I immediately put a helmet on my head. At 13:38 we were ordered to go to Readiness No. 3. "Germany is on its feet," the radio reported. "Yeltsin ordered the missile launchers to be pre-programmed for targets on German territory. Russia will not allow the subjugation of Yugoslavia and the entry of NATO land forces. Schröder[87] stopped further mobilization of Germany's armed forces for engagement in Yugoslavia. Madeleine Albright stated that Yugoslavia is a testing ground for NATO in the 21st century." The truth was slowly spreading...

I did not participate in previous wars, but this now looks like preparation for World War III. Russia and Belarus will accept Yugoslavia into their military alliance, send weapons, and perhaps deploy their armed forces on the territory of Yugoslavia. It could lead to either an all-out war or indefinite peace. The long-term plan of full US dominance over southern Europe is about to collapse (just a hope). "Europe is, in fact, stupid to consciously participate in the NATO's plan to cut it off from oil resources. Sooner or later, Europe will have to compete with America for raw materials, or it will be America's servant; although according to many indicators it is already a vassal entity" I thought.

Žugić and Golubović from the workshop repaired the radar imitator aggregate. Golubović said that he had "fudged" it as much as he could: "when it stops next time, that will be it - it will be all over." They also brought a bucket of UM-2 lubricant for the missile battery.

At 15:10 we are ordered again into Readiness No. 1, and at 16:00 Dotlić arrived at the combat position in the Niva 4WD instead of Dani. We discussed how to improve logistics support. I requested Senior Sergeant Žugić and mechanic Golubović from the workshop to be with the combat crews (because of frequent failures on the aggregates and motor vehicles), Varga to stay on fuel, and food to be distributed to two locations - near Jović (SA-7 unit) and to the camp. We made a new food schedule for the existing combat units and for the additional combat support units. He was nervous and did not understand the need for the impeccable functioning of this unit. I drove the Niva back to camp.

I sent the drivers, Lukić and Stojanović (signals platoon), to Šimanovci to pick up about 700 m of the communication cable and then to go to Jakovoto store the surplus communication equipment that was not needed here. They carried out the assignment. On the way back, they should have picked up Sedlar and transported him to Ogar. They did not find anyone in Jakovo, neither Mijalković nor Sedlak were there. At around 20:00, Kosta Ćurčić, a courier in the Command, reported that a roasted pig was brought for dinner. Before that, I talked to Jović, who was on the radar imitator. I requested for him to be in the motor vehicle that carried the equipment, in order to work

---

87   Gerhard Fritz Kurt Schröder is a German politician, and served as Chancellor of Germany from 1998 to 2005,

faster with the imitator[88]. He found a thousand reasons to avoid it. Fear is a miracle. He mastered it completely. I assured him that it was harmless to operate the imitator and he will not radiate for more than 5 to 10 seconds, because we did not radiate any longer. He could not do it. Then, I explained to him that it takes time to prepare the airplane for an attack, to prepare an anti-radar missile, to launch it, its flight time[89]. He said he did not understand why he needed to change his routine now, when he worked from the trench in the past 15 days. He did not understand that the situation in the air had changed completely.

I went to sleep after dinner and Dani woke me up around 23:30. He came back from the meeting. Our Brigade acknowledged that our battalion was the only one to have downed a plane with the material evidence – a wreck in the field. He said that he brought me the underwear Danka had sent me 7-8 days ago. He also said that he brought along a modified imitator and it was in the car. He also brought the last two issues (numbers 4 and 5) of the "Vojska" (Army) journal. In one of them, I guess in number 5, was the article about our unit that shot down the plane. All our names were invented – nom de guerre. I was named Anđelko Đorđević. At the meeting Toša, a Colonel from the military academy, took off his Colonel rank insignia and gave it to Dani. From tonight Dani has the rank insignia on the uniform. He told me that we will all receive ranks, medals, decorations and who knows what else. I told him that one cannot live from these laureates. First of all, we need to survive all this shit, and think about glory later, in some quiet time. He told me that we were the most mobile unit. So far, we had moved five times, and tomorrow we will move again, with the God help... Tomorrow is Easter. I was born on Easter 41 years ago, 13 April 1958. Someone said tonight: "Children are the decorations of the world," and I add, "We also have children."

I was chatting to Danka and told her to go to her father's place tomorrow because "I will see you there". She said she had dyed the eggs[90,91] and bought me something for my birthday. "You shouldn't", I replied. Still, I was touched by her attention. I visualised a mental picture of her face worried for me. All fears would go away - both hers and mine. They are different, but they are tied to the same people. This is a biological struggle for survival. Just like that in nature. I love and respect nature. Nature is a great teacher.

---

88   Earlier, he was in the trench, located about 100 meters away, and then had to run to the vehicle to manually direct and switch on the imitator IRR.

89   Mike Mihajlovic: This is correct. during the war I was able to get a F-16 manual which among the other things also had an AGM-88 HARM employment procedure. At that time, it was classified document. Information was sent to the proper authorities in the air defense command.

90   It is an old Eastern Orthodox custom to dye, paint and decorate chicken eggs before Easter. On Easter Sunday young kids would duel with them saying 'Christ is resurrected, Indeed, He is', breaking and eating them. Friends and family would hit each other's egg with their own too.

91   Easter eggs are dyed red to represent the blood of Christ with further symbolism being found in the hard shell of the egg symbolizing the sealed Tomb of Christ— the cracking of which symbolized his resurrection from the dead.

I am in the shift from 00:00 to 06:00 tonight. For tonight I brought the last two issues of the wartime edition of the Vojska journal, No. 4 and 5, to the missile guidance station. Everyone read about us. We laughed at Dragan Matić's nom de guerre - Taško Načić, as the legendary actor and Dragan were look-alikes. Senior Sergeant Volf slept on some bags on the floor. Lieutenant Nikolić replaced the "no launch" lamp on the second launch ramp. Captain Muminović helped him not to screw something up. That equipment keeps us alive, so we must look after it too. The respect is mutual.

We went into Readiness No. 1. On the screen, on azimuth 330 degrees and from zero to thirty at a height of 6 km, I watched eight targets. They were coming to us. They were still far away. Our transmitter to the command was turned on and the ramps were powered. We waited in ambush. We became patient hunters. It is a great game of nerves. The stakes are high - our lives for a downed NATO airplane. The pilot would eject anyway, if he is lucky. Their airplanes are designated with certain safety factor and backup systems. He may be caught, or maybe not. We can only be losers. Our tin can van is not armored. Alternatively, if he passes away, there will be some new destruction and new victims.

Are those people in our society aware of that? Those people who belittled or underestimated us until yesterday? Do they know how much anxiety, trembling and trepidation we have at night? The night, on the other hand, has absolutely no meaning to them. They are safe somewhere, and who knows what they think about while dodging military duty. Tomorrow, they will be the loudest. I am disgusted with them and I feel sorry for their ill will, motivated by self-interest.

Everyone here would like to be relaxed as they are. Why do I love this country more than they do? Why was Nataša's former boyfriend Todor so delighted with a piece of the downed F-117A airplane I sent him? He does not like to kill, and his present was a part of the killing machine. It must be because of his immaturity and adolescence. I am not bitter, rather I have just been thinking a lot in these long night hours, waiting for the phone buzz and call to tell me that they are coming after us. I do not know if I would like to hear the phone buzz for the rest of my life. My life could end after that sound. The organism relaxes and then tightens as a string, unlike the brain. Does my heart beats at all? I often think about it. I cannot hear my heartbeats. Perhaps I should not?! Maybe my heart shrank a bit, so my chest became big and wide?! Are we the heroes of our days? It is stupid to fight for ideals. Our ideal is freedom and a free country. Yeltsin said that he will not give up Yugoslavia. Yeah… Who pulls the strings behind the scene and plays with us, and what was our price? Whose trading cards are we? The truth slowly comes out into the world. What is the truth for and for whom? I am someone's child too. On this day tomorrow someone young and beautiful struggled for my life and gifted it to me. For this reason, my life should be appreciated, others as well. Just wait until the war ends, I will go to visit my father's and mother's graves and light the candles[92]. I know they are guard-

92   It is a custom to light up candles. According to the religious belief we

ing me. I felt my eyes tearing up. Was it a moment of weakness? I was left alone. Danka is the only person in this country who is truly worried about me. My great co-warrior. She is my friend from my thoughts. By comforting her, I was comforting myself too. It may look mean, but it is true. We are very small indeed, but the little ones do make miracles. Miracles are often happening. I trust there will be a miracle here, sooner or later. A few days ago, I heard that Colonel Savić was sent to assist Colonel Djević. His improper conduct towards me was inexcusable, in my opinion, although I knew he has good qualities. I buried that past deep into myself. We used to be good friends. I noticed that I was chewing my gum again. Was that because of the memories, or not? I will think about it after the war. What is my sister doing in Italy? I know that she is not calm, and she is tense, weeping and bewildered. She needed to calm down. The most important thing is to settle your nerves. It is necessary to socialize and to talk more and laugh. She needed to try and relax. All this is a beautiful saying and an illusion. The reality is something else. The night is our spasm. It brings to much strain on the psyche and body. Tonight, is Easter, the greatest Christian religious holiday.

On the other end of the telephone line is soldier Radovanović, manning the surveillance radar. My voice was calming him down. I felt that. Does his family now know where he is and what he is doing? They probably do not know. They will find out one day. One day, we will all have something to talk about. They (NATO) respect us a lot, but they have also been trying to kill us. Fuck the respect! Staying alive is truly the highest priority. How much fighting is required to save our lives?! In some rare moments a man can only say that he did not care about his life. Danger gives rise to other thoughts, much more meaningful and sincere. Senior Sergeant Jović told me tonight that he is going to resign from the army after the war. I watched him and I saw all of us in him. We have just learnt how to overcome fear and anxiety. He feels fear and that fear suppresses all positive thoughts. He has just confided in me that he had counselling. His family vortex irretrievably took his expertise away from him. These years have taken their toll on him. He does not see an exit from this new vortex of war. He knows that he left his children behind in the darkness of the city. He knows that he is defending them here at the salt marches of Srem, but only when he is thinking positively. Tonight, he is obviously feeling hopeless and overwhelmed, as he was all of these past evenings, and the question is whether he will ever recover. I felt sorry for his situation. Being afraid is a natural thing. I have a feeling that the fear is a part of nature. The only question is how we manage our fear.

The time base on my radar screen rotated slowly but no enemy approaching. The war seems idle. Is it a sign that they honor our Easter? They flew on their own Easter; they flew and killed. Who are they really? Great believers in God and democracy that fly combat mission, drop bombs, kill the enemy than have a nice meal and pint of beer and call their kids to ask how they slept last night and are they ready for school and tell their wives and girlfriends that they love them?! Is there any God's commandment or Church's rule that they have not broken yet? The morning is far away. It is 02:00 now.

We always have the same preparation for the night shift: helmet, flashlight candles for dead in order to light up their journey and warm up their souls by remembering them and letting them know that they live in our life.

light and notebook - my war diary was just for me and Danka; two packs of cigarettes, one in the blouse, in the right pocket, and one in the vest, in the left pocket. Are these parts of my habit or my superstition? The same uncomfortable chair, the same pose. Only the situation in the airspace changes every night. Boris Stoimenov is napping. At the instant of changing to a more comfortable position, he asked me "What are those guys in the air doing?" "Nothing," I replied to him" it is Easter today." "Yes, yes," he confirmed dreamily before dozing off again. The only light on is at my workstation. The others are in the semi dark, with the uniform humming noise from the equipment and heater filling in the air. All communications are idle. I sit busy with only my thoughts and surrounded by five phones and nine communication lines.

Noskov went with his unit to Pančevo to defend the liquid ammonia fertiliser plant at Azotara Petrochemicals, together with Mijović's unit. The air-defence ring around Pančevo is too small to be effective. Other units are covering other directions. Behind me is Djević with his unit. The Fruška Gora mountain ridge, my great love, is too close to our position now, causing me big worries. I hope it will not let me down. It extends from azimuth 330 to 350 degrees. From there airplanes leap and go after us. The distance is about 30 km. Too close to defend from a massive attack. On the opposite side of the ridge Is my other great love – city of Novi Sad; the city of my childhood, that is having a restless and ruined sleep. We did not verify the correct operation of the emission by the target acquisition radar, in order not to reveal our location. I guess that everything is okay. Dani told me tonight that Djokić had been keeping high voltage on the transmitter antenna of their radar all the time. Could they detect the frequency if the radar is switched on to the equivalent[93] mode of operation? During these 17-18 days of war, we had radiated our radar for no more than a few minutes in total. Of those, 20-25 seconds during downing of the F-117A.

Senior Sergeant Varga looked at his fortune-telling pendulum. He said the pendulum had shown that we will be shot down another airplane. When will it happen? We all secretly asked ourselves, and who will down it? It is not about the glory. We already got it. And more importantly, the pendulum also told him that we would not be hit. We just need to play safe, and not be fooled. They will punish any foolish move or our error. They will punish our weakness if there were many of them. Varga said that Milošević would sign a peace agreement between the 15th and 20th of this month. That is on a string and far away. Our lives are decided here in seconds, and theirs too, but to a lesser extent. How many seconds until that time comes?

We listened to the news at 03:00. They said that at 15:45 one plane was shot down somewhere near Prizren. They also said that at around 00:15 the air defense hit another plane in the Bački Brestovac village near Zrenjanin [94]. Today's newspapers reported that the 19 countries participating in the

---

93   Equivalent is when the radar is not switched off but doesn't have any emission and the energy is encapsulated into the system. See the appendix for more explanation.

94   Indeed, Harrier was hit and jettisoned the fuel tanks and electronic warfare containers. Mike Mihajlovic found the parts and identified the type of the equip-

attacks on the FR Yugoslavia have an aggregate population of over 900 million people and are among the richest countries in the world. There are about 10-12 million of us; so, the ratio is one to ninety (1:90). 'Congratulations,' I said sarcastically! Over the past 7-8 years our country has been hampered by a trade embargo and all kind of sanctions, although it is among the poorest countries in Europe.

I must save these wartime editions of the Vojska journal to give them to my son. Whose life do I live and who is the master of it? My life is like a novel. I know that everyone thinks so negatively about himself and probably the way his life is, but what I have been through has greatly strengthened me. I wish I were not so strong. The loss of my father, the bloody disintegration of Yugoslavia, the sanctions and trade embargo unprecedented in history, the dissolution of my marriage, the loss of my mother before the war, and now the war. That part of my life now belongs to the past. I wish this past were shorter lived.

Today Žugić brought three soldering tools to Muminović and requested his signature as a proof of delivery. Signature in wartime!? As if he handed him ammunition or weapons. Peacetime rules enforced by the bureaucratic minds. Muminović complained to no avail. Dotlić, a veteran from Bosnian war, should better manage the logistics support. A man needs to be born for some things, to have them in his genes. Volf was playing the video game Tetris or similar on his handset that had commands on it. 'What a youth,' I thought. My generation did not have video games. His generation has war. Every generation has something. I guess that must be karma. I was good at writing essays in Serbian (then Serbo-Croat) language assignments during my school time. They say that only a soul that suffered makes good writing. If so, then the next flow of thoughts and a blink of my soul will bring something to write about. Carefree times vanished long time ago. I often remember my childhood. All of sudden, from the depths of my subconscious I evoked the image of Pop's children running rampant in the living room, while I dropped in once, and their parents not trying to control them or saying a word, even after they had broke the wardrobe door. I compared my childhood with that of the Pop's children. They would never become responsible adults. Or perhaps they would. If they do, then my belief on the necessity of strong discipline and Spartacism for good upbringing of children would be wrong. We have a natural tendency to raise our children the way we were raised. Perhaps, we do not use creative rudeness, humiliating and insulting display of contempt in words or action when raising our children because we are more educated than our parents and have wisdom from our schools. That may have softened my generation and blurred our boundaries of acceptable. Our life wisdom wise, however, is probably behind that of our parents, who possessed wisdom beyond their years: knowledge of what is true or right coupled with just judgment as to action.

I lit a cigarette. Volf did too. We were both busy, just with different ways. I was busy writing and he was busy playing games. We were spending our time and our lives. We were both indifferent, as if these were someone else's

ment. The ECM (electronic countermeasure equipment, part of EW) equipment was burned which confirmed explosion and fire. The airplane later crashed inti the Adriatic Sea but was officially declared lost because of the technical malfunction.

lives. Volf's fingers were skillfully clicking the video game controls. His cigarette was in the corner of his mouth. He was breathing irregularly. Finally, a long smoke came out, then he shook ashes from the cigarette. "Rest your lungs and keep your health safe," I thought to myself, "Take it easy. The new game is about to start under the dimmed light of the indicators of the missile guidance officer station. It would require some new winning sequence of controls"… It was 04:20.

Would it be possible that they took off at the beginning of our shift to wish us a happy Easter and then returned to the base?! Unlikely, they are not so humane. Maybe they respected us?! The answer could be in the pilots' motivation? What was his true motivation to take off, regardless of the name of the particular machine he operates, and take course of throwing bombs on the heritage of one nation? It was not worth thinking about it. If all the thieves put on my thinking cap, then there would be no thieves at all[95,96,97].

The new shift to replace us came at 08:00. At 09:00s we were ordered to prepare for the march. Our 'circus caravan' was on the move again and we, as the crew, will be again sleepless and exhausted. Our destination was in the region of Karlovčić village. I was trying in vain to call Armuš to come for the logs. I took a car and went for him. Two reservists hitchhiked with me along the way. I stopped and gave them a lift. I informed Armuš about the time when he should arrive in Popinci. He said that he had solved the problem with the FAP truck. "What a great guy," I thought. "He had found the spare parts and installed them in the truck engine. What an amazing job." At 11:00 I returned to Karlovčić. Danka had not arrived yet. She came about 15-20 minutes later, together with Nataša and Aunt Mara. We had a coffee.

I went back to the new combat position, as the vehicles had arrived and were spreading across it. Several attempts to park the missile guidance station van failed, as the cable of the target acquisition radar was too short. The

---

95   At that time, the author underestimated the importance of his own question about true motivation of the NATO pilots. It transpired after the war that many Italian pilots who opposed the war and bombing of their neighbor chose to dump their bombs in the Adriatic sea which separates the Balkans from Italy, where these could cause no harm, and faked their bombing air raids over Yugoslavia.

96   That was revealed when unexploded NATO missiles washed on the Italian beaches and unexploded bombs were caught in the fishing nets of Italian trawler boats, causing panic of their crews and safety concerns after one cluster bomb exploded, injuring three fishermen. The munition with depleted uranium dumped in deep sea was not recovered. It remains the source of radioactive pollution along the Adriatic coastline and islands of Albania, Croatia, Italy, Montenegro, and Slovenia.

97   One might ask why Italian pilots were 'singled out' as conscientious objectors to the bombing. A simple reason is they reflected their society: a strong streak of pacifism coupled with old-fashioned leftwing anti-Americanism have been running through Italian politics for decades; and the stand of the Vatican which preaches the uselessness and immorality of war as a means of settling disputes and has an enormous influence in this still overwhelmingly Catholic country. Italy remained the only country taking part in the bombing whose embassy in Belgrade had been up and running and whose ambassador was on poste during all 78 days of the war.

radar station footing was not leveled up. I called the earthmoving machines team to come and level it up. A party of four men and women arrived. They said they were from the Serbian government. They came to visit a reservist - the son of a woman who was with them. They used the government jobs as cover for coming here?! I chose the location where to set up the radar emission imitator and explained to Jović how to work with it. The control equipment for remote turning of the device, which Dani brought yesterday, was not a bad solution. Perhaps simple and primitive, but it worked. This was the most important.

Leveling the radar is manual labor-intensive work. Typically, enlisted troops are doing that under the supervision.

The transition to the combat configuration was moving slowly. The missile battery must relocate the launch ramps. The cables became short after Maletić had to move the power supply vans to the other side of the missile guidance station van, in order to place the logs around it. I ordered to place ground protection mats (a rubber mantle of about ten millimeters thick) on the roof of the missile guidance station van. The missile battery crew normally used the ground protection mats around the launch ramps to protect the cables from the fire that occurs when the missile is launched. We were putting the mats on the roof for the first time during the war. The engineers did the earthworks and erected berms around the equipment on the combat position. "Not bad," I thought, considering how fast it was done. Later I went to Milan's place for lunch and shower. It was already 16:20. The last time I slept was two nights ago: all day, all night and again all day today; and my shift will end at 24:00. The telecom installers woke me up at 17:30. They came in and installed a civilian telephone number. I decided I would sleep at the Milan's place after my shift ends. This would give me an opportunity to sleep seven, eight hours which is premium...

I returned to the combat position around 19:00. Along the way I met Tiosavljević. He set off to Šimanovci in Ural truck, but the truck was not pulling.

It runs like crazy while the engine is cold. As soon as it warms up, it will not pull. I told him and the mechanics that it could be a faulty pump.

We had a photo session in the afternoon: the missile batteries[98], the crew that fired and others. Captain Golubović and Senior Sergeant Žugić took the photos. It was 21:30 sand we had not yet gone to Readiness No. 1. Trgov-čević from the Operations Center reported that there was an unmanned air-craft in our vicinity, at the altitude of about 200 meters above us. If true, then it meant that we were discovered and filmed. We were not afraid of anti-ra-dar missiles, but bombs… Bombs are our greatest threat.

We had a malfunction. We were bridging all microswitches on the target acquisition radar in order to find the fault. The missile guidance battery team spread all the blueprints: drawings and schematic diagrams. "Guys, do not bother yourself with the blueprints," someone said, "The fault is probably in cabling." In the end it turned out to be true. "What a colossal waste of time that was," I thought.

The rain drizzled all day. Senior Sergeant Tiosavljević and Radivojević were orientating the missile guidance station van. Their battery commanders were not present. I ordered to commanders to come to the station van. They were not happy. Captain Golubović told me that he had not slept since this morning. "My shift has not slept since yesterday morning," I replied, "So what?!"We made a few attempts to orientate the target acquisition radar. Our tiredness took its toll. For this reason, we made mistakes where we do not usually make them.

At about 20:00 Crnobrnja called me. He finally re-joined his formally as-signed[99] unit. The Noskov's battalion went to Pančevo. They passed through Belgrade in just 25 minutes. Aca, a guy from the military police unit, orga-nized that. Very capable man. People are nervous and exhausted. I was calm-ing them down. "A cool head thinks properly, a hot head never," I thought. I offered Dani to sleep at the Milan's place. Anyway, we are always in dif-ferent shifts and we had been sleeping in the same, field cot bed since the beginning of the war. He told me, "In the end, we will start sharing women too ..." I laughed and replied "That is out of consideration, forever".

At 22:55 Blagojević called me to go to Readiness No. 1. I questioned him "Who told you that we are ready?". "Well," he replied, "Half an hour ago, you had only orientation outstanding." "He must know that after the orien-tation, it is necessary to determine the corners of the base and to place the missiles[100]," I thought. I told him, "Tell them that I will report as soon as it's over." He replied, "They did not ask, I was asking you." Then he asked me "When do you expect to complete it?". "It is raining and people are tired. I'll let you know when we finish," I replied. I was close to telling him to go

---

98   See the organizational structure in the Foreword to English Edition section.

99   Assigned unit - is the unit within the organization where one is formally employed and one's employment data were kept, including that of the salary level, rank, promotions and other entitlements.

100   This is a routine procedure to establish redundant "surveying like" topo-logical references, so the commanding officer could quickly cross-check for correct orientation, which is critical for operations.

fuck himself. Why did he only call me when he was on the commanding post? Lieutenant Colonel Djuro Duvnjak and Martin Djurić from the 250th brigade personnel service was visiting this afternoon. They were looking for an experienced missile officer to send him to Obrenovac. Dani and I did not give them any man, as we have had no surplus officers. We had a good team. In Dani's shift, the assistant commander is Golubović, and in mine it is Stoimenov. The respective missile guidance officers were Janković and Muminović. We were only waiting for Roksandić to load missiles onto the ramps before we could report to the higher command that we are ready. We worked together like clockwork, or myriad cogs of a Swiss watch. We can really fight.

Loading missile onto the launching ramp - PR-14A/AM transporter and 5P73 launcher.

Upon his return from the meeting last night, Dani told me that the Brigade officially had hit only one target, as they were able to find only one wreck in our territory which is unquestionable truth and material evidence that the airplane is downed and that is the one we shot down. Today, we could not do anything properly. We had a lot of work, but too many problems. I told them today is Easter and it is a day for joy and relaxation not a day to play with the combat equipment, but it is also a war time. I offered home made chocolates, which Danka packed for me, to the men. They all took them in silence. They said they were good. After the dinner, around 22:00, one roasted pig and grilled meat were brought in. No one bothered to ask who sent it or who brought it. We enjoyed the feast. Todor's family sent me a painted egg, which read: "Congratulations to the F-117A!"... Varga was on the surveillance radar.

Dani told me that today he scared Jović by telling him that he felt sorry that he had to tell him that the anti-radar missile would destroy the vehicle that carries the radar imitator. Jović was astounded and flabbergasted. I replied that I had asked him to be in the vehicle and radiate in five-second intervals. He was scared to death. We both laughed at this war joke...

During the transition to the combat configuration, Captain Senad Muminović injured his right middle and ring fingers. He said he felt a tingling pain in his fingers. The fatigue was slowly taking its toll. I did not know if anyone picked up Kosta and the reservist soldier from Popinci. SA-3 is not a mobile system and require time to set up. We were using it as a mobile one and that was tantalizing. At 23:30, I informed Blagojević that we are in Readiness No.1. He said: "Are you tired, buddy? Your people must be exhausted?" I told him "We have not slept for 36 hours and we transitioned under very bad weather conditions." "I know, I understand you, mate, regards from your friend," he replied. I was astounded. Just half an hour ago he told me something completely different and he was not interested in people. "Then, who really cares about the people?" I asked myself. "That is not the way, my brother Srba, to wage the war," I replied to myself, "The people are the basis, potential, and value. Without them, one cannot do anything. If you lose them in any way - mentally or physically - you are fucked. Motivated people can make miracles happen."

I will sleep at the Milan's place and will feel like real a man, for the first time in a very long-time. I will sleep in bed; freshly showered and in the clean underwear. It was really a big deal. And I appreciated it.

I talked to Danka. She arrived well in Belgrade. She told me that she was proud of me, one of the heroes of our defense. She must have known how many of us there are in this war...

Monday April 12

Milan gently woke me up. His soft pronunciation of my name did the job. I opened my eyes and looked at my watch. It was 07:30. I jumped! After a brief stay in the bathroom I walked into the living room. Nada had already made me coffee, tea and fried eggs. Russian salad and cooked ham were on the table too. I was in a hurry. I did not eat much. The food and its arrangement on the table looked surreal to me; the attention to detail resembled that of an ikebana.

I arrived at the combat position before all others from my shift. The thick mud of Srem was everywhere. Access to the equipment and vans are awful. Milan gave me a pair of rubber boots. About 25-35cm of deep mud was firmly sticking to them each time I stepped. I had to pull my legs out slowly and carefully in order not to lose them.

Last night they bombed Pančevo, Novi Sad, Kragujevac, Kruševac and more.

Dani told me that they had radiated three times, each time for about five seconds. The Brigade Command Post directed them to the potential targets, as they had not seen them on our battalion's surveillance radar. Nothing showed up on our fire control radar when they turned it on.

Dani told me that Noskov was a coward last night, "He had 6 to 8 targets above him about 8 to 10 kilometers away and did not dare to turn on his target tracking radar. Others around him launched their missiles, while Noskov was silent." I thought to myself, "He who has been hit once becomes fearful – once bitten, twice shine... the trauma takes its toll."

According to Varga's plumb-line based prediction, today or tomorrow, the second shift will launch and shoot down an airplane. That was my shift.

After the rest of my shift arrived, I ordered them to check the alignment of the station and ramps, as well as to inspect contacts on the microswitches on the target acquisition radar that we had shunted[101,102,103] last night. It was raining. They offered me some small cookies that someone had brought in a shoebox. I couldn't eat and I politely declined them.

At 08:12, Luka Trgovčević told me go to the Readiness No. 2. We immediately commenced the equipment check up procedure. When checking the alignment, we found that the missile guidance station deviated from true north by 1 degree. I chose not to rectify it, as it was not so important when looking for a target[104]. The correct alignment of the missile launch ramps was much more important[105] than that of the radar. These must be perfectly aligned, which will be checked next.

Today is my dad's birthday. If he were still alive, I would be able to celebrate his birthday and wish him a long life. Unfortunately, I cannot do it anymore. I will call Danka and ask her to go to church and light a candle to commemorate him. I loved him a lot. I regret that I never had an opportunity to get to know him well.

Rain continued to drizzle. I told Dani to go to Milan's house to sleep and shower. I was not sure if he would go there. The best I could do was to offer him accommodation.

Our verification of the alignment of the second launch ramp showed the

---

101   Shunted – bypassed by wire.

102   Faulty microswitches were shunted in order to bypass one protection in the circuit that controls movement of the fire control radar antenna by the azimuth and vertical elevation.

103   This improvisation immediately made the air defense system combat ready. The tradeoff was the need to check if the shunt wires were holding in place, typically after each shift.

104   Because the missile guidance officer is manually searching the area of about ± 5-6 degrees around the target (like with the beam of a search light) in order to find the target and bring it into the crosshairs. Its success ultimately depends on the experience of the missile guidance officer. The 1-degree alignment error is not critical as it represents less than 10% of the area the officer needs to search anyway.

105   Because the missiles need to enter into a very small "expected" volume of space that lies within a very narrow cross-section of radar beams for target tracking and missile guidance.

error of three thousandths[106,107,108,,109,110]. I chose not to rectify it, as there were four missiles there. This error amounted to about 10.8 angular minutes[111], which was well within the allowed fifteen angular minutes.

We than checked the first launch ramp. The error was one thousandth, which was ok.

We were ordered to be in Readiness No.1 at 11:00. This morning, on the Easter Monday, Maletić and I cracked Easter eggs[112]. He won, breaking two of my eggs. We were laughing. Maletić decided to keep the "winning egg".

I stepped on a wheel of the Target Acquisition radar during its repair. The wheel spined and, in a fraction of second, I was "flying" forward through the air and fell into a muddy pond. Luckily, I did not fall backwards on the trailer. Had I fallen onto the trailer I could have broken my arm or leg, or even something worse. Under these circumstances, my fall into the soft mud was preferrable one. I cleaned the bracelet of my wristwatch. Everything was covered in sticky mud.

---

106   Thousandth (sometimes also referred to as mils in plural) – is generic name for few similar but slightly different practical small angle measures used to fine tune the artillery or sniper fire, for example by 1 meter for a target located 1,000 meters away. Its name, "one thousandth," stems from the ratio of the "length of the correction required" to the "distance to the target," 1 and 1000 meters respectively in this case. In other words, one "thousandth" can be thought of as the angle between the two ends of a 1 meter long stick seen from a 1000 meters distance.

107   Different measures for the absolute value of a "thousandth" unit largely stem from the need to approximate, for practical calculations, otherwise infinite, number of digits in the number "P", for example to P=3.14.

108   The thousandth angle unit used by the Author in Yugoslavian army is defined by dividing the circle into 6000 equal segments. Smaller units are minutes and seconds. The advantage of this definition is that allows simple conversion between degrees, minutes and seconds. These units were officially used in the 19th century Serbia (after 1867 liberation from the Ottoman occupation). To remind you, one circle = 360 degrees, 1 degree = 60 minutes, and 1 minute = 60 seconds.

109   The thousandth units used by some other armies are based on dividing the circle into 6300 or 6400 segments.

110   The military compass used by the Author (thousandth based on 6000) divides the 360 degrees circle into 60 coarse segments (6 degrees each), each of which is further divided into 100 small segments termed thousandths. The notation: for example, the full circle (360 degrees) is 60-00 thousandths. Hence, 01-00 equals 6 degrees.

111   Conversion of 00-03 thousandths to degrees, minutes and seconds. One thousandth has 3.6 minutes (calculated as 360*60/6000=3.6). Three thousand multiplied by 3.6 equals 10.8 minutes. Since 10.8 ≤ 15 minutes of the allowed error, no further calculation is required.

112   Cracking or tapping the Easter eggs symbolizes Jesus Christ's resurrection from the dead. The goal of the game is to crack the other player's egg. The winner, then, uses the same end of the egg to tap the other, non cracked, end of the opponent's egg. The winner is the one whose egg cracks the eggs of all the other players.

I was waiting for my trousers to dry, so I can clean them with a brush. Dani was at the "safe place" in Milan's house. I could not take that place just for myself and be there alone, and I did not. We had been sleeping in the same bed since the beginning of the war. It was like a "hot bunk" in a submarine. Perhaps Milan and Nada didn't like that, but what can I do now? It's going to stay as is.

At about 10:00, Lieutenant Colonel Stanisavljević, an engineering officer, called to ask me for the next combat position which his unit is now preparing in the area of Deč. He told me that they will finish it today. I called Dani at about 16:30 and passed that information to him. Today is the Easter Monday. On Saturday, while we were still in the Popinci village, Maletić wanted to go to his home in Golubinci. He postponed it for Easter Sunday, but on that day, we moved to the next position and he was quite unhappy. Later we came to village of Karlovčić.

Constant stress during the combat duties and running the battalion business can be hard and require some rest to retrieve just a bit of energy. The author during one of the rests in the home atmosphere.

This morning I came to the shift in rubber boots. My army boots are drying now in Milan's house. Today or tomorrow, as per Varga's prediction, we'll launch again. We are preparing ourselves mentally for that. Maletić told me that it was not fair that only Nikolić and Dani got promoted, and that Nikolić was also decorated with a medal. We should not allow discord and battalions among the people in the battalion. I replied, "The brigade is probably keeping the things quiet as they probably didn't want to publish our names. When the war ends, and I feel that it will end soon, we will all be adequately rewarded."

Lieutenant Colonel Joksimović, from the brigade logistics, called and told me that he will send a reel of the PTK cable to the signals platoon and lunch for the troops. He came to take Vučković, who broke his arm, to the VMA (military hospital in Belgrade). How? When? Which arm? I didn't know. The equipment was functional and working fine, so it was better not to talk too much over the phone. Caution is the mother of wisdom.

Strong wind was quickly drying the soil of Srem. It was already drier around the equipment and the mud was not sticking that much. The diesel generator crew was cleaning the deposits of soot. Maletić was tying the cables. I set on the radar ladder, took my diary and started to write. I told Lieutenant Jović, "We need to send a camera to Lieutenant Colonel Bajić via the lunch delivery van, so he could forward it to the Institute."

Someone said: "We will be staying two to three days in each village." I replied, "Fuck it. There are 125 villages in Srem. So, when will this shitty war end?" Everyone laughed.

As each day of the war passes by, the anxiety and fear are less and less present in the unit. I ordered Senior Sergeant Jović, to thoroughly check everything on the radar imitator and report back to me. We must be combat ready at all times. You never know when they may pop up. Wesley Clark[113] said that NATO was very surprised with Serbian air defence toughness, tactical actions, and readiness. Personally, I think that we had a room for many more tactical actions. One of them would be to leave the surveillance radar to work for some time at the previous combat position, while we relocate to the new one. This should trick them to think we were still there. This trick would be particularly effective on combat positions from which we had not radiated from our target acquisition radar.

We had radiated last night from this position. Dani radiated three times for five seconds. That was not very good, especially as the target did not show up on our surveillance radar. Well, it is what it is. We cannot change it now.

Danka told me yesterday that she had spoken with my sister Ljubica. She was scared and cried. The war propaganda is relentless in Italy where she lives. She was worried about me. Danka jokingly told her that we had plenty of food and that we can eat as much as we wished. "Do not fuck with me," said Ljubica. I know very well what she meant with that. I could hear her voice. Her kids are good. Bojana was recovering from surgery.

NATO foreign ministers are meeting today. So will the G-8. We'll see what will transpire from these meetings.

It is the second day of the stalemate the Hungarians caused by stopping the Russian humanitarian aid convoy comprised of 70 trucks from transiting through Hungary. If this escalated into a wider war, the Russians would retaliate. Hungarians had been opening every truck, every crate, every single package... Bastards... Or they are doing what the big boss told them to do...

---

113   Wesley Clark – in his capacity of the Supreme Allied Commander Europe of NATO, was in charge of the 1999 military assault on FR Yugoslavia and subsequent invasion of the Serbian province Kosovo and Metohija, under the code name Operation Allied Force.

Whores sold themselves... no wander.

It was announced how long it would take to redirect Russian missiles to targets in NATO member states in Europe. The maximum redirection time of 12 minutes applied to the UK! Shorter times for other NATO countries.

The FRY Federal Assembly will meet today. The key agenda item was confirmation of the Government's decision to enter into an alliance with the Russian Federation and Belarus. In January, we received the status of a special observer in that organization and alliance. If NATO was everywhere around us, then once again, sooner or later, a new war would erupt in this region, I was quite sure about that. NATO would not be safe in the south of Europe if we were in Russia's sphere of interest. We would be like a thorn in NATO's flank. It is not good that we are cut off from Russians by Hungary.

The rainy day turned into a sunny one. It was windy, which was good. Maletić said that he had thought he would be working in Batajnica, however they dropped bombs and destroyed his workplace at the airport. It was inconvenient for him to travel from his village, Golubinci, to our base in Jakovo. I told him that the municipality would build an apartment for him in Jakovo. He laughed. He said: "The local government of Jakovo should give a block of land to all military employees to build their own houses." "They can do that in Belgrade as well," I said jokingly. "Oh yes, it will happen when pigs start to fly!" He commented.

The sky was clear and blue. A few light white clouds seemed determined to disturb that indigo blue sky. It suddenly seemed so beautiful. My sky... Free sky... It should always remain free. Volf was playing Tetris again. Reserve soldier Slaviša, tidied the power supply van; he and Maltić worked well as a team. The soil had almost dried out. We were not walking through the mud anymore. Finally...Our physician, Dr. Djukić, had not arrived yet to change bandages on Muminović's fingers and bring the foot cream for Maletić. He got blisters on his foot from boots and sweat.

For the third consecutive day, Albanians had been attacking us at the border posts. We had been repelling and pushing them back behind the border, probably inflicting considerable casualties on them. Madelene Albright would propose further air strikes until they achieved their goals, and probably her personal too. That was sick and insane. The Pentagon and the CIA criticized her because she didn't listen to their warnings that Yugoslavia was not Iraq. They should change something or someone. I can only wish that those lunatics of the new world order would one-day experience the same stuff they had been doing to other people in their own countries.

We have not repaired the epsilon drive[114] yet, and it was already 14:15. I cracked eggs again with Maletić. - cracked the pointy top end of his egg, and he cracked the bottom of mine. He was leading 4:2 in the aggregate score. I had not been able to reduce his lead. The pen and cigarette lighter with

114   Epsilon drive– is a complex piece of equipment that enables centralized control (from the missile guidance station van) of the target acquisition radar, which is comprised of four antennas that simultaneously operate in a coordinated manner. Its name "epsilon" stems from the "elevation error" variable of the computer model of the control system.

Zoran firm's logo had still been working fine since he gave them to me in Šimanovci when he fixed our communications.

"Lunch has arrived," I thought to myself after seeing the pickup truck coming to our combat position. Stoimenov handed the camera over to them. They will take it to Progar village and Bajić will try to fix it. It was good that NATO had not been flying combat sorties during daytime yet. We were all tired and exhausted. I gave Lukić a key from my Zastava 101 car to take out some bearings for the pickup truck from the car. He will return the key to me when his shift comes at 16:00. I have to cut a new car key, because it started to crack. Varga had not brought the fuel yet, and he should have brought it early this morning. He should leave two barrels at the combat position. At 13:00, Tiosavljević, Golubović and Janković came from base camp because of the antenna manipulation and positioning system broke. Stanković was at the operation center (OC). Around 18:00, a breakdown on the drive was fixed. The three wires on the cable on the fire control radar SNR-125 (NATO Low Blow) were broken. We replaced them. In the UK-64 block, some resistors were burnt. Straight after his shift Dani came to Milan to look for an electrician. He had lunch, bathed and shaved. At that time, he told them how many times his father had married. Twenty-three times!!! Well - Congratulations!

Milan asked me to go to Obrad, an amateur painter. He wanted to paint a picture about the F-117 downing and present it to Dani and myself as a gift. It wasn't clear to him what kind of missiles we launched and how the airplane looked like. I showed him photos in the war editions of The Army magazine.

I went through the mail. Crnobrnja should bring Sedlak to Ogar to do his job. A few days ago, Lukić and Stojanović could not find him in the barracks. I went to sleep around 18:10 hours. Danka phoned me around 21:45. I was a bit nervous and simply didn't like when she wakes me up. She told me that she was worried. She heard the shooting, but there weren't any bomb detonations in Belgrade. She felt the smell of gasoline or something similar in the air. They bombed the Pančevo oil refinery[115] again. Who knows what they hit[116]. The phone calls were her old weakness. I couldn't fall asleep again and got up. Nada made me stewed fruit. I ate it and it felt good.

Danka went to the church and lit a candle for my father, and another two for all the dead and alive. Milan came into the house and said that the sky was red from the bullet tracers. Nada and I went out. I watched and heard the anti aircraft artillery fire from Bofors, Praga, and triple 20/3 mm cannons. They were shooting at something. We couldn't hear any airplane. If they were up, then they must be very high. It was more likely that the artillery received information about the approaching Tomahawk cruise missiles. It occurred twice, around 22:15 and again around 22:35. Milan watched me to see how I would react. I was calm and without any visible emotion. He told me it was his habit that had become an almost involuntary one. He con-

115   The oil refinery in Pančevo is located about 30km away from Danka's apartment.
116   The oil refinery is just one of many plants in the petrochemical industrial complex in Pančevo.

gratulated me for my calmness. His wife Nada was worried. "My child, how are you going to go through the night? It's a long night. I am praying to all the saints, as if I am your mother, for you to stay alive. When all of this is over, go get drunk with your friends and sleep for five days and nights if you need." "I may do her advice," I thought for myself. It sounded good, but I had no time to think about it.

For the first time since the beginning of the war I tried to telephone my sister. I succeed in the third attempt. She was happy to hear me. Her children were fighting for the phone. I was chatting for a bit with both of them. I wished my niece Sandra happy 17th birthday. She had grown up into a big girl. Bojana was fine too and she gained some weight. She weighed almost 4 kilograms more than Sandra and was 2 years younger. "Uncle, I now have to catch up with my school and homework for all the time lost because of my surgery." My sister told me that the anti Serbian warmongering propaganda campaign was very strong, ordinary people opposed it, getting organised and that the demonstrations of enormous proportions had been spreading all over Europe. There was chaos in the Aviano air force base in Italy. They talked so much nonsense on TV when the F-117A was downed, lost credibility, people do not trust them and want the war to end. I told her that she had a hero brother. She understood it right away. She told me through the tears "I felt it," and then added, "Just to let you know, the Enterprise (aircraft carrier) is in the Adriatic sea[117] and it is bothering me a lot." I laughed and told her that it might come one day into our scope[118]. Her children wished me a happy birthday. My sister was overjoyed that we spoke, so was I. Pajče was sick, and my childhood friend Steva, a car mechanic, was thinking about returning home with his wife, Sladjana, and daughter. Albright promised that the bombing would continue until 24 April, when NATO celebrates its fiftieth anniversary. There will be a feast in Washington. She is fluent in the Serbian language, as she had lived in Yugoslavia until she was twelve years old... Bitch...

I noticed that the phone was ringing, and long conversations made me very nervous. I had been spending hours on the phone holding the handset, so my hand and ear hurt a bit. These are probably the consequences of the phone pressing onto my ear. I quickly got dressed and went out. I searched in vain for my simple, inexpensive, flashlight. I couldn't find it but found out later that Senad Muminović had found it out and took it with him to the camp. Hopefully nobody would take it. It has the most common insert, dates back to 1996 when I was posted for a short time in Martinci and still works well. I met a police patrol along the way. We greeted each other. I passed two village checkpoints manned by the local hunters. They greeted me as well. I was in a hurry. My midnight shift is from 00:00 to 08:00.

117   This was misunderstanding, as the US officials announced diversion of the 2nd aircraft carrier USS Enterprise to the Adriatic Sea to strengthen the NATO naval force comprised of the USS Theodore Roosevelt battle group operating along with British and French carriers attacking Yugoslavia from safety of the far west end of the Mediterranean Sea.

118   Neither a NATO aircraft carrier nor a major naval ship entered the Adriatic Sea during the 1999 war, as that would probably put them in the range of coastal missile defense systems or missiles launched from fast 'missile boats'.

The bus with our shift has just arrived. Dani told me that he had radiated a few times before midnight last night for about a minute and a half in total; continuously for 30 seconds in one occasion. I asked him "Why? We agreed to radiate[119] only when we see a target on our surveillance radar." He replied, "Colonel Stanković provoked me by saying that we were not radiating and seeking targets." Dani continued, "In fact, I think that some mistrust prevailed in our brigade. Perhaps, towards some in our brigade and for a particular reason." I replied, "But there is no need to mistrust us. We were the only ones who destroyed the plane, moved six times so far to a new combat position and did everything that was required. If we do not see a target on our surveillance radar, then it is logical that we would not be able to see it on our target acquisition radar at the guidance station van!". "All this should be analysed after the war," I thought, "...and by starting from the very beginning. " Someone said sarcastically, "It is not okay if we do not radiate and do not look for something that only Vučković and nobody else sees." The other night we counted that he 'saw' between fifty and sixty cruise missiles on his radar. And what then? If we radiated so many times[120], we would have revealed our position and been destroyed. If so, then we would have been judged as an untrained crew and our conduct would have been assessed as stupid. What a contradiction?!

Stanković asked me for some data and I gave it to him. After that, we decreased the use of our surveillance radar, in order to fully stop at 00:45. I spoke with Captain Vučković and told him that it was a bad idea to radiate with our target acquisition radar before I see a target on my surveillance radar. I told him that radiation from the target acquisition radar is unnecessary and it would only reveal my location. "You are right," he conceded. After that, we switched off the high voltage on the target acquisition radar and power supply from the launch ramps. There was no need for these to be switched on and energized when there was no single target in the air. "For God's sake, today is my 41st birthday," I suddenly popped up. "I am not too young, nor too old." I thought, "These are the best years of my life." Then, I corrected myself: "Probably the best age is one's own age." Then I realised: "It's not a good time now to think about it." My whole life flashed before my eyes. My life is like in a novel.

Major Stoimenov talked with Vučković. Vučković gave him instructions on how to detect targets on the surveillance radar under circumstances of radio disturbances and jamming and lectured him on the radar operation modes. Boris then went to Ljubenković on our surveillance radar, to double check everything he recorded while talking to Vučković.

It is 01:45. Time passes slowly, and I do not know the current situation in the air. My visual observer is silent. So, there are no problems in the immediate airspace. I wish there were no problems all the time. My shift is napping. Their sleeping positions are different, just like children in a kindergarten. The station equipment works monotonously. I lit a cigarette. How about hav-

119   With our target acquisition radar.
120   Each time he saw a cruise missile.

ing coffee now? Double the water, medium strength. Lately I had just been drinking that one. I went to the toilet. It felt as if I was about to get a cold. Senad looked after the phones, whilst I was away. I met with soldier Slaviša outside - he controlled the generators. One of them consumed 20 liters of oil per day. The workshop mechanic was here the other day to see why. The job to repair was huge. Most likely, it would work like this until the end of the war or a new truce.

Sima, the retired Colonel, is really a great man. When his son announced that he was called to go to the war, he shook his hand and congratulated him. Then, he said to the nearby farmers: "Why are you surprised people, it is war. If they need to go into your house to get your tractor, then so be it. We are defending our country!" He was a real officer with an attitude. Varga said that his "plumber line" told him the war would last a while. That they would invade by land troops and that it would be fierce. We were supposedly returning to Jakovo in mid-June. The war will be wider, maybe the new World War.

Yesterday, the Federal Assembly adopted the Government's proposal to join the Russian and Belarusian alliance. There was a new polarization in the world. Pandemonium... It should be that way. Otherwise, there would be no one to stand in the way of this crazy hegemony of the West. Had Europe and the world, human dignity and freedom, international law and the United Nations been defended in this area? All these great thoughts, great creations were in fact shit and a common farce. It was a dictatorship. This was the true truth and the order of things in the world.

Once again, they dispatched the war machine to loot apiece of someone else's skies and rob them of their heritage, minerals and energy resources. They were plundering us today. Whose life is on the line? Who will they attack next? I would very much like that only part of the suffering of our people could be felt by the creators of this new world order in the West. What kind of mothers gave birth to those sick kinds of people, and whose blood were they? To create, live on and feed off the misfortune of other people! They are great unbelievers[121]. Their publicly stated high moral values and objectives are just a finely crafted public relationship smokescreen for their true motivation. All they cared about was the damn money. Their tools of war are goods like all others, but because of the money they were waging war and people were losing their lives[122]. Madness...

My shift ended at 08:00. I went to the local school to meet with Crnobrnja. Kosta was boiling coffee, "The usual for me: large black, medium strength" I said. Bora told me that Draganić had fired last night and downed two Sea Harriers[123].One was found in Bosnia, and the other had not been found yet, as far as he knows. The pilot failed to eject. His charred corpse was found

121   The way I think of it these days is the West is everything opposite of what the Ten Commandments recommend we should be.
122   In other words, the misery and death of other people is the 'sacrifice' they are eagerly prepared to take.
123   Sea Harrier is British naval short take-off and vertical landing/vertical take-off and landing jet fighter, reconnaissance and attack aircraft; in the Balkans conflicts it mainly operated from aircraft carriers positioned within the conflict zone.

near the aircraft. I would not be surprised if they had disabled the pilot's ejector seat, as they did in Vietnam. In Vietnam, they deliberately disabled the ejector seats after realizing that pilots were leaving their aircraft mid-flight 'en masse' by ejecting (and parachuting on the territory not controlled by their foe – the Viet Cong).

Bora had a shower at Milan and Nada's place. We had coffee and breakfast. I went to Ogar. Armuš sent me a message that we should meet. We agreed to meet in Ogar at the Dotlić's office. I took the battalion mail with me and told Sedlak what should be done while I am away. He looked at me dumbfounded.

He joined the unit just yesterday. "I will do everything you say," he replied to me. Senior Sergeant Barvalac told me that the carburetor[124] on Ural truck in the missile guidance battery probably failed. He had returned the camera to Lieutenant Colonel Popović, "That skinny guy from the school center, I know him well, he is my good friend," I replied. He wanted to show me the camp. Everything was arranged and separated. They were cooking bean soup, and a pleasant scent was filling the air. I brought to his attention that the guard at the entrance must be armed and have ammunition. A general warning about the operation of the enemy's commandoes, saboteurs and other terrorist groups had been issued.

On my way back I met with Armuš on the road. I told him to wait for me in Pećinci and that we will meet in an hour. Dotlić was not in the camp. A group of soldiers from the reserve approached me and we greeted each other. I asked them whether they rested. They said they were. I sat in my car and drove off briefly stopping at Žika's house to say goodbye. At the same time Milanka, a hairdresser, appeared; the other night I reprimanded her husband when we were setting up the combat position in Ogar. "Would you like a coffee," she asked me. I refused, explaining that I was in a hurry. Time was running out and Armuš is waiting for me. She said that I have not changed much: I had only gotten a few more gray hairs, since the last time she saw me, seven or eight years ago. Nice conversation but I had to leave.

I went to the entrance of Pećinci to wait for Armuš. I went to the local headquarters of the Civil Defence administration to obtain a purchase order for 400 liters of 'D-2' diesel fuel. At the headquarters, the mayor of the municipality told us that they were no longer responsible for fuel, but instead it was the Interior Ministry. According to the new regulations, fuel can only be obtained through vouchers issued by police. However, Kovačević was not in the police station. He was in Mitrovica. We could not get vouchers. All in all, the procedure was not the clearest and the question was how to solve the problem. I gave the mayor the war edition of the 'Vojska' journal, as well as to the cops. Our cooperation was excellent. They brought us juice because we refused their offer of hard spirits, and then we left. Armuš went home in Šimanovci, and I went to see Pošarac to make me a spare car key. He did it manually, because the machine was not there at the moment. I called my son from Pošarac's phone. I had not called him until then, but I missed him a lot. He arrived quickly. We hugged each other. He is proud of me. He told

---

124   Carburetor is a device for mixing vaporized fuel with air to produce a combustible or explosive mixture, as for an internal-combustion engine.

110

me that every night he and his mates would sit on the kerb of a street, gazing into the night sky and waiting for us to shoot down more airplanes. My little boy was seventeen. He said that he was studying a bit. I told him that the war would end soon. It must end one day...

Our neighbors Nana and Mile Vauš approached us. They hugged me and said, "Where have you been, man? We have not seen you for the past 2-3 years. You have not changed." They saw the war edition of Vojska journal at the rear seat of my car. They asked if I cane give them a copy, and I gave it to them but did not have issue No. 5 to give them... only two or three copies, one of which I had already given to my son. He liked my 'nom de guerre'. I was hurrying home. I asked my son if he had money. "Five more dinars," he replied, so I gave him one hundred dinars, just in case and left Milan's house. Danka and Nataša arrived. We had a coffee. I was tired and felt like sleeping. I layed down in the living room and slept like a log for one hour. Obrad woke me up. He brought me an unfinished painting to look at it. He wanted to gift it to me once he finish it. Danka liked it. We had a quick lunch. Danka packed me a birthday cake to bring it to the people, who were delighted when I brought it. The whole shift came, including the officers from the radar emission imitator, surveillance radar and the guards. There was a piece of cake for each of them. Everyone liked it. I did not have a slice, because I did not feel like it. That was strange, as I knew it was made just for me, and with lots of love. Danka asked me if I was not in the mood. I replied, "No, I am just tired." Everyone hugged me and congratulated me for my birthday.

Pauljević was up at the Operations Center. He asked me if I was rested. I replied that I was, whereas in fact, I was not ... Time flew when I was not in the shift, but it stopped when I was in. I was unsuccessfully trying to get comfortable position in my workstation in the cramped missile guidance station van but could not fall asleep. At 17:02 we went into Readiness No.1. That was our routine work during active operation of the air-defence system. The atmosphere was pretty relaxed. It had become our daily routine. Ivanov[125] and Albright met in Oslo today. They were seeking a political solution.

I told Senad that, perhaps, they may choose to negotiate until the 50th anniversary of NATO on 24 April 1999, in order to get out of the Balkan's mud. Then, they could choose to publicly announce that "in the name of peace" they would be ceasing, effective immediately, their own military operations; that will show to the world NATO's "humanity" and that they were not the alliance of aggressors. This was my wishful thinking. Although, I would like to believe that this could materialise.

It was reported on the news tonight that they hit the Military Medical Academy[126] where sixteen people were wounded. What was agreed in Oslo, we might never know. Tonight, Slavko Ćuruvija, editor-in-chief of the Nedeljni Telegraf journal, was murdered in front of his house in Belgrade. He seemed to have known a lot, or he had found something very important. My shift was busy playing with untangling Boris's wedding ring from the rope.

---

125   Igor Sergeyevich Ivanov - The Foreign Minister of Russia from 1998 to 2004.

126   The Military Medical Academy of the University of Defense, is a military hospital center in the Banjica neighborhood of Belgrade.

He showed them some puzzle. They were trying to solve the enigma. After several attempts, they succeeded. One by one they wanted to figure out how to set up the puzzle and what was the solution. It was also reported on the radio tonight that last night our air-defences inflicted enormous losses on the enemy and that 10 cruise missiles were destroyed. It was raining and drizzling, making a 'beautiful' Srem clay. I had been sitting outside in the rain and enjoyed the cold raindrops, which refreshed my face. I used to love the rain and the beautiful feeling of nature immediately after it stopped raining. The radio reported that Serbian security forces had entered into the northern Albania. "Maybe it was part of the agreement. Who knows?" I wondered. "One just has to endure, persevere and survive," I thought, "Every war ends with an armistice, so would this one; I am sure about it."

While sitting in the cabin, I thought, "We had spun a web like a spider. We were waiting for the victim to be mercilessly killed by one injection of poison." Further observing, "Nobody gets excited about it, nor does anyone care about it." And realising, "Kill him in order not to be killed. This is the fundamental rule of war. A bit crude, but true, expression of the key survival rule in the Darwin's theory; in which natural selection was the basic mechanism of evolution."

I nearly forgot that, around 16:30, I had received a message on my pager: "Dad, Happy birthday. Lots of love from Vlada." I smiled and thought, "In that earlier frenzy, he either forgot to do it earlier, or his mother reminded him now. Who knows? Last year he gave me a bottle of whiskey as my birthday present". I then recalled, "When I took the money to give to him, he saw my pager. He asked for my number, and I gave it to him."

At 19:30 hours, Dr. Đukić came to do a quick health check up on my shift. "We are fine, but who give a fucks anyway", commented Tiosavljević. Everyone laughed. I sent him to Maletić, the joker, to cheer him up and let him know that "Something was wrong with him, and we did not know what that was."

We all concluded that NATO had brought Europe to a dead end. I realised that I had Danka's letter, she had sent it on 3 April via my classmate Matija, together with other things. He gave it to me the other day. I remembered earlier today that he had mentioned the letter, so I brought it to my shift. I read it and found nothing new in it. Did she write it in a moment of weakness or some dilemma? That was all I can conclude after reading it. I watched her furtively today. She hardened. She no longer discussed whether the war is justified or not, and now her understanding of the war was the main cause of our numerous quarrels. But now, in this situation and at this place, I did not want to think about it.

Today, Stoimenov did not keep his promise. He had promised that he would not bathe until the end of the war. "They screwed me," he said, "the war has prolonged for too long." We all laughed, and someone said, "It was not a long time – only about twenty days without showering." It was strange how things could turn out. At 14:30, Russian humanitarian aid finally arrived in Dobanovci. Only 68 trucks arrived. For now, we did not know where the others lost their way on the 2,000-kilometer journey. At 20:10 we were ordered into Readiness No. 2. I watched my people, and they were incredible. At the sharp and shrill sound of the phone alarm, they all automatically grasped for their helmets. They all had one thought: "We are either hunting or being hunted." They could not believe it when I ordered them to switch off the equipment. Then, a great sigh of relief erupted. Indeed, I could see and feel that they were all firmly and subconsciously tied into an invisible mental bond.

Dinner was served. Boris said, "Let's eat before night falls." That was funny. We had to stay in the dark because we had to conserve fuel. At 23:40 we went into Readiness No. 1. There was a pair of plains at the azimuth of 270 degrees, at a distance of 85 kilometers. Shortly after we received an air danger signal for Tomahawk cruise missiles. "Who are their targets tonight?" I wondered, "Their control system is guiding the tree trunk of metal and explosives to destroy something somewhere in a city that is now coming to life awoken by the sirens and the hustle and bustle of the air-raid shelters."

Wednesday, April 14

I finished my shift at 00:10 after the usual information exchange with Dani and a farewell handshake for good luck and success in his shift (like miners…). I told him that we had searched for a low flying target with the fire control radar. Vučković informed us about the target. Did he personally see the target, or was he told by radio-amateurs? They helped us a lot. Of course, we are their army. It is amazing how well they are organized.

I went to Milan and Nada's place to sleep. Everything was locked. I rang the doorbell three times. Nothing happened. I thought maybe I should go to the school building and try to sleep there because I felt unconformable for disturbing their sleep. I knocked on the living room window; Milan heard me and came out to open the door. I had a shower and was so tired and exhausted that I couldn't call Danka. I fell asleep as soon as I hit the bed.

A sharp phone buzz woke me up at 07:00. Dani was on the line. He couldn't recognize my deep and raspy morning voice. I stayed in bed for further 10-15 minutes, as Milan and Nada got up later than usual this morning. I had coffee and herbal tea with honey but no time for breakfast. What I didn't want is to be late for my shift. The feeling when the replacement shift is late pisses me off.

By 08:00 my shift was on the combat position again. Dani told me that during the night they didn't radiate with the fire control radar. They had a target 15 km away, but something was wrong with the radar. He told me that they had changed the generator and after that "everything works fine now." At 08:40 we were ordered to go to Readiness No. 3. We turned off the equipment.

We had breakfast: one hot dog, a piece of bread and cheese. That was quite enough food for me, but not for some others. They complained and criticized the logistics. Barvalac and his guys weren't good cooks. Yesterday's bean soup was awful. One soldier from the engineering unit was delivering the meals. Officers were not happy with his work. I have to check what was going on. My shift will end at 16:00.

Around 12:00, just after the Belarusian president Lukashenko's plane landed in Belgrade, we heard two loud detonations. We were in the shift on standby with our equipment turned off. After that we heard the noise of an airplane. Because of the plain terrain it was hard to determine its distance and altitude. Everything seemed closer than it was in reality. We immediately went into Readiness No. 1. I knew that there was no chance we could find that particular airplane. We needed three to four minutes of preparation time to get ready to fire, and in the meantime the airplane will leave our engagement envelope[127,128].

Around 15:00, Colonel Stanković arrived at our station. He shook hands with everybody. We discussed our work. I raised the issue of absurd requests coming from the Brigade Operations Centre to search for helicopters and cruise missiles with our radar. All riverbanks[129] are overgrown with willow and poplar trees. Why they didn't ask the Riverine navy[130] to close the river paths[131] and army air-defence to cover waterway directions with the light anti-aircraft systems, such Bofors or Praga, or MANPADs. The Air defence is working like crazy while others are scratching their balls in the neighbouring villages. Colonel Stanković wanted us to send one missile guidance officer to the battalion in Obrenovac.

I finished my shift at 16:00 and went to Milan's place for lunch, and after that, to meet Dani and Bora in the school. When I got there, I met reserve Captain Lukić, the commander of SA-16 (9K38 Igla) shoulder launched missile unit, his driver Kosta, and Lukić's brother Mića who served in that unit. They were 1-2 km from us. One guy from security joined us. Dani ordered a coffee and Mića went to bring two cases of beer. I was not drinking alcohol at all, so I took a standard double shot medium strength coffee. Kosta

---

127   Engagement envelope – is the range of the missiles within which it can destroy targets.

128   In theory, the airplane could remain within the engagement envelope for the duration of the fire control radar preparation time (three to four minutes) and show up on the radar screen; however, it was highly unlikely that it would be shot down. This explains the Author's pessimistic note. The crew searched for the target but did not find it.

129   Belgrade lies on the confluence of two large rivers, Danube and Sava, each of which has relatively large tributaries that are further connected by navigable channels. These provide the shipping route from the Black Sea to a few countries in central Europe.

130   Riverine navy (or Brown-water navy) exists in these waterways since the ancient times, protecting the key cities and their shipping routes. This is, for example, illustrated on Belgrade's coat of arms.

131   During the 1999 war, the small navy boats represented an invisible threat and insolvable puzzle to NATO's air force, as they easily camouflaged under the large canopies of willow and poplar trees along the riverbanks. Every night they would relocate and anchor under a different tree, typically just a couple hundred meters upstream or downstream, or across the river; and often without the need to additionally camouflage the boats.

already knew what coffee I liked, and in which mug he would pour.

Dani started to speak to the laymen about tactics and how we downed the stealth. I watched a TV show and occasionally gave approval when he asked for it from me. I was getting annoyed from all that dick swinging. His ego was astronomical. He ascribed the work of the whole unit exclusively to himself. "Well, do what you want," I thought to myself. He had been showing off and presenting himself as an almighty being, which I saw as an inferiority complex. He was extremely cunning. It is our job to shot down enemy airplanes. Yes, we downed the stealth, but the war is not over yet and we have to be smart. Dani had too much beer that he could not stop talking. He was talking to everyone about how he had downed the airplane, as if the other people did not exist at all. If he behaved like this when some people from our unit were present, then I could just imagine how he talked when none of us is around.

Around 18:30, the other guys left and Dani, Bora and I discussed the security of the combat position. The conclusion was that it was not safe. I suggested the creation of a rapid intervention platoon to combat any sabotage and terrorist[132] groups. They both agreed. I further suggested the platoon to be under the separate command, so the brigade command (Dani and I) should not waste our time by organizing checkpoints, village guards and managing volunteers from the local villages' hunter's groups. That was Bora's job. He was the battalion's security officer. Other than approving the creation of the platoon, it was obvious that Dani didn't like the rest; he would no longer have an excuse to go around the local villages, meet people and present himself as the one that downed the stealth.

Bora's thinking was quite different. He had already been collaborating in setting up the protection around the combat positions and camps, but he wasn't formally responsible for their security. "What is your job than?" I asked him directly, "If everything turns out ok, then you did that, and if not, then what?" Our security officers had organized their job as "sniffing around". They had their own communication channels to their superior[133,134,135,136,137] in the brigade command. It was logical to me that we, in the battalion HQ, must have access to all the information available in order to

132   Terrorist group–The Author referred to the Commandos and Special Air Services (SAS) groups from NATO countries and their proxies - armed and trained by NATO military to attack the air defense and other sites. From the Author's perspective, all these groups required equal treatment - as per the manual for managing terrorists.

133   The security officers in the missile brigade had been sending their reports, observations, assessments and suggestions in sealed envelopes directly to the Chief Security Officer of the brigade command.

134   **This practice bypassed the chain of command in the battalions.**

135   Consequently, the battalion commanding officers (Dani and I in our battalion) did not know what their security officers (Bora in our battalion) had been reporting to the Chief Security Officer of the brigade command.

136   Two separate communication channels to the very top of the Air Force Air Defense had been created.

137   That was not good practice as it put the chain of security officers above

115

gain the best situational awareness. At present, we were subjected to select security information sharing on "as need-to-know basis" at the discretion of the security officer. I found this to be unacceptable.

Dani kept on reflecting on the Stanković's visit earlier today. He asked for a missile guidance officer for Djokić's battalion. The repair of his UNK missile guidance station van will be completed soon. Dani objected the requested transfer and told him that we were unable to give away either Golubović or Muminović, because of the people's moral and completeness of our command structure. They both performed dual critical combat and non-combat combat roles: Golubović is the combat shift deputy commander and battery commander; Muminović is the missile guidance officer and the second platoon commander during relocations. "You can take away one of them only over my dead body or if you dismiss me from the battalion commander position," Dani told Stanković. Just before Stanković left he told Dani that he would receive the orders in a few days time.

"Be ready to arrest me," Dani told to Bora jokingly. When asked would he arrest Dani, Bora replied, "Not for now".

"Djole, you will be promoted. Get ready to take up command of the battalion in a few days" Dani said to me.

I replied him, "In my opinion, both of you were either angry or emotional, and Stanković will probably think twice before deciding."

Dani cried out loud, "Fuck Djokić and his excessively long radar emissions!"

I asked Bora to which unit he was now assigned to, to our or Noskov's? Namely, I had a feeling that Bora had been spending as much time as he could with Noskov, because he couldn't stand Dani. However, as soon as Noskov had left to Pančevo, Bora returned to us!

Dani did not go today to his afternoon shift at 16:00. I noticed a pattern of his behaviour in the last few days: Dani fails to go to his scheduled shift if the preceding shift crew radiated with the fire control radar. I wondered if this pattern was just a coincidence. For example, after we searched for the target earlier this morning, Dani didn't show up for the afternoon shift. He sent Dotlić to replace him. He had already done it before, I couldn't remember on top of my head which location that was; but I do remember that, at the shifts' changeover time, Dani and Bora went to the local municipality mayor and who knows where else…

At 20:00 I went to Milan's place. After a quick shower I called Danka. She worked today. She got a new mobile phone; it came unlocked and she gave me her new number. "It must be some embezzlement with the phone," she told me. I urged her to be quick as I was exhausted, "You will explain it to me in details when I see you."

It took me a while to fall asleep. Shortly after Milan woke me up. My head was heavy, I had no thoughts and my mind was blank. I had to put an effort to get up. I slept and felt better at Kosta's place. The smell of fresh double shot medium coffee at the table filled in the whole kitchen. I hoped it would that of the command officers.

keep me up all night.

We came to replace our buddies at the combat positions at midnight. The surveillance radar was broken. Everybody was nervous. Captain Golubović suggested calling Ristić and Vučković to come and resolve the problem. The tension in the air was high. Blagojević from the brigade operation control center told them that they had just been fooling around whenever the situation was dangerous. They had left and we took over.

The task remained the same. I sent Major Stoimenov to the surveillance radar. A few minutes later, Balgojević phoned me and asked, "Do you have anything on your Number Two[138,139,140]?" I replied, "Nothing, how I can have anything when you know that we have a malfunction? People are working to fix the problem." Shortly after, Major Stoimenov requested a new radar vacuum tube 6M15P. I didn't have it here, at the position, and I didn't have it in the spare parts van. I told Ljubenković to try to find a second-hand one.

The receiver was not working well. I could see that from the reflection of the Fruška Gora Mountain on the radar screen. The quality was less than a third good of what it should be. Blagojević got pissed off. I told him: "You are a missileer, why don't you come to us, take a seat and work with us the best you can." He realized what he was asking from me. He said: "Djole, please don't be angry. Hurry up. They are very close to you. C'mon, I'll guide you."

I ordered the high voltage to be turned 'on' on the missile guidance radar antenna, and preparation of the launch ramps. I warned Blagojević to be careful when giving me the azimuth of the target, to be relative to that Vučković will see on his radar. Otherwise, he would fuck me up. The weight of the whole shift was in his hands. I felt very uncomfortable. It was quite a different feeling when I can personally see the whole airspace situation on my radar screen, all planes, including he one who is attacking me and from which direction; to that it is very tricky when I see nothing and someone else is directing me towards the particular direction of the target. Under these circumstances, correct use of the radar imitator is crucial. I wondered "Would he be able to remember it and correctly re-calculate the azimuth of the target in the heat of the moment?"

"I'll call you when I have something 15 km from you and don't ask me for permission to launch, just launch it," Blagojević told me. "Go to hell," I jokingly replied, "I didn't come here to pick up wild strawberries".

---

138   Number 2 is jargon and an acronym for the local (battalion's) surveillance radar. Similarly, Number 1 is jargon and an acronym for the local (battalion's) target acquisition / fire control radar. The battalion relied on these two radars for its autonomous combat operation during the 1999 War.

139   The air defense officers regularly used these two jargon words when communicating with each other.

140   These two jargon words cannot be translated into the English language in a manner that the translation retains the linguistic property of brevity the original words have in the Serbian language. For these reasons and for ease of reading, this translation uses full English description of these two radars.

In the meantime, Ljubenković and Stoimenov had been trying to fix the radar. We had armed the missiles[141] three times so far:[142] the first and second missile, then the third and fourth missile, and then the first two missiles again.

I asked Blagojević for a half an hour break because Ljubenković had found a second-hand radar tube 6M15P.

"Djole, you have all your life to take the break", he replied, "You are the only one left. They hit the first and the second battalion while you were off."

"Go to hell Srba, you are the one who guided me. Why didn't you give me any target? This means that they didn't even come into my envelope," I replied and asked, "What did they use to hit the others?"

"An anti-radiation missile and laser bombs," he told me.

"Motherfuckers," I thought to myself," How did they find them? You have just dearly comforted me," a stream of thoughts ran through my mind, "How did it happen? Why did they target two of the three units Srba had guided?" I couldn't get his words "You are the only one left" out of my head.

I told my guys that there were no casualties, just wounded. Everybody dipped into their own thoughts, probably thinking about how they found them and what mistakes they had made. A hush descended over our crew in the van. Swear words and spasms filled the van. Was there something new in their tactics that we had not been aware of? We really needed to think about it.

"I'll call you later to tell you everything," he said. His voice was strange, it sounded like he was laughing. I didn't understand it. Perhaps he was just fooling me that our guys were hit. Maybe our guys launched. In any case, I heard news about dire calamity through my headset.

Dani had also told Stanković that they have missile guidance officers in the brigade, but someone must have the balls to risk coming to the combat position. It was much safer being far away from the missile guidance station van. It was much more secure to be in any house, building, field, forest or who knows where else, than to be here. Everywhere else, just not in the van. The prey is in the van, and we are part that game.

Around 02:00, Ljubenković reported that they had fixed the radar and tuned it. There were so many blips on the screen when he turned it on. I didn't have such a "rich" picture since the beginning of the war. The fixed reflections disappeared when he turned on the filters and eliminated the clutter. It would be fantastic to be able to see the targets clearly without the interference.

---

141   Arm the missile–means to prepare the missile for immediate launch, i.e. to bring it into the "hot start" state.

142   There is a limited time, say 30 minutes, the missile can be in the hot start state, before it is required to "cool down". In order to maintain the combat readiness for immediate launch, another pair of missiles has to be brought into the "hot start" state. This process was alternated three times by using two pairs of missiles (first and second; third and fourth) on the single launch ramp.

I didn't have one fucking vacuum tube and I had been fighting against the whole NATO! If they just knew which "slingshot" had been downing their planes... Hearts and brains against the computers and all weapons money can buy...

I remembered Major Tepić blowing up an ammunition depot during the Siege of Bjelovar Barracks. On 29 September 1991, unwilling to leave the ammunition depot to the enemy. Our nation had been forgetting our heroes very quickly. His death in selflessly drawing the line and saying "no further" to the puppets of the assertive hegemonic power transcends our physical space and time; it symbolizes the eternal battle between good and evil, and should be remembered in the history books via stories that should inspire future generations. Territories were lost.

I learned from the first reports that nobody died in these attacks but there were some who were injured. How many, how seriously, I didn't know. All I know at this moment is that we will have to analyse that quickly. Learning lessons is very important now; in order to never again repeat these mistakes, if any.

They destroyed almost half of the brigade's equipment. Colonel Bajić and his men had been trying to fix and put back together whatever equipment was broken or not completely destroyed.

Lukashenko was in Belgrade. I didn't have the time nor the willpower to write what he said after his visit.

Near Prizren, NATO bombed a column of Albanian refugees returning home from the hideaway. The horrific pictures were broadcast throughout the world. We were fighting against sick minded people. They are destroying monuments much older than their own existence. The mudhole was too deep.

The state of the air defence was of concern. Unit after unit had been eliminated. There was no one left to watch my back or to rely upon. Slowly but steadily we had been entering into the vortex from which only the luckiest of us will get out.

Last night we radiated twice with the radar imitator. We emitted in 10 second bursts.

If a nation does not feed its own army, it will feed a foreign one. For years, no money had been invested in the defence forces. The standards plummeted; paychecks were late, and armed forces were subjected to widespread disrespect. And now everybody was expecting a miracle! It was already miraculous that we had been fighting more than 20 days and we were still alive and strong. The question I asked myself was: "How much longer will we be able to survive?"

How long would the heart, the quiet companion of man's soul and master of his strength, be able to endure? Everybody was suffering this trying test of history in his own way. Patriotism is a great thing but only if it is in the majority. Is patriotism something that could unite the nation, or will people just be sheep like many times before. I had just realised a muffled sorrow coming from the bottom of my heart. I know that ordinary people, including us, soldiers, will pay the highest price. Many people in this country are now sleeping in their houses with their families, looking after their wives and children and having a much higher quality of life than I'll probably ever have. Fuck this injustice and politics, madness, and the war. Throughout history we had always been trying to do the impossible and "straighten the river bend". We're proud and I'm proud as well. I won't hesitate to die for the truth, but, perhaps, everything could have been done a bit differently. Now, it is what it is.

Horrific photo of NATO atrocities – bombed column of Albanian refuges while they tried to get back home.

Varga's plumb line screwed us again. Today is Thursday and according to him we should have launched on Monday or Tuesday. We all hope that we will never be hit, and if it would be possible, we'll launch again – there is no dilemma about that.

I listened the news at 03:0. They bombed many cities again. Instead of stealing from the country and embezzling money, politicians should have developed the armed forces. The political agenda they pursued inevitably led to the war. I don't care about the intentions. I can see the outcomes and consequences, and these consequences are catastrophic. My generation lost the right to a normal life. The country was destroyed. God helps us that casualties are not that high.

Kosovo and Metohija are burning. Everything started there, and everything will finish there. I see the situation as an arena with a lot of mad lions and we are alone. The whole world is just a spectator. I have been looking for the position of the thumb – would it point up or down. I wish I had a strong stick, so when they open their jaws to swallow us, I can ram it down their throats.

We have learnt the secret of being content, whether living in plenty or in wain. There will be re-construction after this war ends, advocacy of special interests and unequal wealth distribution. On average, we will eat cabbage rolls stuffed with meat again. Ordinary people will end up eating the cabbage and will find it difficult to make ends meat. Others will eat the meat. Ordinary people will end up with pride, whereas others will end up with everything plus whatever the ordinary people have. One cannot live from pride and defiance.

I realized that our wives are not entitled to use our officers' fuel rations unless we show up in person at the petrol station. Tomorrow, this stupid rule, "in person only," may apply to any future food rations. Fuck that senseless "in person" rule when I'm now in the "centre of the arena" at the combat position, not voluntarily, but unfortunately not by pure chance either. I wondered what the price of is being in the arena, who and how would they pay for my time here. The stakes are high. Any life is worth more than a bridge, equipment, or anything else. "I don't care about the people!" I recalled the exact words that drunken asshole Blagojević said during the relocation. "Then, what are you interested in? I thought to myself, "You are a miserable piece of shit and ass-lover! One hundred lashes on someone else's back wouldn't bother you at all! Or "in the others ass a telephone poll is not too much." You have never been interested and never will be."

At 05:40 hours I called Colonel Stojanović and asked him about the news. "Nothing good," he replied and then asked, "What happened with your surveillance radar last night?" I told him that we had found a broken radar when we came to our midnight shift. "But yesterday the radar worked," he said. "It worked yesterday but not the last night," I explained and asked him, "Do you think that I wouldn't like to have functional equipment instead of having to rely on you to guide me?" "Blagojević told me that those were interferences," he replied. "Screw Blagojević, he was sitting "up high" with you, not with us," I replied and tried to engage him, "What did Ljubenković fix at the end?" He cut our conversation short by saying: "I'll talk to you later in person. Don't have time right now." That was not good sign at all. I got the impression that something bad had happened when he cannot talk about it via the phone. Someone was most likely killed. They can point laser guided bombs to almost any target. It was much easier to fight against anti-radiation missiles and outsmart them. Even that became a luxury – to choose what to be hit with. We had log protection around the van and rubber mats from the launch ramps on its roof to protect us from shrapnel's in the case of a HARM attack. I had recently ordered that additional protection for people, as it increases their chances to survive.

The sun rose up. This morning was magnificent. The sky was light blue. I didn't like it, as it had hidden the killers last night. A desire for revenge started to rise up[143]. Why didn't we have better weapons?? If we had them, then mothers, wives and sisters other than ours would cry as well.

Last night when I was trying to fall asleep at Milan's house, Senior Sergeant Tisoavljević shot in the air[144] right in front of the pub. Dani and Bora

---

143   *And if you wrong us shall we not revenge?"* Shakespeare clearly thought revenge was as normal and predictable as the sun rising.

144   Celebratory gunfire is the shooting of a firearm into the air in celebration.

spoke to him and reprimanded him. He said he was exhausted and stressed, in part because of no clean clothing and underwear; the song from the tape player "hit him hard emotionally" and he needed to relieve the pressure a bit.

We were born to live and now someone wants to take that divine heritage from us by force. Someone that you don't know and who doesn't know who you are. Why? Is what they have in their own houses and countries not enough for them? The greed and avarice must be stopped. Why were we chosen for that role?

Slaviša Pavlović brought me a pack of cigarettes from my Zastava 101 car. I felt tense and I couldn't fall asleep. I wasn't so stressed for any particular reason, but it felt as if I had a bad premonition that something calamitous could soon occur, as it did indeed. It was the omen I felt inside me, like when animals get agitated before an earthquake.

Stanković asked me if we have camouflage nets. "Only one, that had been set up and that you saw yesterday. The others are pure rotten garbage," I replied. "Oh, fuck it!" he uttered with a sigh. "Oh, fuck it as well," I thought to myself, "Someone should be asked to explain the reasons for that."

"Why are we here? Why are we doing what we are doing? And why had we been given nothing. Someone needs to be held to account. Fuck this country and its military! These two go together, they are inseparable," I thought to myself. "We are glorified now, honoured with praise and admiration. We are their hope and they rely on us[145,146].

Our unification through hope should genuinely be strong. Hope is beautiful if feet are shod with the preparation of the gospel of peace[147], otherwise our heartbeats sound much louder than the thump of our steps[148,149].

It provides an emotional discharge and stress relief; hence it has beneficial psychological effects. It is culturally accepted in parts of the Afghanistan, Balkans, India, Middle East, Pakistan, Russia and United States, even when illegal.

145   The political leadership and people expected the military to defend the country in this difficult time of war.

146   The Author questioned himself if that was feasible by using the obsolete weapons they had.

147   "Hope is beautiful if feet are shod with the preparation of the gospel of peace" – is the Author's adaptation of the line of the (King James's translation of the) Bible, Ephesians 6-15, The Armour of God, to suit his particular situation.

148   "Our heartbeats sound much louder than the thump of our steps" – The Author feared for his life, that someone else decides by sending him to the boxing ring "to fight Mike Tyson" without any chance to defend himself, and his mates.

149   In this metaphorical sentence, the Author addresses the expectation of the state officials and people that the military will defend the country and protect people in this difficult time of war. He wondered if that would be possible by using the obsolete weapon systems they had at their disposal. No money had been invested in the military for years, which the Author metaphorically describes as [their] "hope was not shod", meaning their hope was not backed up by equipping the military with the "tools of war" needed for the assignment. His ill-equipped unit was sent on the front battlefield line of the homeland defense, which the Author metaphorically describes

Did our hearts become one? It could be, but only temporarily while we are here together. I am afraid that we will go in different directions after all this madness ends, and the beats of our common great heart will be forgotten, like many times before. This is who we are. I told that to Dani. We have to respect and look after each other after the war ends.

Unfortunately, Dani's behaviour so far showed to a large extent that he thinks about and cares only about himself and his personal success. In other words, he started his own Munchausen Syndrome[150]. We are all on the margins now.

Thursday, April 15

The new shift came at 08:00. I talked to Dani for about 40 minutes about last night's work. He knew about the radar and its malfunction. Blagojević had already called Dani to tell him that he was angry with me because of the malfunction. "We were ready to shoot upon his information order to engage the target," I told him, "My shift is my witness." I continued angrily and spontaneously, "What does he think, that if he is in the Brigade Command, that he is worth something more than me? Does he feed me or dress me, or will he look after my family tomorrow? Fucking asshole! He is a pretentious fool." I was surprised with my own outburst, however the emotional discharge instantly helped, and I calmly concluded "Or should we do nothing, so the 'barbarians would remain eternally primitive'." I was sure that Dani knew the truth. We were all upset. After returning to the camp, Boris Stoimenov told him the whole situation and asked him to check whether all conversations were still recorded at the Operations Center.

I found out that the 1st missile battalion was hit last night, sometimes between 21:00 and 22:00.

So, an Infra Red (IR) guided missile or a laser bomb hit them even before my shift commenced last night. The 4th missile battalion was also hit last night during combat work. They fired at one target and were carrying over fire to the other target without pausing the high voltage radiation. They continuously radiated for too long. Courage is needed, but not craziness. What did they achieve? They were left without their air-defense assets and Belgrade was left defenseless from the direction that is in their jurisdiction. They were HARM-ed, literally. Major Vasiljević and Captain Stojanović were slightly wounded. Their equipment may be repaired, depending on how much it was damaged.

<u>We will not go to a new combat position today.</u> Lieutenant Colonel Djord-

as "our heartbeats sound much louder than the thump of our steps", meaning they feared for their own lives.

150   Munchausen Syndrome- was named after a German cavalry officer Baron von Munchausen, a man who travelled widely and was known for his dramatic but untruthful stories. Remembering Baron von Munchausen and his mythical tales, his name became a synonym for a great layer in former Yugoslavia.

jević and Lieutenant Colonel Draganić will do so, as they shot last night. We will probably go tomorrow. After firing the missiles last night, Djordjević was ordered to leave the equipment immediately. They were running away so fast so Bora said that they set "A world record for running 1,500 meters". "That order was probably made because two other battalions were hit", I thought. "I am terribly angry at Srba. Who gives him the right to ask Dani if I was working at all? There are many witnesses." The frequent attitude of the higher command towards the combat crews was that of distrust, vilification, insults and superficiality, and that arrogance often resulted in misunderstandings. We were stressed, exhausted from the chronic lack of sleep, overtired, largely disconnected from the real world, overwhelmed, desolate and uninhibited from being continuously on duty, moving the equipment from one combat position to another and fighting air defence warfare. We could have lost our lives, but they were safe.

Dani did not come to his shift today. Captain Golubović was alone. I went to Petrovčić to pick up Ristić to check if the surveillance radar was operating correctly. We arrived at around 11:00 and I went back to the camp to sleep. He had just finished when we came to the shift around 16:00. He said "The radar works well now. We will get you a new generator soon."

Milan said he was in severe pain, as the stone in his kidney started to move. I went to bed to rest at around 11:15, as I will be in the shift from 16:00 to 24:00. Loud noises woke me up at about 14:00. They were removing planks from the smokehouse; Sloba arrived and started shouting loudly at Milan to hurry up and go with him to bring flour, which had been allegedly delivered somewhere in the village. They left and, of course, they did not bring anything. I knew Sloba. He came to Milan's front yard only when he needed something. "He never enters the house, just shouts from the outside," I thought to myself while trying to fall asleep again.

As the sun was setting while we prepared ourselves for our shift, I was told that the Local Community Headquarters had designated unarmed village guards. I told Bora and Dani that it was necessary to takeout the rifles from the Territorial Defense warehouse, that were in the police station in Pećinci, "Two rifles for two guards for each guard post".

I ate some onion dish that was garnished with bacon, coffee after and then went to the school. I gave my car keys to Lukić to check the oil, top-up the fuel and fill in the logbook. The minibus took my whole shift to the combat position. As soon as the bus departed my officer's mind subconsciously drifted into professional topics. People were complaining about the food again. The fish soup was stinking. People were hungry and they bought various treats.

The camp was finally properly set up for the combat crew[151], so upon

---

151   The logistical support platoon finally got into the routine of doing the beds for the combat shift crews, as it was unheard of until then one group of solders was required to do beds for another. The purpose of this wartime tactic change was to provide additional rest time for the two combat crews that were countering the around-the-clock attacks of NATO aviation. Namely, the officers and soldiers returning to the camp from the combat position were too tired after completion of their

return from the combat position the people went directly to the 'hotel-like' accommodation. I could not provide them all with sleeping bags because each unit had a certain number, as per the pre-war planned head count[152]. We decided to mobilise the infantry platoon[153,154] and forma special antiterrorist platoon for physical protection of the combat position[155,156]. Barvalac and combat shift and even more tired after relocating their combat assets to a new combat position (and transitioning them from the marching to combat configuration) that they needed an immediate rest. The additional rest time marginally improved their combat performance in the next shift, to the maximum feasible level under the given circumstances. The highest benefit occurred when the combat crews arrived to a new camp/accommodation.

152   The logistical support platoon failed to provide additional sleeping bags for soldiers mobilized after the war commenced. This was revealed when someone asked the author for a sleeping bag and he did not have one. The soldiers were exhausted and often nervous, loudly cursing and acrimoniously commenting that they were relocating the assets, driving and waging war, only to find out when they returned to the camp, that the logistical support platoon failed to provide them with basic accommodation necessities. In other words, the logistical platoon was caught 'sleeping on the job'.

153   The infantry platoon was part of the wartime reserve component of the entirely Soviet made Neva S-125 air-defense system, as per the Soviet doctrine Yugoslavia adopted, based on the multilayered airspace defense systems. However, in contrast to the Soviet Union, Yugoslavia had a single layered air-defense; that made the Neva S-125 air-defense system and its combat crew intrinsically vulnerable to enemy attacks. For example, following a helicopter landing in the vicinity of the combat position, the enemy's Special Forces or rapid deployment expeditionary units could quickly destroy the assets and kill soldiers in their unarmored vans.

154   At that time, elimination of the Yugoslav air-defense was the top military priority for the NATO pact irrespective of how that was done. By that time, it became obvious that their first preference of destruction by launching conventional and smart weapons from the air had failed to deliver results after 23 days of war. It was necessary to protect the air-defense battery in case the enemy changed their tactic and decided to attack from the air by either parachute airdrop of special forces/rapid deployment units, or by an unexpected helicopter landing of special forces troops/terrorist units (in a similar manner to when they evacuated the pilot of the downed F-117 stealth plane on 27/3/1999).

155   In order to overcome the vulnerability of the combat position it was necessary to additionaly arm the infantry platoon with man-portable anti-aircraft missiles (Strela-2M MANPADs), rocket propelled grenade launchers (often called "RPGs" or "Bazookas") and sniper rifles. The standard infantry weapons and existing measures were deemed adequate against the conventional sabotage and spying.

156   The plan was to select 15-16 of the most capable soldiers for the rapid response antiterrorist unit; arm and train them with different types of the infantry weapons, including practice firing with live ammunition. This included MANPADs, RPGs/Bazookas and snipers. The remaining soldiers, from the new fully manned infantry platoon, would be assigned to guard duties around the camp and combat

Dotlić were instructed to communicate my oral order to Sedlak, who should make the mobilization list[157] and deliver it to the military logistics department for execution, either personally or via a courier.

'Dog tags' arrived. They needed to be sent to the soldiers in the camp to fill in their personal data by using waterproof markers. I asked Dani "Did you bring a dog tag for me? Žugić told me that he had made it for me and for you and gave it to you to give it to me. I have not received mine?" Dani replied, "It stayed with Žugić, and I only took mine." "He is lying again," I thought for myself in disbelief, "I had spoken with Žugić before I decided to ask him this question. We share the same bed, and he's lying to me. With this guy anything is possible."

I had spoken with Danka before I went to my shift. Milan asked me if I could somehow come to Belgrade and take my fuel vouchers to Danka and top up the fuel without waiting in the queue. I replied that "People are nervous, somebody would tongue-lash me. They would not know that I have been fighting for more than twenty days. That would be unfair to other officers and reserves, who do not have a car like me and are unable to do so for their families. I do not want to differ in any way from others in our collective. Danka will have to do what all others have to do. She won't drive, and that'll be it."

Milan was not happy with my reply, but he abstained from commenting. Danka told me that she had spoken with Ljubica yesterday and that she was worried. Rumors were spreading that the infantry units were to be deployed in anticipation of the opening of a new front – NATO's expected land attack. At 16:53, the Operational Center issued a ban on the use of the MANPADs. The NATO campaign had been extremely strong and relentless. Wesley Clark, NATO commander in Europe, requested an additional 200 planes.

"Yesterday, NATO targeted a column of women and children refugees on the road[158]", the news reported. My first thought was, "Indeed, NATO

---

position.

157   The list of reservists for the infantry platoon remained in Deč with Sedlak. For this reason the message was orally communicated to Major Dotlić, Deputy Comander of the Logistical Support Platoon, to pass it on to Sergeant Barvalac, who was delivering food to all units, to transmit the order to Sedlak, with the next food delivery.

158   The video reports were horrific: scattered body parts and children's' toys. Witnesses reported that the pilots returned and raided the column three times in total. The victims were Kosovar Albanian refugees returning home from Albania to the Serbian controlled territory, after being given assurances of their safe return by the Yugoslav authorities. Some say that their safe return and peaceful resolution of the conflict did not suit the military agenda at the time pursued by some great powers, and they were executed by NATO and their locally trained paramilitary militia KLA.

126

is prepared to wage war until the last Shqiptar[159,160,161] is dead. This is the sacrifice they are willing to make". The combat positions in Deč and Sibač were fortified; the mounds were reinforced. The combat positions in Popinci and Mihaljevci should be reinforced next. Dani said he had found a good location in Mihaljevci, just a few kilometers from here. We messaged Bajić to send someone to install the new video camera that Popović and another lieutenant colonel had brought us yesterday. Further to the Dekes's shooting last night, Dani ordered the mayor of the local community to close the tavern by 20:00, otherwise he will close it by himself. We would not allow that we fight, while others live normally and enjoy loud, live music in the restaurant until late in the night.

It seems that a NATO airplane had sneaked under Lukashenko's plane yesterday, came close to Belgrade, made a U-turn, accelerated to quickly escape across the border, and broke the speed of sound somewhere between Belgrade and Novi Sad. No one saw it, but we all heard the sonic boom it created. We were in Readiness No. 3 at that time. By the time we went to Readiness No.1, it was too late. In the period from 18:00 to 19:00, I had a conversation with Aleksić's son, Miroslav. I knew him as a little boy from Skopje. He told me about his life in the community, about divorcing his wife, and how much he loved his daughters. I knew he was a having hard time and I did let him talk. I had gone through all that before and I know very well what to say and what not to say. He was hurt, but he was psychologically strong. "How small is the world," I thought, "After so many years, he is a reservist in my unit. His father was my commander when I was a young officer. Now I am his commander. Aca has not changed, neither has his mother Mileva. He respected them and was repenting for many failures in his life. He went through hard times, the child of a soldier. He is an honest person, not a misfit." His penetrating blue eyes stared deeply into my soul. Not like those watery ones that made me shiver. The stress made him bold. He grew up and became a real man. At 19:10 our conversation ended as the

---

159   Shqiptar is an Albanian language ethnonym (endonym), by which Albanians call themselves. They call their country *Shqipëria*.

160   It is interesting to note how great powers change the name of the particular ethnic groups to suit their political agenda. During the cold war Kosovar Albanians called themselves Albanians, when creation of the Great Albanian state was on the political agenda. In other words, in order to make the claim more credible, the name of the group should match the name of the land. After the Cold War ended, the political agenda shifted in favor of creation of the independent Kosovo state (rather than merging it into the Great Albania), so did their name, used by the great powers that run the agenda and their locally chosen vassals.

161   This practice of name changing seems to have become routine in recent history of "nation creation" projects. For example, the official title of Islamic population of Bosnia and Hercegovina changed from "Muslims" (with capital "M" to indicate their ethnicity, not religion, the latter of which is spelt with small letter "m") to "Bosnians" at the time; in another part of the world, the Imperial British term "Bengali", for forced settlers brought as laborers from the north-west shores of the Bay of Bengal to Burma (now Myanmar), was replaced with the term "Rohingya" in order to better match the name of the land – the Rakhine State in Myanmar.

order came to go to Readiness No.1. I was reporting to Blagojević by using the crypted codes. I only wanted to communicate with the 'alcoholic' formally. I felt that the night would be long. Would my knowledge and 19 years of experience as a missileer be enough to pass the practical exam tonight, if it comes to those critical seconds? I felt like it would suffice. Everything was quiet and then, at 20:15 hours, the spotters reported a large fire about 100 metres east of our combat position. I reported it to the Brigade Command Operations Center and sent Senior Sergeant Tepavac, with a spotter, to check what was going on. "What caused a fire at this time of the night, and why now when we are in Readiness No.1?" I asked myself. The Operations Center requested Dani to urgently report to them. Dani went out to see what was going on and was on the road somewhere. I could not reach him. The headlights we saw were those of a tractor. The local farmer who drove the tractor said that he had seen two silhouettes around the fire. The truck tires had been burning. "The tires cannot burn by themselves," Tepavac said "Oil or gasoline was poured over the tires. We hardly extinguished it". "Was the fire some kind of a marker for the aircrafts?" I wondered. "Maybe it is just a coincidence, or maybe there are too many coincidences in such a short period of time," I tried to think rationally. At 21:2 two targets approached us from the azimuth of 270 degrees. They initially flew at us and then turned towards Novi Sad. Observers reported that they had heard three muffled explosions. The couple (two planes per flight mission) returned along the same route. At 22:30, there was active noise interference on the radar display at the azimuths of 315, 180, 80 and 60 degrees. We started combat actions in the zone of our responsibility around 23:30, when observers reported they had heard distant airplanes. For a while, we did not have anything on our radar. It was like the whole screen was a black hole. We tried switching to all the different modes of the radar operation; then we tried the raw picture (unprocessed image); we then changed the angle of the antenna – with no success. We could not see anything below 30 kilometers. At distances greater than 30 km we saw many targets, going towards us from all directions. All targets suddenly disappeared by the time they came to 30 km from us, as if they sank into the sea. "This is classical interference," I thought. "Now, when I need radar the most, I do not have it." Blagojević asked me if I saw anything. "I have nothing close, fuck them!" He told me, "Djole, do not swear, it is all being recorded." "What a pleasure," I thought to myself. "This may become an issue only after the war ends; if one decides to listen to the recording, he will find out how who did what." Tepavac warned me of an approaching aeroplane from the azimuth of 70 degrees, flying over us towards the azimuth of 210 degrees. It was in the blind spot of our surveillance radar and I did not see it. The whole shift was pissed off. We had been sitting here for days and nothing entered into our zone. Now when the target was in our zone, and I was sure that there was no anti radar missile, we could not shoot at it. I had no overview of the situation in the air around me. I took a risk, for people and resources, by switching on the target acquisition radar and started searching for the target following oral instructions from Tepavac. We did not find it from two attempts.

The replacement shift came in time. My shift went to the camp, while I went to Milan. The door was locked but they were awake. They said the anti-aircraft artillery was ferociously shooting all night around them. I did not launch tonight, and I was greatly disappointed because of that. I told them that I could not do anything because I did not see them. Nada told me: "Let it be so my child, maybe it was needed to be so. Maybe it is a destiny." I went to bed but could not fall sleep. I called Danka to calm her down and after our conversation out to smoke a cigarette on the veranda, thinking "Oh my God, I had him from the rear side; it was an ideal opportunity to punish him, and I did not see him… What a mess"

Friday, April 16

The shift arrived on time. My shift is from 08:00-16:00. Major Stoimenov went to the combat position and I am going to talk with Dani about today's relocation. Our next position is in the vicinity of the Deč village. That is affirmative. As soon as somebody is ready, they leave. That was agreed. We will not be going in large groups. From the village of Šimanovci our vehicles started to arrive. I'm not going to send them to the combat position right away. I sent the bus driver, Lukić, to Ogar to pick up our men. They arrived around 9ish and Dani informed me from the combat position to start to get ready for the move – to pack or "suitcases" and the circus is again on the road.

Dani, Bora and I set and discuss the next steps. Dani wants me to perform the training for the people that I chose and train them for counter-diversion actions and probably against the helicopter incursions. He told me that he thought all night long and after the last night fire he realized that I was right, and my warning that our combat position is exposed and utterly unprotected to any attack was correct. I expected him to tell me many things, but this was really unexpected… I was shocked… Did he really want to separate me from my shift and practically eliminate me?! I asked him directly was that order from the "above". He told me that it is not ordered by anybody. I really don't trust him. On many issues I got in verbal confrontation with Blagojevic. With the others is ok, for now. I'm glad that all conversations are recorded and one day it will be known who made mistakes. I understand the importance of the stuff he told me, but I can't believe it. No, I can't do that! That is against my believes, with my shift and my men. Why he wants to kick me out from the game? Is he cleaning the path for himself and marginalize myself or is that competition fear? All of that is of no importance to me… My men are important to me. What will they say? He waited for something to eliminate me from the equipment and for all of us he doesn't give a shit. Maybe somebody will wait for something like this but not me. I felt humiliated and rejected. I felt the pressure and can't believe it. I'm asking him to explain to me why he is doing that and tell me the truth and I'm only interested in that. He told me that he has nobody else to do that. Major Dotlić can't do that. The only remaining officer is me. He will go to my shift with Stoimenov and Golubović and Dotlić will be in the other shift. I know why. Dotlić and Stoimenov will argue and get in altercation for sure… Chaos is in my head. They are removing me from the equipment….Why??...A thousand of "why" without an answer. I don't want to go! Definitely NO! Bora told me "My friend, did I ever screw you up?... I swear to you, this is

129

not a set-up. Please do that in a few days and come back to your shift. Please tell me who can do that better than you... Many though about me that I'm coward because I didn't go with Lieutenant Colonel Noskov to Pančevo, but that was the order and I stayed here. I was hurt as well."

I realized that it was an order from the above. I also thought for a moment that Bora was a coward but that was an order and order mean to be executed, no matter what. I told that to Bora. But still, my brain can't process this... Dani also swear to me that this is an order...I have to believe him even that is hard for me. Still, my brain didn't process that.

Bora and I went to the car. Kosta will go with me. Bora turn the car and I got in. One more time I asked him what is going on... "Djole, back off...you insisted that our security on the combat position is not good and that we are exposed to the ground attacks and we all agreed...Train that group man and do not think about the stupid thing." He is probably right...

I have a lot of work today. I have to go to Jakovo to pick up individual files of our reservists. Kosta is with me. In the garrison I found Mića Mijalković with four reservists. One of them is Dejan Tomović, Captain which left service six years ago. He is now commander of the logistics platoon. He asked me how are the things in the battalion. "It is war," I told him... "If you have somebody to lead the battalion in the war, that is good but if you don't have a leader than better to put the lock and close it". We got a mail and among them were some samples of the punishment and sentences for the breaching of the military rules and discipline. Nobody got less than a year and a half... Even for a guy who went to his home for five hours...It must be some fighting while he was absent... on the end he was treated as a deserter.

I'm giving directions to Mića what he needs to do. What is missing is 50 sets of uniforms. Mića told me that Joksa went to our position to bring cigarettes and tetanus vaccines. Everybody needs to get a shot. This is reasonable. I shook hands with everybody and left to the Jakovo combat position. I haven't been there since it was bombed the first night of the war. Everything is quiet, like nothing happened. Only from the outside it looks like that. The building looks undamaged but there are a lot of glass debris scattered all around. Detonations were strong and broke a lot of windows there. In the guard house a lot of windows were blown out. Private Brković waited for us there. There was one other reservists, Predrag (I couldn't remember his family name) and our carpenter's son. Down there, the ammunition warehouses look terrible. Bomb or cruise missiles penetrated from the north side. Batajnica warehouse disappeared, like it never existed. Everywhere there are debris of concrete, steel bars, missile parts and dirt. "God, these buildings were very strong with the steel bars 20 mm thick"...It look like the cemetery... Warehouses looks very small to me... Across the road there are few holes from the booster motors and missiles... they look like a foxholes. How those missiles are small and all in parts. They are scattered everywhere. Our guard dog Efa was on the guard duty that night and her fur is burned on few places. She was so scarred that she torn the steel cable and ran away. More than 80 missiles were buried there. In the night when our brigade commander Colonel Lazović got injured in the car crash, in Sremčica warehouse almost 40 missiles were destroyed. In total, about 120 missiles were destroyed. Damage of minimum 10 million dollars. How those missiles were dear to me. It looked that I lost somebody dear. It is so sad.

The nature is waking up after the winter. The grass is green and the fruit trees blossom. Spring is here but like there is nothing around. All around there are fields of scattered debris. My eyes got wet. I went to our fire control radar position. Direct hit… Crater is 4-5 m wide and about 3 m deep. It was good that we left decoy at this place... everything is just a pile of twisted and burned metal. Bunkers are undamaged except that plaster fell off on few places. Electric cables from the launching platform No. 4 are melted right at the bunker entrance.

We are getting into the building. Brković told me that he doesn't have any money and cigarettes. I took one box of "Classic" from the trunk and gave to him. He was very thankful. While we toured the position, warrant officer Mijalković came and brought a lunch for three of them. The offered me as well. The bean soup was very tasty. They started to sort the salad… will they took this or that… I took an onion. The soldier's bean soup is very good. I am glad that they offered me a lunch. Very nice from them. Kosta, the courier, is not eating. I asked him why not… He told me if he looks like a hungry person to me… He is a young guy… almost 100 kilos… big and nice… like a teddy bear. He told us that is the first time since the beginning of the war that he is coming to our base during the day. The village of Jakovo is full of troops. Many vehicles parked everywhere… mostly military police. While we eat, on TV there is on American movie… it is disgusting… I know that the movie has nothing to do with the American bombing but still it is disgusting. Their movies are full of shit. I'm tired of their language, their "bravery" and their "fight for justice". Just wandering where is the justice now??

We have to go to Surčin to make a car key copy. The one that I'm using now was hand made and it is not the good one. In Surčin I found the guy. I interrupted his lunch. Everything for the army he said… oh yes, everything for the army but you are siting at home with the family, sleeping in your bed and I'm craving for a normal pillow and clean uniform…

While I was on the combat position, I looked at the parts of the downed airplane. It was really nice machine… a technical marvel.

I went to the local police station to enquire about the fuel ratios for the people in my unit. The boss is not there. The other cops looked at me like "over the dick". It seemed that they wandered from which shithole I popped up… They are so arrogant… I couldn't get any information… those guys behave like they own the place, like they are untouchable… "In the name of the people, everything is permitted…". What a difference between these policemen and policemen in Pećinci. I left with the thoughts that this war is only mine and the other don't give a shit. No wander why their guard post on the way to Surčin was demolished by somebody. I had a feeling that I'm going to cry because all that anger and bitterness accumulated since the beginning of the war.

Equipment is almost set up. Missile guidance station van is secured by the logs. This position looks nice if anything can be called nice in the time of great uncertainty. We have to finish everything by 19:00.

Major Dotlić came and bring a new uniform for Dani. Why he didn't order one for me, I thought... He brought a new pair of boots for Armuš. Armuš performed a lot of work for us. Dani assigned 40 liters of diesel to him and to the crane operator. We must try to conserve the fuel. We are fighting for the country but can't do anything without the fuel. Dani, Dotlić, Armuš and the driver of the Ult truck went for a drink. After that they will go for a lunch and my shift is going to wait until they finish their lunch and come back... We are on combat duty from 00:00 again. When they came back, we left.

I put the radar imitator not far from the guidance station, like many times before. The brigade command issued the operation instructions, but we used them differently during the combat engagements. On this way we avoided antiradiation missiles. I found a system solution for the optimal use. What happened today is that I saw how one log which was leaned on the van, fell right behind Major Roksandić. I was about 30 meters away and it looked to me that he will be hurt. In desperation I raised my arms to my head. Fortunately, the log fell behind him.

Sergeant Tepavac took the key from the local football club building so we can use their bathroom. At least we can have a shower. I went to Karlovčić around 19:00. Milan was in his bed. He doesn't feel good because of the kidney stone problem. In the dark there was also Grandma Danica and Nada. Somber atmosphere. I took my stuff and left. At the gate, I gave 50 dinars to Nada. The same amount I kept.

I went to sleep around 20:00 but can't fall asleep so I took two cigarettes. Thinking about todays day... When I was on the way back from the combat position, the owner of the container which was on the position gave me the key and told me that it is for the guards if they need it. I found out today that some people from Karlovčić are not happy that we came to their village. They were afraid that "those above" will target their village because of us. What a stupidity... actually total ignorance and egoism.

I woke up at 23:30 and found Bora and Dejan Tomović in the hallway. They were in the middle of conversation. Tomović told me that he would like to do something useful. Well, your job will be very useful because you know how to work with the people and have a good organizational skill. Maybe you can improve the logistics. "There is no computer here" he said. "Well, we'll bring you one from the barracks in Jakovo. You will need it for your work." I told him.

I went to the shift. I told to Dani that we have to order that all streetlights in the village are turned on because that was an order from the municipality. Jović need to be relocated into the communication center and instead of him, Sergeant Dančev shall be assigned to the radar imitator because he is younger and faster. With this, I'm creating a space for Tepavac so he can be assigned as a battalion counter diversion task force commander.

Camp in Ogar need to be relocated because the workers are coming to that place on 27 April and Žika, who is director there, will need that space. Today, on my way back from Jakovo, in Petrovčić, I met Lieutenant Colonel Joksimović. We passed by each other but than we backed up and shook hands. I asked him if he can secure 50 uniform sets for the reservists. He told me that he may have about ten. The best think will be to call Lieutenant Colonel Duvnjak, brigade commander aid for logistics. We, the officers, also need to replace ours because they are worn off. "You look like crap" he told me… And he was right, my uniform was muddy, all camouflage almost disappeared and washed away.

He brought cigarettes, vaccines, and some stationaries.

Saturday April 17

We are in the shift. By 00:00 hours we were in standby mode with the surveillance radar. We have an active noise disturbance from 310 to 320 degrees. Another radar is nearby, and it is interfering with us. It is probably the radar of Vučković and Ristić in Petrovčić. Up in the operations center is Popović. But I don't know who is on the radar for detecting low altitude targets - the P-15. Once again, I explained to my shift how to work simultaneously with the radar imitator. In principle, there should be no consecutive shooting of two targets. It all depends on the situation in the air. By firing from one target to the next they would have been radiating for too long. That is how Draganić was hit. I reminded Lieutenant Nikolić that he must keep a record of the length of time missiles spend in the "preparation" state.

I told them that, due to other commitments, I will not be with them in the shift tomorrow. I knew that I would be back as soon as I can. I am not sentimental, do not feel talkative tonight, so I am succinct and specific. They stared at me in amazement, worryingly, and as if they understood nothing. They told me that they got used to working with me as their commanding fire control officer and gained confidence. Last night Varga shared his ration of cigarettes. Each of us received five packs. I don't know for how many days, probably for ten. If so, the daily ration is ten cigarettes. That is really comforting, not to say ironic, at this time. Fuck their ration allotment rules and the budget allowances.

There is a dead man in my head. I do not see his face nor know who he was, he's just there. I want to visit my parents' graves. How big is the grass in my backyard now? Two blasts at the azimuth of 180 degrees. Far away, it seems. "No, it is not that far", I thought, "all blasts are close as they are across our country." They are harassing us because they can. I wish we had something that shoots further, like S-300, so we could make the evening much jollier. Had we had one, perhaps, there would be no war. What we have is not a deterrent for their aggression; they know very well what we have at our disposal. I have heard they would suspend air strikes if Milosević resigned. Who are they to tell us who should be our president here? Even if I passionately wanted him to go, I would have changed my mind in defiance to their interference into our internal affairs, just in spite.

Some say that children acquire most of their genes from grandparents. I just don't know from whose side. Anyway, my blood is from Lika and Bosnia, and I was born and raised in Srem. This looks like a winning combination: cheeky and cocky, proud, and indomitable. But I see there are quite a few like me around here. We don't let anyone interfere in our affairs. I disallow it, full stop·

I called Danka last night. Milutin and Goca were with her. They sent me their regards. Danka works tomorrow. She will go to visit the apartment with Goca. She also spoke with Jelena Rauš from the Post Office in Ruma about obtaining a telephone connection for the house in Vrdnik.

Yesterday, during the relocation to the new combat position in Karlovčić, we were ordered to change the encrypted communication code from 12:00 on 16 April, to that titled "Elektron", Annex 4-11.

It came to my mind that had we taken the missiles out of the depot on trolleys and safely spread them under the trees, they would not have been destroyed with just one hit. That was a lack of our experience. We had asked the brigade command for permission to disperse the missiles; we presented to them our comprehensive plan: the new locations, the schedules, and the security, but they disallowed it. We heeded their order to leave them in the depots. We anticipated that the missiles could be destroyed if the depots were targeted first. The only good thing was that none of the missiles went airborne, self-activated and flew towards the village or town. In fact, the art of war must be learnt in practice. I wished no one ever had to learn it. What would have remained of a human body when the bombs can destroy concrete and steel? I remembered the missile warehouses as bustling and lively places.

It was very eventful last night and today is too. The Russian Duma has adopted a proposal to allow FR Yugoslavia into the union of Russia and Belarus. It was sent to drunkard Yeltsin for approval. My shift napped again. I didn't like it. The sleepy ones are sluggish and unable to clear their heads straight away, which is crucial for our work. I let them nap because they worked hard all day today to relocate to the new combat position and they are very tired. I don't even know how we endure all this, but we do and it's true. The jokes and laughter are probably the only things keeping us going. I have not noticed any activity from the reserve so far - there is no drinking of alcohol and their seriousness and concentration is at a high level. All actions and procedures are implemented without any problems. There are some minor misunderstandings, like the one with the wrong launch pad orientation, I no longer remember where, but in principle, our morale and enthusiasm are high. I wish I could talk to them more often, but I don't have time.

Because of the stress, fatigue, and exhaustion I lost a lot of weight and feel it by the holes of my belt.

Our accommodation is in a kindergarten. I was nostalgic seeing the small toilet bowls; the partition walls were about 1.5 meters high, small washbasins and low-mounted mirrors. They are our youth and our pride, our children, and future generations. They may remember the war when they grow up. Oh yes, they are the children of the war. One little girl came in today. She encouraged herself to come in through the doors. She was so cute with a normal face lines, neatly trimmed black hair and curious eyes. From the perspective of her eyes we must have looked like a dark green sea monsters dressed in camouflaged uniforms. She quickly entered, stopped and said that her dad was a soldier too. I gave her a soldiers' candy. She did not know that her daddy did not like being a soldier; that he would have preferred to hug her and kiss her and to cuddle her soft baby skin. She was so proud when she said, "My dad is a soldier too," unaware of all the dangers, strain and struggle for her to grow up free. No one can replace her dad. "He is a soldier too," she says so gently and proudly.

Senior Sergeant Jović came to his senses. I don't know how much my conversation affected him, but the fact is that he calmed down and composed himself. We got one additional man yesterday. Dani and I had to share one cot bed again. We work in two different shifts. Bora told me yesterday that, in his opinion, those from the brigade command did not know what they were doing. Demolition of the bridge across the Danube River would leave three missile battalions, commanded by Mijović, Noskov and Draganić, stranded on the other side. Nothing was clear to him. "Fuck it, there are pontoon bridges." I thought, but I didn't comment.

If I were to give a title to this war diary one day, then title "The Shift" would be appropriate: short, sharp and to the point.

I have just got an idea on how to eliminate the sidelobes from the target acquisition radar radiation chart. We should utilize the adversary's technology and cover some parts with the absorption material - about 1 millimeter thick coat taken from the downed stealth planes, This is only a fantasy for now, but after the war it should be tried and tested.

Djević's battalion was hit in Banovci, I remembered. He did not radiate. Their position was either laser illuminated or marked with a locator. A lot of spies have been traversing FR Yugoslavia. They are probably looking for our locations and reporting to their controllers via some pre-established channels. There are many of them here and very few of our spies near their military installations. It seems to be destiny. The bad guys are always up for grabs. At 04:40 we were ordered to go to the Readiness No.2, in which we spent the reminder of the shift, half open eyes napping and waiting to engage.

How beautiful is peace, and how much would we appreciate it after this war ends? Does this have anything to do with the decision of the Russian Duma tonight? I heard on the news that there were only two explosions tonight, in Valjevo, at the Krušik industrial plant. These were the two far away explosions that were seen from the camp. After the shift, I tried to fall asleep, and I did. I slept until 13:00.

When I got up I saw Colonel Stanković and Lieutenant Colonel Samardzić from the Brigade Command and Crnobrnja sitting and talking. They did not want to wake me up. I was unshaven and tired. We greeted each other. Bora loves me. We touched on Blagojević's attitude towards people. I told them he was unfair towards everyone. It is a pleasure to work with Stanković and Pauljević. Samardzic replied, "Djole, you know Srba, he is who he is..." "I am no different, Bora" I replied and asked him, "Why do others need to understand him, and he does not need to understand others?" Bora shifted conversation towards correct operation of the equipment and away from Blagojević's terrible attitude towards others. I replied "He must never say, even in frenzy or madness, that he did not give a shit about people. If he is nervous, then he must understand that we are nervous too. The launch ramps and other equipment do not wage war for him, but people do. People are a fortune and they should be looked after." I also told him, "It was extremely difficult for me to accept the order to do other things and not be in charge of the combat work and assets." Bora replied "Djole, I work the least with the equipment, my role is more that of a politician. Fuck it, everything is important. I disagree with you."

Boško Dotlić, who was present at the conversation, added that in one occasion Blagojević pissed him off so that wanted to leave the equipment: "With all respect sir, we're tired too, but we're not insulting you. Neither you should insult us. "Boško said that on another occasion Srba told him "By the way, I have nothing to talk to you, asshole, get me Captain Golubović right away! ". Boško gave him Golubović on the line and Srba reprimanded him. Golubović was so pissed off, "Who the hell does he think he is? Who the fuck is Blagojević?! If he respects me, I will respect him, and if not – I will fuckoff the motherfucker!"

Stanković agreed that there have been failures in work, "Try to be positive and do your best." I explained to them that the work on the radar imitator takes time and that man is not a machine. If they can understand, then fine. And if they cannot understand, then it is their problem. "We report on everything and we won't lie. I reported the fire, and it turned out that I would have been better off if I did not. "Dragan comforted me and said I did the right thing. "Steva Djević was screwed up too." "Do not take it too much to the heart, we are aware that mistakes are made and that there are problems."

I told Stanković about the 50 sets of outstanding uniforms for the enlisted soldiers and the grenades for RPG launchers and rifles. I also reminded Bora that one unit consumes a lot of oil and that I needed Ljubisavljević for the target selection system. "No way," he replied, "It is not a combat system and you can do without it." He showed admiration for the availability of our equipment and its state of combat readiness, considering for how long it has been working. He was concerned that the generators may start failing. The equipment had been overloaded, not to mention the people.

Dotlić handed out the salary advance of 300 dinars. I need to go to Ogar to check the mail and have a meeting with the enlisted reservists. Bora left first, and five minutes later I left too.

I called Danka at about 14:10. She was at her neighbor place. Nataša, her daughter, answered. "Mom's working today, and she'll also work on Tuesday," she. They talked to Ljubica, my sister. My sister and her husband moved to the new apartment in Trieste. They invite us to come and visit them in summer, only if the war stops. Lieutenant Stojanović, the commander of the signals platoon, secured a radio station from a friend through a radio amateur club in Belgrade. I ordered it ten days ago. We'll go get it, probably tomorrow. We'll put it in the missile guidance station van and listen to it. We will listen to radio amateurs and have complete information on the situation in the air from them as amateurs' observers airspace throughout our territory. In the peacetime, we used our own observers who were located 20 to 30 kilometers away from the equipment, in the expected direction of the incoming enemy aircraft. On the way out of Deč I was stopped by the military police. We said hello and my classmate, Colonel Trajković, approached me. He greeted me and invited me for a coffee at his mother-in-law's place nearby; she was my first wife's aunty. I replied I was in a hurry. "Fuck it, you do not want to hang out with your classmate. Fuck it, you divorced my mother-in-law's niece, not me..." He was right.

I had two "Cipiripi" chocolates in the car and gave it to his kids. His daughter Jovana had grown up, I don't remember the little one. He was in diapers. Inside the house were Vida, his mother-in-law, my classmate's wife Jasmina, and Irena, the wife of Jasmina's brother Dušan, with their children. They made coffee. They told me that I haven't changed. No one mentioned the past. That was very good. Finding the truth always requires two stories - one from each side. They heard my unit shot down the F-117A. I told them some details. My classmate already knew these. They told me that they always liked me, and what happened with my marriage it just happened, it is not their business... life is going on They did not want to interfere. Maybe they were right. Who would like to peek into other person's problems and try to solve them? They have heard that the woman I live with is very beautiful. I told them that she is beautiful indeed and that we get along well. Vida's husband Jovica went fishing. He was out of job, and Dule had a work obligation[162]. I finished my coffee and left.

In Ogar, I explained to Sedlak how to manage the mail and ordered him to make a list of emergency contacts. I am responsible for the assignment, from the very way of printing the identification plates to the organization and training of the enlisted soldiers and reservists. I gave Captain Tomović, in charge of the logistics support, all the important information and phone numbers and drew his attention to the shaving of the reservists and gave him specific assignments. He made notes of everything. Later I held a meeting with the reservists in the camp where I processed the information received about each of them. I made some preliminary decisions and introduced them to Tomović. After that we had dinner together. I gave Sedlak the file for the whole unit. It was already 19:30 and I headed for Deč. It was very dark by that time. On my way back I visited Armuš. He wasn't at home. He was also looking for me, but I did not know why. In Deč I found Šumarac, Brigade Chief of Security, Bora's boss. We greeted each other. "My people," a thought went through my head, "we all greet each other by hug and giving three kisses in the cheek, like family. This is what we all are in this situation." Bora felt guilty because he stayed with us. As if he deliberately left Noskov when it was tense. Šumarac said to him "We have a man there. You are needed here." He and his driver shook our hands and bid us farewell wishing us good luck

Dani is in my shift, as we agreed. Sergeant Žugić went to bring back the Zastava 101 to the camp. I left the list of requirements for motor vehicles in Ogar. In the camp in Deč, I found some pie and strudel with cherries and nuts and had a slice of each. At 22:20 there was an urgent call from the combat position for Matić to come immediately because there was a problem in the combat section of the station. I woke him up and he left in five minutes. The

162   Work obligation - a wartime decree required essential services and small business to remain open.

sky was light up with tracer munition from 20/3 mm cannons, Bofors and Pragas. They were shooting at something. We did not know at what. There was no airplane sound. Something or somebody was in the air. Which lunatic sent 'that' here and engage this groups of people to shoot at him? To do something that everyone else avoids. One should not wage senseless wars, but if you have no choice than to fight back, then it is something else.

Bora told me that he did not understand why General Bane Petrović, Commandant of the Air Defense Corps, landed in a helicopter near Noskov while visiting the brigade. I don't understand it either, and probably neither they do. The helicopter flew a ta low altitude and exposed their position. The general ate, drank and had fun. His attitude told us he didn't give a fuck about us, because after he left, we would be in the shit because he exposed our location. It is amazing how different we are in the unit whose lives are threatened.

We want to bring back our former officer Slobodan Jovanović to the unit. The brigade's security could do the necessary paperwork with the Department of Defense, by presenting justification along the lines of their responsibility. We need such man, an all-rounder. He has the intimate knowledge of several air-defence systems, has a crane operator's licence and experience, and can be a manual tracking operator in the guidance station. I am no longer responsible for the unit... I lay down to sleep but could not fall asleep for long. I was awake when Dani returned from his shift and prepared to go to sleep in the dark, without turning the lights on.

Sunday, April 18

The phone in the kindergarten rang around 02:30. Dani picked up the call. I didn't know what they were talking about. He hung up. For about five minutes, Dani had been walking around the room and then he woke up Crnobrnja. He had been whispering something in his ear. Bora got up and got ready very quickly. I was in some kind of semi conscious state. I asked Bora what was going on. He told me "P-15 radar[163] was hit[164] - the height measurement radar[165,166]." Then he invited me to go with him there. I got ready very

---

163   The P-15 "Tropa" (the NATO reporting name "Flat Face A") is surveillance radar developed in 1955 in the former Soviet Union to detect aircraft flying at low altitudes (observed at 2-14 degrees).

164   Regarding its combat work, the P-15 is vulnerable to HARM attacks, as it works in the dm (decimetre) wavelength range (UHF band, wavelengths from one metre to one tenth of metre; radio waves in the UHF band travel almost entirely by line-of-sight propagation).

165   Security Officer Bora Crnobrnja was wrong in saying the P-15 is the height measurement radar, which is ok for a Security Officer. In practice, an experienced radar operator can approximately determine the height of the target from the two target parameters which P-15s and the other 2D radars provide: Distance to the target and its Azimuth.

166   Height finding radars -The Integrated Air Defence (VOJIN) had height-find-

quickly and we were on the way to Petrovčić. While driving my "business" Zastava 101, I told him, "The P-15 isn't the height measurement radar, as it detects targets flying at low altitudes."

There were no streetlights in Deč. We passed through Captain Putnik's combat position. His 20/3mm anti aircraft cannons were ready. They warned us to turn off the lights and drive slowly. Shortly after we arrived in Petrovčić, ahead of us, we saw a few firefighter trucks and police cars with their flashing lights on. They were trying to extinguish the fire. The radar was burning. All that was left of it was a pile of rubble. We passed by a stretcher with the body of the reservist Gajić from Borča. His back was exposed, probably because they pulled him up by holding his belt, which lifted his shirt. His head was covered in blood. None of his clothing had caught fire. Captain Vučković was walking around and smoking one cigarette after another. It was cold outside, and he was only wearing sweater. Captain Vučković told me that he was unable to pull Sergeant Smiljanić from the radar van and that he burnt there. God bless his soul. Both men from the radar van were unmarried and they left no dependents behind them. I remembered Smiljanić, his face and big body. He is charcoal now. It is most likely that my classmate Matijević would have to inform their parents. It is a very difficult assignment.

Vučković's son was agitated. I didn't know that his son was in the same unit as his father. He told me that he saw a few flashes of light, similar to a flashlight, from the house near the football field. They searched everything but found nothing. Both Smiljanić and Gajić died at the same moment. They were unaware that they had been hit. Right beside the radar van I found a cylindrical body from the missile. It was about a meter in length and about 0.3 m in diameter. Its one end was stuck into the ground – HARM[167]. We had not touched it. We requested a bomb disposal expert[168], a pathologist and the military police to come. They were needed to pull out Smiljanić's remains from the wreck. Military firefighters had arrived, and thick streams of water were spraying the metal and burning radar wreck. Vučković told me that he had ordered that only one man works in the P-15 radar van at a time. It is most likely that both men were scared to be alone, and for this reason both were on duty.

I approached Vučković and told him, "You are not required here anymore. There is nothing else you could do here." I secured the place and then went

---

ing radars: PRV-11 (the NATO reporting name "Side Net"), PRV-13 (the NATO reporting name "Odd Pair"), etc., but not the 250th Brigade. Similarly, the Army used M-85 Žirafa radars (based on the Swedish Giraffe 75 radar, locally improved under the licence agreement) that communicated directly to Bofors anti-aircraft artillery guns.

167   HARM seeks for targets that radiate in the cm (centimetre) and dm wavelength ranges, but not for those that radiate in the metre range. Radars that radiate in the metre range are immune to HARM attacks, for example P-12 and P-18.

168   Bomb disposal expert –is an explosive engineering professional who renders hazardous explosive devices safe. An alternative terminology is Explosive Ordinance Disposal (EOD) expert.

to the house where the detached radar screen from the P-12 radar[169,170] was located[171]. Vučković's son asked him, "Dad, are you ok?" "I'm ok son, go outside, stay on guard and secure the place," he responded. The house host made a coffee for us. Vučković was very upset and had been smoking non-stop. This was the first loss in his unit since the early 1990s war in Bosnia and Hercegovina.

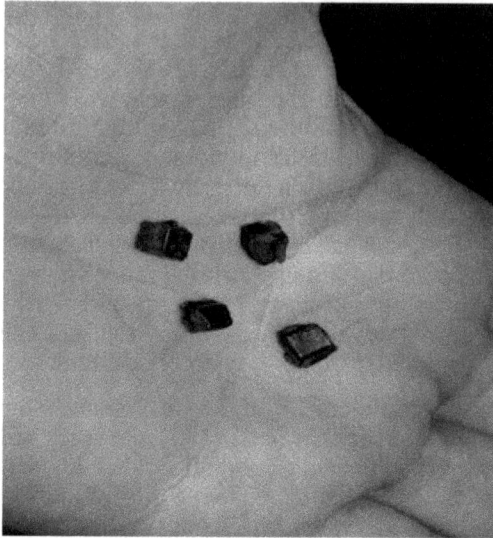

HARM warhead particles – intended to shred radar or any other electro-magnetic sources. The speed is more than twice speed of sound and can penetrate through any unprotected surface. Beside the fragments, the blast is also very strong. The effective way to stop these fragments is to use armor or improvise with the raw logs. The 3rd battalion was targeted at least 22 times with this kind of missile, but it was never hit (except few near misses that didn't cause any significant damage).

Vučković felt guilty. He told me that he had requested the Brigade Operation Center to discontinue operation of the P-15 surveillance radars[172,173],

169   Capt. Vučković's radar unit operated two surveillance radars, P-15 and P-12. They reported the airspace situation to the Brigade Command Post; his non-combat field unit had no missiles and was part of the Brigade Command.

170   The P-12 "Yenisei" (the NATO reporting name "Spoon Rest A") is surveil-lance radar developed in 1956 in the former Soviet Union to detect aircraft flying at high and medium altitudes.

171   Capt. Vučković used the extension cables to relocate the panoramic radar screen from the P-12 van to the nearby house that was located at a safe distance away.

172   Capt. Vučković was able to see the "whole" airspace from his P-12 surveillance radar screen, so there was no need for the P-15 to operate at all.

173   Although the surveillance radars P-12 and P-18 (the Author's unit) were

because NATO could easily detect their location and launch anti-radiation missiles. The P-15s were dangerous to operate. Their antennas radiated electromagnetic waves directly into the airspace (not into ground in order to reflect into the airspace), similar to our fire control radar. He told me that around 22:30, during the first air attack wave, he had ordered Smiljanić to go to sleep. During the second attack wave, around 01:30, Colonel Stanković from the Brigade Operation Centre ordered the P-15 on. After Major Popović's secondment to Vučković's radar unit had ended, he returned to the Brigade Command Post and a new crew was put to man the P-15 radar.

I thought to myself, "Was Smiljanić properly trained to work with the P-15 radar: not to continuously emit radiation into the airspace, but rather be in the passive regime and wait for an order to turn on the emission and search for the low flying targets in short "bursts" of radiation? After the short bursts he needed to switch back to the passive regime. And so on again, as required. This should have been the appropriate training procedure. In other words, Smiljanić's operational procedure for the P-15 surveillance radar should have been similar to our procedure for operation of our fire control radar.[174] I doubt that he knew how to apply this procedure, and for that mistake he paid the ultimate price."

At that time, Dotlić and Golubović, with their team, were in the combat shift in our unit. They had unsuccessfully searched for the target twice, on altitudes 4 km and higher. In hindsight, the airplane approached the P-15 radar in Petrovčić at a very low altitude, perhaps at around 100 m, and launched a HARM missile from about 12 km distance. That missile hit the heat exchanger on the P-15 at the base of the antennas (right at the connection of the antenna post and van). The missile penetrated through the upper part of the van, exploded, killed the two-man crew and completely destroyed the radar. They are two new casualties in our 250th Brigade, in addition to Tepavac before.

Vučković told me: "Djole, thanks for coming". Lieutenant Colonel Nikola Stanković from Karlovčić, an engineer from the logistics support, soon arrived at the site.

Other units equipped with anti-aircraft cannons and shoulder launched RPGs didn't have any information about the target; obviously because the airplane approached flying at an extremely low profile. This also showed that the Army Operation Centre and the Air-defence Operation Centre were not properly connected.

Bora stayed with Crnomarković and the military police to wait for the coroners and investigators to come.

I left for Deč around 05:00. I wanted to sleep but I couldn't. My thoughts and my mind were overwhelmed with the images of Smiljanić and the re-

designed to detect aircraft flying at high and medium altitudes, they can also detect aircraft flying at low altitudes, which depends on the terrain topography. In the lowlands of Srem, there was no need for simultaneous operation of the P-15 surveillance radar.

174   Because both radars have at least one antenna that radiates in the cm and dm wavelength range visible to HARMs.

servist's bloodied face and body on the stretcher. I don't know his family or relatives, but I can only imagine their reaction when they get the news.

I eventually fell asleep but woke up at 09:30. Dani had to go to Šimanovci. His wife was coming, and I had to go to see Armuš and to somehow try to find a radio station. We desperately needed the real-time information the radio-amateurs broadcast. They are the best visual airspace observers in the entire world, and they provide their services free of charge. They are very passionate about their work, numerous volunteers providing intelligence on the enemy air force movements, cruise missiles flightpaths and the corridors they use.[175] Armuš requested to be in the anti terrorist task force group, as he wanted from the bottom of his heart to hunt and kill the enemy commandos and special forces, preferably in bulk. I had difficulty explaining to him that the rapid intervention team must always be together around a single place, and that I needed him to perform some other assignments at other locations, which others could not do. He was stubborn, but in the end, he accepted my arguments. His final request was to give him an assault rifle with ammo, explaining that it is war and he may need it, just in case.

At 11:30 hours Mika Stojanović and I left for Belgrade. By 12:00 hours we had to arrive to Aca Ekmečić's place. He procured a radio-station for us. He is Mika's very good buddy. They worked together a while ago. Aca's son found out on the Internet that the F-117A with the registration number 806 had been promoted at numerous airshows as a show-off; its photographs had flooded the Internet. This is the exact airplane that we had downed; by downing the show-off plane we had also drowned the "American dream". I gave them some F-117A parts, and they were overwhelmed with joy. "I doubt that anyone will give you such a gift," I said jokingly.

I met Srećko Morić, the President of the Radio-Amateur Society of Yugoslavia. They got the radio-station for us; probably directly from the President of the Republic of Serbia, Milutinović, personally or form someone from his cabinet. The most important thing was that we will have a radio station. It needed to be decoded and its memory erased. They will be able to do that. Hopefully, it would take them a few hours to do that, so we could use that time to quickly go to our homes and have a decent shower and meal.

Mika hadn't seen Belgrade since the beginning of the war. I called Danka to tell her that I'm coming and to prepare lunch. Soup and stuffed capsicum with meshed potatoes waited for me. I was hungry like a wolf. Lunch first, then shower. I was so dirty. The water from my hair was so muddy.

At 15:30 Mika Stojanović called me to inform me that the radio station is ready. We have to go to see Srećko, and than to the Belgrade Water Supply Authority. These radio-amateurs rock! They come from all sections of the society - physicians, electrical engineers, policemen, farmers, handymen, mechanics, trades, etc., just ordinary people, great buddies, and patriots. Their Operation Centre is fully stuffed with the equipment. It seemed that they have "everything"! Srećko gave each of us one big and one small icon

---

175   Mike Mihajlovic: for example, my connections from Italy, Slovenia, Germany, Croatia and Hungary provided on-time information about enemy movements, particularly aviation.

of Virgin Mary from the Hilandar Monastery[176]. He had been there for about ten days and the monks blessed these icons. By the custom, he wrote his name on the back of the icons, reminding us that we would have to write our names as well if we decided to gift them to someone.

We rushed to get to Karlovčić before dark fell, so Mika could put the radio station in service. We needed it to be operational for the night shifts tonight. Everything worked fine and after some time the station was on. Now we are connected with the radio-amateurs. Mika had tested the station for correct operation in the city, while it was raining, leaving no doubts that station would work as planned.

Around 21:30, I went to my bed to try to catch some sleep. My shift starts at midnight.

Earlier today, Bora told me that even the birds knew that we had downed the F-117A, as Dani has been telling everyone that he is the commander of the unit that downed the stealth. Then, I replied, "it became much more difficult to protect and defend the unit under these circumstances.[177,178,179,180]" Dani also told Bora, "I now need to get a designated driver." "Maybe he's right," I said to myself, "I should get a designated driver as well. Perhaps, I should take a son of my former commander from Skoplje, who is in the special police unit."

Around 23:30 Kosta woke up Dani and he told him to wake me up. As ordered, Kosta woke me up. I asked Dani if he had slept well. "I did," he answered. "Could you go to the shift, I'm so tired," I asked him. He responded, "Not a problem".

I slept until 07:00 the next morning.

---

176   The Hilandar Monastery- is the Serbian monastery in Mount Athos in Greece, founded in 1198 by Stefan Nemanja and his son Saint Sava.

177   The Author knew that the enemy (NATO, particularly the US) was enraged by the worldwide distribution of the sensational images of their downed stealth bomber and having to publicly admit own initial lie that all NATO airplanes had safely returned to their bases on 27 March 1999.

178   The Author also knew that the US could not afford to explain how that occurred nor to objectively discuss the matter in public, as that could only reveal the true characteristics of their stealth, and allegedly "invisible", airplanes and further adversely affect their public moral, military leadership and contractors, as well as their commercial interests.

The US could not allow a grain of truth to spoil the "remarkable stealth narrative," and they desperately needed a "media distraction" away from the 27 March 1999 events.

179   In the Author's opinion, in order to restore the "perception" of their prestige and reputation, the enemy had no choice but to mobilize all their resources for an immediate revenge now, not soon or ASAP.

180   Dani's unnecessary self-promotion to random civilians and journalists could have only helped the enemy to narrow the search area for the unit, or even worse.

When I woke up, Dani, who returned from his shift at 08:10, told me Lieutenant Colonel Podovac had been hit tonight; it wasn't that bad, there were no casualties, and no one was injured. "So, the protection was effective, and it was my invention," I thought, "3 to 4 units have already been hit, and no one except Tepavac had been killed." To be fair, I didn't know if they had that protection.

I left to replace Dotlić in the shift as he was supposed to go and sort out our accommodation. Aleksić told me something low flying was coming towards us. We were already at Readiness No.1, so we searched for everything but could not find anything. "Switch to passive mode," I ordered.

Blagojević called me and asked if I knew where Noskov was supposed to go. "I know," I replied. "Get ready to go there," Blagojević replied. We sent a telegram to the Corps and were waiting for a response. They would certainly approve relocation to the new combat position. I informed Crnobrnja, who was in the camp. At 11:00 we received the signal to move on. We quickly transitioned the equipment into marching configuration, and our convoy of vehicles went again to another ambush location to knit a new net. In the meantime, we received a new GI19B vacuum tube for the surveillance radar. Its installation would slow down the transition back into combat configuration as we will need to do the full set up procedure and then re-tune the transmitter and receiver.

We listen to the radio amateurs' communication. Someone is constantly interfering with them, probably a radio amateur from Bosnia. While we were in Deč, Bora repeatedly insisted that we turn off the lights in the dormitory. I realized that he was scared. Last night, while I was asleep, there was a noise near my desk. I opened my eyes. I saw Bora touching something and looking for it. I asked him, "What is it, Boro, what do you need?" "Nothing, nothing, just need to leave something here," he replied in a confused tone. I thought he wanted to leave me a picture that had been taken earlier on top of the downed F-117A. However, in the morning, I found his mobile phone there. Why he left his mobile on my desk? I think his true intentions were completely different - he wanted to take my war diary and read it. I interrupted him; he panicked and made a mistake.

The equipment at the new combat position was transitioned into combat configuration, tuned, and tested for correct operation. There was a breakdown of the 50 Hz insulation. We replaced cables Š-4 and Š-5 on the UV-102 block. The PR-46 fuse on the 36 Volt AC distribution board in the power supply transformer cabin blew up disabling the signaling of air-pressure in waveguides and that of the "remote switching".

In the evening, at dinnertime, Barvalac brought me 12 angular reflectors for the early activation of the anti-radar missile warheads. I installed them in pairs around the combat position, 50-80 meters away from the center.

Armuš did his job and brought the tree-trunks. They were unequal in length and protruded above the missile guidance station van. This posed a risk in case of a HARM attack, regardless of the direction of its approach, as the HARM could hit the top of the tree-trunk and explode above our heads. I ordered him to shorten those that were protruding too much. Dani found a remnant of an anti-radar missile, about 2 meters long, in Subotište - Miškovci. He brought it in the car.

I am in the shift with my team until 00:00. Today, as I did each time before, I installed the radar emission imitator at the new combat position, taking into consideration the anticipated direction of the enemy's incursion. Panić checked it thoroughly for correct operation. Captain Golubović asked Janko Aleksić for the new switch for the imitator, as the old one was damaged. At 21:34 Ljubenković began to radiate from the surveillance radar in order to adjust the receiver. We set up the combat position near the village of Bečmen, the one that had been prepared for Noskov. We do not understand the complete idea of the set-up. The target acquisition radar remained inside, protected by the battlement. It would be better if it was located outside, but now we have to make with what we have at site. We did not mount the camera because it was defective and completely useless when mounted onto the target acquisition radar.

It was raining from very low hanging cloud sin the evening. Now I remembered: Danka told me yesterday, when the war is over, that she would give me something to drink to calm down, and then she would talk to me. I think I know what that would be about, though I can only guess. She was unhappy with my boldness and attitude to defend the country at all costs. She told Nataša that I would return from the war as a hero, and she would end up like the "partisan Mara"[181] [182].

Today I told Senior Sergeant Tepavac and Soldier Aleksić that I was planning to set up an emergency response group and asked them to help me to choose the guys. They agreed and warmed up to the idea. Tepavac told me tonight that something was shining in the graveyard. People went to the cemetery today, it's Monday. I don't know what saint is celebrated today.

At 21:55 I reported to Lieutenant Colonel Luka Trgovčević at the Operations Center that my surveillance radar was defective. Ljubenković cannot adjust the receiver in any way. He cannot store the selected frequencies in the memory. I asked for Senior Sergeant Ristić to come and help us if he was available. I told him to find out where Rile was now if he was anywhere nearby? Ristić was there, but Trgovčević could not let him go, as they were expecting an imminent air raid and Ristićwas required to be there. Instead, he would send me Sergeant Ivković. I told him "Ivković has no idea how to fix the radar," to which he replied, "Why did you not train him. He is your reward for your laziness. And, you sent him to us in the Brigade as an expert." "I told him it was not time for me to talk about it now. "You know very

181   She is a character from a WW2 story about a young peasant maiden who joined the partisan war against the Nazi occupation of Yugoslavia. These women were often romanticized in literature, for example, in the 1946 Vladimir Nazor's lyric poetry book "Patizanka Mara", the title of which became a generic name.
182   After the war, when the fighters got hold of city girls who smelt nice and wore beautiful costumes and dresses, the Maras were left behind because they were mostly girls of rural descent. The name Mara is synonymous with them.

well how the unit was formed and that I am the least responsible for Ivković not being trained. Ask Dani, he was his boss before we joined in the brigade. "He made me upset. I told myself that I would not get nervous anymore.

Everything was calm. Radio amateurs were reporting markers in various parts of Yugoslavia. Vučković called me and asked, "Buddy, what's the problem with the radar?" I replied, "Buddy, he either does not know how to fix the radar or is too tired to do it as we moved to the new combat position today." "He has always been making mistakes," Vučković replied. I called Bora in the camp and told him to go and get Ristić. At 22:35 we are ordered into Readiness No.1, only with the missile guidance station. Blagojević had sent us the signal. His communication changed, it was succinct and focused on core commands only, just: "Receive the signal this and that." I concluded, "So, Colonel Stanković brought to his attention that he was incorrect in dealing with the units." At 23:45 Ristić arrived on the surveillance radar. I reported it to Blagojević, who replied that Ristić could stay with us tonight. I passed it on to Major Stoimenov, who I had sent on the surveillance radar to assist Ljubenković.

Tuesday, April 20

The shift ended last night at 00.00, Ristic repaired surveillance radar P-18 by 01.00. He stayed with us all night long. He left with Dani's shift this morning. Ljubenkovic sleeps... I still don't know what was wrong with the radar. During the shift transfer, Dani told me that there were two targets at the distances 20 and 22 kilometers. Far away to perform the combat work and launch. Radio-Amateurs have repeatedly welcomed us through the radio stations. Our "name" is 'Lasta' (swallow). We're only in the reception mode, without any emission. When we woke up, Bora told me he slept very bad last night. Before his eyes was Smiljanić and his burnt body. Maybe he didn't have to attend the site examination. Now I understand what the police inspectors face working on blood crimes scenes investigations. They're looking at that almost on daily basis.

At 08.00 I'm coming into the new shift. We're going to be on standby readiness No. 2. I immediately ordered the private Miroslav Alekic, from the P-18 radar, to go out into the field and to check the corner reflectors and to affix them to the posts, if they fell off. There was a heavy rain and a storm tonight. I'm letting Ljubenkovic to sleep. It is more important to me to let him take some rest than information about what was wrong with the radar last night. I'll find out later anyway.

P-18 radar became a bit problematic. It is breaking more and more often. Was that because of the exhaustion of the people that are tasked to work on it? Ljubenkovic is alone at the radar and today is 27th day of war. Even when he is on rest, he is sleeping inside with all the noise from the equipment around him.

Yesterday I really felt completely exhausted and broken. I felt tired before – going with a minimum sleep for two-three days but yesterday it reached the breaking point.

I've got an information that all actions with SA-7 "Strela" must be stopped between 09:30 – 10:00.

I'm trying to call warrant officer Jovic on his civilian number, but he is not responding. The reason was that the we got a fuel and the wheel from the PTL cable somehow got caught by the wheels and break, so we don't have a connection. Stoimenov is trying to fix it but I'm not able to establish a connection with the communication center. The good thing is that Jović got information about the ban of any SA-7 "Strela" activities. He told me that he passes the orders to all his position commanders except one because there is no phone line. "You have a vehicle! Use it." I told him. He is not really organized.

Discussion and arguing between Stoimenov and Maletić about the sleeping bags took another level. Exhaustion taking a tool on people and they started to fight about totally unimportant things.

The paper said they bombed Batajnica airbase last night about 03.00, Dani's shift... I spent the pen, which I received from Zoran Armuš, who was in Šimanovci to mount and connect our phone line. Armuš called me. I sketched few drawings, so he can make corner-reflectors, and now he's asking me for the height. I'm explaining to him that they have to beset up as high as possible. They'll make a mounting post around six meters in length. He asked how many pieces we need. I told him a dozen. That man helps us a lot. We'll try to keep in touch after the war.

The drinking water in Bečmen is awful. It stinks. They are so close to Belgrade, and don't have decent drinking water. It is a shame that fifty years have passed since World War II and nothing has been done. It is actually very simple – if you need a water, then you have to pay...The state doesn't have time to deal with everything and everyone. I'm just curios about the water quality in Dobanovci, in those places were the big assess, shots and politicians hunt and fish in their luxurious resorts. There are a lot of crows around us. They are picking the food leftovers. I aimed my gun at one but didn't shoot her. On the end she is also one of ours.

Stojanović is checking communications. He is calling me from the different phones. It is funny how he is meticulous with that task, and obvious proof about his professional involvement with the State Security Service. He is leaving nothing unchecked and for him everything is of equal importance, every piece of puzzle. That reminded me of Smiljanić and how he was kicked out from the regular service after the second negative mark during the review. The story was that he couldn't go home to tell that to his father. Now he went home, forever, in the coffin, burned like a log. He had father and junior sister. He wasn't in good relationship with his father and often had fierce arguing. He was a bit flimsy. The life doesn't have a price and if he is still alive, everything would be forgiven. For him personally it would be better if he left the military for good, at least he would be alive.

The officers asking when it will be an opportunity to go home for a few hours. I'm telling them that we will talk about that and make some decisions. All of them want to go home and see their families. They are craving for home environment. At 12:38 Stoimenov spoke with his wife and she told him that from the other unit, located in Smederevo, two guys got killed when their unit was hit. That was Blagoje Radić and Robert Lajčak. The whole town is talking about that, but we have no idea what is going on around. Maletić commented that the brass is hiding that from us like we are going to run away. It is a sad spring.

The other guys lay down and tried to catch some sun, like lizards on the rocks. Everybody is in his own thoughts. From our position we can see Jakovo silos. The Belgrade defence is shrinking. Smederevo battalion was hit with two missiles. At 13:20 from the Brigade operation center we were ordered to get into the Readiness No. 1. At this very moment something popped up in my memory. One of those peace time stupidities which higher command always liked to play. To reconfigure the radar frequencies on the fire control radar in the war time! Utterly stupid thing. That is a peace time exercise, but not in the middle of the war. What was the purpose of all of those charts and tables and all of the paper spent on it and classified as a top secret? It's pure junk, which should end up where it belongs - on the garbage.

High voltage on the transmitter cannot be raised. The time necessary to reconfigure frequencies is minimum four hours with the necessary instrumentation warm up. This is the old technology and need a time to warm up. God, what madness, and that was very well known before the war. the other side have computers and electronic equipment on the airplanes that can receives 740,000 information per second. They applied everything in the military industry--whatever and whenever it was discovered. We are really like Indians to them. Like bow and arrow against the firearms. All we have is just a heart and nothing more. Still, it's a big heart… And a lot of pride. We're not going let some foreign boot to step on us and our land. I hear determination that many people just waiting them to start with the land attack, so we can "fuck their mothers" for good. President Milosević is right when he said that they can come as an observers, but not from those countries that bombing us right now. Now we are putting conditions, right from the Balkan mud. Let them destroy the stuff… they don't know anything better. We will rebuild it.

I'm thinking how these events will make a gap between the ordinary people and government. The foreign credits and help will start to arrive but one thing is for sure and that it will be a lot of thefts…Who is going to pay for all of this time in the dark and fear to this shift and to many other shifts… The shift is where the technics is operational…the life became a shift. Minimum number of people to operate the equipment may reduce casualties… logical and realistic. The people are just the numbers on ID's. I would love to see Smiljanić's ID. For sure he had one, like Vučković, and maybe it didn't burn. The problem is how to find in that wreck of burned metal and ashes. The heavy tool was paid. The operation band of P-15 is very well known. Why then the radar worked unprotected and who ordered that??? That one who ordered that is to blame for Gajić and Smiljanić death. Vučković know that and he rose a lot of noise about that. He requested that separate screen to be relocated from the cabin. Unfortunately, that was never approved by the command. Maybe Danka is right… Someone sits "higher on the ladder" and makes mistakes without endangering their own lives or functions but their moves and commands or ignorance endanger people lower on the same ladder and unfortunately someone pays for their mistakes with ultimate price. Who was the one with more "stars on the shoulder" at the brigade level and who was responsible for the radars and why that one allowed this kind of operation? I'm going to investigate this after the war…Where was the brigade "tactician", Janko Aleksić, with his vast knowledge??? Fuck their tactics which is breaking on the other people backs and heads! Who in fact will have any satisfaction because of knowing the truth? How to tell somebody that his son got killed because somebody made mistake? The unit in the field can rely only on itself. Who protected us with the logs? Who is making corners reflectors posts? Who is transporting logs from site to site, who is working on the radar emission imitator?... and so on and so fort… Everything is on us and we have to do everything by ourselves! Those people for brigade are there to issue an orders - very lucrative business far from the danger and on the end they are also mad on us! Hierarchy and everything is twisted and skewed. The truth is in the justice and love and those bad guys are product of the time and the bad system in which we live. Misery, what else to say!? For many of them it is not a war at all. Some of them behave like the bombs are not falling every day.

I'm warning Lieutenant Nikolić not to sleep on duty. I'm not going to let anybody in my shift to sleep while on duty. In just a moment when is the most critical, somebody may make mistake and that can be very costly.

I took a half of pill of Ranisan for my ulcer, after a while. Maybe it is because I'm chewing to much of bubble gums. Our psycho changed and we are not all the time under combat stress. That first stress passed some time ago. Now we have a wish for revenge. But we need to control that urge otherwise we may fell into the trap. Everything that is out of control is simply not good. Our buts are moulded like they are permanently attached to the uncomfortable chairs. We are real sufferers. Our working and living conditions are crappy… almost zero quality.

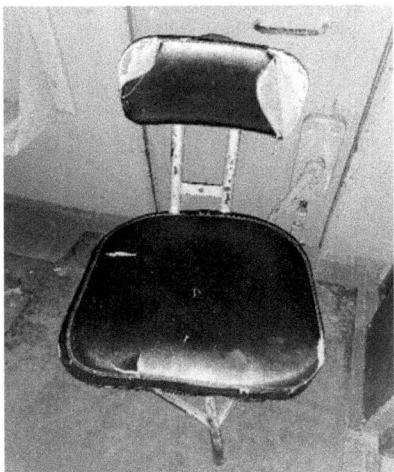

A very uncomfortable chair on which the author spent hours after hours on the combat duty. The look and the state of this chair may represent the actual state of the Yugoslav defense – something that was neglected by the political leaders. Even with these miserable conditions, the military gave their best and far beyond the call of duty fighting nonstop against the mightiest alliance in the history.

Golubović told me this morning that radio-amateurs saluted and gave their greetings to "Lasta" and that the guys from the shift called to thank them. I'm curious did Dani told anybody that he is "Lasta" commander. The man who downed the stealth - that is his way how he introduces himself to everybody. It is disgusting that he talks about that to everybody and with us he is playing conspiracy. My partner Danka profiled him very well. I must be careful of him. He is covered with a many layers. It is without any doubts that he is trying to push himself up. He doesn't give a shit for anybody else. He is exploiting others. I wander did he asked the brass why only two guys (himself and Nikolić) are promoted out of the whole shift. I understand secrecy but promotions do not need to be published to everybody. Well, it is not going to finish on this for sure.

I'll call Tomić from brigade HQ as soon as I catch some time and ask what happened with the proposals to promote to the higher ranks the whole shift, or if that proposal exist at all.

Around 14:50 Lieutenant Stojanović dialed a number and gave me the phone. He told me that one guy wants to talk to me. That was Lieutenant Colonel Davidović, HR boss in Air Defense Corps. After the usual greeting, which started with, "How are you, legend?" I asked him about the promotions for the shift that hit and downed the stealth. He told me that nothing came from the Brigade HQ. He told me that last night he spoke about that with Colonel Vukosavljević and General Karanović. "Is it possible, David?", I asked him "Dani and Nikolić got promoted but still nothing came from the Brigade, but still they were promoted and Nikolić was also decorated." "The brigade had no idea about Dani. General Bane Petrović proposed promotion." He told me. Maybe that was the way how general thanked Dani for the fishing trips and parties that they had before the war. "Put the paper into the typewriter and type the same suggestion for the promotion to other combat shift members…Dani and Nikolić did not act alone." I told to Col. Davidović. "I really have to do that" he responded.

Mića Mijalković came with Captain Tomović to the combat position. He brought me a sleeping bag. "Mićo, you will get a cold beer for this?" I'm in the military for 19 years and still don't have a sleeping bag. And someone who came to the unit yesterday got it right away. The other night I was looking for blankets to cover myself because it was chilly. Not a single one to find. Shameful. I pointed that to Varga. He told me that Dani ordered him to distribute blankets through the unit but how come that nothing left? Dani is playing on two tracks again. He tells me one thing and he does the others. I gave to Mića keys for the office and safe in our barracks. He told me that he needs these keys for the mobilization room because the computer is there. I explained to him that the room key is in the drawer in my desk. Orders for the days were: Jović to stop any combat activities from 17.00 to 17.20; Standby Readiness No. 1 from 15:42 to 16:00; At 17:30 Captain Cvetić and Lieutenant Jović need to go to Dani for a meeting; Varga to bring an ammo box to the SA-7 "Strela " launchers, personal weapons, helmets, masks, blankets and anything else they may need. I'm going to sign the documents so everyone can bear arms; Bring notebook to Cvetić.

Dani and Crnobrnja went to meet the members of the local crisis headquarters around 18:30 and I tried to lay down for a bit, just to try to take a rest. Just before that, Dani said that he had decided to put the computer from the mobilization room to safety, which is at his house. "So how are we going to do it?" I asked him. "We'll manage it somehow." Just wandering who on earth put this guy to be a commander?? I'm looking at Crnobrnja because taking official computer home (and the only one in the whole battalion) is a matter for the arrest. And here, we will use the typewriters for the documents like at the beginning of the century. The time of war profiters started. I can't sleep…No wander why…Soon after, I've got a call from Armuš. He made those corner reflector posts and holders. They'll bring them tonight. He didn't get a chance to paint them, but I couldn't care less about the paint. We will paint them if we have time for that, and if not, who cares… let them rust.

Slavko Sedlak told me that somebody from the police called and that they arrested reservists Simović. Major Dotlić probably let him go out. Today, he said he let the two guys out from the missile battery, two from the guidance battery and one from the logistic and supply platoon. At 20.00 with Slavko, I'm trying to deal with the numbers - how many people called to duty and how many showed up. Miloš Vladović came to our unit with his son. We have to solve this issue as soon as possible. After the divorce, the child was assigned to him. He doesn't want to avoid military commitment and his duty. It was emotional to listen his story. He needs just a few hours to talk to the woman who is babysitting his child and to prepare the child for his longer absence. He's here for days. Nobody handled it. Seem that Major Dotlić do not care at all. He is in the camp for days with the man and his child and didn't do anything. Tomović spoke with a babysitter and she's willing to take care of the child until the war is over. That was such a nice thing from her. Very noble. Tomović shaved his beard in front of his two-and-a-half-year-old son.

The reservist Boris Vakanjac can get a computer from his faculty; In a base camp in Deč, the toilet is clogged; The units are not formed properly: there are guys on the list and with the certain speciality but assigned to completely different units that actually does not need that specialities; Sedlak has not yet finished with the dog tags, although it should have been done a few days ago; The "Strela SA-7" MANPADS should be formed and organised properly… I ordered to Barvalac what I need for tomorrow.

Stojanović came with me to Deč. On the way back we bumped inti the three civilians, by the road Petrovčić – Deč. This was suspicious so we reported it to a unit located on a farm. I went to my cot bed at 22:30. My shift is tonight from 00:00 to 08:00… A very busy day behind and uncertain night ahead… I'm laying on my bed in the dark and talking to Bora about the situation…This situation is not good. To many still unsolved problems.

Dani, without informing me, decided to put two enlisted men on the surveillance radar and Sergeant   Ljubenković to be with him during his shift. He also issued an order that the car must be ready in the base camp to pick him up. That is at least half an hour back and fort. That period is to long for the combat activity. As soon as I get to the combat position, I banned to Captain Golubović to do anything similar like Dani. I'm asking him: "Is it better to put enlisted men during the day, when most likely it will be no combat tasks and let Sergeant Ljubenković to do night shifts when is most likely that the enemy will pop up from somewhere". I have feeling that this is just the start of the game of "putting the stick into the wheels".

Dani pretends to be a big boss in surrounding villages... he got what he wanted, and he doesn't give a shit for anybody else. On my insisting to propose some stimulation for the other crew members, he told me that there is no need for that, and that brigade will do that. I stick to my first idea because Colonel Davidović from the Corps told me that the idea and proposal must come from the base unit. Bora told me that he hoped that the order to promote the other "stealth shooters" will come. He told that to the brigade chief of staff, Colonel Stanković. It is almost comical what he is doing. If we serve under Saadam Husain, he will pay us in gold and look what is happening here... those assholes from the HQ don't care about others... they care only about themselves. Bora told me that he keeps notes of everything but what is the value of that. Is the only computer in the whole battalion safer at Dani's home?? Can anybody just grab what they need from the unit inventory and bring it home?? Is that the official green light for the theft?? I'm thinking to tell that to the others but that may undermine the morale. I must think how to let people go home for a day or two to rest and also to place new men into the proper duties. People need permits otherwise somebody may think that they are deserters.

I read today observation which General Smiljanić wrote during and after the visit to the 4th and 5th battalions. His, to say, negative comments were that the units march during the day, that there is no engineering preparation of the combat positions, that the half of the men are unshaven and when on march, it is individual and not in the proper columns. God, what the stupid things that man wrote!!! Is he normal and conscious that we are in the war! These kinds of generals every enemy would love to be in charge of command to his opponents.

Typically, we are out of combat readiness between 09:00-11:00 and combat readiness usually around 19:00. If the unit must be ready for the combat and can't do any relocation march during the day, then when it can do that and how on earth to be ready to engage the enemy in the middle of typical relocation recommended time, written for the peacetime exercises?... We are led by the incompetent donkeys...

Missile battalion column is usually few kilometers long while marching. That stretched column is an ideal target for the bombers. It makes more sense if we dispatch vehicles individually and disguise them in the traffic. Well, seem that our general is still living in peace time of gala dinners and wasting of time meetings of the brass.

I called Armuš around 00.10 and he told me that he delivered posts for the corner reflectors. Golubović and Djordjević were there. It was around 22:00. As soon as we have the daylight, we have to mount those reflectors. In the meantime, the shift spoke about the short home leaves. Everybody agreed and suggested that if somebody need to go, it should be at 08:00 and be back by 14:00. This is reasonable. Captain Muminović wants to move his family from Obrenovac to Belgrade. There is a plenty of chlorohydrin acid in the local refineries in Pančevo and Obrenovac that was not dispersed and moved to safer locations and if those guys above somehow hit those tanks, that would be enormous catastrophe. The both places are almost at the edge

152

of panic. Whoever can, ran away from the town.

This night we worked with the radar imitator on azimuth 150, 180 and 210. The attack wave came from the south. Guess, those guys above got our radar signals, and nobody even dared to enter into our zone of destruction.

Major Stoimenov wandering if he can really take a bus home because nobody knows if there is operational civilian bus line at all…

Wednesday, April 21

We commenced our night shift from 00:00 to 08:00. With God's help, the crews of this shift and the next shift will respectively see their families tomorrow and the day after tomorrow.

The air raid began around 01:00. The closest targets on our radar screens were 28 kilometers away and they were disappearing. I orally communicated to Blagojević the location and movement of all the targets he had asked me to track. No target entered our zone of engagement. During the second raid around 02:30 our radar was jammed. The jamming caused saturation of the receiver and the frequency drift, so the selected frequencies cannot be stored in the memory. I saw the Fruška Gora Mountain peaks as two small reflections on the radar screen.

The surveillance radar failed again: from the 30 kilometers circle mark to the periphery of the radar screen there were fan-shaped patterns. I could not see anything. I was blinded and reported it to Srba Blagojević. The surveillance radar operator, Sergeant Ljubenković, reported to me that the receiver had failed. He requested 6M15P vacuum tube for the oscillator to fix it. First thing in the morning someone should call Paunović from the central warehouse to see if he maybe has that vacuum tube in stock. If anybody going to the warehouse, then the compressed air bottle should be filled-in as well. There is about 40 atmosphere of air pressure left in one bottle.

I was nervous, and so was the whole shift. I could not see anything within a radius of 90 kilometers. There was nothing even on the base up to 190 km away. Srba replied, "It is ok Djole, don't be upset, you're just blinded." At around 03:30 it looked as a target had briefly appeared 12 km away. Ljubenković was not sure if this was a radar noise breakdown. Neither was I.

The operations center no longer insisted that we search for targets by using the target tracking and acquisition radar if there were no targets on the surveillance radar. Several battalions and P-15 radar had been hit so far. The body count was known: five dead. Probably for this reason there had been no recent screw-ups, in contrast to those at the beginning of the war.

Colonel Stanković called us at 06:30 and asked for Dani's phone at the camp. I gave it to him. He probably wanted to talk again about the radar. Shortly after that, Dani called me and asked for an update on the surveillance radar. I told him everything. He replied, "Then it must be a malfunction." Captain Golubović and I had been signaling for over fifteen days that the radar was faulty and not working correctly. In case anyone wanted to doubt me, I was not the radar operator who reported it. There is an officer at the radar station who would report the malfunction to me, and then I would report it to the brigade. In addition, the soldiers and officers from the combat shift were also present. There were many witnesses.

Our shift ended and we left for the camp.

I told to Dani that it was not okay for him to tell command that the radar was working when it was not. I had tried everything in all modes, including live (unfiltered) images with reflections from stationary objects. I also asked him about the trickery yesterday when he sent two soldiers to man the surveillance radar P-18 without consultation with me. He replied that he had told Captain Golubović to sort it out and that he had nothing to do with that decision. He was lying. Golubović should not have made that decision on his own and without consulting me first. I prevented that from occurring last night.

I tried to fall asleep but failed. Dani will go reconnoitering today. Later at lunch, I heard from Senior Sergeant Mijalković that Dani had already "reconnoitered" the mobilization room this morning and had taken the computer and other equipment for safekeeping - to his home.

I was unable to fall asleep because numerous phone calls kept waking me up. They were calling me from the command and subordinate units. I conveyed to Stojanović, commander of the signals platoon, the problems with the communication equipment and ordered him to fix them.

I went for a tetanus vaccination. Bora was standing when I entered the room. I took off my vest, rolled up my left sleeve and received an injection. Bora asked me if it hurt. Dr. Djukić said it would protect me for the next ten years. I went to the combat position to check the placement of the corner reflectors and the camera. Bajić had sent a Lieutenant Colonel to solve the camera problem and he fixed it before I came. Everything was working, so I went to Deč. Dani was coming there. In the camp, he held a meeting with the newly arrived reserve troops - mobilized soldiers and officers.

I am falling asleep while writing this… I slept until 17:00. Tomović and Sedlak went out for a walk so I could sleep in peace. After that I told Sedlak to sort out the personnel files. The mood in the camp was quite peaceful, without tension. We needed to bring Ristić from Šimanovci to help us with the radar. Dani's driver went to pick him up in the Opel Ascona. Barvalac went to Paun in the warehouse to get the vacuum tube and fill-in the compressed air bottle with air. After that, he went to Jakovo to pick up everything needed for MANPADS unit.

I wrote a proposal for incentive measures for the 250th Air Defense Brigade, to be sent by the first next mail delivery, which reads:

Proposal of incentive measures,

To Command, 250th Air Defence Brigade

Based on the successful outcome of combat operations on 27 March 1999, when the symbol of NATO aviation and the lat-

est stealth military technology of the 21st-century US aircraft F-117A was shot down over our air-space, we wish to point out to the ensuing omissions of superior command. As experienced air-defense missile operators, you should know that the two people who have been promoted so far do not represent the entire combat crew that participated in the combat work, nor the two individuals could have achieved the success of slapping NATO and delighting the entire progressive world. By using a second-generation weapon we shot down a fourth-generation aircraft as a team. This success will be remembered in history. Your ensuing conduct so far has hurt members of the combat crew, as all its members were not treated equally, hence we respectfully request from you to equally treat all members of the combat crew as follows.

The following officers have been stimulated so far:

> *Lieutenant Colonel Zoltan Dani was promoted to the rank of Colonel,*

> *Sub-Lieutenant Darko Nikolić was promoted to the rank of Lieutenant and decorated by the President of the FRY with the Order of Courage.*

We also recommend promotions and decorations for the following officers and soldiers:

> *Lieutenant Colonel Djordje Sava Aničić, Deputy Combat Shift Commander,*

> *Captain Senad Ejub Muminović, Missile Guidance Officer*

> *Senior Sergeant Dragan Branislav Matić, Manual Tracking Operator on F-2,*

> *Sergeant Dejan Radiša Tiosavljević, Manual Tracking Operator on F-1,*

> *Senior Sergeant Djordje Slavko Maletić, Power Supply Unit Commander,*

> *Sergeant Vladimir Ljubiša Ljubenković, Radar Section Commander,*

> *Sergeant Zoran Dušan Tepavac, Signals Platoon Commander,*

> *Senior Sergeant Igor Andrija Radivojević, Radar Emission Imitator Operator,*

> *Private Vladimir Selko Radovanović, Electric Generator Operator,*

> *Private Sead Alija Ljajić, Radar Emission Imitator Operator,*

> *Private Davor Slobodan Bložić, Notetaker and Manual*

Plotting Board Operator,

Reserve Private Slaviša Milovan Pavlović, Diesel Electric Set Operator.

The incentives proposed here would eliminate the injustice done to the combat crew as a whole and would have a positive effect on the members of the combat unit, and beyond. We further respectfully propose the unit to be decorated, and that all other officers and soldiers who supported the combat work of the unit be, at least, commended.

Commander

Colonel

Zoltan Dani

Amazingly, we had to fight for our rights and equality if we were even equal at all. Dani was nowhere to be found to sign this letter and other documents that had to be mailed to the Brigade Command. So, I had to sign again all the correspondence, as I had done many times before, including the letter. In my capacity as the battalion deputy commander (executive officer - XO), I have the right to use my own seal (to stamp or authenticate hard copy documents). I checked that the typed list matched the names on the files. I also needed to compare the folder with the mobilization orders before signing the respective outcome reports going to the Military Service Department.

Dani will replace me in my shift duty. Dotlić will replace Dani in his next shift. Earlier today Dani jokingly told Bora to be his deputy combat shift commander and work with the radar emission imitator and other communication devices. Bora replied that he had never done that and that he was not trained for these duties.

Bora came from Šimanovci around 20:00. Some Pakistanis were captured there. The villagers had surrounded them, and they were shaking with fear. Barvalac completed his assignment. We talked about the composition of the Emergency Response Team: weapons, training and shooting practice.

My shift rested until 15:00 today.

At 21:05 I called Dani who was in the guidance station. They were not combat launch ready yet. Ristić went to fine-tune the radar. Bora told me not to tell Dani that he had returned if Dani asked about him. He was afraid not to be called into the missile guidance station.

I spoke with Danka. She was depressed for the second day. I did not understand it and it annoyed me a lot. I insisted on her telling me the reason why she was so sad, but she didn't want to.

I gave Tomović my diary to read. "Nothing has changed in the past six years since I demobilized and left the Air Defence," he later said. "You're a very strong man. Reading this, I can see what you've been facing for the last ten years. I don't know how I would have endured it if I were you."

Last night I slept in Deč, in the camp, without my shift, which became an integral part of me and my life. NATO bombed Belgrade and hit the business center building "Ušće"[183]. It's all on fire. It's near my building in New Belgrade where I live. I'm wandering now what happened to all windows and glass on my building. The good thing is that there were no people at the business center. Beside the business center, on TV I also saw President Milosevic's residence which was targeted as well. I never supported and never agreed that he moved there and now I'm sorry for the residence. It was an old historic building, very nice architecture. Seem that NATO wanted to decapitate the country leadership, just the guy was not there…Not really smart move from the NATO mission planners.

Business center Ušće the day after NATO bombing. In the foreground is a monument called "Winner" on the antic Kalemgdan fortress. Destroying landmarks is one of the tactics that NATO used to show the shear dominance and disrespect to the national history.

Dani called around 10:00. He asked me about the intervention group and what is the status. Last night he had the announcement that the helicopter was somewhere near him. He is scared now. I suggested an intervention group to counter any diversions or helicopter attack a long time ago. Now when the upper command realized that there is a real danger, we have to form, arm and train the group, and that is the lengthy process and require a time and men and we didn't have either. We could have done this before, but

183   Ušće – in Serbian Ušće means "confluence", as the tower overlooks the confluence of the Dunav and Sava Rivers.

Dani and command didn't want to listen. Now, we're at the beginning and it will take time, the same one that's been missed for nothing.

He wasn't listening to me. I organized a meeting with the unit commanders in the camp. We need to perform chemical, biological and nuclear attack protection basic training as well as the basic infantry tactic training. I also had a meeting with the infantry platoon. From the forty reservists, so far only 16 came... not real great number. The platoon commander will be Sergeant Tepavac. I really hope that when the rest of the men arrive, we can relieve other guys for the specialist duties as per their qualifications.

On my pager I got a message from Armuš that our "Ural" truck has been repaired.

Friday, April 23

At 07:00 it was announced in the camp that the bus is coming to move the unit. The troops had breakfast and prepared for the move. They boarded the bus immediately upon its arrival and headed to Bečman. In Šimanovci, the order came to bring the vehicles to the combat position. I went there too. By the time I arrived, the work had already begun and progressed to a great extent. I informed Armuš that we were packing our suitcases again.

Dani, Aca, his driver and Tepavac are searching the terrain around the position. We were shot at last night. The parts of one anti-aircraft missile were found about 600-800 meters away from the centre of the combat position. The shift had been radiating extensively tonight, looking for the target. They couldn't find anything with the target acquisition radar.

Tepavac said that one missile flew over the position, just above the signals platoon field HQ.

At the explosion place, the crater was about one meter deep. They also found the "cap", the front tip of the missile. It was coated with Bakelite.

We analyzed the combat work by time and onset. Dani, Stoimenov, Golubović, Dotlić, Roksandić and I were present. Three pairs of aircraft came to the proximity of the missile battalion, from three 120-degree spaced directions. That was a classic way to neutralize air-defense units. I know that airplanes bombed the combat position near Smederevo. They were almost completely dug in. A shell fragment of about 1.5 to 2 kg weight was found in the missile command transmitter antenna. In contrast to the battalion in Smederevo, Draganić was targeted by anti-radar missiles. They were protected by logs, as we did. A small shrapnel slipped through the logs and wounded Šilja, one of the operators, in the leg. Nothing serious. The bombs are fucked. Bombs show that Draganić's battalion was located, photographed, and marked as the next target.

A decision was made to go between the villages of Petrovčić and Ašanja, to a new combat position near Petrovčić. Ašanja is very close to the river Sava, which should be avoided; and Noskov had also fired from somewhere there before. By 09:00 the equipment was taken away from the combat position and the column of vehicles dispersed into the village. We were waiting for the command to go individually to the new combat position.

The biggest problem in our combat work is determining the target altitude. If we had the correct information, our combat would certainly be far more successful. I suggested that I go to Belgrade with Stojanović and try to get some device through astronomers. Professor Ninković and geophysicist Perović were extremely welcoming to us. They tried to help us. Ninković, who was married to a Russian, said: "It wouldn't be good for us if they target the Arkan's[184] house". He wanted to say their house was near the Arkan's. Stojanović thrilled me again. He was a real otter and left nothing to chance.

We stopped by Srećko Morić, the president of the Radio Amateurs Association. They had no cigarettes, which were difficult to obtain in the city. I left him a box of "Partner". He was overjoyed. We got in touch with radio amateur Dragan, on mountain Cer. He had stationary equipment, which was useless to us. Its IR device could not meet the distances we needed. Finally, at around 16:00 we found a theodolite in Energoprojekt engineering consulting company. They gave us the training until 17:30. We figured it out pretty well. The only issue is optical visibility. It magnifies 25 times during bright nights.

The Serbian Broadcasting Corporation HQ in Takovska Street was hit tonight. Finally, the Vuk Drašković's old wish to tear down the "TV Bastille" had been fulfilled. It is very sad. Another accomplishment of our people and our nation was hit last night. We have no information on the number of casualties. At 18.00 Mika drove his car and dropped me to my house on his way home. Once we were in the city, we all needed a quick shower and to change our underwear. The deal was to catch up at 20:00 and then go back. I had a coffee with Danka. She fried eggs with bacon for dinner. I haven't eaten that for a long time. She had cooked beans too. I eat beans every third day and I refused it. I enjoyed the salad and took a quick bath in a tight bathtub, after carefully removing a barrel of reserve drinking water. We did not spill it. She made another coffee. I told her that Smiljanić was killed. Her eyes were full of tears. "They were shooting at us last night," I said. "I knew. I had a bad dream," she replied. The phone rang; it was Danka's father Milan. He went in Petrovčić to buy 'dilcoran' medication for Nada's chest pain and saw the destroyed radar. It looked nasty. When will I come, he asked. He wanted to have a chat. I have nothing to tell him about the death of a colleague and officer, who used to be in my unit.

Stojanović came to pick me up.

By the time we arrived the night had already fallen. No air raid warning was issued yet. The lights in the villages were turned off. We found the school. Bora was there. Dotlić was asleep. Dani was with my shift manning the combat position. At about 23:00 a local hunter came to tell me that he had noticed some light on the football pitch, like a spotlight. I immediately recalled the Ića's son's story that there was light from the direction of the football pitch before Smiljanić was hit. Stojanović, Bora and I immediately left the camp for search. The guards found a man. The terrain around

184   Željko Ražnatović Arkan is controversial figute. For some he was the leader of the criminals, the boss of all bosses, and for other he was a hero.

the house should be searched. He was crouching. He lived in a newly built house, had a legal gun, binoculars and a phone. Who knows, maybe he was okay and maybe not. He was a Montenegrin. Stojanović and Bora searched his house and found a cassette where Ljubiša Trgovčević, local mag and self proclaimed seer, spits on this country and the people; the words: "I don't give a fuck about Television ..." echoed from the tape. Good-for-nothing and depraved. The Montenegrin went to see him because he wanted to check if he had been under any spells, since he was not married and could not have an erection. He was born in 1961. Stojanović can handle this situation...

I had enough and went to bed late, around 02:00.

Saturday, April 24

Dani's words woke me up: 'You don't give a shit because Hungary doesn't have a see and has a navy"..."You are right" I told him and we both laughed. We are talking how to get theodolite and how we can benefit from that[185] . He and Bora need to go to the local police station in Karlovcić. Locals found some kind of sensor. In the meantime, I'll go to Deč. Before that I spoke with Major Roksandić and I told him that private Janić did not come to the radar emission imitator because he is sick, and the doctor told him to take few days off. I put Warrant Officer Jović back to the signals center, and instead of him Sergeant Radomir Petrović on the radar imitator. Sergeant Denčev is on the antitank launcher (LAW) instead of Sergeant Petrović. In Roksandic's group one of the assault rifles is missing. That was private Vladimir Milić rifle. The rifle was in the truck, TAM 150, and it disappeared in less than 10

---

185   The practical engineering problem of concern was how best to quickly determine the height of the target, in order to put it in the cross hairs (lock on the target) and fire the missile. The key objective was to reduce the radiation time of the fire control radar; as that would reduce the likelihood of the battery being hit by the HARM anti radar missile and increase the likelihood of the crew's survival. The hardware of the S-125 Neva air defense weapon system included two 2D radars – surveillance and fire control. 2D radars provide information on the azimuth (vertical crosshair) and distance to the target, but not that of the height (horizontal cross hair) of the target. Generally, it is possible to quickly align the target with the vertical crosshair by relying on the azimuth data; Typically, it takes longer to align the target with the horizontal crosshair because 2D radars do not provide the height of the target; and the target could be at any altitude, in theory up to 20km above the ground level. The practical engineering problem for the guidance officer was to find the target in the vertical plane (in order to align it with the horizontal crosshair), whilst keeping the target in the vertical cross hair. The search time to lock in onto the target increases as the range of the heights [from, to] to be searched increases, all other parameters being equal; largely due to the narrow beam of the fire control radar operating in the target acquisition mode. In order to reduce the search time, the Author's idea was use a theodolite to measure the elevation of the target; and use the measured value to quickly align the target with the horizontal cross hair; ideally to simultaneously bring the target in both crosshairs.

minutes when the truck was in Deč. Roksandić ordered him to write a statement. Boris Radenović, one of his soldiers, also need to write a statement why he is not going to shave his beard and private Boris Hadžibabić to write a statement why he doesn't want to take a haircut. Let see how Roksandić will solve this... Seem that some men do not give a shit for the military discipline...well, it is a war time and some more important things to worry about, but still, discipline is the discipline...

When I got to Deč, I found Jokić in tracksuit and snickers. He told me that he washed his uniform and boots, but it didn't dry yet. He's asking me about some soldiers that want to go home. I'm criticizing him. How come that an officer doesn't know how and when to dry his uniform and boots. It is not his fault... He is the product of one year of education and training in the military academy.

Today Slavko Sedlak need to go to bring mail...Still no money for per diem...Last time he delivered our mail including a proposal letter for the promotions. I signed all documents, like many times before, because Dani is always absent. Barvalac and Tepavac need to work together and train the intervention platoon. We also got an address for the "Mile Dragić Production" in Zrenjanin. That company is making personal protection equipment that is really need. So far, we have just a few. In that company there is also development of camouflage systems and decoys[186]... Bugarin brought to me a volunteer, Nedeljko Radjenović. He served in 63rd Airborne Brigade. He is scout and leaves alone. Born in 1973...kind a good looking and an easy-going guy. When he was 17-18, he went to fight in Bosnia. I have opinion that he can find hard himself doing anything but be a soldier and fight. He told me that he's is not hungry, and I gave him a pack of cigarettes. His address is in Palilula municipality. I can't take him into the unit because we are not accepting volunteers for now, so I sent him to the regional 1st Army command because they have a place where they are accepting volunteers. Later I found out that he is a bit lazy guy.

After this, I went to check Žugić and his men in Šimanovci. Every vehicle has a designated driver. There are a few vehicles from the guidance and missile battery over there. Guidance battery does not have a designated driver for their vehicles! How come?! I have to fix that as soon as possible. For now, they have some temporary solutions. Guys over there did not received tetanus vaccines and I have to send our doctor as soon as possible... Varga is complaining about the reserve and the lack of fuel because they are positioned on two different places. He moved weapons and ammo to Šimanovci. "Handover that to Žugić and let him take care of that", I ordered him... "Fuel is of strategic importance and it need to follow the unit. Without that we are just sitting ducks!" Bugarin left for Deč to drive a bus. Lukić has obturation for his mother and he need time to prepare and go. Dani suggested him to postpone everything...Lukić came to me and beginning to talk about Dani... Maybe Dani is not familiar with our (Serbian) customs" I told Lukić..."Ok, we'll find a solution". Sedlak is giving two flasks, for me and Dani. They are nice little souvenirs... Žugić and his men were happy that I visited them and heard their issues...Varga need to go home for a leave...Barvalac pick-

---

186   Mike Mihajlovic: I was involved in development of this equipment prior to emigration to Canada and the equipment was indeed very good.

up was hit today from behind by a truck. That pickup is our supply vehicle which is on lease for the military use and now we have to call the owner on Monday. We need to go to the collision center for the damage estimate.

Later today I went to Armuš because he called me few times. I couldn't go earlier and didn't have chance to call him back. Milan gave him 150 Deutsch Marks for the material that he used for his smoke house just before the war. He is asking me now can he give me that money for the diesel. I can't believe this! He helped us a lot with the phone landline so we were able to establish the communication with 250th brigade operation center... He helped us a lot with the other stuff as well...I can't believe that he is now offering me a shitty 150 DM for the diesel and I don't want to disgrace my-self taking that. I just wandering how come he can't understand that for me the money means nothing and that stuff that I'm doing now is something that I'm doing because I believe it is the right thing to do to protect our country. He really dropped a lot in my eyes... I'm leaving very disappointed. He is asking for a fuel and that fuel is our lifeline. This is not Bosnia where every-body trades with everybody including the enemies. Is it possible that people just think how to make some dirty profits? Yes of course... Dani found a "safe place" for the battalion computer and who knows what else while here I'm trying to save as much as it possible and secure lives – my and my men.

The shift became my obsession. I haven't been there for two days. I know that the stuff that I'm doing at the moment is important, but the shift is an essence. She is there... In the ambush and fear...

Today, with the mail, we got a nine flack vests – seven for the missile guidance van crew and two for the power supply van. In the camp I found out that Dani criticized Tomović because Tomović didn't call him and tell him about the incident and why he didn't inform him that he will go to pick up supplies. "Why you didn't tell Dani that as a supply platoon commander you need to know the suppliers and places where to pick up the stuff" I asked Tomović.

Captain Golubović called and asked is there any photo studio because he need passport photos. Seem he is going to Russia for a training on S-300. I'm so happy for that! Dani never mentioned anything about that to me. Doesn't matter who is going there... It is important that we get that system. Whoever going there need to study and work day and night to be ready to execute all combat procedures. If I stay here, we must hold on until the new system arrive than we'll give a lot of shit to those yanks! Can you imagine: 150 km range?! And now he is shooting at us from 40-50 km distance with HARM and I have to wait him to come 14-15 km. Their advantage is enor-mous. If we have the new system than we will have that long-range advan-tage. Simply a game changer.

In Vietnam, according to some estimates, they lost 3,350 airplanes, not counting helicopters. At that time there were no antiradiation missiles or they were rudimentary one.

So far, over Yugoslavia, as per the information available to us, we hit about 40 airplanes, 160 cruise missiles and 5-7 unmanned aerial vehicles (UAV). If the S-300 come on time, it will be plenty more hits... Just we need to be smart... I wouldn't launch all 24 missiles at the same time, but rather wait and every night launch two or three and get a few airplanes every time. I am so excited that I forgot almost all negative things. My big hopes and expectations... "Just one step at time and we'll fuck their mothers!...They will have no idea what is going to get them!" Tomović looked at me and told me "Djole, take it easy man! don't be excited to much"... How not to be excited man?!" I'm telling him. "If anybody is going to Russia in the middle of the war from the combat unit the meaning is only one – to get ready for the new system!?" The west is underestimating Russia and does not care for the Russian opinion. It must be that the Russian had it enough and decided to sell us or just give us their most advanced system. What is the real reason is not important anymore. The most important is what will happen. Victor Chernomirdin seem seal the deal. Is it possible that I got so excited because of the weapon and not for some ordinary thing? I think that my feeling got dulled. I told Mika that on our way from Belgrade. Maybe I became to rough? Maybe I'm just insulting people around, the same people who care about me. I remembered Danka's face, standing at the door, and looked at me with a very worried look. I knew she was sad. Well, priorities are more important. My priority now are my men and to wage a war. I don't have time for the ordinary things. Seem that I don't have that time for a long. Did I really realized that level of feelings or I just got forged in the cruel reality of war that I can't see the right thing and disgrace any human weaknesses?...

I'm reading reservists statements - one about the beard and other about the hair. God, what is, and what can be important to people... Well, on the other hand, it is a part of their personality and without these personalities they are not who they are... And what is the part of me in that personality? I'm asking myself...

I haven't spoke with my son since 13 April. He even doesn't know when my birthday is. Just wandering how much I really mean to him. Lies, all of that is just a lie...Damn with my hope in something that never happened. He was always afraid of me. I insisted that he must study with the work and discipline. The other side didn't insist on that at all. The line of the less resistance and my son leaned to that side. All in all, in all that story I was that hard way...The way to the irresponsibility. A man without responsibility and a firm believes is not a man at all. He is like a mass and just look as a man. I'm really sorry that my son is not like me. When I think of him, I get sentimental...always. Am I ever going to be strong and firm when it is about him? Am I ever going to grew up regarding to this...?

Sunday, April 25

Tomović and Sedlak are watching a movie. It's similar to *The Call of the Wild.*"

I feel restless. Dejan told me the other day while reading this diary, something caught his attention: "What did you say that if you survived until you were 42 years old, you would live long? You will survive, but not for that long, perhaps until 60 or 65 years. Man, you're really worn out. Life is consuming you." I sincerely hope he was wrong.

I talked to Dr. Djukić. He received eighty tetanus vaccines and vaccinated seventy eight people. More doses would be needed for all people to receive tetanus shots. Crnobrnja returned after delivering the list of names of the unit to Roksandić in order for him to know who will be in his sub-unit and to re-distribute the reserve force to other sub-units. Mića Mijalković drove Lieu-tenant Nikolić and Captain Golubović to Belgrade. They took new photos and brought their citizenship certificates to collect their passports. So, two men from our unit were going to Russia. Dani told me nothing about that. The deputy commander of the police in Pećinci, Kovačević, had organised a passport photo session in Pazova for them. Bora said six anti-radar mis-siles had been found around us so far. They shot at us, but we had perfectly timed switching off our radars. We did a good job. This was my idea and our combat tactic since we had downed the F-117A fighter. It has been working well for us.

I had a meeting with the commander of the SA-7 missile battery. We iden-tified the following problems:

-   Soldiers going home without authorization,

-   Changing positions - arbitrary choice,

-   Lack of military ID card - private Dragan Branković,

-   Lack of phosphor for marking night sights[187],

-   Need to get "Bronal" eye drops for private Igor Stojisavljević.

At about 12:00 we received a signal to move. We are heading back to the Ogar village area. The setup was the same: the same combat position and arrangement of the combat equipment. Dani went to the front of the column, and I stayed at the rear end. We had implemented this routine many times so far. SA-7 "Strela" battery remained to secure the combat position. The vehi-cles began moving very quickly, in just an hour and a half they transitioned into the marching configuration. No one picked up the corner reflectors. I sent Boris Stomenov and some soldiers to dismantle them and load them into the Kraz truck. They loaded ten poles and twelve reflectors. Someone fucked up and didn't load two of the poles. I called Armuš to load the logs. Along the way I hooked a trailer with spare parts. Unless you order them, no one would do anything on their own initiative. I am still convinced that we have to know exactly who is doing what, name by name, task by task, as it does not work otherwise. It is more like circus than the combat battalion. Soldiers Hadžibabić and Jeremić did not take part in the preparation for the march, because Stomenov sent them to the village to buy a spoon, fork and knife. Weird... two guys for three small items. Should I laugh?...

Bora, Dani and I got pissed-off during the transition to the marching con-

187   The night sights gradually dim over time, as the tritium has a half-life of 12 years. The electrons emitted by the radioactive decay of the tritium cause phosphor to glow, thus providing a long-lasting (several years) and non-battery-powered fire-arms sight that is visible in dim lighting conditions.

figuration when we saw a Honda Civic with the Smederevo license plate. Inside the car were a disabled driver and two other men who did not have any documents. I took the driver's car keys, driver license and passport. I gave it all to Bora, our security officer, who had just arrived to see what it was all about.

The Ural truck could not pull it, so the Kraz crane truck towed it. Dušan Milojković came and brought a repaired stand for the radar emission imitator. The imitator was on the TAM 110 truck. I decided to hurry up and catch it upon the by-pass road in Subotište to test the repaired stand for correct operation. I asked Dušan if the Lola Institute could give us a computer for the needs of Sedlak and Vakanjac, the latter of which worked at the Faculty of Mining and Geology. Dani knew we needed the computer to do the mail, but he took it home. What a great commander, one who does not give a shit about his unit.

I told Roksandić that Senior Sergeant Jaćić, who was the least engaged in transitioning the launch ramps, was now solely responsible for mounting and dismounting the corner reflectors. By 21:00 the combat equipment was secured and transitioned into the combat configuration. I'm not going back to Deč because all my gear is with me. We slept in a nursery in Ogar. Dani, Bora and Dotlić were with me.

Monday, April 26

I spoke with Danka. She told me she spoke with Ljuba, my neighbour from Vrdnik. They cut the lawn and fixed the fence around my house. There is nobody to take the flowers from the cellar. She called my sister's godfather and god mother, Suzana and Dule, to ask them to water the flowers in the lobby. Ljuba is reluctant and cranky. Her phone bill is somewhere around 52-53 dinars. It seems that Ljuba has no money to pay the bill. The phone has not been paid. After my mother died, September 1998, I had to pay to get my phone line back, like I never had it in my house. "Reintroducing the line, so that someone else doesn't get a number". Sadness and misery - that the way of the telecom business operates and prey on people. I don't have time to go and visit the house.

Crnobrnja should go to Smederevo to organize arrival of Lieutenant Colonel Noskov's battalion. Dani went home about 08.00. He came very late. I told Crnobrnja that Armuš is checking the position after every transfer. Maybe he found assault rifle No. 131171 which may be left by the soldier during the transfer. We should test him on the way that we intentionally leave one rifle at the position. Last time he brought two posts and corner reflectors that we forgot at the position. This "forgetting the equipment" is very upsetting so I told Major Roksandić to task Jaćić and few other men for putting in and dismantling corner reflectors.

The intervention group is formed. Group commander is Tepavac and Aleksić is the deputy. The group consists of 16 men... one section. We started with the training. I decided to arm them with two snipers, two shoulder antitank launchers, two machineguns, one SA-7 "Strela" MANPAD, one "scorpion" automatic pistol and two hand grenades for each man. Beside this, everybody got an assault rifle. They are based in Ogar, in the community building. Horsić and other drivers are based on the community farm. They will sleep there and also guard the vehicles and fuel.

Varga is looking how to get home for a leave. He found out that the road is blocked. I gave him a permit to go home. There is only one bus to Novi Sad and the departure time is mostly unknown. He is not happy with that. He hasn't seen his son since the beginning of the war.

My neighbors, Djordje and Zora together with their son Aca, from Pećinci, searched for me and invited me for a coffee at their place. Zora made a pie and cookies. During the blackout, there is no phone lines in the village. That was the reason why Stojanović and I went to find Pošarac in Obrež so he can show us how to reconnect the phones in the phone communication building so we can have a stabile connection during the blackouts. The key of the post office is with my school friend Goca. I looked at the working conditions in the post office where my friend need to earn her pension…Sad environment.

Mika Stojanović, signal platoon commander, wants to speak with Dani to not put him into the shift. He s opinion is that in the shift shall be missileers and he is signals specialist.

Even Žika invited me but I can't go because I'm exhausted. Dani brought cookies from home. They are very tasty. Aca, Dani's driver, told me that the Askona (the car) is like a warehouse. I believe him. Later I went to see Captain Cvetić and his battery. They are trying to work on unimportant things but can't fix the most elementary one. They got two new guys and basically whatever they asked for.

Aca, accordion player and Cvetić's driver, told me: "You are very competent. The people adore you."

Soldiers from the infantry platoon which are not on duty will guard the Captain Tomović camp. That will be their only task.

Lončar stayed the last night on the radar imitator. The commander didn't provide any replacement for him. I have to check why.

Tuesday, April 27

It is a public holiday today, Statehood Day, and I will go home later on. First, need to finish some work in Deč to ensure the weapon systems are complete and to process the mail. After that I have to go to Jakovo to meet with Colonel Milenković and Liutenant Colonel Mileusnić, and to pick up my civilian clothes.

My task in Deč was finished around 13:00 and left for Belgrade. Danka was upset and I told her that I would come and fix the problems. She didn't even have a single bank cheque. My daily allowances were not coming. Fifteen days ago, I received my 300 dinars field allowance advance for the whole month. I left her two hundred. I decided to look for Mileusnić and Milenković on my way back as I have to pass through Jakovo anyway. They targeted the Ušće Business Center again last night. My apartment is close by. The tenants moved out; I should inspect it and authorize Danka to use my bank account, including drawing cheques.

Just when I arrived, a family friend Maksa from Novi Grad, formerly from Bosanski Novi, arrived too. He brought me a box of Winston brand cigarettes, saying, "You are my brother. I know what is needed in a war." Danka was crying. Until recently there was no one in the house and suddenly two of us were there. I was calming her down.

Business center Ušće targeted again. The author's apartment is in the building just behind.

Along the way to my apartment a public transport bus broke down between the petrol station and sawmill on Ledine. A mass of people was walking in two columns: one towards the sawmill, another back to the Surčin village. A man and woman were looking to hitchhike with me. As always, I stopped. I drove them to Tošin Bunar. A woman looked at the cigarettes and asked me, "Where did you get them?" I replied, "A friend from Republika Srpska just brought them to me". There was a shortage of cigarettes in the city and they were unable to buy any. I gave her two packs. She wanted to pay. I refused. Through our conversation, I found out that she worked at the Medical Center near the Mercator Shopping Center. I asked her to see

167

if there were any "Dilkoran" medications in her pharmacy; for Nada and Milan. They had Angina Pectoris, but they had no medications. She mentioned that she lived in Jakovo. Oh my God, how the war drew people closer together to simply make a contact and help each other.

The war was raging, and times were bad.

We finished very quick authorization in the Post Office Savings Bank. Danka deposited her signature and got authorization for the cheques. I got six cheques and gave them all to Danka. My account balance was 300 dinars. There was no other customer and they locked the doors of the bank as we were leaving.

On the way back we dropped to my apartment. The windows and doors were open. The shock wave from the explosion did not break anything. "We have to buy aluminum foil," Danka said, "in case they accidentally shatter." She reminded me a lot of myself, she thinks through everything in great detail. This is very useful now. There were many things in my head and items on my "to do" list. The most important thing was to stay alive. Everything else comes second.

We went home to Danka's apartment. I had a shower and then we had lunch. She is so much more beautiful than any other women I've had eyes upon. I was getting ready. It was time to go. Nataša and Danka farewelled me to the car. Nataša went her own way and Danka went back home. The neighbours will come soon, and she won't be alone. The children were going their own way. They are selfish; I had reinforced that for God knows how much time. A colleague from work got petrol for Danka. She told me that one of her female colleagues at work had an abortion yesterday; the baby was conceived with someone out of marriage. Her husband was in the army. Somewhere in the mud of Srem under the shadow of stars he was farewelling the discharges of cannons and firing bursts of Bofors. It was a sad thought and realisation. Oh my God, how cute are the girls. Where does their loveliness disappear when they become women?

I dropped by Jakovo pharmacy to pick up the medications. The cleaner had not bought them. The pharmacy had "Dilakor" medication. Maybe she did not have money? One box cost 25 dinars. I gave her 100 for four boxes. I have to work out how to get back my money from her. Most likely I will talk to Mićo Mijalković.

It was not easy to find Lieutenant Colonel Mileusnić. Jakovo was full of troops and it was buzzing everywhere, from the Command to the Operations Headquarters and even the Communications Center. Everything seemed to be more important than missiles and airplanes. Their "Giraffe" radar position was bombed. They had vacated it on time and there were no casualties.

I requested "Osa"[188] and "Zolja"[189], "Šilo"[190], M-57 handguns and training ammunition. Milenković replied to me that he had to seek approval from higher command at the Department of the Army. I realised that I would return empty-handed. Those 'up' in the Army command chain will be considering my request completely ignorant of what was going on in the field. While we had coffee. I told them, "Those up the chain of command are crooks who were doing nothing. They failed to close[191] the corridor of the Sava River and formed the field command post instead. Bullshit." The reservists were watching me. "Those wearing blue berets[192] are really tough guys," said one older major from the reserve.

At about 22:00 I left for Ogar. Two soldiers hailed me near the farm. I stopped to pick up the hitchhikers. One was silent and got off in the center of Bečmen. The other got off after Petrovčić and went straight to his combat position. He carried a rifle with him. He had some alcohol but was not drunk. His father had cancer and sister just gave birth. Radovan is his name. He fought in Bosnia for four years and was a true warrior. The military police stopped him in the city when he was carrying his rifle. He told them, "Get out of my face!"

He offered me a cigarette. I did not refuse. Fuck, I hadn't smoked my Drina cigarettes yet. He wanted to take me to his Pragas or his Bofors and show me parts of the downed cruise missile. "A souvenir," he said. I replied, "The Lieutenant Colonel will give you a real souvenir." I gave him a piece

---

188   The M79 Osa (wasp) is a Yugoslav-made portable 90mm anti-tank weapon made of fibre-reinforced plastics. It is an improvement of the French portable anti-tank launcher 89 mm LRAC F1. It consists of the launcher, a CN-6 sighting piece, rocket and carrying case for the rocket. The M79 shoots unguided projectiles in direct sight and is effective against armored fighting vehicles and fortifications. The M79 Osa was designed and manufactured in Serbia by Sloboda Čačak.

189   The M80 Zolja (other name for the wasp) is a Yugoslav-made portable one-shot disposable 64 mm unguided anti-tank rocket-propelled grenade, designed and manufactured in Serbia by Sloboda Čačak. Constructed from fibre-reinforced plastics, the M80 Zolja is designed to be used by an individual against armored fighting vehicles or fortifications. The M80 Zolja is similar to the American M72 LAW in both appearance and performance. Its two models 9K310 Igla-1 with its 9M313 missile (NATO reporting name *SA-16 Gimlet*) and 9K38 Igla with its 9M39 missile (NATO reporting name *SA-18 Grouse*) were manufactured in Serbia by Krušik Valjevo under the licensee.

190   Šilo is the jargon name for Iglas (gimlet) because these missiles roll in flight (900 – 1200 rpm). An improved lethality on target achieved by a clever combination of the terminal maneuver to hit and corkscrew into the fuselage rather than jet nozzle, and then explode inside by setting off the additional charge and any remaining rocket fuel.

191   To close the corridor by setting up Army air-defense artillery positions along the banks of the Sava River, so no cruise missiles, neither helicopters nor airplanes flying below 5,000 meters could use it.

192   The Air Force and Air Defense wore blue uniforms in the peacetime and blue berets. They were responsible for targets flying above 5,000 meters.

of F-117A. He loved me like a brother. "Mate, I wish and hope you live for a hundred years. Come with me, let's have some brandy and coffee together. "I refused because I was in a hurry. He hugged me as if we are brothers.

I felt an instant rapport with him and wondered why. Was that because we lived in the same conditions or because the night was our ally? Or because we are waging war and our adversaries are on the same mission? The poor people had always been waging wars. I remembered Book about Milutin[193]. I felt it was very easy to gain people's trust these days. We should share stories together, both good and bad. A person should be energetic, solve problems simply and quickly, and without philosophizing. People would love you and appreciate you more. My high school pal Srbe told me once that I had fucked up when I went to the Military Academy. He told me, "You have excellent communication skills. You would be very successful in a civilian career."

I arrived at camp driving most of the way without lights. The road was through the anti-aircraft artillery combat position and I did not want to un-mask them. As the drive was slower, I arrived late. Dani will be in the shift until 00:00. After that Dotlić will replace him as I had been relieved from my shift duty and was instead assigned to mobilize and train the new sub-unit until they become fully operational and functioning flawlessly.

I tried to fall asleep, but couldn't, so got up. Dani returned from his shift and was having a beer. We talked until 02:00. He is a great jokester; tech-nical knowledge was not his strongest skill, but he was very cunning. This personality feature is perfectly suited to our situation.

I told him that I got an extension cord, soldering paste, insulating tape and a tin wire for Muminović and the van. He laughed like crazy. He said he liked that we worked outside of the box and that we were managing the situations very quickly. Seem that I caught a little cold because I kept going to the toilet frequently. It happens to me every time I have a bath. As if my body had become dependent on dirt and uniform to function flawlessly.

Wednesday, April 28

Kosta woke me at 07:20. He made me a double, medium strong coffee. It was drizzling outside. Fog had descended on the area. I enjoyed the coffee and smoking cheap cigarettes… What a life? Today I supposed to go to the Nikinci shooting range and arrange the shooting exercise or the guys. After breakfast I hit the road.

The hand grenades for Tepavac arrived. Once a SA-7 "Strela" MANPAD come, the rapid response unit will be completely armed. The fuses are with Captain Cvetić. The combat training had already begun. I forbade them con-suming any alcohol. The meeting with the unit was brief. I saw that they had

---

193   *Book about Milutin* is a novel about Milutin, Serbian peasant and former soldier who tell his story from jail after World War II. He talks to an imaginary lis-tener about tragic fate of Serbian people, his family and Serbia. Written by Danko Popović.

taken their roles seriously. I brought key details to their attention. It wasn't easy to concentrate in order to come up with ideas and arrange them to be more detailed and cohesive, so these could be succinctly presented in a logical sequence. I would challenge anyone who says that solo brainstorming work is not difficult.

For some time I have been feeling pain on the sides of my heels but have no idea what caused it, the sweat in the boots or, perhaps, the walking. I had not been walking much, neither too far nor for too long.

Later I called Danka on my mobile phone. I wished she was a "queen." She deserved to be one, because her life, like mine, was difficult. She's a really good friend.

Nikinci is kind of a shithole of a village. I thought of my aunt Anica from Vrdnik. She regularly goes to Nikinci. Her sister lives here.

People say Colonel Nikolić is a good man. Maybe, but when he's sober. I have nothing to talk about with him, simply we are on completely different wavelengths. I made arrangements with his aid, Lieutenant Colonel Filipović.

"The First Army Command banned all combat actions today" Lieutenant Colonel Filipović said. "They must be afraid of bombing," I thought to myself. "Come tomorrow, we'll arrange something," Filipović comforted me, "I'll show you the place where you can finish everything." We shook our hands and hugged each other as old friends. It felt kind of weird because that was the first time I had ever seen him. They all wore civilian clothes. Their HQ was located in the dirty motel in the center of the village. I went back along the same route, through the village of Brestač.

Along the way, I stopped in the village of Tovarnik to visit Cvetić. The locals had brought them a roasted pig. We had lunch together. There was fresh spring onion in every plate. It was delicious.

After the lunch I went to Ogar. Žika was waiting for me to take me to his house for a coffee. He told me that in a day or two seasonal workers will be coming and that there are some beautiful gypsy girls among them. He begged me to order the troops to stay away from them and avoid creating a potential mess.

Some of the soldiers based in Kupinovo went into the shop and took the cigarette boxes without paying. The same happened in the pub, drinking without paying. Bastards! Those soldiers were not from my unit, but still they were from our armed forces. Those guys are just pricks who are abusing the situation.

I tried to convince Žika not to worry and that everything will be sorted out. He replied that my unit was ok and that he had never had any problems or issues with my men. I looked so dirty that he offered me to use his shower. I politely refused. I showered last night. Having a shower every day is an unsustainable luxury during the war. We somehow adapted to the inevitable circumstances and adopted belief that the body has to get used to the sweat and dirt for most of the time during this war. The worst is when I get a rash. It hurts. I can't use a soothing cream because it would make my uniform greasy and there are plenty of other odours in the guidance station anyway. Extra ventilation would help.

Žika's wife made us a snack – ham and boiled eggs. I took few bites but couldn't take anymore. I was simply not hungry. Even if I were hungry, it would be the same, as I was so sleepy. I took an hour-long nap then went back to Deč to pick up some reservists and the battalion mail.

On the way there, I briefly saw Milan and Nada. They were working in their garden. I told them that Maksa, Nataša and Danka may visit them tomorrow. I left them 500 dinars out of 700 dinars I had received in lieu of my per diem allowance, to give to Danka; if she didn't come, then they can courier it via their neighbor who will go to Belgrade in a few days. I also brought them two months worth of medications, with more to come from that lady from Jakovo. This made me at peace with my conscience, for at least this item is off on my to do list.

I had a meeting with the unit commanders in Deč. I stressed that they have to keep their men under control. After that I had a conversation with Hadžibabić, he was still refusing to do the haircut. He may be punished by the court-martial. The procedure is simple and straightforward. Anyway, it is up to him. Maybe he was just sick of all this military crap. After that me and Slavko went through the battalion mail.

Thursday, April 29

This night I was in the camp. Just after midnight we heard aeroplanes passing by and went out. The sound was coming from Deč direction. The anti-aircraft artillery fire was coming from all directions and tracer ammunition was lighting up the night like fireworks. We could not see the aeroplanes, but we could hear them very well. Despite looking vigilantly, we couldn't see even the dimmest trace of their exhaust flames. They were probably flying very low, below our horizon line. Dani was with my men in the shift in Ogar. "One seems to be circling above Deč and then heading towards Belgrade," Barvalac said. We heard the sound of aeroplanes for about three hours, until 03:00. I went back inside and recorded it in my diary. This attack will also pass.

Yesterday they beat Priština by day. They became bolder. Also, yesterday, Bulatović fired Vuk Drašković after his controversial media conference.

We again heard the artillery fire, this time coming from the direction of the quarry. "Keep firing guys," I said to myself.

On this moonless night, with caprice and audacity, perverts in the town preyed on the soldier's wife to lust after her. I would send them into this ocean of darkness to feel the pounding of their hearts, and to once and for all to erase from their mind the idea to go after the soldiers' wives and girlfriends. It makes me sick when the perve relished in his triumph. It hurts so many souls, children, and families; it increases suffering during this misfortunate time, for what? Where did those cute little girls with innocent looks and fond eyes go? It looked like they grew up in someone else's bed. Fraud. Adultery... What was she thinking? What she wanted from the first encounter? Was that curiosity, desire, lust, or whim? Was she trying to be romantic, saucy, steamy, or was she not sure of herself? How did it evolve? Why she did not put a stop to the cheating? As they kissed, did she find herself carried away by a fantasy of such pure ego that she couldn't admit to herself what she was doing? How did she feel after, both physically and mentally?

We heard the airplanes again and the night was instantly lit by straight beams of light tracer bullets that looked straight out of Star Wars. They were shooting towards the sound. At one point I saw a plane. I showed it to Barvalac. At that instant in time the air defense artillery guns, "Pragas" and "Boffors," triangulated it. I enjoyed seeing the plane sharply climbing up, making 180 degrees turn and running away. After about ten minutes there was a flash of light on the sky on the north. I saw the exact moment the missile was launched from the plane. I couldn't identify what was that plane. After that the fighting was brought to a stop.

Did our battery fire tonight? Dani called me around 07:00. He told me that they had fired tonight and said, "We'll talk when we see each other". I thought, "My shift had fired again, except I wasn't with them this time. Fuck it!... I was forced to do this job. If I hadn't, I would have been with them tonight." I expected that we would relocate today. Did they hit it? I turned on the TV. They didn't say anything about the downed plane. I started to doubt it. The Chief of General Staff, General Ojdanić, gave an interview the day before yesterday. So far, 46 planes, 182 cruise missiles, 6 helicopters and 8 drones had been hit. The enemy also suffered losses in manpower. I ordered Barvalac to wake up the soldiers. They should have breakfast, get ready and wait for the bus. Tepavac called me. He asked, "Will we go shooting today? It appears that ours fired last night."

Yesterday, Milutinović and Rugova met in Priština.

Around 09.00 I arrived in Ogar.

The truth is that our guys did shoot. We had a target. We found it very quickly, within two seconds. Parameter[194] 6 km, altitude 6 km. We launched. The target was two kilometres away, approximately 1.5–2 seconds before <u>the encounter,</u> the jamming[195, 196], about a finger thick[197], appeared on the

194   Parameter–is the distance between the radar station and the horizontal projection of the course of the target. Once the target is acquired the fire control computer automatically calculates the parameter of the target, as part of the assessment if it is possible to shoot down the target.

195   Radar jamming and deception – is deliberate tampering with electromagnetic waves intended to interfere with the operation of a radar, including to "blind" the air-defense radar by saturating its receiver with noise, multiple reflections or false information. The ultimate objective is to prevent radar operators from identifying the location of the real target.

196   Radar sweep arc – The side boundaries of the radar screens F-1 and F-2 are boundaries of the 15 degrees wide sweep arcs for target and missile beacon transponder tracking via UV11 F1 and F2 receive antennas.

197   A finger thick jamming– (in this case) indicates that a relatively "narrow"

marker cross and three missile baits were seen in the front hemisphere,[198,199] two to the right and one to the left. That was observed on the screen of the missile guidance officer.

The aircraft, concealed by the jamming, suddenly changed its course by turning 90 degrees upward[200].It avoided the missile, which passed through the radar's crosshairs and went onto self-destruct. Congratulations to the pilot. Either he couldn't eject, or he was so skilled that he had enough nerves and patience to stay alive in the only possible way. This guy was a pro, no doubts. Any moment before or after would've meant certain death. He may have been guided by AWACS[201] or he may have been a member of the SEAD[202] Group. SEAD, comprised of 28 aircraft, was specially formed for this war after we shot down their F-117. Their sole task was to destroy us.

The manual tracking operator on F-1 reported that, "I cannot see the target, I have strong jamming in the front hemisphere of my screen, so any tracking was impossible." The manual tracking operator on F-2 did not report jamming. This meant that, due to the width of jamming in the horizontal plane, the manual tracking operator on F-1 was very "close" to the target, whereas the manual tracking operator on F-2 had not "found" it yet.

We quickly packed our equipment and decided to relocate to a new combat position near the village of Ašanja. However, when we arrived, we found that the Army Corps had already stationed a battery of their SA-6 (Kub) anti-aircraft missile system there. What a chaotic situation; the Brigade and the Army Corps were totally uncoordinated! Why did they send us here at all? On the spot, we decided to go to Bečmen and wait there. Once dark fell, we set up a new combat position near the village of Petrovčić.

Dani found me in Ašanja and told me that he had some good and bad news for me. I chose to hear the bad news first. Dani said, "Your boss has arrived." I did not understand him, "What do you mean 'my boss has arrived'?" Dani replied laughing, "I saw Danka, she went to her parents." I asked, "and what's the good news?" He replied, "Your wife has arrived." That was funny!!!

He also told me that the villagers found some parts either from a bomb or a missile. I went with them to inspect the parts that were around the house of Sreten Tešmanović, in Tovarnik. They showed us parts of the boosters. In Mitar Kostić's wheat field, which was nearby, I found the complete missile

volume of space was jammed, within the radar sweep arc. It probably originated from the target itself since it emanated from the cross of the markers.

198   Front hemisphere – (of the radar screens F-1 and F-2) is the area on the screen located between the intersection of the horizontal and vertical markers and the bottom of the respective screens.

199   Front hemisphere shows the space between the target (traveling towards the missile guidance station van) and the missile guidance station van.

200   Pilots practice maneuvers to avoid missiles; typically to change direction of the flight by a certain angle, usually 90 or 180 degrees. In this particular case the maneuver was in the vertical plane.

201   AWACS – Airborne Warning and Control System.

202   SEAD – Suppression of Enemy Air Defense.

booster. It was dug in at a depth of about half a meter. I told Žika he didn't need to secure it, as there was nothing dangerous in the empty booster shell. He informed his boss. Soldier Kosta accompanied me. We were invited to Tešmanović's house for a coffee. We drank it quickly.

SNR-125 radar components packed and ready for the move.

We will start transitioning the equipment at around 17:00. Until then, I had enough time to go to Karlovčić. Kosta was with me. Danka arrived in Karlovčić with Maksa from Novi Grad. They came in his Ford company car. He wanted to see her parents. We had a coffee and lunch afterwards. The neighbor Sava joined us. He was a little drunk and kept rumbling on. No one else could speak. Maksa went to lay down. As per the old custom, Milan washed the windscreens of both of our cars. I felt like sleeping too, but my time was up. Kosta and I left without saying goodbye to Maksa. Sava said that someone from the Agricultural Cooperative shot down the F-117A, and that they found an "Igla" warhead in the aircraft's engine. Nonsense, "Igla" cannot reach an altitude of 8.5 km where the plane was hit! I chose not to argue with him, so I briefly stated, "There is a lot of talk..."

We left for Petrovčić. Around 17:00 we commenced transition of the battery into combat configuration. Upon arrival at the camp we found a group from the military establishment "Dedinje". They said they had been sent by the Headquarters Joint Operational Command. They brought a roast pig and cookies. When I showed up, Dani introduced me politely. There were a husband and wife among them, who brought medications worth DEM 10,000 from Germany. The man told me what the mood was of our people in Germany and the West. The media campaign was relentless. They were proud of us for being so brave and holding on.

Around 20:00, Dani called me to come to the combat position. Armuš had requested fuel for the relocation. I went there. I said to Armuš that it was not okay from him to charge us for the corner reflectors' tubes. "Why didn't you tell us upfront how much it would cost? We would have worked out how best to proceed then. We would have found a sponsor, had we needed one, instead of paying you now for your work in fuel. That fuel is crucial for our work and our lives!" This time he was not modest at all, I had the feeling that he was stockpiling the fuel. Who knows how much fuel his truck consumes? Him and his mate bowed their heads.

Dani left the position sometime around 20:15, saying that he would return by 21:00. The camouflage and protection set up was nearing completion. Around 20:20 General Grujin called and left a message for Dani to call him back. I passed the message to Dani when he returned around 21:00, and then went to rest. The setup was complete by 21:30, including the log protection. In contrast to quickly transitioning the equipment into the combat configuration, arranging the logs around the equipment was time consuming. Dani asked me, "How much more time do you need to make the group combat ready." I replied, "We need to do firing exercises from personal armament and hand grenades. I had hoped to do it today, but I haven't heard anything from the Nikinci firing range. The group works in harmony, like a fine-tuned violin." "Okay," Dani replied shortly.

I went to bed around 23:00. Dotlić, Bora and I slept at the school. Dotlić will replace me in the shift at 00.00 tonight.

Last night, while ours were launching, they were also shot at. They turned off just in time, and this, for now, had been saving our lives.

Friday, April 30

Bora woke me up around 03:00, telling me that our boys had just launched two missiles. He saw something engulfed in flames falling from the sky. I jumped and we both went out in front of the school. As soon as we got out, we heard a whistling noise above our heads, followed by a terrible explosion in the direction of the battalion position. We thought of our men who were there. We quickly got into the car and drove towards the explosion.

Just before the road curves right in Petrovčić, we came across a gruesome scene in front of a house: a concrete power pole had snapped in two, as if someone had moved its top half next to where it was before. It was leaning on one side, touching the ground, its top held in the air by the overhead power lines. The road was scattered with debris from the roof, plaster, grass, and dirt. People started to gather around. A lot of broken glass everywhere. The plane shot at us with the anti-radar missile "HARM". The missile went after the bait - the radar imitator. The entrance gate from one of the houses was blown away and fell onto the porch. Fortunately, no one was on the street when the warhead exploded. There were some light injuries from the broken glass. There were no shrapnel injuries. This was the ninth time they had targeted us.

I went straight towards the combat position. From the base of the rapid intervention group, located at its perimeter, I called Dotlić who was with his shift in the missile guidance station van. I asked him if he needed help, and if he wanted me to come. "No need for it," he answered. He was on the call, reporting on the combat work to the brigade HQ. They asked him about the result of the shooting. Crnobrnja said it was a hit. The spotters on the SA-7 (Strela 2M) and Tepavac saw the shooting; the first missile exploded in the vicinity of the target, and they saw thick black smoke and a plane leaving[203,204,205,206].

Our battalion doctor was also involved in providing first aid to the injured. The ambulance came from Surčin.

I was surprised that the brigade command had not yet issued an order for immediate relocation to a new combat position. It was the middle of the night and we could have relocated before the daylight.

I created a list of injured men and one woman and gave it to Bora. He himself, as usual, did not take any notes about what had happened.

I went to sleep at 05:00, two hours after the HARM exploded and slept until 07:00. The morning TV news reported about an earthquake that shook the city of Valjevo at about 06:00. I didn't feel it, I was so exhausted.

We started relocation at 08:00. Our next staging position is in Mihaljevci

---

203   The latest confirmation that another stealth F-117 plane was hit on 30 April 1999 was published on 1 December 2020, on The-War-Zone page of the popular Thedrive.com website by Thomas Nedwick, *Yes, Serbian Air Defenses Did Hit Another F-117 During Operation Allied Force In 1999*.
The article referred to (the latest at the time, 24 November 2020) The Afterburn podcast, in which "*retired Air Force Lieutenant Colonel Charlie "Tuna" Hainline, a former F-117 pilot, confirms what had, for many years, been a rumour: that a second stealth jet was hit by the Serbians, but managed to return to base.*" Note that Thedrive.com concluded that the incident occurred on 30 April 1999, though pilot did not mention the exact date explaining the event was still classified.
(See   https://www.thedrive.com/the-war-zone/37894/yes-serbian-air-defenses-did-hit-another-f-117-during-operation-allied-force-in-1999?s=08)
204   There are, at least, two other independent confirmations that another stealth F-117 plane was hit, without specifying the date.
205   The first was published on 31 December 2001 by Benjamin S. Lambeth, NATO's Air War for Kosovo: A Strategic and Operational Assessment. Santa Monica, CA: RAND Corporation, 2001, page 108, 3rd par., 2nd last sentence; "*…another F-117 sustained light damage from a nearby SA-3 detonation…*".
(See https://www.rand.org/pubs/monograph_reports/MR1365.html)
206   The second was published on 8 March 2005 by Everest E. Riccioni, Col. USAF Ret., Description of our Failing Defense Acquisition System as Exemplified by the History, Nature and Analysis of the USAF F-22 RAPTOR PROGRAM a National Tragedy — Military and Economic, page 10, footnote 18; "*Of the three aircraft shot down during our incursion into Serbia, ... two were the most stealthy F-117 Night Hawks, one of which staggered back to its home base never to fly again, so it is seldom counted…*".
(See http://www.pogoarchives.org/m/dp/dp-fa22-Riccioni-03082005.pdf)

and we will return later to the new combat position in the area of the village of Karlovčić. I had realized a while ago that if we put our vehicles on multiple staging locations and have a firm schedule of taking up the new combat position, everybody knew when it was their time to arrive there.

We left the signals platoon in Karlovčić, two "Strela-2M" sections, medics and Varga with his logistics, as well as the radar imitator. A bit later Sergeant Petrović arrived with his ZIL truck loaded with two new missiles. The rest of the battalion including Dani left for Mihaljevci. On my way there, I briefly went to Deč to find Slavko to hand him the battalion's mail for the brigade, to tell him to find Armuš to move the logs, and to determine where to bring lunch for the men.

In Mihaljevci, while we had coffee, we got news that one airplane crashed somewhere between Bečmen and Petrovčić. Tepavac and I decided to go there to check. One Major from the army air-defence units, equipped with 2 x 37 mm "Praga" cannons located at the community farm at the outskirt of Bečmen, told us that nothing had fallen in this area. Since a few days ago, his unit was also securing the area around an unexploded airplane bomb that had fallen at the outskirt of Petrovčić towards Bečmen. We decided to go back. The information about the crash was false. On our way back we dropped by Milan and Nada's place for a coffee. They also made us a nice snack – two fried eggs each with freshly picked spring onions and garlic shoots.

At 14:00, we left. I had to check whether or not the group that I had ordered to check the new combat position near the village of Karlovčić completed their assignment. The boys had done their work very well. I personally inspected the radar imitator, and after that went to the school building to try to catch some sleep.

At 16:00 someone woke me up because General Karanović with two colonels and one lieutenant lolonel just arrived. I got ready and went to the general. I knew one of the colonels, Vita Andjelković, but I didn't know the other two. They asked me about my experiences, "How many times have you launched?"

I started with the latest launch, "Last night we caught an airplane at a 7 km altitude, acquired the radar tracking in 2 seconds, and launched 2 missiles. The first one exploded in the vicinity of the target and the second one just passed through the center, it missed and after a few seconds the missile fuse activated self destruction."

Then, I told them about the launch in Ogar, when the first missile was launched at such a high angle that the blast threw the soil around. The blast made a one metre deep crater that was about two and a half to three metres in diameter. The blast disconnected all cables and connectors, so the second missile didn't even blast from the ramp. The soil was very soft.

We then went to the combat position, where the radar installation was nearing completion. General Karanović told us that Mijović's battalion was hit by the bomb. It was most likely located earlier on. "Be careful with that," he told us. I gave them some part of the F-117 and they were overjoyed.

I used this opportunity to talk to the general about the mistake that not all crew were awarded, just two individuals. "I had no idea about that and all that came through via some other channels," he told me. "You were the first ones who should have been be awarded, before anyone else," he continued.

The General also wanted to see our staging area in Mihaljevci. Vita went with me, and the rest followed in their Mitsubishi car. Dani and the other guys were already there. We spoke about our experiences, the way in which NATO had been executing their attacks, and how we had been protecting ourselves. From our conversation, I could also see that they were not happy about how the upper brass and the high command had been performing.

"NATO made a "show" last night in Belgrade," the General told us, "they targeted General Staff HQ, Foreign Ministry, Kalenić green marketplace and a few other places."

They left at 17:00, and we continued to assemble our equipment. The ZIL truck overheated and Sub Lieutenant. Janković didn't know how to bring the trailer van into its designated position. The clutch was most likely broken. Stominenov called via his dedicated line. I informed Dani about the problem at 20:05. The problem of setting up the fire control radar was a big one. We had been at this position before and the terrain was not very good. The soil was porous, pretty wet and subject to flooding. The officers hammered the pikes in more than 30 cm deep. Whenever we finished and tried to place the radar, its pads started to sink. We couldn't put in its designated location (where it was located before) and the cable[207] was too short to try to relocate the radar anywhere else.

At 19:45 the first truck with logs arrived. Armuš was still not here. I called Stana, Armuš's wife. He was still at home.

The mosquitos were a great nuisance. There were thousands of them. Swarms of mosquitos. You couldn't even open your eyes because of them.

The hole[208,209,210,211] where the communication cable ran through between

207   The cable – (Military: RPK kabl) is a special high-speed communication cable between the missile guidance station van and fire control radar. Its length is about 12.5 m. There is a cable connection box on a side of the van and radar. The fixed length of the cable and height of the connection boxes effectively limited the maximum distance between the van and radar to about 10 m.

208   The hole – is an opening of the sewerage pipe used as a duct to run the cable through, the two ends of which were plugged into the connection boxes in the missile guidance station van and fire control radar.

209   The sewerage pipe was laid into the embankment.

210   The embankment – is the artificial elevation of earth shaped as a dam or barrier. Of concern is the embankment erected between the missile guidance station van and the fire control radar. It had a defensive purpose, to protect the van and its crew from nearby explosions targeting the fire control radar and shrapnel they release.

211   The embankment was 4 m high and about 8 meters wide at its bottom, constructed from natural materials excavated or obtained nearby and located over soft ground. It was designed in such a way that stability of the embankment was maintained during construction and its immediate aftermath.

the van and the radar was filled in[212,213] now. "We learnt the lesson to never go back to a previously used position the hard way[214,215,216]," I told Dani. He told me that the general and his team wanted to return and see the position. Well, they could wish for whatever they want, but the position was not ready yet. Anyway, let them come and see our misery.

On my way to the position, I met Milan and some of his cousins. They were looking to buy a house. Six thousand Deutch Marks, with eight acres of land. Our heads were at stake and they were looking to buy a property. Well, everybody had their own worries and concerns. They were refugees[217].

Kosta was sitting in the front seat beside me, hunting mosquitoes in the car.

Warrant Officer Žugić wanted to go and tow away the ZIL truck. "Stay here until we fully secure and protect the equipment. Send our mechanic Golub, nicknamed Binke, to tow it and try to fix the problem," I told him. He was angry. In fact, he was looking for an excuse to leave the combat position. "It appears that everyone wants to do whatever they want when I'm not here. WTF!" I said to myself.

There will be a huge storm tonight. The black thunderclouds piled up and brought rain. The lightning weather front was quickly approaching, making the resounding noise of thunder increasingly louder and more explosive. My vest and jacket were completely wet. Kosta and I arrived at the camp under bucketing rain.

Around 21:15 Colonel Dubajić arrived at our position.

The transfer belt for reloading the missiles was located in Dobanovci.

---

212   Due to the intrinsic short-term use of the combat position, the long-term settlement of the embankment was not considered essential for its design, so its outer walls were not compacted.

213   Consequently, and in part due to heavy rains, the embankment landslide occurred sometime after the battalion had previously left the combat position on 25 April 1999, which buried the pipe duct.

214   It was very difficult to find the buried 'hole' (an endpoint of the sewerage pipe) in the 10-12m long leg of the embankment, nearly as hard as finding a needle in the haystack.

215   There was no choice but to find the buried hole in order to run the cable through the sewerage pipe duct as it was not possible to lay the cable over the embankment due to its short length.

The power and other communication cables were easily laid over the embankment, as they were 30 m long.

216   There was an unwritten rule not to return to the combat position after you left it. Yet during the 78 days of war, the Brigade Command ordered the 3rd Battalion four times to return to the same combat position they had previously departed from, which was, in the Author's opinion, utterly senseless, ignorant and incompetent decisions bordering lunacy.

217   The refugees – were Serbian refugees from Croatia, from the Banija region; expelled by Croatians earlier and unable to return.

We needed to send two ZIL trucks to bring three missiles. One of our ZIL trucks was parked in Šimanovci and was in good driving condition. Another ZIL truck, with the missile already loaded on the "beam," was parked in Karlovčić, but was not in good working order and could not pull the load[218]. I hope that somehow it would be able to get to Dobanovci. I ordered Major Roksandić, missile battery commander, to send Sergeant Denčev and a driver to bring the missiles.

In our camp, Vita Andjelković, Dani, Bora, Colonel Ivković and one Lieutenant Colonel (I don't know his name), Dani's classmate from the academy, were discussing something when I arrived.

Major Dotlić called from the camp to tell us that general Bane Petrović, Air Defense Corps Chief, had promised "a double rank promotion to anyone who hits and shoots down an airplane tonight."

"Nonsense!" Dani commented. "Fuck the airplane if we lose our heads. We had downed an F-117A and received just a few promotions in return. All shift members have not been promoted yet."

General Karanović told us today how he felt that his work in the Air Force Command was very difficult, because of the perception that they were just a service to the General Staff. That service had been functioning flawlessly in the peacetime, but quite the opposite during the wartime. "I am not surprised," I thought to myself, "because the big brass focuses on getting their "chairs", ranks and privileges during the peacetime."

Lieutenant Colonel Nikola Stanisavljević, from the engineering unit, lost two men today. They were setting up a new combat position near the village of Bogatić when an airplane popped up from somewhere and hit them. He was not sure yet if they were dead, but he looked very upset. In contrast, I thought to myself that I seemed to be indifferent to last night's launch and explosion in Petrovčić that caused wounds, blood and one dead dog. After Smiljanić and Gajić died, who would be next?

General Karanović told me today that Robert Lajčak's mother, who was killed a few days ago, had found him, "She was crying for help, any help. Robert left behind two little girls and she needed something so she could feed them." Her cry for help upset the general. "Well general, who else she can ask for help? Who could the other mothers, sisters and kids of dead soldiers ask for help? You are "the General"! You have the power! Resolve it!" I replied.

It was clear to me that he was sidelined. He just waved his arm, as if he was acknowledging that no one in his power circle cared about him or his opinion, implying that those in the General Staff room did not know what they were doing anyway. It was a fucked-up situation. This certainly raised a big question if the subordinate units knew what was really going on in the upper echelons of command, would they discharge their duties at all.

Last night, the missile guidance battery made the following catastrophic mistakes:

---

218   The truck either lacked power during acceleration or it suddenly failed to reach normal driving speed.

- The combat position was not surveyed properly prior to returning to it; the sequential order of setting up the equipment was not determined; the pipe duct that the PRK cable ran through was not unearthed.

- The holes in the ground made by outriggers[219] of the fire control radar were not leveled after previously leaving the combat position. The radar's position was not leveled[220].

- ZIL saddler truck's[221],[222] clutch burnt[223], so it was not possible to correctly position the missile guidance van in the embankment[224] – Sub- Lieutenant. Janković,

- Maletić reached the position[225],[226] before the wooden log protection was set up blocking the approach for Armuš's truck to access the missile guidance station van[227].

219   Outriggers – are the legs of a crane or similar heavy vehicle, radar in this case, that are extended for mechanical stability when the vehicle is stationed for operational use. The outriggers are comprised of the beam, which is the leg of the outrigger, and the pad, which is the foot. Sometimes, "floats" are placed under the pad to dissipate the force of the crane and the load over concrete, pavement or soil.

220   Clearly, during the previous deployment of the radar at this combat position, the weight of the radar produced sufficient vertical forces on the pads to make holes in the soft soil. These holes were not leveled then, causing problems now: the radar was not aligned, which took time and effort to correct.

221   The ZIL saddler truck – (model: ZIL 157) tows the missile guidance station van (named locally: StVR).
Its adjective "saddler" stems from the word "saddle" or the "fifth-wheel" that describes the type of coupling between the towing truck and the towed vehicle: the front edge of the towed vehicle extends over the rear bumper of the truck.

222   Parking of the missile guidance station van by reversing it into the narrow space of the pi-shaped embankment on the combat position requires good driving skills of the ZIL driver.

223   The role of the missile guidance officer included driving the ZIL truck. Sub-Lieutenant Janković, a young officer at the time with just 1.5 years' service, hadn't had many opportunities to drive the ZIL truck, let alone to practice reverse parking of the guidance van. He had always been erroneously parking the van in a slanted position, never parallel with the two legs of the embankment; without releasing the clutch in the process of multiple attempts, so the clutch eventually burnt out.

224   The missile guidance station van (StVR) weighs about 12 t, so no manual adjustment is possible.

225   The main embankment on the combat position – was a horseshoe shaped embankment, 10-12 m long and 4-5 m wide. It sheltered the missile guidance station van and Maletic's switchboard and transformer van (RKU).

226   Maletić parked his vehicle behind the missile guidance station van before the log protection around the station van was set up. This was a commonsense error, as the arm of the Armuš's crane truck could not reach over the combined length of the station van and Maletić's van.

227   The proper sequence was to: a) park the station van in the embankment; b)

- The radar imitator was left completely unsecured, without a supervisor[228,229,230].

- Žugić and his drivers must drive out all the vehicles, they had brought to the combat position; note the officers and leave the equipment and combat position before all work was finished[231]; As soon as a vehicle delivers the equipment and the equipment is correctly positioned, the vehicle should immediately leave the combat position.

- Sedlak did not contact Armuš on time. He said the phones hadn't been working. I gave him a lot of shit. "Manage it, don't spend all

---

Armuš drives in, puts the log protection around the station van, and then drives out; c) Maletić parks his vehicle behind the station van; d) Armuš drives in, puts the log protection around the Maletić's van, and then leaves the combat position.

228   A soldier or an officer brought the vehicle with the radar imitator to the combat position and then left it unattended there, because he had to go back to his base unit, the missile battery in this case, to help transition the launch ramps into the marching configuration and load the missiles (they were carried ready-to-fire).

229   The Author came to the vehicle in order to instruct the driver to go to the designated location, to find that there was no one around. That was unacceptable.

230   Regardless of that, in the Author's opinion, the vehicle with the radar imitator (IRR) should have been left within their eyesight, so no one could approach it unnoticed.

231   The root cause of this problem was quite a novel method of accommodation of the combat-support motor vehicles. For the whole duration of the war the vehicles had been stationed at the Agricultural Cooperative in Šimanovci, regardless of the actual location of the combat units that changed 22 times.

The driver-soldiers were seconded, from their base units, to the commanding officer in Šimanovci, Žugić. He was responsible for them while they were in Šimanovci.

Prior to relocation of the combat units, Žugić was informed where his drivers need to bring their vehicles. Upon arrival at the combat position, the drivers were working within their own base units – the missile battery or guidance battery.

The overarching rule was that the vehicles and drivers should be present at the combat position for as long as the soldiers were required to assist in the process of transitioning the equipment. At the instant in time the driver was not needed any more for the transition, upon receiving permission to leave from the commander of his base unit, the driver would return to the motor vehicle base in Šimanovci.

These two rules, in theory, ensured the minimum number of vehicles and people were present at the combat position at any one time; because the battalion is most vulnerable during this period of transitioning equipment, because it has no defenses. In practice, some individuals, mainly officers on their own initiative, or upon receiving approval from their superior officer, sat in the vehicle and drove it back to the base in Šimanovci. Should the need for these officers arise after they left the combat position, we would not be able to contact them nor bring them back to the combat position (there were no mobile phones at the time). The simplest way to avoid that problem was to implement the rule "who brings the vehicle to the combat position has to drive it back to the base".

day long laying on the sofa and watching TV. The local post office is working, and you have enough people to do the job!"

- Captain Golubović and Lieutenant. Nikolić went to Russia. Captain Muminović, deputy battery commander, must organize a much better job in the battery, so that today's mistakes are not repeated.

May 1999

I was in the shift from 00:00 to 08:00.

The communication line with the officer on the radar imitator was down. I sent private Golubović from the signals platoon to go to Sergeant Petrović and see what it was all about. A wire had been disconnected on their field phone was the reason that stopped the communication between us. Was that accidental or intentional? If the situation were dangerous, he wouldn't be able to help us. Communication was re-established at 01:02.

Armuš reported that the driver of a civilian vehicle had unhooked the trailer with logs and went home. They were still putting up the log protection. Colonel Stanković wanted us to hurry to be ready to launch because the activities in the air had started. I told him we were down to our knees in the mud and we hurried as fast as we can.

I analyzed today's work and glitches with my shift.

Volf has to have a replacement on the crane, as the logs took 3-4 hours and he was tired.

A few times last night a pair of airplanes approached us from the azimuth of 290 - 310 degrees, launched their missiles and quickly turned back. On one occasion we put our missiles on preparation to launch after they came to within 42 km of us.

I was listening to a fool on the radio station. He kept saying, "NATO bombs are falling down." "There is nothing left of Serbia."

Ljubenković had prepared the radar for operation and was awaiting for the command to turn it to high voltage.

Signals code need to be changed tonight at 00:00. The code tables for the second quarter are in Deč with Sedlak.

I felt like a turtle in the new flack jackets. I was sweating profoundly, and my wet clothes stuck to my whole body. We had helmets on our heads. The air condition worked, yet it was oppressively sultry in the van. I stink to myself. It was 04:55, the worst period of the night. My shift was napping. I was awake looking after myself and them I was contented with the fact that we were so reliant on each other and that they were at peace with me. Our bulletproof protection wests looked like a baby's bib. It made my neck itchy.

General Karanović remained the same in appearance. Only his face revealed that he had aged a little.

Around 03:00, the announcement came from the operations center that General Slavko Biga was coming to visit us. By 05:05 he did not come to the combat position. Maybe he was in the camp.

If I can sleep, the armor collar would firmly hold my head in one position. I suddenly shuddered after having such a crazy thought. A moment of weakness and carelessness means we could lose our heads. I wished for 08:00 to come sooner, so I could fall asleep.

I told Dani last night that we can't go on like this any longer and that the shift crew must have a proper rest, without hearing the sound of boots and shouting. They should sleep at private houses if there was no other alternative; the only sure thing was that the current arrangement can't continue anymore. During our meeting I handed him my notebook which had my list of lapses of the missile guidance battery. "We'll have a meeting tomorrow," he said.

My shift shot at the first plane. They shot at the second plane too, when Dani replaced me in the shift. The 3rd launching of our battalion or the 5th missile was fired by Sub-Lieutenant Tiosav Janković. I was happy that he did it. He was the best student in his class. He was a little nervous and answered back quickly. He was very knowledgeable but didn't know what the launch looked like before the war commenced. Comparing to more experience crew members, he never completed his air-defense training at the Kapustin Yar firing range in Russia; he made his first missile launch in his home country. Before he left for Russia, his roommate, Nikolić, had messaged him that the "Alternative 2 applies". This meant that Nikolić had left the key of their apartment at the location known, only to them, as "Alternative 2". They shared one key.

My pager fell silent yesterday. The battery had run out. I told Danka to buy it for me if she found one, and also another one for Miki Stojanović.

Some Croat or Muslim[232] was turning on and off the radio transmission handover switch of his radio amateur station, hence hampering use of that frequency. Other radio amateurs were swearing at him. They had short fuses. He knew that he annoyed them and thus became more persistent. One should let the fool alone to heal his own complex of inferiority by himself. He didn't sleep all night in order to tease others. He was persistent or maybe he was paid to do it.

My shift ended at 08:00. We did not radiate from the surveillance radar.

I went to Milan and Nada's place and laid down to sleep. After waking up I had lunch, took a bath and had coffee. Lastly, before going to the new shift, I went to Deč for the signals code for this month. Tiosavljević and I changed them. Earlier this morning, he went to Armuš's to repair the Kraz crane. The guy who had worked for him and who just off-loaded the logs the previous night and fled was fired. I was not pleased, but he turned out to be a coward last night.

---

232   Muslim – One of the 1974 changes in the Constitution of the Socialist Federative Republic of Yugoslavia (SFRY) was the establishment of the new ethnic identity – Muslims (with capital "M") from the citizens of Islamic faith (muslims – with small "m"); former Christians (largely Serbs) that converted to Islam for various reasons during the 500 years long occupation by the Turkish Ottoman Empire. People can change faith but not language, so they understood each other.

A HARM missile that was fired at us last night was brought into the court-yard of the school. We lost count of the number of missiles that missed us. The missile wreck was about 2 m long. It looked deadly and peaceful at the same time. However, this impression was just an illusion. There were three guides for hanging points on the plane on the body of the missile: two parallel ones at the rear and one in the middle of the front section.

Senad Muminović and the soldiers masked the embankments with green bushes. The equipment, so far, had always been masked to blend into the environment. We used tree branches, rows of the clover cut-outs that was grown as a crop, gray bushes that mimicked the ponds, etc. We had always been camouflaged to look like the environment around us.

While I was at Milan's place, the leaflets were falling. The plane was dropping leaflets about 20 km away. Nada commented that dropping leaflets is a sure sign that they were and would lose the war. Germans had been dropping leaflets during WW II and they were defeated too.

I was in the shift again from 16:00 to 24:00.

At 18:02 we were ordered to go to Readiness No. 2.

At about 19:30, Armuš came with his son and brought a thermos of coffee, lemonade, and apples. The kid was 4-5 years old and very curious. He came to untie the trailer for logs. At about the same time Maletić's godfather with another comrade and directress of the Brickyard from Golubinci came. They brought us a roasted pig. In vain I told them to go to the camp and leave it with Varga. They also brought a lot of food to the combat position. They said that next time, when we shoot down another plane, they will bring us a roasted bull.

At 19:45 the Operations Center requested someone to wait for General Veličković when he plans to arrive at 21:15 at the Local Municipality offices. I told Bora in the camp to find Dani. At 21:00 we were ordered to go to Readiness No. 1. General Veličković arrived at our combat position at 22:00. He came to visit us in anticipation that, if he was lucky, he would be able to see us shooting at a target. He had visited Djević's battery the previous night around 03:00 but was unlucky to see them in action. We reported that our flack jackets are good, but we were sweating a lot. General Veličković had a long talk with Dani outside the guidance station. Upon entering the van, we discussed our combat tactics[233] with him, the creation of a horse-

---

233   The author shared with the General his intimate thoughts on the possible air defense combat tactics (not that of the attacking air force).

189

shoe[234,235,236,237,238] and an ambush[239,240,]. Politicians had not been investing in the military for many years. For a while they had even wondered if they need an army at all. They invested in the police, who was unable to catch the pilot when we downed his plane. Weird decisions were made in our weird state. We told him that we didn't need the air force as it was[241,242,243]. The air force has two principle functions: defence and retaliation. Our air force had not been able to fulfill either of these two functions, nor it will do in the future[244].

234   The fundamental air defense problem of concern is how best to locate individual air defense batteries, at the brigade level, in order to ambush and trap the incoming enemy aviation arriving from the anticipated direction; as a better alternative to random distribution of the air defense battery sites.

235   It is a graph optimization problem. The nodes of the graph represent (available) locations for the air defense sites. Its salient feature is that constraints are made on the nodes and edges of the graphs that represent feasible solutions. It bears all features of a combinatorial optimization problem.

236   Horseshoe- is a jargon name for the "horseshoe air defense network configuration".
The horseshoe air defense network configuration is created by connecting the nodes of a graph (individual air defense battery sites) by a line in the shape of a horseshoe.

237   Horseshoe airspace – is the airspace directly above the air defense sites, which make up a horseshoe air defense network configuration.

238   Ambush in the horseshoe - is similar to that in the canyon, for example, between cowboys and Indians in Western films.

239   Trap - the horseshoe airspace represents a trap. Once the airplane "enters" into the airspace of a horseshoe it becomes trapped and cannot leave without it being shot down.

240   Opening of the horseshoe - faces the anticipated direction of the incoming enemy aviation.

241   Futile Air Force -The author also conveyed to the General his opinion about the futility of small countries relying on their own air force against threats posed by neighboring countries that were members of the NATO alliance or in favor of that alliance, as NATO would always have more advanced and newer generations of planes.

242   That was intuitively clear to the author at the time as his country was completely surrounded by either NATO countries or their vassal states over whose airspace, airfields, and other key civilian and military assets NATO had effective control over.

243   In hindsight, the real events confirmed the author's opinion about the Air Force. Up to that day, 1 May 1999, FRY's Air Force had only 8 (eight) take offs. Three days later Colonel Milenko Pavlović would die in what was the last 9th flight of the FRY's Air Force during the war (of course the author did not know any of that at the time).

244   For completeness, the author shares the opinion of Miroslav Lazanski, a military commentator, journalist and current (at the time of translation into the English language) Serbian ambassador to Russia, that Serbian Air Force needs half a squadron (about six) airplanes, the peace time purpose of which would be to ensure civilian airplanes do not fly outside designated corridors for civilian air transport.

Where were the pilots now? A strong air defence is the guarantor of peace of small countries[245,246].General Veličković told us tonight that the shift that knocked down the F-117Ashould have been the first to be honoured, promoted, and celebrated. "It was the first time anyone had done this in combat. We are proud of that," Veličković noted.

At about 23:00 the Operations Center ordered us to turn on the surveillance radar as the target approached us. We armed the missiles to Readiness No. 1 and commenced search for targets with the surveilance radar. There was a target 18 km away and it was heading towards us. When it was within 15 km of us, I ordered everyone to search for it with the target acquisition radar. The routine sequence of combat actions started. Veličković was silently observing the work of our crew. We radiated for 10 seconds when I ordered the search to be stopped. We had found nothing. That was another fruitless attempt[247]. God, how difficult our work is without having the target elevation data. Veličković was now convinced of that[248,249,250]. He said we had naively lost our height finder radars[251]. He saw firsthand our combat work and that

---

245   Effective Air defense -The author also conveyed to the General his opinion that small countries must rely on their own air defense against threats posed by neighboring countries that were members of the NATO alliance or in favor of that alliance.

246   In hindsight, the real events also confirmed the author's opinion of how important the Air defense of small countries is. The FRY's Air defense had been fighting non-stop for all 78 days of the war, being a constant threat to NATO aviation, as is documented in this war diary.

247   In hindsight, the author explained the crew was looking for the target at altitudes between 5 km and 7 km, whereas the target was flying much higher. The 10 second period of allowable radar radiation time (in order to avoid HARM missiles) was insufficient to search the whole vertical sector, all the way up to the ceiling of the missile range. The crew had no elevation data for the target (the target acquisition and surveillance radars provided only 2D picture of the location of the target, which did not include its height); it had to initially guess the elevation (altitude) of the target and search the airspace around that initial guess for about 10 seconds, before switching off the target acquisition radar; hence discontinuing the search.

248   The General witnessed firsthand our attempts to find the height of the target by guessing it within the 10 second short time interval available, and, as a pilot, the General finally understood how valuable that information was.

249   Had the crew had that information from their height finding radars, the missile guidance officer would have been instantly finding the target on his radar screens and the crew would have been immediately able to shoot at it.

250   Unfortunately (as a result of the unavailability of the target height data) due to the firing time cycle, the crew had to stop searching for the plane in the air, which consequently made them unsuccessful.

251   The Air Defense had mobile height finding radars PRV-11 (NATO Name: "Side Net") and PRV-13 (NATO Name: "Odd Pair") that were very quickly destroyed by NATO HARM missiles because they radiated continuously.
For that reason General Veličković said, "We naively lost them" (because of the length of their radiation time).

one of others. "Write, write everything, who commands you, what you feel, combat actions, state of the equipment. It will mean a lot for post-war analysis." He could not have known that I an implementing his advice, that he is now giving to us, since long time ago… Nothing significant happened for the rest of my shift.

At 00:00 Dotlić arrived with his shift. I commanded the removal of everyone's vests. One by one they were swapping them out with the incoming shift crew waiting outside the van. The combat crew changeover was complete. With Dotlić, we analysed the situation and drew his attention to the fact that we had radiated for about 20 seconds. Everyone left by bus. I smoked a cigarette with Veličković and Dani. After that I said goodbye to the general and left. One thought was on my mind: I could not get over the opportunity we had tonight. My mind kept rewinding the events. He was alone in the zone, everyone else was far away. I felt terribly bad that we failed to get him.

Sunday, May 02

I drove to the school without turning on the headlights. Bora was sitting in front of the entrance. I sat next to him and we talked about the tonight's missed opportunity to shoot down the plane because we didn't have information on its altitude. He told me he hadn't seen or heard a single airplane. It means it flew very high. We'd been looking for him at 5 to 7 km altitude. Bora told me that Jaša (wartime nickname for Major Dotlić) would shoot tonight. I told him that Dani was still at the combat position. Tonight I will go to Milan's place to try to catch some rest because I was so exhausted.

At about 02:10 hours Milan woke me up. He told me that there had been heavy firing and that something flew overhead. It made a terrible whizzing sound. There was also an explosion in the direction of Šimanovci.

At about 02:08 Dotlić had a target on azimuth of 315 degrees. They received a warning when the enemy was 20 kilometers away. The surveillance radar was turned on and the target was acquired on the fire control radar at the distance of 16 km. The target was a pair of planes. Missile guidance officer's crosshair went onto the farthest target. The closer one was a bit aside. Sub-Lieutenant. Tiosav Janković was able to cover the closer target[252,253] with his crosshairs and to hand it over to the manual tracking operators. They launched two missiles. The target was hit at the distance of 12 km. Target speed 300 m/s, target altitude 6,000 m. The target made a small maneuver. The first missile acquired the target but the second didn't. This was the second time that the second missile failed to acquire the target. Obviously, there

---

252   The generic air defense rule – is to always shoot at the closest target, because it enters first into the destruction zone of the missile.

253   The missile guidance officer's quick thinking realized that the closer and dimmer target was the real one, and that the other, slightly brighter dot on the radar screen, was a towed decoy; both targets were on the same course.

Part of the crew that downed F-16 front to back:
Lieutenant Tiosav Janković, Senior Sergeant Dragan Matić and Major Boško Dotlić.

was an issue and we have to fine-tune the coordinate system[254,255,256,257,258]. Functional checkups didn't show that anything was wrong. Every time the shifts change, while the commanders exchange the handover information, missile guidance officers check the equipment for functionality. So far, no one had ever reported malfunction of any component on any of the two mis-

---

254   The coordinate system – is a part of the missile guidance station van that controls fine turning of the missile flight towards the target. The initial phase of the flight of the missile puts the highest demand on operation of the coordinate system; the missile powered by the booster motor rapidly accelerates and the target may take an evasive action.

255   Tuning of the coordinate system – is the process of adjusting the so-called "target tracking strobes" on the S-125M Neva air defense system.

256   Target tracking strobes – are used for the measurement of high-speed motion of the target.

257   The self-test system (KFS) - in the missile guidance station van (StVR) did not report any problem (as no self-test system can identify all malfunctions); however in practice, the 2nd missile repeatedly failed to capture the target, which required inspection and tuning of the coordinate system by S-125M Neva technicians.

258   S-125M Neva / SA-3 Goa Technicians - commissioned officers in the missile guidance van (StVR) were trained as technicians for the system (to disassemble & reassemble it); non-commissioned officers were trained to operate the system.

193

sile guidance channels. In reality, obviously something was wrong because the second guidance channel has not been functional. In other words, we had been operating at 50 percent firepower! We will be able to check the major systems once the equipment is not required to be in a combat ready state. The problem was that people were exhausted. On the other hand, who would dare to approve, in the middle of the war, for the equipment be taken out of service for an extended period of time in order to do a thorough check up?

Part of the crew that downed F-16 (left to right):
Standing: Sub-Lieutenant Tiosav Janković, Major Boško Dotlić, Lieutenant Miodrag Stojanović, WO Dragan Matić
Kneeling: Sergeant Igor Radivojević, Major Milorad Roksandić.

Our frequent relocations did not help. During the launch in Ogar, the second missile didn't blast off because the exhaust flame from the first missile booster motor disconnected the power supply cable for the launcher platform. Most likely, the crew didn't tighten the cable joint enough. "What else could have caused it? I asked myself, before concluding, "I'm quite sure that the loosely connected cable joint was the true reason for the malfunction."

Danka phoned me yesterday. She was in a state of panic. She told me that there had been many break-ins into the apartments. My apartment in Belgrade was vacant, a potentially easy target for thieves. I tried to calm her down and persuade her not to worry and told her to take a step back and think what we can do. It worked and she started to think calmly and coolheadedly. Last night, they targeted us for the tenth time with a HARM missile.

Around 03:30 Dani woke me up. He told me that our guys had downed an airplane. We hugged and congratulated each other.

I got up and Nada made me an extra strong coffee. When I got to the combat position the equipment was in transition and the battalion's relocation was in full swing. By 05:30 the last vehicle departed the combat position. Only the wooden logs were still left there. The craters from the missile blasts are visible. The tow truck couldn't approach the launch ramp platform to tow it away. This was a great problem that required special effort.

We relocated to a waiting position near the village of Mihaljevci. As per usual, Dani found a place for himself in the last house. The hosts are very hospitable.

During breakfast we discussed the whereabouts of the next combat position. It should be a new position near the village of Deč. It would not be wise to go to the position previously used in Deč. Roksandić, Muminović, Stojanović, Dani and I scouted the Deč vineyards. We found a few good locations and decided on one. There were many cottages owned by were retired military people. They were happy to see us. We returned to the waiting position around 10:30. Just before we departed, Air-Defense Corps Commander, General Bane Petrović called, asking for the names of the crew who downed the airplane. I also informed him about the names of the other shift crewmembers who had not yet been rewarded for downing the F-117A.

Last night's crew which downed the airplane consisted of Major Boško Dotlić, Commander; reserve Lieutenant Milan Stojanović – Deputy Commander; Guidance Officer Sub-Lieutenant Tiosav Janković; Warrant Officer Dragan Matić, Manual Tracking Operator on F2; Senior Sergeant I Class Igor Radivojević, Manual Tracking Operator on F1; and Missile Battery Commander Major Milorad Roksandić.

Colonel Stanković visited us at around 13:30. We spoke about our experiences. I told him about last night; as soon as I had turned on the high voltage and emission on the fire control radar, I saw, what looked like, two imitation targets, both located 25 km away, but on different azimuths.

Sergeant Ljubenković used the internal communication link to inform us about the distance and azimuth of the targets. He informed us after every sweep of his P-18 surveillance radar. Major Boris Stoimenov used the radar emission imitator to cover our fire control radar during the target search. I had trained him a long time ago how to do that, when exactly to turn it on and for how long.

We had downed the F-16, the wreck of which was shown on TV. There is a guy in our Operations Centre who listens to the NATO pilots' communications in real time. They heard that the pilot radioed that he had been hit and that he needed to eject (bailout). The airplane crashed in vicinity of the Cer Mountain.[259] The rescue helicopters picked up the pilot. We heard about the firefight during the rescue mission and that one NATO helicopter with about 20 commandos was allegedly downed. I wondered if this was true (the media like to exaggerate on both sides).

As per the previously agreed schedule, around 15:00 the surveillance radar went first to the new combat position. The radar emission imitator and signals platoon vehicles followed. Others would wait until 16:30, and then move in small groups in 10 minutes intervals.

259   He attempted to leave the Serbian territory, flying towards the NATO controlled parts of Bosnia and Herzegovina.

F-16 in Aviano base before taking off for bombing raid in Serbia.

F-16 engine wreck.

Major Roksandić's missile battery was scheduled for 17:30. We took a route via the abandoned combat position near Karlovčić, and Mika found the grounding electrodes from the power switchboard and transformer van that we accidentally left here last time. We took it with us. In the future, each time after we leave our combat position, we will send someone to survey and sweep it to ensure that nothing is left there.

I spoke with Danka. She assumed that we worked last night. She told me to be very careful and not to worry about the apartment, as she will somehow find a solution. She took the fuel vouchers. Well done.

Everyone was occupied with their own problems…

I went to Milan's place to try to have some rest from 14:00 - 16:00 but couldn't fall asleep again. He was pouring concrete on the clay earth walkway to his garden with Zdravko and Dragan. They had been speaking loudly, and almost yelling while moving the concrete mixer, the loud noise of which was irritating. I couldn't fall asleep, not even for a minute despite I was very tired.

Our circus was on the move again. Tepavac was very nervous. We said goodbye to our hosts and went to Deč.

Major Roksandić erroneously ordered his missile battery to move at 18:30 instead of 17:30. As soon as I found that, I ordered the first ramp to move at 18:00, ten minutes later the second; ZIL trucks with the missiles to move at 19:30.

I arrived in Deč. Armuš with his driver was already there. He brought a chainsaw to cut the large mulberry tree that was in the middle of the wheat field obstructing the missile launchers. I felt sorry for the tree. Who knows how old it is[260]. So, I ordered him just to trim the branches and leave the trunk. We'll use the branches to mask the fire control radar trailer and other vehicles if needed. It seemed that all works had been proceeding as normally as they could. The MANPADS were located on the opposite side of Deč towards the village of Petrovčić; just outside of our old combat position in Deč, on the vehicle entry side.

Major Dotlić thought that it was the signals platoon people's job to collect all the phones after everyone else leaves the combat position, and for this reason he had told Stoimenov to leave earlier. Until now, Dotlić would depart the combat position last, informed the operation center that everybody else had departed it, disconnected all the phones and take them with him. This time Dotlić had changed the order, and the previously well-rehearsed drill was not implemented. Consequently, we lost our phones. Someone had found them at the recently abandoned combat position and, of course, stole them.

The first section experienced difficulties loading the missiles onto the launch platform. It was already dark. Crnobrnja came to the combat position around 20:15. I told him, "General Slavko Biga called, he will visit us tonight and I need someone to wait for him. The meeting is scheduled for 21:15 in the center of Deč. He didn't know where Dani was, neither did I."

Dotlić didn't come to his shift at 21:00. So I had to replace him. He must have been celebrating somewhere. He had rested all day long. I had been non-stop with men. I permitted Sergeant Tepavac to change the location of his rapid intervention group.

Žugić requested permission to return all trucks to the equipment base in Šimanovci; explaining that he had a lot of work ahead, he needed to organize fire pickets[261], etc. "Eh, my friend, I left you the troops, vehicles and designated drivers, and instead of everyone knowing their own job and duties in the Šimanovci base you are trying now to assign them something new. Make the schedule while you are in the camp and help us here now! After completing relocation each driver soldier should have asked the commander

---

260   It is an old custom to plant a tree in the middle of the field to provide a shadow for those cultivating it, to rest or have a meal during hot summer harvest days.
261   Fire picket – a soldier or small unit of soldiers maintaining a watch, relieved at a time.

of his base unit if he or his vehicle is required any longer on the combat position; if not, they should immediately return to the base in Šimanovci in full knowledge of who should do what and when there. At the combat position, we should all work together to set it up as soon as possible. We do not stop work to go to a meeting and have a discussion. All meetings have to be held and plans made before arriving at the combat position."

He found it difficult to put the logs around the vans again, to protect us. We already had the same discussion at the previous combat position. After we set up the combat position, the logistics support people will leave, and the combat shift crew will stay. It seemed that there was no rest for us.

Dani spent all day in Kupinovo. He went there to bring more logs but had achieved nothing. So far, I had secured 104 or 106 logs, delivered in two lots. One lieutenant from the reserve finished that. No one actually knows where Dani goes and what he does when he is not in the unit.

When the logs were put in place, we started with the masking. The guidance station was operable and in function. The remote radar screen (VIKO) from the surveillance radar didn't show any picture. I reported "up" that we were functionally and operationally ready but without the picture on the VIKO screen in our van. Colonel Blagojević was "up" at the Brigade Operation Center. He told me that the sergeant operator from the surveillance radar should guide me, and that, in the meantime, we have to fix the problem. The problem was that the sergeant operator was the same person who should have guided me to fix the problem. Obviously, Colonel Blagojević didn't know the physics - no one can be at the two places at the same time...

I ordered Ljubenković to lay out the reserve cable. While Ljubenković was working on that, Blagojević asked me "Are you reporting to me that you are in combat readiness?" I told him: "Not yet! Suppose I should inform you, not the other way round!" Ljubenković stretched the cable but it was too short. He needed to disconnect one cable form the power supply unit so he could extend the first one. After he connected it, we finally got a clear radar picture on our VIKO screen.

Dani's shift is scheduled from 00:00 to 08:00.

Around 22:30, General Slavko Biga, Air-Force and Air-Defence Chief of Stuff popped up. He was accompanied with Lieutenant Colonel Milenković and one major whose name I didn't remember. They wanted to take photos of us wearing flack jackets and helmets, "for the history books" they said. We had a nice conversation after that.

The General was not aware of any of our attempts to promote all members of the crew that downed the stealth. Fuck it! Those guys "up" had no idea about the shift that downed the stealth! They had not been even considering promoting or rewarding the crew. Shameful!!I lost my temper in that moment. Every second in combat engagement, every minute, every day, and every month we had been risking our lives and the guys "up" had just been fucking around! General Biga was a missileer and understand us. He realised the magnitude of the injustice inflicted upon us. The upper echelons were not functional. They shifted the burden of air defence work to us,[262]

262   The Air Defense – was comprised of the air force and missile air defense;

missileers in the Air-Defense Corps.

This created new experiences that brought a whole new perspective to me.[263,264] The general[265] summarized his understanding of my combat experiences by saying, "You strike a balance between orders and reality, and try to keep your head on your shoulders?[266,267,268]" I confirmed by nodding my head.

Who can trust those guys "above" us[269] anymore? Who can trust that they

it had two Corps during the 1999 War: The Air Force Corp (VAK) and The Air Defense Corp (Ko PVO). The Air Force Corp was solely comprised of the aviation defense force. The Air Defense Corp was comprised of the aviation and missile air defense forces.

263 The hierarchical command line from the General Headquarters' Operations Centre to the Author's battalion had a few intermediate operations centers. This structure introduced communication delays and 'purification' of the information flowing in the upward direction to such an extent that the top echelon had often been presented with an idealized field situation that differed from the reality on the ground. It adversely affected the morale on the ground.

264 The (lack of) recognition of the missile air defense crew that shot down the F-117is a case study example of the corrosive impact of the double standards of the top brass upon the morale of the people on the frontline.

265 The General was an excellent communicator.

266 To balance between orders and reality–is a practical decision-making process on whether to execute an apparently unsound order or to ignore it?

267 A typical combat situation included the Author receiving a direct order from the Operations Centre of the 250th Brigade to do something. By considering the airspace situation on his surveillance radar screen, the Author has to independently make a decision on whether to execute the order or to ignore it.

268 For example, the Author was ordered to search for (low flying) a helicopter (or cruise missiles).

As the combat crew Commander, the Author knew from his experience that there was no chance of finding the helicopter (or cruise missiles) by using the fire control radar and that its radiation would only reveal his location to the enemy. For these reasons, the Author decided not to execute the order and to ignore it. For selected details, refer to the notes of the:

3rd April, at around 23:10, exchange with Colonel Blagojević and Colonel Stanković;

5th April, at around 07:00, conversation with Colonel Pauljević;

14th April, recollection of conversation with Colonel Blagojević, and; at 17:40, conversation with Colonel Stanković.

269 There were many reasons for the mistrust. In a nutshell, one needs to comprehend that the Commander of the shift crew at the firing position was on the (hardwired) telephone line with someone from the Brigade Operations Centre. Readers of this book would recall the character of Srba Blagojević – the alcoholic. The Author had no way of knowing whether he was sober or not when he was on the line from the Operations Centre. Obviously, the Author did not trust him. In addition, the Author could not trust the system that had appointed such a person to a position of power to make decisions about the lives of those at the firing position.

were trying to save our lives more than they were trying to save their own. That would be unnatural.[270,271,272,273] I've known that for a long time.

I just swallowed my pride and listened to the General, thinking about his words that consoled me.

Danka was right… absolutely right.

The General spoke to us about everything, not only about the professional military issues. He spoke to us not only as a general, but also as a missileer and human being. He heard about the stupid decisions our upper command had made from us. He took part in the war in Croatia and was of the opinion that many things should be changed after this war.

I replied, "An unrealistic picture is presented to you and other top military brass in the Supreme Command. That deception must be rooted out, once and for all," while thinking of the 'we can do anything'[274,275,276,277] attitude that facilitated it.

I started to be very suspicious about the reports on downed airplanes. How hast he public been shown only two of the airplanes that we downed?

---

270   That would be unnatural – was a summary of an outburst of involuntary thoughts that flashed across the Author's mind that analyzed the sum total of the mental, emotional, and social characteristics of individuals at the Operations Centre.

271   There were poltroons among them who would not bother considering if the order was unsound (or not) and whose sole objective was ensuring it was executed.

272   In the Author's opinion, the poltroonery may have worked in the middle ages or in the last century.

273   It was logical to the Author that one should execute the order and save people. If one loses people today, then who would fight the war tomorrow?

274   We can do anything – is a sentence that epitomizes the widespread attitude and practice in the Yugoslavian army of falsely presenting things to be ideal or much better than these were in reality.

275   There was an unwritten rule to beautify and cover negative issues, rather then addressing them. The content of the reports to the upper command often did not match the true state of the field troops.

Inspectors from the higher command were rarely presented with the true state of affairs; instead, they were routinely presented with glib vacuities intended to impress. For example, after conscripts were leaked an advanced notice of the forthcoming 'surprise' night alarm, some of them would sleep in their uniforms, and the unit would arrive at the assembly point in an unrealistically fast time.

276   Poltroons in command positions were hiding the real state of affairs and didn't have the guts to bring out any problems. By doing so, they were creating an idealized picture as the result of their own success.

For example, if an engineering unit with no mechanization and trained people was ordered to prepare embankments for a firing position, they would reply, "Yes, I understand," and leave an impression that the order could be executed, in spite of knowing that it was practically impossible to do.

277   The "We can do anything" attitude screwed up the army, because the truth comes out in times of need and by that time it is usually too late.

Something was fishy and not quite right. Have we been lying to ourselves and to our people? I wish I were wrong about this...

This night I realized something unexpected and big: almost everyone appreciates their own lives more than we do here at the combat position. We are the biggest risk takers. I am not a natural-born gambler, but our job and our combat work here is a very big gamble. The stakes cannot be higher - our own lives.

After our shift ended, the general went back with me. My Zastava 101 was parked just outside of the combat position. He offered to give me a lift in his "pooh"[278], which was how Danka would have said, because she didn't know to properly pronounce the name of this brand. I'm laughing whilst writing this.

NATO "collateral damage" – destroyed civilian objects.

While we had been waiting for completion of the photo session of the other shift, the General spoke with the guards and reservists. There were two of them. They were not moved that Biga is a general. They couldn't care less. My boys from the intervention unit. They are ready to execute any order I may give them.

Cigarettes before going to sleep instead of the toothbrush; we don't have any electricity or water.

Last night between 22:00-23:00 they bombed Obrenovac. Everything on the horizon was dark. They bombed the major power station there. So now we can say goodbye to the fridges and freezers and all the food stocked. Damn them! And a few days ago, our President, Milošević, released three

---

278   The General came in the Pinzgauer high-mobility all-terrain vehicle. This name was too long to pronounce, so Pinzgauer was nicknamed Puh /puh/, probably after the logo of Puch on the Pinzgauer (after the originally Puch family's factory in Graz, Austria) where it was manufactured.

of their soldiers that had been captured on a clandestine mission in Kosovo and Metohija to mark up the targets for the bombers by using laser markers. Those bastards from NATO have being doing what they want to do. Whenever they hit a civilian target and kill innocent people there, they simply say it was "collateral damage." How pathetic!!!

Monday, May 03

Dani woke me up at 05:30 and said that we were moving because we had been discovered. "How? When?" He didn't know any more details. I was getting up. Transition of equipment had already began. Last night we had relocated to the new combat position and completed set up into the combat configuration by 22:00. The strain on the troops was enormous. Biga said that he would rest his people and equipment tonight. The second missile couldn't be guided for the third time and no one seemed to understand why. Why was it not guided at the target? Karanović, Veličković and Biga, three generals. visited us for the past three nights. Everyone had their own vision and tactics, with, of course, our heads on the line.

I am missing fishing and beekeeping a lot – the activities which do not endanger human lives.

The decision was made to relocate the missile battery again to a new combat position in the region near the village of Mihaljevci, for the third time. Several trucks had already gone to the village. "That is not good," I said to Dani. I redirected the remaining part of the missile battery to the region near the village of Šimanovci. We left the surveillance radar in Deč. It was parked in a shadow of poplar trees that lined the Main Street Boulevard. That wasn't the perfect spot, but I didn't have any better spots at the time. The crews were sent to rest and have breakfast. We will continue the relocation in the afternoon. After that, we will either set up the new combat position for ambush or be hit by a HARM missile. Let it be as it had been so far. Just be smart. Sea Harrier jets were buzzing in the air, waiting in concealment, sneaking and prowling. They were predators too, like eagles, stalking their prey.

At 10:30 Blagojević, from the Operations Center, ordered the missile guidance battery to go to the new combat position near the village of Mihaljevci. Just as we had been expecting. Dani, Bora and Dotlić were sleeping while I wrote our experiences, difficulties and problems in my war diary. I wrote about a part of my life. As we were leaving the combat position, Dani's cell phone rang and he was ordered to immediately suspend operation of the MANPADS that had been dispatched to protect the convoys of trucks while they were relocating to the new combat position. He replied, "How can I pass on the order when everything was pulled apart and is on the move? The signals platoon and all other people are on the move. I cannot notify them right now?" The guy from the Operations Center could not care less. In case an incident occured, he would have simply said that he had passed on the order to the field units. I thought for myself, "God help usto deal with with our communication channels and our command in their armchairs.

After the war, I will also only think about myself."

My son had my pager number. So far, he had called only once, on 13 April to wish me a happy birthday. He wouldn't have remembered it himself.

"My wish came true," the words echoed in my ears[279]. "And what was my wish? Where was I? I had to deal with everything in my life. Truth was my great ally", I thought for myself.

I called Danka. She was worried about me, the electricity, the freezer."We will feed ourselves somehow, even without the freezer," I comforted her.

As we were having breakfast this morning, Dani said he and Dotlić had shot down the plane. I coldly told them, "If so then, from now onwards, the two of you should go alone to the guidance station and shoot the planes as you please. Everything you shoot down will only be your kills. You don't need a shift." I kept on joking with Sedlak, Tomović and Bora, "You are missile shooters too and you were in the station before. We will hire you too. The times are tough."

There were no comments. That led me to believe that, if required, each of them would find a reason not to go to the missile guidance van, which we jokingly called the mausoleum[280]. Everyone probably thought for himself, "Don't let my name be there. Maybe one day, when old age kills me, or technically speaking, when my resources run out."

I hope Tomović is wrong. I was annoyed by the imperfection of people and by them not thinking about moves and actions. I had to overcome that bitterness in myself, so it did not upset my abdomen whilst keeping my stomach calm. Achieving that objective was a big task for me. Had we really been discovered tonight? If we did, why didn't they go after us? Why didn't they fire or bomb us? Something was wrong here. They probably have a lot of information about our location and it's probably very valuable. If they knew our location, then why they did not come tonight? Dani is technically inferior, however he is very street-smart and very cunning. I didn't like that he was not honest. He secretly enjoyed gaining some personal benefit, whilst pretending to be virtuous and uninterested. Everyone mentioned his name when talking about our unit.

Blagojević told me in an unencripted call that the new location of the combat position was the site in the village of Sremski Mihaljevci, and this morning he told Dani not to set up the combat position there, because it was too open and without any shelter that can be used as a camouflage. It was a

279   These words, his ex-wife said when they formally divorced in early April 1997, haunted the author.

280   Mausoleum– Is a simile for the missile guidance station van as it is a place of potential death during combat work. Death lurked above them, ready to pounce at any second. If death came, they knew, a monument in their honor would be erected after the war, with the names of those who died carved in stone. The author said, "However, we all aspired not to have our names listed on any such future monument."

The officers mentioned had hoped not to be included in combat work and therefore would avoid the risk of death.

joke.

The last time Colonel Stanković visited us, the allegation was made that Dani and Mića Mijalković quarreled so much so that they did not speak to each other. The whole Brigada burst into a whirl of gossip. That was insane. Someone had nothing else to do. He said that Toša, a Colonel from the School Center and Colonel Miodrag Savić[281] [282] from the Center for High Military Schools were expelled from their respective air-defence units. That was the destiny of another man that I used to be a great buddy and friend with. A long time ago he had told Danka[283] that he would be the first General from Belgrade. A Belgrader by birth. I thought that he was definitely not going to get his twigs[284]. I hated such sick ambition solely reliant on networking and poltroonery[285]. That was diametrally opposite from my life views that progression in the military ranks should be earned by hard work, self-sacrifice, knowledge and true professionalism. The cost of that virus was high: the face under the tail.

And again the same familiar sequence of transitioning each peace of equipment one-by-one into combat configuration. Dani and I agreed that he will be in the first shift that ends at the midnight, and me from 00:00 until 08:00. He went to the combat position and I went to the school to rest. I told Kosta to wake me up, and my shift, at 23:30.

Boris Stoimenovand a mechanic from the village worked out how to power the municipality water pump from our generator, so the village could have uninterrupted fresh water supply while we were on the nearby combat position. Well done Boris. "Yipee!" - his famous saying.

Kosta woke me up. I got ready, took my helmet, and waited for my shift to start. Dotlić got up too. He told me that at 21:00 he had made an arrangement with Dani replace me in the shift. He commanded the shift to go. I was hurt by Dotlić's conduct. I decided to talk to Dani and Dotlić in the morning. I didn't want to argue with him in front of the soldiers and other officers. I will not let anyone fuck with me, especially not the assistant-commander for logistical support.

I was waiting for Dani to come...

---

281   At this instant in time Colonel Savić returned in the author's life. Long time ago they were family friends when they served in Skoplje. That friendship ended after his former wife complained Savić had been indecent towards her while he was on a six months assignment in Banja Luka.

282   Mike Mihajlovic – I met Colonel Savić and Colonel Tošić during the war and had a very good cooperation with them.

283   Savić met Danka when he was a student of the military academy and she was in a high school; hence many years before the author met Danka. It's unbeliev-able how small is the world.

284   Twigs – Is a part of the insignia for commissioned officers of the rank of General (equivalent NATO codes OF-6 to 8).

285   In the author's professional opinion, Savić did not have true qualities that would support his ambition; he was an average missileer, whose peacetime progression in the ranks could be largely explained by personal networks and luck.

Dani arrived around 01:00. He looked tired and wanted a beer.

I angrily told him that someone here is crazy, "You and I had a deal before you went to the combat position." He replied that he had reprimanded Dotlić for not showing up to his shift the last night, so I had to stay for another shift instead of him; that it was really not right of him and that Dotlić needed to come to the shift tonight instead of me. I didn't know that.

We sat and smoked in the dark. Seem that the situation is getting very "sparky" and we need to prevent anxiety and discord among the people. "Don't worry," Dani said. They had a problem with the launch ramp tonight. They couldn't properly position it[286]. The missile guidance station van had to be moved next to the embankment, because of the length of the command cable. The logs at the front end of the missile guidance station van protruded about a meter above its roof and blocked the line of sight between the fire control radar post and the ramp. Fuck it... Well, another experience. No one had considered that at the time and the ramp had to be moved by 10 meters away. The complete positioning work had to be done all over again. They didn't touch the protective logs at the front end of the guidance station van.

We went to sleep. I couldn't get it out of my mind that they had detected us so quickly. Yesterday, around 14:30, there were three explosions. They found Vučković's P-15 radar, which had been reassigned to him. The radar was destroyed. This time there was no one in it. The VIKO screen was relocated to a secure remote place. The previous lesson had been learnt. Smiljanić had paid with his life for that experience.

Yesterday, around 17:00, we commenced our relocation, and shortly after that, at around 03:30 we were ordered to move again, because it had been reported that our position was compromised. It was done very quickly.

Yesterday in Deč, while we had been waiting, we saw Captain Senad Muminović carrying a bag with some English words. Dani asked him, "Why are you wearing the enemy's bag? Throw it away!" "This bag is not mine; it is Volf's," Captain Muminović replied, "I have Deutsche Marks and dollars, but I didn't throw them away... What does that have to do with anything?" We all laughed.

Last night, when I was taking off my uniform and getting ready for sleep, I saw that Dani wore a compact black bulletproof vest, designed to be discreetly worn under the suit. In the guidance station, he was putting on another one. He was protecting himself very hard. He must have gotten it from the police, only for himself and who knows when. I found it hurtful that he <u>had never offere</u>d that vest to me or any other combat member of the combat

286   The positioning of the launch ramp–is the process of aligning the launch ramp and the fire control radar to the same point. Typically, the North Pole becomes the zero degrees horizontal reference for the radar and ramp. An optical instrument, called "panorama," is affixed on a designated spot on the radar pole and ramp. The operators of the radar and ramp aim the two instruments at each other, which requires a clear line of sight.

crew. We were not in the same shift and if he is not selfish one, he would do that. I was not important to him. He had started my elimination a long time ago, and I had been feeling it at each step since then.

I ordered Jović, from the signals platoon, to come and wire us the phone lines away from the guidance station and other combat equipment. We should go away from our combat equipment when we're in Readiness No. 2, i.e. when the equipment is not working. It's better to be away, as you never know if your position has been photographed and compromised, and airplanes may suddenly pop up and obliterate it in a matter of few seconds. This is the greatest danger for us. The rest depends on us, and our luck. Luck is a very important factor indeed.

The other officers in the shift had a fun time discussing the topic of our unit after the war; I will be their commander after the war, and I will be fucking them up every step along the way. We all laughed. They were telling me: "Djole, don't forget us. We are war buddies". I told them: "You can never forget that. Never!"

Volf was working on the leave schedule worksheet. Travel plans should be handed over to logistics so they can issue us new permits. The administration was almighty. In the middle of the war, we had to justify our fuel consumption through the papers. Bureaucracy... Some people, who are sitting up somewhere far from any danger, are justifying their existence through the paper pushing.

During last night's equipment positioning at the Deč Vineyards, a van approached us with its high-beam lights on. I ran in front of it. Some officers were inside. I started yelling at them. "What should I do!? Damage my van driving at night on a dirty road with out my lights on?" one officer replied. "Fuck your van, damage it, crash it, do with it whatever you want, just don't illuminate my equipment!" I angrily told him.Then he recognized me. He said, "Are you Aničić?" I didn't know him. Probably from the newspapers or who knows from where. It did not matter at all. The tension dissipated. He immediately apologised, saying he was sorry. Then, he congratulated me for downing the F-16 as well.

Around 09:30, Dani called and we spoke about the security guards for our combat position. I told him that we have security guards on all four sides. Somewhere on the azimuth 120-130 degrees was the radar emission imitator, slightly to the right was the intervention group, and we also have two guard posts on the two field access roads.

There is a solution to fix the problem with the corner reflectors. When driving[287] the support posts into the ground the corner reflectors (hooked at the top) were falling off like pears from the tree. A solution was to weld another ring bracket at its high end. A rope should be pulled through the hook at the top corner of the reflector and then run through the pole top ring bracket. Once the support post is erected and stable, someone should pull the rope to raise the angular reflector and tie-in the rope, like when rising

---

287   Two hammering brackets were welded at the opposite sides of the post, at about 1 meter above its end. The heavy eccentric pounding was violently shaking the post, so the corner reflectors were falling off their hooks.

the flag.

Tonight was cloudy and cool. Good weather for us, which prevented them from performing the visual reconnaissance and taking aerial photography. With a set of relieve, we are ordered into combat Readiness No. 2. We shut-off the equipment... We were allowed to rest, finally.

Yesterday in Deč, we found that Private Oskar was selling cigarettes to the local peasants. He was so slimy. In his defense, he said he had shared his cigarettes with the other fellow smokers, and then he started selling his daily cigarette rations. He realized that it was not right and that he had tarnished his uniform and the whole military. He promised that he will not do that again.

Bora went to Mihaljevci because they reported that they had found a missile. It fell in the field about 2 kilometres away from the church, on the right-hand side when looking from Karlovčić to Mihaljevci. The missile was in one piece. It was our missile, damaged by the fall. The missile didn't acquire the target during the launch. It was the guidance channel issue again. The missile blasted off from the platform and continued its flight along the ballistic trajectory. We talked about it this morning. We checked the control's functionality, and everything was in order, and yet the guidance channel wasn't working. What can be wrong? We only have one guidance channel in operation, and yet all the controls showed that both channels are working properly.

At 11:55 we are ordered into Readiness No. 1. Colonel Blagojević was at the Operations Center. We got in full combat readiness within five minutes. Colonel Stanković was talking to our pilot. I heard their communication. NATO was attacking Valjevo. There were plenty of their airplanes in the air. I listened to radio amateurs. We received a no launch order, as our MIG-29 entered into our zone of engagement. He took-off to try to intercept them. I saw him on the azimuth of 180 degrees. To his left side was a pair of NATO airplanes. Somewhere on the azimuth 190 degrees, distance 65 km. We prepared our radar emission imitator or operation.

"They are getting bold," I thought to myself, "NATO is now flying by day attacking the targets in the field, and by night they are attacking the targets close to the cities, because of our air defense." We also provided cover to one of our battalions. We had to use our radar imitator to simulate the fire control radar emission and try to lure NATO airplanes away from the real fire control radar. We emitted with the imitator three times in 10 second intervals. Once at the azimuth of 100 degrees and twice at 210 degrees.

At one moment, the radio amateurs reported that one airplane was shot down above Valjevo and the pilot's parachute was seen. "Bravo, Yugoslav Army," echoes from the radio station in the booth. We were happy. We need our comrade to come back and land safely. It seemed that this tactic was working. NATO airplanes were obviously confused as the "sky was cleared" very quickly.

Blagojević asked me if I had seen him. The last time I saw the MIG-29 was 45 km away, at the azimuth of 210 degrees. I called our visual observers. Somehow, I felt something was wrong, but I didn't know what. Around

12:10, they heard the sound of the airplane but couldn't see it. God, if only he is ours and was on its way back. If it was still true that he had knocked down one enemy airplane than all congratulations to him. The pilot is a hero. The air-defense covered him. He probably had a double fear - from ours and from theirs.

The NATO vultures began to concentrate in Eastern Bosnia. They probably covered the rescue of the pilot of the downed plane. It all happened very quickly - between 12:05 and 12:15.

I shaved in the van this morning. While the equipment is on, I certainly have an electricity supply. I need to get a new electric shaving trimmer. This one's become dull.

For the first time today, I saw Captain Muminović reading a book. His concentration returned. This is a big thing. This means that the guidance station actions have been done without spasms and fear. I'm happy about that.

Admittedly, comments were made during the radar imitator emission that we had been protecting our fighter-interceptor while revealing our position.

"Vujić" TV had recorded the plane crash and showed it immediately. We listened to the radio news. Senad lifted his thumbs up. The first league! It was just said that the airplane had been shot down by the air-defense. No way, but it did not really matter at all at this moment.

Armuš came to take the chains to paint them in white. They are not visible at night when thrown on a truck or when they fall to the ground. This guy thinks of everything. Congratulations! Yesterday, as he was repairing the horn on my Zastava 101 he found the cause of the oil leak. The leak was on the oil dipstick. He offered me lunch. Roasted baby potatoes. I love them, the first crop this year. Spring onions and bread baked on wood. Hot-dogs and smoked Kulen salami. Stana, his wife, prepared everything very quickly. Their little son wanted to wash the car. He was playing in my car. He was so cute. He was interested in vehicles and his dad's business. You could see that.

I rested in the afternoon. Later I spoke with Danka. She worked today. There was no electricity in Belgrade. She was concerned that someone may break into my apartment. Other than that, she was fine. She will work again on Thursday and will have a day off tomorrow.

Dani came around 21:00. He was in Pećinci and had a haircut.

He told me that the hairdresser told him that he had heard, but did not believe, that some guy, Djordje Aničić, the Pećinci's son-in-law, shot down the F-117A. He told him that he is my commander and I am his deputy and that this was true. He was a bit tipsy. Everyone has their own unique tension and stress coping mechanisms... Lukić brought a bunch of the Yugoslav Army war edition magazine.

I was thinking about how better to protect the guidance station roof. A great idea flashed through my mind: to loosely tie two logs at both ends about the width of the van, and then to lay them along the two roof edges of the van like two side barriers. The logs should be further secured in the position by wrapping the ropes around and under the van, in the square shape around the van's longitudinal axis. Additional logs should be placed on the roof between the two secured logs – side barriers. The metal plates[288] should be placed on top of the first layer of the roof logs. The second layer of logs should be placed on top of the plates, therefore creating an excellent "sandwich" protection from HARM missile shrapnel.

Dani secured a truck mounted log loader. Tomorrow we have to go to Kupinovo for another 100 logs. We shall not stop thinking about how to make our protection more secure. I had a feeling that the diplomatic activity would bear fruit. The missile guidance van should be protected in the next expected area. We need another strong rope. If required, I would send someone to pick it up from the rope maker in Ruma tomorrow.

Tonight, we discussed again why the second missile didn't acquire the guidance link. In the guiding process, only coarse selsyn works, and during the tracking, the fine selsyn is turned on. Therefore, when switching to tracking, we should wait a few seconds for the tracking system to completely actuate and then launch.

I have a feeling that it would be a mess tonight.

We learned the sad news that I was afraid of. The MIG-29 pilot was killed today at Valjevo. The downed aircraft, as seen by the radio-amateurs, and the pilot's parachute was ours. In the back of my mind, I knew it was true, but I wanted to believe the news at 14:00. They stopped reporting about it. They didn't show a clip of the downed airplane. Tiosavljević called his uncle in Valjevo. He told him the markings on the airplane were Russian. Everything was crystal clear to me.

I ordered Jaćić not to go alone to the radar imitator tonight and to take Sergeant Petrović with him. Petrović had allegedly been training him and wanted to send him alone tonight for the first time. I didn't allow that.

At 00:00 hours, when we took over the shift, Dotlić told me that they had a quiet shift, but it seemed now that a big commotion is about to come forth.

Wednesday, May 05

During a short bus journey to the shift, we saw a glowing ball, somewhere on the azimuth of 280-290 degrees. I didn't think it was that high. It glowed for a while and then it diminished. It lasted for about 10 seconds, then it ignited again. I drew it to the attention of the spotters and the SA-7 man portable missile air defence crews; to pay more attention to it and, if possible, to down it. It was probably a marker or something. Along the way, I received a pager message from Armuš to call his landline in Belgrade. I picked up the handset but there was no signal, the line was dead. Even if there was a sig-

288   The metal plates were laid around the launch ramps to protect the power supply and communication cables from the thermal and mechanical stresses due to the missile launch exhausts. The metal plates were readily available, as the battalion used only one or two, instead of all four, launch ramps.

nal, I would not have called him[289]. One should have taken all precautions, just in case. I trusted no one[290].

An idea came to my mind to schedule a meeting with the Mayor of Pećinci and all 16 Local Community Executives tonight. Roads should be closed at night. Village security guards should be established. The safety of the unit really must come first. Aleksić, from the emergency response group, told me that about 40 Romanians[291] had come to the village today.

During dinner last night I spoke with Mika Stojanović. I tried to break his fear. He didn't want to go to Dani's shift. If he had to go to the shift, he wanted to be with me.

The Operations Center told me to reduce the operation of the surveillance radar from continuous operation[292] to 2/2 (radiate high frequency energy during two full turns of the antenna, and then do not radiate for the next two turns of the antenna). I warned them that the proposed reduction of the radiation pattern, from continuous to 2/2, would not do the job, "If I am an enemy, I would know that there is a real combat unit there because the surveillance radar works non-stop and the crew is required to switch the radiation on and off. If your true concern is that our radiation is too "visible" for the enemy, then we should not radiate at all." They accepted my argument and changed the order to not radiate high frequency energy into the air from the antenna of the surveillance radar. We put the radar into "silent mode": its antenna was turning without radiating high frequency energy into space[293].

---

289   In 1999, digital telephone switchboards were installed in the Belgrade metropolitan area, whereas old analogue switchboards served the surrounding rural and semi-rural areas, which "eased" potential for eavesdropping of calls.

290   The author was cautious and inquisitive, as he explained later: *"Even if I had a signal and I could have dialed, I would not have, as I was not sure if someone unwanted had the ability to eavesdrop our conversations. We trusted no one. We all played safe and avoided all risks."*

291   This group of Romanian migrants seems to have chosen the cover of the turmoil of war to sneak through the border between Serbia and Croatia (that was located about 20-30 km away) on their way to the Western Europe. Due to dire economic situation many Romanians temporary worked in FRY before the 1999 war. After the war commenced some of them returned to Romania, whereas this group apparently decided to go to Western Europe. We didn't know if any NATO spies were inserted into that group or not, which posed a significant military security risk, as their unannounced route went through the area that was heavily traversed by anti-aircraft artillery guns and mobile and semi-mobile missile air-defense units that had been shooting at, seriously damaging and shooting down many enemy planes, two of which fell down "like a stone".

292   During continuous operation of the surveillance radar the radar radiates high frequency energy non-stop into the air during the full 360 degrees turn of its antenna.

293   During silent operation of the surveillance radar the Operations Centre of the 250th Brigade provides information on the allocated target to the crew and orders them to shoot it down.

Muminović was reading a book. Boris was napping, as he usually doing in every shift. No wonder why he was so well rested after each shift. In contrast, I had been constantly on guard and restless.

Varga said he heard an owl hooting tonight and that he felt that we would be at shootout tonight. I replied to him, "Owls are helpful. They feed on mice and rats, rodents and pests."

My body armor had been soaked in sweat and stunk of my own body odour.

Bora went to Noskov yesterday. He left around 15:00. He spent the night in Belgrade with his family, and then planned on going to the village of Grocka in the morning. Senad Muminović suggested that we should arrange for the officers to go home for 24 hours. I acknowledged the merit of his suggestion, but thought, and told him, it might be better to endure a little more than to spoil the quality of the shift crews. We needed to be very smart.

Last night, before our shift commenced, I came up with another reason on why we should not go back to the combat positions we had already occupied. Someone can place radio locators on the battlements or around the combat positions. The villagers would certainly not do so. They did not understand much about the security of the unit. They would want to help, for sure, but this was beyond their knowledge and resourcefulness.

Yesterday, after almost a month, I called my son Vlada. My former mother-in-law, Radmila, answered the phone and said that he was in Belgrade. She told me that my ex wife and Vladimir were no longer residing in the apartment in Belgrade that I had rented for them, and that Vladimir was in Bilja's apartment[294]. That news upset me greatly[295,296]. I didn't tell Danka so as not to upset her. When I was leaving his life and community, he was cleaning the barn. He decided. If I hadn't called him and asked him where he was staying, our parting, as father and son, would have happened at a distance of 50 meters. "Fuck our genes," I said to myself, as my son failed to exhibit my personality and did not react as I had expected at that tense and highly emotional situation. Geneticists' saying that children inherit most of their genes and personal traits from their grandparents, not parents, subconsciously flashed through my mind; leading to a conclusion that I must find out whose genes he had inherited by "researching" his grandparents and finding out all I know about them. I might have been too much of an ambitious parent, as that question surfaced again from deep down inside me, haunting me to find out an answer.

294   When the war broke out the author's ex left that apartment and moved with Vlada to their neighbor Bilja in the same apartment block. Bilja's apartment was on the same level as the author's apartment, with their doors located diagonally opposite to each other.

295   The author's first thought was that of desperation, "Why go to Bilja's apartment when my ex had so many relatives in Belgrade!"

296   The author considered the relocation to be an atrocious conduct by his ex for two reasons. To much of an unnecessary burden on the neighbors, and to psychologically upset their son, who could see the doors of his apartment (where they lived as a family) but could not enter into it.

Mika was supposed to contact Srećko Morić last night in order to bring him in to join us at the guidance station tonight. I did not understand what Dani wanted to achieve with it.

Dani bought over 230 packs of cigarettes for soldiers at a wholesale price from Luki. He was selling three packs for the price of two at full price. In return, Dani promised to loan our 15 horsepower diesel generator to Luki to power his pasta and juice production line. Luki also had to give juices to the soldiers. The deal included Luki's obligation to return the generator to us right away if we needed it. Who knows what else was included in the deal and who benefited from it. It looked fishy anyway. I wondered why Dani needed to get into all this.

Radio amateurs reported that two planes had been shot down over the Rudnik, Maljen and Povlen mountain ranges. After that, they made a correction that two helicopters were actually downed. They congratulated the Army and Air Defense.

We had to turn off the air-condition after droplets started dripping from the ceiling above the VIKO radar screen. The humidity was high. and the cabin was unbearably hot.

Tonight, I heard from Tiosavljević that General Veličković said at a news briefing in Pančevo that he could find as many missile operators as he needed at the Zeleni Venac Market, but not air force pilots. I recalled his last visit here, and I wish I had told him to bring those missile operators here to replace us, so we could go home. Some were going home, and they were not us – these were probably the esteemed pilots, who play cards in a house or some other hole, while waiting for the war to end with the "vexation" of being powerless. "Fuck chess when you're stupid and you don't know how to play," I said to myself.

Today I procured a manila-hemp-rope to set up the corner reflectors. "Has anyone, other than me, been thinking about improving our combat work and making sure everything works?" I wondered. I was disappointed by the lack of ingenuity and indifference of individuals, including their frequent superficiality.

The southern parts of the country were attacked tonight: Užice, Čačak, Ponikve, Rudnik, Povlen, Maljen, Cer, Bajina Bašta, Kragujevac...

Had it not been so "dens" in the air, I probably would have been writing much more tonight and much more emotionally, especially when thinking about my son. There were many undefined things and emotions.

Tonight, by chance, I spoke to a reservist, who was a child of divorced parents. Tears were in my eyes. Will I ever gain the strength to hold myself together when it comes to kids? They are an endless story, like an ocean.

Last night, Dani told me he was going to send one of the officers to take souvenirs from the F-16 wreck.

At 03:30 we are ordered to Readiness No. 2.

At 05:15 I received a signal for no-action.

At 06:00 I spoke with my classmate Matijević. He told me that Colonel Čikić, Assistant Commander for Morale, and him will come to visit us today. Outside, the wind amplified its moans. I remembered Vojislav Ilić's poem "In the late fall", I had learnt in childhood. It blows and hustled through the ajar doors of our missile guidance station van... The equipment was in perfect peace...

At 06:20 the Operations Center sent out a signal "Air Danger Over".

At 06:35 Bora Crnobrnja called us from Noskov's unit. I talked to Noskov and my classmate Đorđević. They also had a peaceful night. Nothing had been happening in this area. Noskov told me that when they were at some location, an old man approached them and asked, "Soldiers, would you like to fuck girls? I have two good, clean ones." "It was pity that we had no time." Noskov concluded. We all laughed.

I told Bora that 40 Romanians came here. He said, "Come on, could you check it out for me." "I'll see when I get off the shift," I replied. Đorđević told me that he cannot wait for the war to stop and return to peaceful family life. It was the first time I heard from him since the beginning of the war.

I listened to the news at 07:00. Clinton is in Europe. He will visit a NATO base and meet three American soldiers that Milosević released. In contrast, our President did not receive the team that shot down the F-117A. What a shame. That proved to me that an orderly system respects the individual. Serbia remained consistent in disrespecting its heroes. At 07:16 Janko Aleksić reported that from 08:00 Air Force testing will begin in the area of Dobanovci. All air defence activities are prohibited at that time. That order was forwarded to the MANPADS and emergency response groups.

At 07:38, the Operations Center ordered us to go to Readiness No. 1. I wondered if this aggression had been a birthday gift to the NATO alliance - justifying their existence.

Dani told me to go to Military Recruitment Centre and complete the administrative formalities for the volunteers that had joined our unit. "Who knows where Military Recruitment Centre is located now?" I thought. Sedlak, got me their phone number."

I made a note to return the theodolite to Energoprojekt Consulting. It was a precise and accurate tool, but useless to aid our quick combat work.

This time again, many issues suddenly popped up just when I had to go home; all of which had to be resolved "my way"; it didn't matter when I was scheduled to going home. I was disgusted with the Dani's conduct.

I conveyed all my thoughts on improving our combat work to Kosta, marked with an asterisk on previous diary sheets. He agreed with me on many things. We had breakfast. I had delicious scrambled eggs with bacon and spring onions. Kosta made a double shot of coffee, as usual.

Armuš arrived and brought 88 logs on the truck that had a loading crane. Dani signed the invoice from the Kupinovo State Forrest Corporation.

Dani sent me, with the driver, who was a refugee, and Armuš, to the combat position to explain to them how to set up the log protection. We left,

213

although Dotlić was on the combat position with our shift. It was an absolute fuck around. The sole purpose of this was to make me not go home or to make me go home later. He needed to show me who the boss was, not in words, but by unnecessarily delegating me assignments. He said that he must go scouting south for new combat positions that area bit closer to the camp than the current one.

Upon returning from the combat position, where I explained the log protection system to Armuš and how to set it up, I found my classmate Matijević, Lieutenant Colonel Zeljković of the Corps, Branko Kopunović, journalist of the Vojska magazine and one cameraman in the kindergarten where we were housed. We greeted each other.

I took my bag and went home. Stojanović came with me. I checked if the theodolite was loaded. "long time ago," Mika said.

A shadow of doubt came over me, and on departure I called Matijević outside to ask him something in private: "long time ago we sent a proposal for awards for the downed F117-A. We have not received a response from the Brigade so far, and Davidović from the Corps told me that this will be urgently considered and resolved quickly."

Matijević replied that the proposal was considered and that he did not recall seeing my name on the proposal that was sent to the Corps. At that moment everything blackened before my eyes… a torrent of rage, fury, powerlessness, hurt, and dissatisfaction poured out from me. All the injustices of this world seemed to have follow me. I couldn't control myself and I went into the kindergarten where I told Dani not to count on me from today, that it was an injustice from here to heaven. I was shouting and excited. "I am not fighting for decorations and ranks, but if there were six officers and a soldier in the team, and if the proposal for awards included all names except mine, then it is over for me!" I took off my pistol and insignia and handed them to Dani. They all kept their heads bowed. They realized the magnitude of the injustice. One hero of the air defense no longer existed. He was anonymous, as he was - Anđelko Đorđević. Dani said he didn't understand why I was angry, everything's going to be okay and we were not fighting for ranks and decorations. "I agree with you, but then why did you accept the rank of colonel?! You're playing a poseur! You have been introducing yourself to everyone as the commander of the unit that shot down the F-117A, while we have been hiding the identity of the unit! You said you were promoted before anything was known!" He replied: "It's not true." "It's true, and don't make me confront you with that man. At the Žika's house in Ogar, that man has no idea about ranks, you talked and bragged about being promoted!" Dani was silent, he realized that I found out what he did. I would have said a thousand other truths to his face, that I knew about him, but I managed to control myself at the last moment. I was emotionally discharging my frustration while walking around the kindergarten thinking this was all true. Everyone was silent and he was writing, probably every word I said. "So is it possible that social connections were working even during war time, and that the "boys' club" is keeping for themselves and their favourites? Why was Lieutenant Nikolić immediately promoted, he who had a year and a half experience, whereas everyone else, except soldiers and Tiosavljević, have over 15 years of tough air-defence missile operator's experience behind them?" I burst out. The injustice made me wish I could die on the spot. I have never been able to adapt to falsehoods and lies, to half-truths and posing, as well as profiteering. I was surrounded by all this. This environment was not for me. I was too honest…

I apologized for my outburst of anger. They totally understood me and told me that I was right. Matija, my classmate, told me to calm down and that he will check everything. He called Djuriša, a Brigade staffer, and asked him for the proposal and list of names. He pretended that he didn't know if my name was among the names on the list. Djuriša transferred the call to Stanković and Matija wisely and diplomatically asked for the names, explaining that he was already here and that he would like to use the opportunity to inform the people. Stanković told him that the lists were forwarded as it was suggested in the proposal for promotions. My name was on that list too. I wrote the order and the proposal. On the other hand, why was there all this secrecy, instead of simply reading the names on the list. Doubt started to erode my confidence while increasing my anxiety. I will trust no one until I personally see the paper Stanković was referring to. I may as well go and fuck myself, 42 days of war, mud, dirt, work, no sleep, thinking and death.

Between 13:30 - 14:00 I said goodbye to everyone and departed to Belgrade with Stojanović. Silence and an anguishing stillness remained behind me. In the car, I told Stojanović to remove the Yugoslav Army sticker from the car. I explained to him that it is a civilian car for military police, and it is a military car for civilian police because we are in the uniforms. He laughed. He should drop me off at home, then go to Energoprojekt Consulting to return the theodolite, and then to go home to his mother-in-law's house, where his wife and sons are staying.

I could not enter the building because there was no electricity and I was unable to call Nataša or Danka to open the door for me via intercom. While driving, Mika told me that he had overheard Dani's conversation with his family at home and that he realised they were talking about a computer. Dani probably asked one of his kids how their computer works. I explained to Mika that our computer from the unit had ended up at Dani's house. Mika said that he later asked Dani if he had a problem with the computer, and Dani replied that he didn't. "I don't like that man at all," Mika told me. "Not one of the Commanders likes him, Mika. Everybody's complaining," I replied.

I shouted out to Danka to come down and open the door for me. They were both happy to see me. Luckily Danka had already made lunch before the electricity was cut, as if she knew there would be a blackout today. There was no electricity, but the water supply was not interrupted. She made a coffee on the camping gas bottle and warmed up lunch. I particularly liked the hot soup. After lunch I had a shower and went to bed for a nap. Oh, how good it was to be here. I told Danka about my reaction to the injustice. She understood me, she was sick of the injustices, she had been seeing everywhere too. As we talked, Vlada called. He needed money to pay the rent for the apartment. It seemed that he would only call when he needed money. I called my friend Colonel Sidor Mišović from the Military Medical Academy. I told him what it was about. I told him I wanted to talk to him. He was proud of me and what we had done. He had been carrying the newspaper article about me everywhere and showing it to the people. The only thing he did not understand from the article was how I lived in Jasak, not in Vrdnik. I told him I was just born there. Mika brought my car back and Danka and I headed to Banjica to visit Sidor. We were wrong not to tell him that we were coming. He was not at home. His wife worked and he went to his father Rista in the 22nd Block to bring him a piglet. When we walked into his apartment, it smelled like urine. He must have a dog. He was the Chief of Surgery. His wife was the daughter of a general. We did not linger for long. His daughter was home alone, and she called her grandfather. We told Sidor to wait for us there and that we were coming. She gave us a paper note with his address: 19A Milentija Popović street, 22ndBlock. We could not find street number 19A in 22nd Block. So we left for 19th Block. After wandering around we returned to 22nd Block. Somehow, we managed to find the building and the apartment. Grandpa Rista and aunty Nada lived in a nice apartment. I told Sidor about the events today and the problem that bothers me. His advice was to do nothing right now and that we will fix everything after the war ends. He was proud of me. The most important thing was to stay alive and stay sane. The psychiatric criteria were eerily tightened. I didn't want my name to end up on the list of traitors and deserters, but I was terribly traumatised by the war. I was hurt by injustices, being sidelined by posers, cliques, and their social connections. I did not have the connections, and even if I did, I would not knock on anyone's door and degrade myself.

Lucia came in the evening. We discussed war profiteering and the set ups. For many, the war began with a power outage. Many were not even aware that there was a real war waging around. How ironic... We have been at war for 40+ days, and many don't even know what it is. Danka and Lucia were outraged. Many left Belgrade for the safety of the countryside. Now they understand what it means to be a refugee. To leave everything behind and move. Danka was snubbing at all for all the injustices she had experienced. For the first time since the beginning of the war, I had been sleeping in bed with a woman. The alarm clock rang at 05:30.

Thursday, May 06

We had our first morning coffee. Danka is working today.

At 06:40, Mika called via the intercom. I went downstairs. He was in the car with his wife when I came out. We greeted each other and Mika and I left for the battalion in my car. Along the way, we discussed injustices. Many would lose their jobs. There would be hunger and thievery, theft and home burglaries. People will have no or little income.

We arrived in Mihaljevci at 07:30. Dani was already in the missile guidance station with his shift. Major Dotlić came and, as I found out later, went to the engineers to prepare new combat position that we had chosen yesterday. Today is his son's birthday and he needed to go home. Dani learnt from Mika that we had arrived. He called me to come around 12:00 to replace him. I replied that Major Stoimenov should stay with the shift. It wouldn't

216

be his first time to be in a daytime shift. He had replaced Dani many times before, so there is no reason why he couldn't replace him today too.

Dani and I discussed everything. I told him that he can't treat me as he had been treating others. I knew everything and I had been making all decisions in the battalion. I felt I was too honest of a person for this environment, and that this was not the place for me in many ways. I hate posing.

He told me that I, as deputy commander, should not have reacted so tempestuously. "Do you realize that I'm on the edge of endurance? You're fucking around, and all the burden of the unit is solely on me. Get involved man! Do you know that I have lost 10 kilograms just because of the stress? You are exploiting everything for yourself. Who knows what and about whom you talk in the Brigade Command. How relevant is your opinion? We have no right to know, nor have been given an opportunity to defend ourselves," I replied while being seriously pissed off.

Dani told me that he wanted to go to a carpenter, as he had come up with a new idea on how to protect the station van. I was stunned. "He took Mika's idea as his own! Yesterday, when we were in the car, Mika told me about that idea. We have just been talking about this, what a shameless man," I thought to myself and then quickly realised, "Oh my God, I gave him so many ideas and solutions, and he have been presenting them as his own."

Somehow, that behaviour is embedded in his personality.

"No more talking," I said to myself. I gave myself a task to just do what is in the unit's best interest and what keeps people's heads on their shoulders.

Dani told me that the battalion from Mladenovac was hit last night. So, we were the only ones left unharmed... and no one else had been targeted 11 times so far and still is fully operational.

Due to my conscience and because of my people, I left for the shift from 16.00 to midnight. Boris informed me that there was no target acquisition functionality on the second channel. Boris was working to fix it[297] and he already informed the Operations Center. We are in Readiness No. 1.

Only one missile guidance channel had been functional since the war began. It was funny that with only 50 percent available capability to track the target and guide the missiles we downed two airplanes so far.

Muminović[298] came and brought lunch to Volf. We asked for further help. Lukić or Stoimenov went to Djević in Krnješevci. At around 19:55 they brought Ivanović to try to help us solve the problem. I told Luka Trgovčević, at the Operations Centre, that Miša arrived and is working to fix the problem.

---

297   He had already brought Sergeant Zdenko Volf to the firing position to fix the problem.

The fault was in the coordinate system (a part of the missile guidance station van that controls fine turning of the missile flight towards the target), the maintenance of which was the responsibility of Sergeant Zdenko Volf.

298   The Author ordered Major Senad Muminović, the Missile Guidance Battery (BVR) commander, to come to the firing position to help. Muminović came from the camp and brought lunch for Volf, who had missed it while fixing the fault.

217

We could launch only one missile via the first channel. With only 50 percent of our firepower available, the probability of our destruction of the target is reduced by 50 percent.

Someone made coffee in the power distribution cabin. We all drank it.

Senior Sergeant Djordje Maletić and his power supply crew – the Diesel Guys.

At 21:27, one of our fuses blew. Consequently, we did not have a single workable channel. I reported it to Krsmanović, at the Operations Center. The weather improved and the sky cleared... perfect weather for the "party".

Before the shift ended, my classmate, Major Roksandić, told me how much he can't stand Dani anymore. That started when Roksandić was an on-duty officer and his soldier, as an assistant, failed to report to Dani when Dani returned to the brigade command from the party after midnight.[299,300,301,302,303] He was reprimanding him for more than half an hour[304]. Major Roksandić

299   The brigade officers (other than the commanding officer) were rostered on 24 hours duty in the barracks.

300   Each duty officer had an assistant soldier (usually a Private or Corporal).

301   The officer was on duty until midnight, his assistant was on duty after midnight.

302   When the commander or a duty inspection officer visits the unit or duty officer's office for the first time, the duty officer or his assistant is required to report to him.

303   After midnight, Dani returned from a binge drinking party to the brigade command building (where the duty officer's office was located) when Roksandić's soldier was on duty. The soldier did not report to drunk Dani.

304   The next morning, at the meeting with the commanders of the base units, Dani reprimanded Roksandić and humiliated him for about half-an-hour about his soldier, and that he, as his commanding officer, failed to teach him what his duty was.

also told me that the other night, when General Veličković was in the unit, Dani had been drunk and that he did not understand how he sobered up so quickly. It would be fun if General Veličković, a sworn anti-alcoholic, figured out that the battalion's commanding officer was drunk while on duty.

There was a message on my pager to urgently call Armuš. I couldn't, because when there was no electricity in the village, there was no signal and it was not possible to call another area code.

When I arrived at the position, I noticed that 50 percent of the corner reflectors had fallen or just barely hanging. By phone, I ordered Sergeant Jaćić from the imitator to fix them. Around 17:00, he came to the station to inform me that they had been fixed and that everything was fine. On that occasion, Dani told Roksandić that Denčev had not been on the imitator duty for the past 32 hours. My classmate, Roksandić, replied that he would simply solve this problem, "I will pull Petrović off the imitator. When there are only two of you left, you will know whose shift it is. I have assigned the three of you to make it easier for you, and you are not able to agree among yourselves how your shifts will go."

Dani came around 12:00 a bit hunched over. He said that he got an injection and that the doctor massaged him. It was probably hurting him, but he also liked to exaggerate. I gave him the car keys to go to the carpenter, because he gave his Opel Ascona to Aca, his driver, and Dotlić to go home. Askona consumes diesel, "To save fuel," he joked.

Stoimenov called around 17:55 to ask if we are still troubleshooting the missile guidance station. Muminović replied him that he could come to help. "Boris is a good officer and buddy, he will come," he said.

I told Ljubenković to stop the antennas and be ready to work quickly. My task was to the readiness of the communications, the fuel level in the generator tanks and the functionality of the devices. Everything was fine.

I heard on the radio that NATO had dropped illumination bombs for the first time tonight, in Valjevo. The city had no electricity, but it was lit, like it was the daytime. Then they selected targets. Toys and chocolates were thrown over Šabac! Absolutely nothing shall be touched, as these may be booby-trapping. Like when the Nazis used the same method to kill and maim people, particularly children during WWII. Many were not aware that it was war, especially children.

Danka's car broke down. She couldn't put the clutch in neutral. I asked Dušan Milojković to help her as much as he could. He was familiar with the whole situation and knew where I was.

I got an idea to write a letter to the Commander-in-Chief in order to point out to him the injustice inflicted upon me and other guys. I may really have to do that in a few days, after I hear and see the outcome of my previously raised concerns.

I spoke to David and told him about what was bothering me. "That's right, bro," he said, "you've been waiting for a long time." "Is there a time limit for recognition for what we did and still doing?" I wondered angrily, "I can't let them wipe my name off from history. I equally deserved my name to be inscribed into the list of "legends" of our time, just like the names of all others who were in the combat crew that shot down the Stealth. That's my moral right. I will never give up on truth and principles, no matter how much it costs me."

It was cold outside. A cold Northern wind was blowing. The other day we were sweating in T-shirts and it was just 6 degrees Celsius this morning... It was raining..

Last night, on my way back from Sidor, I saw a handful of people occupying the Gazela Bridge in Belgrade. They waved their flags while guarding the bridge from bombs with their bodies. There was about 20-30 of them when I passed through the crowd sometimes between 19:00-19:30.

A large crowd of people safeguarding the bridge by making themselves targets was shown on TV. Many wore the symbolic target insignia, or had Yugoslavian and Serbian flags and protest banners, all protesting against the barbaric NATO bombing. Maybe more people came later or our propaganda was inflating the numbers.

The air raid began around 23:00. We had been informed on several occasions about the targets around us at distances of about 25 km. We turned on our surveillance radar but saw nothing closer than 35 km away, far from our effective engagement range. Those guys up there in the air somehow knew our rough position and avoided us.

Miša Ivanović left us around 22:00. He had to prepare for his shift duty in his unit, from 00:00 to 08:00, so he left early. The analyzer on the second channel was still not working. We didn't have a diode and an oscilloscope for pinpoint testing. In the morning, after an oscilloscope arrives, someone should go and bring Miša Ivanović again. Would our officers be able to remedy the malfunctions under the current field circumstances?

Friday, May 07

The second shift, which replaced us with Dotlić at the helm, was in Readiness No. 2 from 01:00 to 07:00. Armuš came with a team of carpenters to try to realize Mika's idea, which was "appropriated" by Dani. I left with them to the combat position. The idea was to make the palisade fortification[305] around the missile guidance station van narrower in order to cover the van with the horizontally placed logs. After careful consideration we realised that it was not so easy to do. We needed an expert person to assess if the columns would be able to carry the weight of the horizontal logs - measured in tons. There was a risk of instability and collapse under its own weight. In addition, we needed to remove the camouflage nets and some of the palisades, about 25 logs. It would take a good craftsman to construct such a shelter and to put the van inside such shelter. In my opinion, the construction had to be quite strong, with mutually interchangeable logs. I didn't want to take that risk

---

305   Palisade fortification - Tall walls made of logs placed side by side vertically with no free space in between. Also known as "Log protection".

myself so reported it to Dani.

The logs should be stacked from the embankment onto the van. I sent the carpenters, Stojanović and Armuš to Dani to work it out together.

I stayed on shift instead of Dani.

It was reported that Dani must be at the old meeting place of the Brigade Command on the Ibar Highway at 15:00 regarding the stimulus measures. The avalanche was set in motion. If this was the way to solve the problem, then let the dust rise. I wanted to fight for my truth and my justice. If the team was legend then I wanted my name there as well, because I deserved it. After all, I belonged there because I did my job as part of the combat shift. Before Dani left for the meeting, he asked me if there was a legal basis for my promotion to the rank of colonel, since I had become a lieutenant colonel less than a year ago. "Is there a legal basis for Nikolić or anyone else?" I asked him and said,"Wartime promotions are beyond the peacetime rules and the special rule book applies." "Well, then we will request the same for all," Dani reluctantly said. "I did not know that performing a heroic act required a legal basis," I thought to myself. Nonsense and irony. I felt that he will try everything to undermine me. "How about a decoration instead of the promotion," Dani suggested next. I strongly disagreed, "I want the same others have received already. The whole team should receive the same recognition. We are the team and we act as a team, not as a bunch of disconnected individuals. There should be no difference. I don't want dirty games.""Good," Dani said and left.

When we woke up this morning Dani told me that he must beaware of me. "Well, do you think I belong in the category of stupid people?" I asked him. He went out somewhere this morning, allegedly to survey the position, and he needed my business car. He ordered the mail to be delivered today with my car and so on. The game to belittle me and take my car had begun; in a "sophisticated" way, so it was not so obvious. I understood that very well. I chose to be silent. He did not realize that his behavior was cutting the branch on which he had been sitting. I held the unit together, he was a figurehead that no one respects. So, I had been cornered and I had no choice but to start playing politics, not just chivalry.

Stojanović and I went to Karlovčic to check on the construction of the new combat position, but Mika could not find it. I wasn't with them when they scouted it, so I didn't know where it was. On the way, I stopped by Milan and Nada's place. The house was locked and they were not at home. I tied the bag with medications to the window screen next to the front door and left for Pećinci.

I needed to go to the dentist and Mika to Pošarac.

Later, I phoned Danka. Dušan Milojković visited her to arrange a car repair. I had asked him for help when I was at home last time. Well done Dušan. People like him and he should not be forgotten.

Mika told me that he was with Dani yesterday. Dani tried to get close to him and establish rapport, in order to make him speak about me. I instantly thought, "And if so, there is nothing to be found on me. I am clean.""He forgets one thing," Mika continued, "we have known each other for eight years." The time factor was on our side.

Upon their return from Kupinovo, Dani and Mika stopped by Brica for a celebration. The locals were there, as were my ex-wife's neighbors, Nana and Vauš. They greeted me sincerely. As usual, Dani introduced himself as the commander of the unit that shot down the F-117A. There was nothing new in his behaviour. Mika told me how disgusted he was with his obnoxious behaviour, filthy language, and manners. Trgovčević called me to send two Ural trucks that Ića Vučković needed. "I don't have two Urals. I have one Ural and one Kraz truck with a crane. I hope these will suffice. Both vehicles should be located at the entrance to the Deč village from the direction of Šimanovci." Someone from the Brigade will come there in the Zastava Florida car.

Popović from the Operations Centre told me to organise food for his people to be delivered by the logistics support unit or by Stanisavljević. I delegated his request to Barvalac, and asked him to repeat that he understood what I had told him.

The Police Station in Pećinci moved to a new location. I found it. On the way there I bumped into Vesna, Novica's wife. She greeted and hugged me and invited me to come to visit them. I told her frankly that I had not contacted anyone in Pećinci because of the situation. I chose to tell nothing to anyone about my divorce. I heard that there was a lot of talk about me, but to find truth one must hear from both sides. "Well, I know you. When I call you to come, I don't give a fuck what they'll say. I know who they are and who you are" Vesna said. "Great work, " I said,"I don't want to elevate their rating and make them think I'm hanging around their house because of them.""I agree, you're right," she said and we farewelled.

It was already 12:30 and I was in a hurry to see the dentist and quickly climbed the stairs to surgery, but the dentist had already gone home. Fuck it! I have to come on Monday. I didn't even know it was Friday today.

Mika was following me in the footsteps. We walked past the pharmacy and Mika begged us to come inside and see if there are medications his mother needed. She had been a chronic psychiatric patient for 36 years. Vukica, the pharmacy's owner, was inside. When she saw us at the doors she leaped forward to greet and hug me. Oh my God, everyone knew me in Pećinci. She took out the medication out of the corner for Mika's mother and gave it to him. Now he hugged me too. "What a fuck, what's wrong with you people?" I asked them. We talked, they asked how I'm doing. They said I looked good, other than I lost some weight and got grey hair. They also asked when the war will end.

We left. Outside, Suzana, Šilja's wife, approached us. Vesna told her I was here. She hugged me too. "What the hell is this today?" Mika asked me. "Everyone loves you and appreciates you, man." "Mika," I replied,"I didn't bother anyone. I'm a very principled person and people know it. I stayed with everyone in fond memory. That's it."

The hairdresser's saloon was closed, as the owner went to attend to his field.

"Dani is in Pećinci with Luki," Aca, his driver, told us. I asked Mika, what percentage would one get for leasing the gen sets. "Up to 10%, if he is modest," he replied. I absolutely dislike Dani. His evil eyes and shrewd look. I felt sorry for the computer. I knew he can hardly wait for the opportunity to profit and in the end, he did it, he took it to his house. He had plenty of time to wander around under the disguise of scouting for a new combat position and allegedly doing something, that no one knew what, 'on behalf of' or 'for the benefit' of the unit.

His lower back suddenly stiffened up yesterday for a combat shift, but was not stiff for celebrations and meetings... I wondered why he, as a commander, was personally arranging the delivery logs when he had helpers?! He had a need to show off for everybody to see him.

My ex-wife was from here and local people knew me. Everyone asked about me. His jealousness, if indeed, could explain his behaviour?! There were no more benchmarks nor priorities hor him. The unit was left to me. I took care of the unit before the war, and especially now at war. I was the horse that had been pulling the crate the most. My 'true shift' is of indefinite duration and has no breaks. When I was not in the combat shift, I had been liaising with other units, doing administration, as well as a host of other duties. I was taking my job too seriously. Few others were as serious as me, but I wished I could be like most of the others who were not.

I was in the combat shift from 14:00 to 24:00. I gave the keys of my Zastava 101 to Dotlić to go and inspect the construction of the new combat position because the Lada Niva 4WD already left to get the equipment, battalion mail, and spare parts for the signals platoon. Lukić arrived around 17:30. I had a conversation with Colonel Šobota and asked him about Ivanović. The missile guidance officer was in the shift, and his replacement Parađina was not here. I wondered if he would be able to help us. It seemed to me that we only rarely got to go home. My classmate Djordjević had been seen in Jakovo several times so far. Dani didn't care if he went home or not. To be fair, he didn't care about going home before the war either. He often stayed in the unit unnecessarily. It is not my concern how he spends his free time. I and the rest of the unit want to visit our families in our spare time. We had been having the same problem with faggots and hookers, and others who did not want to go home after work. I was absolutely not interested in that kind of lifestyle. Where were the moral norms?

I called Danka and told her allegorically that there was a lot of dust in the air and I was firmly resolved to fight for my rights.

At around 18:00 Cveja Roglić from Mihaljevci, Živa, and Sava, tire repairers, from Pećinci came to the camp. They brought juices for the troops. Živa had a café in Pećinci and, as far as I knew, had graduated from the Faculty of Political Science in Bulgaria.

The total ban on air defense actions for the unit, including Strela MANPADs was announced to take effect from 18:00 to 18:20. The agreement[306] was that

---

306   Providing air defense around operational civilian (and military) airports is tricky due to the risk of error of shooting unintended targets or enemy penetration, hence the author requested redundant confirmation of the critical orders. For

Colonel Milojica will independently re-confirm to me any order immediately before it took effect. He was "upstairs" at the Operations Center. Since he didn't confirm, I didn't issue the order to open the airspace, and all units remained on active duty.

At 18:35 Milojica told me to send a car to pick up Miša Ivanović. "Will you be ok to work with only one channel," he asked me. "I will," I replied briefly. "Then send the vehicle," he told me. I called the school, the reservist Pavlović picked up the line, I told him that he needs to pass that message to Lukić, the driver.

Cveja Roglić invited me to come to his place tonight, to have a bath. "Thanks, tomorrow would be more convenient," I replied.

At 20:34 the Operations Center told us to go to Readiness No.1.

Dotlić sent Lukić to Kupinovo earlier, so Miša Ivanović had to wait from 18:30 to 20:00 before the vehicle with Stoimenov came to pick him up. We wasted hour and a half. Boris eventually went with Maljković's Lada Niva 4WD, and in 20 minutes, brought Ivanović into the unit. We went in the Zastava 101 and arrived at the same time. I will no longer give anyone my Zastava 101.

Popović was "upstairs" at the Brigade command post. He asked me, "How are you buddy?" Was he aware of the problem?

Dani was not in the unit yet.

Earlier today, NATO threw cluster bombs[307] at the green market in Niš, in the middle of the day when it was the busiest. That was true savagery and barbarism.

Boris told me that he saw tonight a Dvina[308] missile launch ramp and a missile guidance station van coming from the direction of Krnješevci. They were setting up a combat position in the area of the village of Šimanovci. Muminović noted that only a madman could send them to take up a combat position that had been fired from before. We shot the F-117A, that glorious day, 27 March, at 20:42. The date, time and minute will be remembered

example, hostile fighter jets can shadow a large commercial plane in order to attack ground targets or to trick the air-defense into error.

307   A cluster bomb consists of a hollow shell with more than 2,000 sub-munitions or bomblets contained within it. Bomblets may or may not explode on impact remaining a deadly risk to kill or maim civilians for many years to come. On 7 May 1999, between the time of 11:30 and 11:40, a NATO targeted the central part of the city of Niš with cluster bombs that hit the Medical Center, the main market and bus station.

About 2,000 cluster bombs containing 380,000 sub-munitions were dropped on Yugoslavia during the Operation Allied Force, in 1999 by US, UK and Netherlands. (Source: Wikipedia)

308   The S-75 (SA-2 Guideline) is a Soviet-designed, high-altitude air defense system, built around a surface-to-air missile with command guidance. Following its first deployment in 1957, it became one of the most widely deployed air defense systems in history. Dvina is local jargon word for the S-75.

in history books. For this reason, I wished to be part of that team, though there were many who would like to dispute it. It was not my first battle in life. I will win this one too. The promotions and awards should be given for the deed itself, not for someone's opinion of me as a person and an officer. Especially not the opinion of an alcoholic.

A very serious air raid started around 23:00. I had the targets on my screen for a long time and had been communicating their coordinates to Milojić and Stanković. After that, there were no targets on my surveillance radar and no indications that it was defective. The images on the screen looked quite normal, but the targets were nowhere to be seen. This was obviously a classic example of electromagnetic interference. At the order of the Operations Centre around 23:40, I directed the antenna of the target acquisition radar to the azimuth 170. The combat work began. The missile guidance officer did not locate the target. The surveillance radar suddenly showed a target at the azimuth 15 km away and in the outgoing direction. During the next turn of the radar, I had fifteen targets around me. After that, nothing again. I had no idea what was going on. Dotlić came with a shift to replace us at 00:00. I told him what we saw.

Saturday, May 08

Kosta woke me up with a double medium coffee. I watched Dani flipping through the mail. I was waiting for him to tell me the outcomes of yesterday's meeting at the Brigade Command. I chose not to ask him anything.

Major Dotlić came around 08:10. Then Dani, the poser, I won't call him by his name again, presented the meeting information to the two of us. At that time, Major Stoimenov was in the shift, as the Commander. Everything was irrelevant to me right now. I was impatiently waiting to hear about the most important topic for me, the one which I had been thinking all night.

He told me to keep quiet and not to write a complaint. He listed three reasons why I couldn't be promoted:

a) I did not spend 2/3 of my military service time in the rank of Lieutenant Colonel (he was ignorant that no such regulation existed in the "Law on the Army of Yugoslavia");

b) I did not finish the Command-Staff School, and;

c) I received all of this very emotionally.

Then he also told me that I resented Blagojević. "What does my resentment towards Blagojević have to do with what the shift did?" "Who asked for that?" I asked him to clarify.

He told me that I signed the proposal for the Brigade Command to promote everyone in the shift that had shot down the Stealth. "How could you sign anything when you're never in the unit. Why didn't they ask you who had been signing the other reports and documents? I replied and thought to myself, "Does he know that I'm entitled to the seal all outgoing correspondence? Envy is in the core of everything."

"Shoot down the airplane and you'll get the rank," he told me. I couldn't believe he had just said that, "So, I was not in the shift crew that had shot down the Stealth. Where was I then? Who was the shift commander? Whose brainchild is our current combat tactic, and who organised its implementation in the combat work we have now been following? Why did I put myself in the position of deputy shift commander? What is my contribution? You either deceived the Brigade Command or intentionally did not want to fight for me," I thought.

My determination was not deterred, on the contrary, "I will push for justice even if I have to leave the Defence Force," I said to myself. I did not know what I should do next at this point in time, as I was hurt, emotionally injured and needed some time to decompress, so I decided to go to Deč and process the mail.

Along the way, I stopped by Milan and Nada's house for a coffee. I told them about the injustice. They couldn't believe it. Trust me. "Just stay alive and well. Everything else will be sorted out," Nada told me as my mother, "Don't lose your mind." Milan uttered curses and swore profanely. He also said that Colonel Sima, who is a high quality person, had also experienced many similar injustices in the Army. He had been waitinga long time to retire and he finally got out. I left them and waws on my way.

Dani -the poser will be in the shift tonight. I had a feeling that his preference would be for a bomb to blow us up, for our combat assets to be destroyed, and that he is deployed to some other place where his life would not be hanging by a thread.

I told Tomović and Sedlak about the injustice that befell to me. "Nothing can be done here. Take care of your health and nerves," they consoled me.

I paced like a caged lion, unable to do anythingn or to concentrate. I really need to learn to control myself. I have to learn to play politics and to socialize with people in the military beyond my beliefs. Is that what I really want? No, I want peace, only peace and nothing else.

Dani told me today, for the first time, what he had allegedly never told anyone else so far, "We sat next to each other, but you thought it was a drone or a bait instead of the airplane".

"So what, man? That was a very important warning that you didn't think about. Do you know what the Americans did to the Iraqis that way? I have to think of everything. It's just proof that we worked together and that I was there. I was doing my job within the combat crew. We were both issuing commands. Are you aware that by interrupting the combat operation, I shortened our shooting cycle by more than half, which gave us a chance to survive? Is there anything contentious about this? What's the matter? " I replied.

He remained stunned. Throughout the conversation, Dotlić merely kept his eyes low. He was aware of the injustice. "It's not about the promotion man, it's about the principle!!! Fuck the promotions! What is hurt is injustice! The award should be given for the deed, not for someone's opinion of me," I said.

When I left for Deč, Dani went to Kupinovo. Of course, I knew he was lying.

Barvalac's troops in Kupinovo were preparing the wood for the shelter. Major Dotlić called Dani in Kupinovo. As expected, he was not there. He never even came, as I though...

It wasn't until late at night that I could concentrate and fall asleep. I watched Tomović's, Sedlak's and Barvalac's steady breathing. Tonight, they went to the centre of Deč and watched the Army's anti-aircraft fire coming from all sides. As if they were watching a 3D fireworks display.

Around 01:00, I couldn't hear anything outside, and I called Colonel Stanković at the Operations Center. I knew he was there at night. I told him that I wanted an official interview with the Air Corps Commander. Hetold me: "Okay.""Write down the questions you want to discuss." We greeted each other. I hung up.

I got a call from the alcoholic Blagojević. Fuck the man who is above you because of his position, and has the inferior moral qualities, far below those required of an officer and commander.

I fell asleep after smoking numerous cigarettes.

I called Danka. She got me the phone number of the Air Defense Chief of Staff, General Slavko Biga. She supported me and felt all my pain. "My darling don't worry," she told me warmly, "be careful and stay alive and well. Nothing else matters." I knew that she is right, but the pain of injustice irritated me. I have to learn to live with that pain and injustice. We needed to wage war with this chaos in our heads. Let's try to focus.

Who is my main adversary? Military bureaucracy, NATO or myself?

Sunday, May 09

I woke up tired after another sleepless night... The first task is to sort out the mail.

I wrote an order to bring parts of the downed F-16 back and assigned it to Žugić and made a roster for guard duty. Later to submit my objection to the list of awards for the two downed aircraft, so my battle on the second front can begin.

In contrast to my first battle, in the shift,which can take my life, my second battle, against the military administration, can take my health and energy. I used the prescribed military procedure to apply for the review of decisions made by my direct superiors in the command chain. I had been a part of that command chain since graduation from the Military Academy and I was familiar with how it worked. It had not been delivering true justice. The justice, as per the command chain, had been an additional star on the rank insignia on your shoulder, and therefore the right to make decisions. Errors had been hard to admit. There had been no place for emotions. "The truth is somewhere in the air and, as such, it does not exist," the Commander of Brigade Lazović used to say.

Dani told me that he had decided to move the unit."You have no right to decide this alone and without consultation with the Brigade Command," I told him. He explained that visited the Brigade Command post tonight and sought their premission to relocate the unit. We stayed on this combat position near Mihaljevci for a week, from Sunday to Sunday, which was unacceptably long. I brought this to his attention earlier today. We will go back to the area near the village of Karlovčić, but to a different position. The rule of thumb was to never return to a previously held combat position. This rule later became an official order.

Unusual news came in the mail from the Brigade Command that Senior Sergeant Mića Mijalković had been ordered out from the unit. No one knew why. My civilian clothes and shoes from the Jakovo Barracks were at his house.

I typed up the complaint letter and sent it with Mića Mijalković for Dani to read it and add the text of his forwarding order[309]. The idea was to re-type the letter together with his forwarding order before we sign it. He didn't understand it, just signed the paper and told Mića that I also have to sign my complaint. I later explained to him that I wanted him to write down the wording of his forwarding order, so that I could re-type my letter together with his order, before we both sign and then officially send it.

I told Mića to find the 1:100,000 scale maps we needed. I handed him my office and cash register keys to get me the requested maps and some other papers. He said he would try get me a new M-93 uniform[310], if he could. Slavko typed the forwarding order. Žugić was transitioning the equipmentinto marching configuration and loading it onto transport vehicles. He returned to the camp. I ordered the CBRN section to take responsibility for camouflage and setting up pallisades (log protection) on the combat position from now on. This was needed in order to reduce the workload of other units.

The situation with my objection came to a climax when all officers of the combat crew who shot down the F-16 were also awarded. All officers of the two combat crews, except me, were awarded. The comparative list of the officers, their roles and awards in the two respective combat crews looked appalling. I hope that NATO one day will not use this list to make a claim for damaged and destroyed equipment. The award field next to my name was blank. Refer to the table below.

Downed aircraft	F117-A	F16

---

309   The military procedure required all complaints to go through the chain of command.
310   New uniforms for the new state FR Yugoslavia (following the breakup of old SFR Yugoslavia).

Role	Name & Rank	Award	Name & Rank	Award
Shift commander, fire control officer	Dani Zoltan, Colonel	Promoted	Dotlić Boško, Major	Decorated
Deputy shift commander, deputy fire control officer	Aničić Djordje, Lt. Colonel		Stojanović Miodrag, Lieutenant	Promoted
Missile guidance officer	Muminović Senad, Major	Promoted	Janković Tiosav, Lieutenant	Promoted Decorated
Manual tracking operator on F1	Matić Dragan, Warrant Officer	Promoted	Matić Dragan, Warrant Officer	Decorated
Manual tracking operator on F2	Tiosavljević Dejan, Senior Sergeant	Promoted	Radivojević Igor, Senior Sergeant	Promoted
Battery commander	Nikolić Darko, Lieutenant	Promoted Decorated	Roksandić Milorad, Major	Decorated

Djordje Aničić

Lieutenant Colonel

VP1205-4, Jakovo

08 May1999

Subject: *Objection to the assigned awards; Military Post 1205-4 Jakovo*

On 27 March 1999, at 20:42 hours, my unit carried out a combat shooting of an enemy target in the airspace we defended. On that occasion, the symbol of the United States Air Force, the "invisible" plane, the F-117A was shot down. The whole progressive world followed that event with great admiration, while NATO strategists remained astonished. Our success was even greater, given that so few such aircrafts have been produced so far, and that the development program and technology were kept top secret. Our weapon system

229

belongs to the third generation of weapons and we have brought down a sixth generation aircraft.

The Russian Army generals, Duma representatives, the Director and Constructor of the missile system specially honoured our unit and personally visited our combat crew.

Unfortunately, my superior command did not honour our unit.

The core combat crew consisted of six officers and one soldier. This crew was located in the command post in the missile guidance van. In case you are not familiar with the composition of the combat crew, which I doubt, I will repeat it here for ease of correspondence. That night, at the request of Colonel Stanković, Chief of the Combat Command Group at the Operations Centre, I personally dictated the names of the crewmembers. The combat crew consisted of:

- *Lt. Col. Zoltan Dani, Shift commander, fire control officer,*
- *Lt. Col. Djordje Aničić, Deputy shift commander, deputy fire control officer,*
- *Captain Senad Muminović, Missile Guidance Officer,*
- *2nd Lieutenant Darko Nikolić, Battery Commander,*
- *Senior Sergeant Dragan Matić, Manual Tracking Operator on F2,*
- *Sergeant Dejan Tiosavljević, Manual Tracking Operator on F1,*
- *Private Davor Bložić, shift clerk and fire control plotting board operator.*

The photograph of the combat crew was also published in the article titled "The game on a knife's edge," Army magazine, War Issue No. 5, published by the Military of Yugoslavia. The caption under the photograph individually listed fake names of the crewmembers for security reasons. My pseudonym in the article was Andjelko Djordjević, and I was referred to as a man who was in the command post that evening. The unit commander personally gave the list of pseudonyms to the journalist of the Vojska newspaper Branko Kopunović and to Lt. Col. Dragovan Matijeveć from superior command.

Further developments were quite unexpected for me. As we were all tapped on the shoulder by world and domestic radio, and TV stations broadcasted a picture of the downed plane, I experienced the greatest disappointment in my life by the responsible commanding officers of my superior command.

The following crew members were awarded for the deed:

- *2nd Lieutenant Darko Nikolić, was decorated with the Order of Courage by Supreme Command and the President of the State and promoted to the rank of Lieutenant by the order of the Air Force and Air Defence Commander.*

- *Lt. Col. Zoltan Dani, was promoted to the rank of Colonel,*

- *Captain Senad Muminović, promoted to Major,*

- *Senior Sergeant Matić, promoted to Warant Officer,*

- *Sergeant lDejan Tiosavljević was promoted to Senior Sergeant.*

As you can see from the above, only Davor Bložić and I were not awarded – neither promoted nor decorated. I would understand if only the unit commander was awarded. I did not go to war for the sake of promotion or decoration, but for the conviction of the need to defend the homeland. That was my sole objective. I have been performing all my duties and tasks very conscientiously and responsibly, which further increased my disappointment. I see this as the biggest moral downfall and the largest belittling and disparaging of me as a person and an officer.

I have been in the missile forces for 19 years and I cannot accept this outcome. It totally knocked me off balance mentally. If there is justice and morality, I trust that by all criteria I deserve to be equally awarded as others were. The state is waging war for freedom and truth, not for poltroons. I have never been a poltroon, nor will I be ever. Can truth be hidden?

Lives are very important to all individuals. For days and nights, from one second to another, my life has been on the altar of the homeland, as well as the lives of the officers awarded above. I am seeking equality. In my opinion, all those who are now, and have been in the past, trying in various ways to challenge the deed and find different ways and justifications not to meet my request are hurt vanities of low morale and consciousness.

There is written evidence about the operation and the mistakes made by superior Command. These should be analysed after the war ends. The central issue here is an award for a historical deed I took part in, rather than an award for one's personal opinion of me as a person and an officer. I request and require that superior command apply to me the same awards criteria that were applied to award the above crewmembers of the combat crew, to award me, so I can find myself on the list where I belong. Otherwise, I would have no choice but to request personal and moral satisfaction through other means. In that respect, I am also respectfully requesting an official meeting with the Air Corps Commander to discuss the issues raised here, since I see no point in discussing it with my direct superior command because they made an unjust selection of people to be awarded. This is also a separate issue I wish to present and resolve with the Air Corps Commander.

As proof that I am telling the truth, I refer to members of my war unit and combat crewmembers, celebrated for excellence in their Air Defence skills.

MILITARY POST

Our Ref.: Int No. 410-166

08 May1999

Jakovo (Zemun)

(Seal or Stamp)　　　　　　　　　　　　　　　　　TO
MILITARY POST 1205, BATAJNICA

I forward to you the objection of Lieutenant Colonel Djordje Aničić
for further jurisdiction and resolution as it exceeds my delegated authority. Everything written above is indisputably true.

Commander Colonel Zoltan Dani

(Seal or Stamp)　　　　　　　Signature

I now have the home phone numbers of Generals Biga and Karanović.
The ball of yarn slowly started to unroll. Danka will get me a phone number
from Živadin Jovanović's driver. I'll get to the Commander-in-Chief. As a
child, I had been brought up in the spirit of chivalry and justice, I must win
this battle.

Today, at 13:30, missile battery commander Golubović called from
Russia. He said he had been working a lot there. "Is everybody there?", he
asked. "Yes, we are and working at full steam," I replied. Our exchange was
deliberately brief and succinct. "Did Tiosav work?" "Yes, he did it twice. The
firsttime he missed, but the second time he hit the F-16." I didn't elaborateon
the facts. He shouted at the top of his lungs in euphoria from the other end of
the wire. He seemed like a nice guy, always making moves to please others,
like a leaf in the wind. Regardless of that I had a feeling that he would end up
like me. Each epoch requires a certain profile of the commander and officer.
I refused to accept human immorality to be a condition for success.

Around 16:00, Nikolić also called from Russia. He asked for phone
numbers to call his friends. I replied, not so explicitly, that the relocation
was in progress and that we no longer have telephone numbers. He said that
he understand. He also said that he expect to return back sometime around
1 June "I will know more details tomorrow," he said. I wondered if it was
careless of them to call us. I was sure the Russians were recording all their
calls and conversations. "Who knows? War is a business that generates
profit. One never knows for sure what is what and who is who…" I wished
I was wrong…

We did not relocate to the new combat position today. Probably because
of the relocation of Noskov's unit and because the log protection was
unfinished.

In the night 7/8 May 1999, Belgrade was bombed and three bombs hit
the Chinese Embassy. Chinese people were protesting in front of the US

embassies around the world. This was not a collateral mistake. This was a deliberate attack. The riders of the apocalypse continued to provoke the whole world... It is as if they wanted to escalate the war to other Balkan countries and accross the world. The UN Security Council reacted very lightly and produced a weak resolution. It had been a mere servant of the NATO Pact for a long time... Useless...

It looks like the war will take longer than anyone expected.

Dropulić provided me with plenty of medicines for Milan and Nada.

The other day dentist Dragan Matić joined the unit. He has his own practice.

Dani had not called me since this morning, when he said to me, "How are you my friend?!" I did not reply. I think he realized that we were no longer friends, nor would we ever be. Friends appreciate and cherish each other. He betrayed me on the first bend. I'll have to do some things, too. I will make my network through Mika Stojanović. He is Dani'sdriver, who need to be recruited, so we could see Dani's itineraries. He is a former member of the state security who would certainly professionally do this favour for his old mate. I will have to talk to him about it.

We, Serbs, had been fools for a long time by having a very naive approach towards politics. I was one of them, and I certainly wouldn't be anymore. In contrast, Dani started politicking very early in his career and prepared the grounds to become a general one day. I am not burdened with becoming a general, but I will be aware of politicking in the future and I will no longer volunteer my opinions so naively. I will surely recognize future traps from now on. A seemingly great friend made small concessions to you while also stabbing you in the back, in order to eliminate you.

Today is 9 May, Victory Day over fascism. To this day, we have been in the ranks of the victorious forces and on the right side of the history; and now our former allies are bombing us. They are worse than Hitler.

I updated the personnel list to be mailed out to HR and Payroll Department next week. Our unit alone will get about half a million dinars cash for salaries and allowances. This is a lot of money. Who will end up paying for it?

I decided to no longer sign any correspondence on behalf of the unit, as a matter of principle. I will cause Slavko to go and find Dani to sign it and take personal responsiblity for all decisions. The order from the 250th Air Defense Brigade came with the mail today, saying that unit commanders must be in the missile guidance stations from 22:00 to 04:00. I doubt Dani would obey the order, but I will insist on that.

Dropulić told me that he will organise graphic preparation for printing my war diary after the war, and that I will only have to find out who will print it. I didn't forget the good old custom of getting to know the people around you. People can always help you, however, only if you respect them and treatthem fairly.

I started the day by sorting the battalion's mail and writing the following orders:

- The guard service procedure and schedule,
- Removal of parts from the wreck of the downed F-16 in the village of Badanja,
- The blank certification form that the person is involved in the war operations,
- The blank certification form that the person completed training shooting from the personal weapons No. 2 and handguns on No. 1.[311]

I went to Deč to pickup the mail and then went to Mihaljevci. There, I met Dani, Dr. Djukić, Major Stoimenov and Dani's driver Aca, in the school. They went to the combat position in Karlovčić to see how the new log protection design had been implemented in practice. Dani cheerfully greeted me, "Where have you been my friend?!" and told me that he's planning to be back by 12:00. The equipment was packed and transported to the waiting area behind the school in Karlovčić.

The status of soldiers from Deč and Šimanovci had not been regulated and the officers there did not know what to do.[312] Lukić asked me about that. I replied with a counter-question,"Why did you not ask the commander, who was here, and now you are asking me?" He told me that he spoke with him and that Dani told him to wait there until further notice. "Then wait! What's not clear with that? Why are you throwing me in the fire now when I don't know the background? Everyone shall remain where they are until they receive an order to move."

It seemed to me that the stay of the troops in Mihaljevci after the equipment left was not planned, and that they simply "forgot" to regulate the status of the troops[313]. The latter turned out to be true.

Major Dotlić was in the room. He was resting on the cot bed. I gave him my letter of objection to proof read. After reading, he told me that his first impression was that I was just looking for a promotion into the rank of Colonel. "It's not about the promotion Boško, it's about the principle." "You're absolutely right," he told me now. "We Serbs are very stupid. We only know how to fight wars, while everyone else is making political moves

311   The training shooting from the personal weapons (assault rifles) and handguns were regulated by the law and required mandatory use of the specific numbering system.

312   The troops from Deč and Šimanovci helped the transition of the equipment from combat to marching configuration at the old firing position in Mihaljevci. The equipment was towed away to Karlovčić and the troops were left in Mihaljevci not knowing what to do next.

313   For example, to tell them when to come to the new firing position in Karlovčić, etc.

and reaping the benefits."

I told him about our battalion computer, who took it, and the situation with the generator.

"Dani did that?" he looked at me in astonishment. "Some things are clear to me now," he told me, "he avoids shifts and other duties."

I also told him about the order from the Brigade HQ about who should be on duty from 22:00 to 4:00. "So, he does not execute the Brigade's Order!" Boško exclaimed in disbelief.

"I do not want to spread negative energy. I just want him to start thinking and behave as a battalion commander," I replied,"I didn't think about everything either, so see what I have experienced; how much humiliation, if not in front of anyone else, then in front of myself."

Dotlić seemed very disappointed and he grabbed a beer bottle and said: "Djole, you're right. We're all a bunch of fools. Just look at the dismissal of the Generals during the ongoing war and who was appointed as the Chief of Security at the Supreme Command. Are there Serbs in other countries in such high military positions?"[314] I replied, "Maybe there is someone, but I really don't know." We spoke about the war in Bosnia and Hercegovina. The same things and treatment of people were being repeated. The conversation lasted about one and a half hours. We laid down to rest.

Dani still didn't show up.

After a brief nap, I sat in the car because they informed me that Mijalković had brought the code maps[315] which I had ordered, to the camp in Deč. He also brought me a new vest. Slavko and I glued and put the code maps together.[316] After that I coded it.[317] If it were suddenly peacetime again, it

---

314   Major Dotlić referred to the appointment of General Geza Farkaš, a native Hungarian from the Vojvodina region of Serbia, who was appointed as the Chief of the Military Security.

315   The maps - were multiple sections of detailed topographic military maps in a scale of 1:25 000.

316   To bond the (code) maps together – individual maps were put together (glued) in the proper order to compose one very large map. Individual maps covered a small geographical area, because of its small scale, which was too small for practical use.

317   To code a map–means to divide a paper map into squares and to inscribe two capital letters, either in the Cyrillic or Latinic script, in each square: therefore increasing the strength of encryption of messages.

For example, a coded message could say: "Go to the square Ruma – Beograd (RB) and do this and that..."

would be a good day to go fishing, though...[318,319]

After that, I went to the combat position in the region of the village of Karlovčić. They were setting up the equipment. The protection system that Dani "invented" could not work. The idea was simple, to horizontally lay the logs against the roof of the cabin and the surrounding berm.[320,321] Unfortunately,the cabin roof gave in and started to crumble as soon as the logs were laid.[322,323,324,325]

Before dark fell, we agreed that Dani and I would go to the Mihaljevci to inspect what had been done. Dotlić remained in shift until midnight. Dani will replace him from 00:00 to 08:00. Afterward, he decided to go home for 24 hours. Dotlić and I will need to cover Dani's shifts during his absence.

In Mihaljevci we talked until 22:30. He argued his view on why I shouldn't send my complaint and tried to convince me. After the war, he promised that

318   The topographic military maps in the scale of 1:25 000 provide an excellent overview of the intimate knowledge of the terrain, showing many useful features for an explorer or a nature lover, including all walking, cycling, and motorbiking paths, field roads, brooks, small streams, creeks, dams, channels, water sources, such as water holes, natural springs, wells and fountains, vegetation, etc.

319   As an experienced fisherman, the Author was reading the map as a guide on where to find local freshwater crustaceans, shellfish, and fish.

320   The roof of the cabin could not bear the weight of the horizontal logs, it started to give in and deform.

321   Mechanical forces when logs were laid horizontally. The Pi-shaped embankment around the cabin was about 4 meters high and had a narrow berm (flattening) at its top that ran along its (Pi-shaped) length. Due to the relative height of the cabin roof and berm, the compression force on the roof was not less than about one half of the weight of the logs.

322   Brittle cabin. The Russian designers made the cabin out of wood, covered with a thin flat sheet of metal, and then painted its outside in the camouflage color. The weight of each log dented it a bit, regardless how carefully these were laid.

323   "Dani's" horizontal log protection design was also used on the next few firing positions. The cumulative impact of the multiple dents made by the horizontally laid logs, observed as an increasingly deformed shape of the cabin, eventually convinced everyone, including Dani, to abandon it. We then reverted to the vertical log protection designs, explained here for ease of communication.

324   The vertical (palisade) log protection design – invented by the Author, comprised of arranging the logs vertically around the cabin, so the full force of own weight was directed towards the ground. As the logs were leaning against the roof of the cabin, they exercised a small horizontal force on the roof that could not deform it.

325   The vertical (palisade) log protection with the sandwich roof design –was an upgrade of the initial log design (see the notes of 4 May 1999) comprised of adding a sandwich of two layers of horizontally laid logs across the roof with one layer of metal plates between them. Due to the distributed weight impact of the logs and the relatively narrow width of the cabin, its roof could withstand the additional weight.

he will leave the unit and I will become the battalion commander.

We were not the children of the Brigade, and a higher rank as the rank meant nothing to me. It's just a huge moral satisfaction, which I must respect. I may be wrong, but becoming the commander of a missile battalion without standing to my own ethical principles would not be something to be proud of. I'd rather be a beekeeper than a battalion commander without morale. I will never be defeated that way and I will, certainly, never give up my intention.

"I do not agree that you write, you are forcing them to reward you." Dani told me.

"Dani, how have you not get it yet? I'm not forcing anyone. I just want to get what you and others got and what belongs to me as well. Nothing more, and nothing less. I don't care about what some individuals up there think of me. The promotions and awards were not given for their opinion, but for the deed we made as a team. I don't care about their opinions, especially if it comes from a person that no one appreciates, and behind his back, they publicly say, who the fuck he is, a drunk and alcoholic at Brigade HQ. I am always straightforward, when someone offended me for no reason. We are all equals here. His insult, and my answer. I have every right as much as anyone else."

He was right in saying that not everyone had been promoted and awarded. I may also be playing the wrong card, but my conscience can't stand that malice. He told me to be patient. "What am I waiting for?" I asked him. "Why should immoral people judge me? No, I can never stand that. Why didn't you fight for me and the other guys, and why are you preventing my promotion? Who am I bothering with it and why? We talked for about one and a half hours and he drank two beers during our conversation. He held them under the cigarette box.

Bora called yesterday and said that he would come to us in a few days. All right...

I went to Deč. Tomović was about to finish the documents and everything will be ready for me to sign. I was content that the forwarding document[326] stated that everything that was said in my complaint was indisputably true. And it was. The battle for my truth will officially begin in a few days' time.

That night our triple-A[327] 20/3 mm, the "Bofors" and "Pragas," fired fiercely.

There was no air raid alarm last night. Probably because NATO had destroyed the Chinese Embassy building in Belgrade, and had killed and wounded some diplomatic staff.

Around 23:30 Tomović headed to the centre of Deč to visually observe the skies. After the work was done, I left too. There, with dentist Matić,

---

326   Forwarding document – is a part of the military procedure where the immediate superior of the complainant forwards the complaint letter together with his own opinion about it. A rough civilian equivalent could be a cover letter.

327   Triple-A (AAA) – is an acronym for the Anti-Aircraft Artillery.

the controversy over blaming the army began. Reservist Matić defended the Army, whereas the former active captain had been spitting on the army in contempt and beyond the argument. I didn't say a word. I was simply very disappointed. "I'm becoming a politician," I said to myself. This was my first lesson.

Tomović needs to take a photocopy of my complaint latter and that of the newspaper article[328] and give that to General Karanović, who is his neighbour. Karan is the Chief of the Air Defence Missile Unit Sector. My battle for the truth has begun. My initial idea was to send a copy to all responsible generals up the command line, to personally see what had been done. Any business conversation, without the solid facts of the matter and evidence, means nothing. I will forward a copy to Generals Bane Petrović, Slavko Biga, Ljubiša Veličković, and Spasoje Smiljanić. If there is no result, I will go to the Commander-in-Chief himself or the Supreme Military Court. If I can't achieve nothing, then this state should not even exist, because it has no moral values. I laid down relieved and immediately fell asleep.I just passed it out…

Tuesday, May 11

I woke up in the school in Deč at 07:15 and quickly made coffee. I didn't like it that way, but necessity made us do things differently. Tomović and Barvalać were sleeping. Barvalac came from home around 06:00. Sedlak went home yesterday afternoon. He needed to bring me the "Military Gazette,"section on the rules of promotion during war times.

After a quick look at it, I left for the combat position.

I gave Dani my objection to the assigned awards to sign. "I'd rather not," he told me. "Is everything written in the way it was and how it is?" I asked him. "Yes," he said and signed. I was personally pleased. The initial step of the formal procedure was completed. The plan should be realized sequentially and no mistakes should be made. One step at a time, when I had been forced to initiate it.

Dani's shift left and Tiosav Janković, Matić, Roksandić, Panić, Radivojević and I remained. We were short of a manual plotting position soldier. I removed his role from the shift crew in order to save one life in case we are hit. There were six of us. I congratulated to everyone on their promotions. They asked me about mine. I read them my complaint and objection to the assigned awards. They were stunned. This was followed by a long discussion about poltroonery, the hardships of the life of missile operators, and injustices in society. The young ones were just listening. My classmate Roksandić told how he came in conflict with Blagojević back in the 80s, and what happened to him during the October events last year. I told them that Golubović and Nikolić phoned from Russia. Everyone was dissapointed that they were not training on the S-300 systems.

---

328   The newspaper article – with the photo of the combat crew that shot down the F-117, as the attachment.

Combat crew enjoying a coffee break. The same night it will fight against
NATO SEAD group.

At 12:00 an order came out of the blue to go to Readiness No. 1. Why do we
need to do standby duty in Readiness No. 1? It was madness to unnecessarily
waste the station's resources and fuel. What justified this logic? Whose idea
was it? Probably that of Blagojević, the alcoholic, who unfortunately had a
huge influence on Stanković, or so it seemed. He was the main reason for my
discontent and injustice. Dani also pointed the blame to him.

Part of the night shift crew members went home on 24 hour leave. The
crew members assigned to cover their absence will have to be on 24 hours
non stop duty, either in the missile guidance station van or on standby, and
vice versa. This work schedule perpetuats cycles of misery and shows how
little we value ourselves. This workload, which is not for humans, shows
how many people become machines. I am not just a machine. A machine
has no feelings and no brain. Those with feelings and brains were not sought
after. The system and the state needs machines. I don't want to be anyone's
toy.

At 13:48 Stanković warned us to expect activities from the west. Radio
amateurs reported planes around Šabac that were heading for Belgrade.

At around 14:10, Tepavac reported that a plane flown over us and that
he fired an SA-7 at it. The missile locked onto the plane, the plane made an
evasive manouevr and released IC decoys; the missile went after the IC decoy, while the plane flew away into the clouds. He was very angry.

I informed Stanković of the aircraft passage above us. The radar was not
radiating yet. After a few seconds pause, Stanković told me to turn on the
radiation. I was watching the air space and could clearly see plenty of targets.
By some intuition I paid attention to a pair at the azimuth 175. They were
about 40-41 km away from us. They were circling us while maintaining their
distance all the way to the azimuth 45s. Another pair also appeared from

239

the azimuth 15, about the same distance away. They knew our approximate position ad for now staying out of our engagement zone.

We saw another target about 10 kilometersin front of these four, azimuth 30. I commanded the rotation of the antennas to 30 degrees. The antennas were directed. The target was approaching us, actually, the complete formation of five targets were approaching us flying at the same azimuths and at the same distance from each other. When they reached 18 km, I ordered the high voltage on at the target acquisitio nradar. In the next antenna turn the target approached to 15 km and I ordered its search with the fire controls. Missile guidance officer Janković was looking for it for about 10 seconds. He didn't find it. I ordered the high voltage down. After five seconds, I ordered another search. Its distance was 8-9 km away. We had two vain attempts at manual tracking. Operators saw it on the edge of their screen, but were unable to bring it down in the middle of the crosshairs. It was too close and the angular speeds were high. We already radiated enough. The danger of an anti-radar missile was high. I ordered the high voltage down.

A few seconds latera a loud blasting explosion was heard. They targetted us and that missile fell very close to us. The cabin shook and filled with the smell of smoke and dust. Slowly, as if someone was howling, the power went out and we were left in the dark. I was expecting another missile. It didn't come. The communication lines with the Operations Center were broken, nor I can get in contact with anyone internally. We opened the van door. Everything was in its place. We remained in the station for about 10 more minutes. We discussed why the guidance officer did not find it. I tried again in vain to establish communication. After that I ordered everyone to leave the station and combat position.

We went out in our flak jackets. The shift officers asked me which way to go. "Anywhere, just run quickly and far away, as there is a possibility of the aircraft returning," I replied. In that case, they will definitely bomb us with laser bombs. God, how silly we were. After the explosion, the six of us remained in the guidance station and discussed how we did not find it at 15 km, nor when it was at 12 km away. This was in sharp contrast to the expected behaviour of people, or the vast majority of, who would either experience a nervous breakdown or would be overwhelmingly fleeing away. In that respect we had become machines.

We hid in the bushes 200-300 m from the equipment. Nothing happened, it was quiet. We listened and observed the airspace. All of a sudden I saw three planesas they flew in a circular arc trajectory overhead, somewhere around the azimuth 270 and at an altitude of about two to three kilometers. They were about 8-10 km away. I first saw them visually: there were three points behind each of which a white mark remained, most likely these were F-16 aircraft.

I decided to go and inspect the equipmentfor possible damage with Lieutenant Janković and a soldier from the power distribution cabin. For the first time the radar imitator did not work. Sergeant Denčev did not know how to start the engine when it was required. We worked without the radar imitator protection and that could have been fatal for the equipment and us. He did not check the generator sets for correct operation when he came on duty.

Any enlisted soldier would have done that job much more conscientiously. Perhaps, we could have fixed it in six to seven hours (from 8:00 to 14:25) if we had the right information on time. What nonsense! we could have paid with our lives.

The bunker with the missile guidance station van inside was not damaged, the target acquisition radar was standing upright and undamaged, the missiles were on the launch ramps, and they remained at a large vertical angle due to preparations for launch and search for the target. They looked daunting with their nose cones pointing high in the sky. We went towads the surveillance radar. I saw a huge crater. "What the fuck, did the bomb make this freakish thing?" I asked myself. Soon afterwards, we convinced ourselves that this was the excavation hole from which the soil had been taken out for the embankments. "So where did the anti-radar missile fall?" It was on the edge of the large hole, about five metres from the junction box. That explained why our communication lines are not working. The cable parts and cable heads were scattered on all sides. They hit the cables near the surveillance radar. For this reason the power, comms and radar images vanished. Parts of the "HARM" missile were scattered everywhere in the grain field.

Senior Sergeant (later promoted to WO Dragan Matić standing at one of the AGM-88 HARM missiles which missed the battalion position.

We went back. I moved soldiers 500 m away from the surveillance radar. Ljubenković didn't work during the daytime.

They started flying by day. The low clouds weather pattern suited them well, their planes just soared above the clouds. We could not see them on our camera, so we had to radiate. We were shot at somewhere betwen 14: 20 and 14: 25.

I decided to go to the first civilian phone to call the Operations Centre. It was amazing how the near death experience did not affect my behavior nor that of the others. Everyone was calm and sensible. As if we went to the theatre or some other harmless leisure place.

Along the way, I stopped at the missile guidance station van and took my notebook and cigarettes. I walked towards the emergency response unit in my flak jacket, helmet on and carrying my tunic in hand. I was greeted with confusion and happiness. "Are there any injured, is everyone alive?" One asked, and the same questions were on the lips of others. They watched and saw everything. It was scary. We, who were in the van, were not aware of it because we did not see it with the naked eye. I replied, "No, everything is fine," and I went to the first phone. They took off my armor, my helmet and tunic and packed everything in my Zastava 101 that was parked next to the hedge.

Tepavac told me that he fired one SA-7 MANPAD, that the plane maneuvered, and the SA-7 went on a flare bait. In my heart, I knew that the SA-7 is an easy solvable problem for modern aircraft. SA-7 is good for an unmanned aerial vehicle, flair or cruise missile. With his firing, Tepavac, the commander of the emergency response group, confirmed the validity of my idea of protecting the combat position. Maybe it saved our lives.

I phoned the Operations Center from Capetain Cvetić office. His field office was in the house of a farmer. Milojica was upstairs. He told me that he know that we were hit because the button on the intercom to connect with them remained on. He listened to our search and commands. As soon as the comms were lost, he knew that something had happened. He asked for people and equipment. I told him that we had lost power and comms and that the equipment, except the cables, at first glance, was intact. "You must get away from there. Make sure you move one vehicle at a time and with as few people as possible on the combat position, so that they do not come back and throw cluster bombs. Send a minimum number of people to check if your equipment is damaged, and then let me know, as well as if you have enough spare cables." I sent private Radovanović to the surveillance radar, and Lieutenant Tiosav Janković and private Ljajić to the missile guidance station van and power sources to check the equipment for any damage.

I told Dotlić to mobilize the people and vehicles and prepare everything for relocation.

Milojica was looking for Dani. I gave him all of Danni's phone numbers, including both of his mobiles. They found him very quickly. He told them that he will come to the unit in 1-2 hours, and he informed me that he was at home and if anyone asked for him to tell them that he was around somewhere. While I be supposedly looking around for him, and he will call Stankovic from home, as if he was with us. He will let me know if he needed anything. He asked me if I was in the shift, and to my affirmative answer, he said, "Well done. We survived the thirteenth missile." "Never mind," I told him, "13 is my lucky number…"

I ordered Jović, from the signals platoon, to establish a hotline for direct communication with the Operations Center. Our end of the hotline was to be located about 200 m away from the combat position. Dotlić to be located there, and he will issue verbal alerts to the people at the combat position if an airplane show up during the transition of the equipment into marching configuration.

Captain Cvetić told me that they saw the explosion, a red hemisphere about 15 m in diameter followed by a huge cloud of smoke and dust. They thought we are all gone. Nobody from the SA-7 MANPAD and the emergency response unit could believe that we were so calm and cool-headed. We were not aware of how terrible it was, so we did not have the feeling they had. They offered us coffee, mineral water, sunflower seeds and cigarettes; and watched us with undisguised admiration and worried glances.

Crnobrnja came in, greeted and hugged me, and said that the 1st and 4th missile battalions were respectively hit by a HARM missile directly into the target acquisition radar, and by a bomb. Pera Masnec, the only son of warrant officer Masnec, was killed. He worked on the power supply and was out in the open at that moment. If he had stayed inside, he might have been alive. For me, it was yet another proof that one cannot escape from their fate.

We were also targeted by a HARM. I knew it by the diameter of the exhaust. The missile stabbed into the ground about 30-40 m away from our missile guidance station van, 10 meters away from the launch ramp and about 100 metres away from the surveillance radar. Their unique feature is regular shaped steel fragments. The explosive charge breaks up the casing with the pre-formed cubes.

Crnobrnja said he spoke with Dotlić who told him about our conversation[329]. He wanted me to putthe computer[330] and the diesel generator[331] incidents in writing. "I won't," I told him[332]. "You asked me earlier to put it in writing

---

329   This conversation took place on 10 May 1999.
330   After Dani took home the only PC computer in the unit, the Author had to ask various people in Belgrade to loan him their own computer (to use it for official correspondence with superior command).
331   Dani planned to give away the unit's 10kW diesel generator to the owner of "Luki" chain of supermarkets, needed for uninterrupted power supply of his pasta and juices production line, because of frequent power blackouts during war time.
332   The Author thought it would be waste of time to write it.

and I did[333]. Where is he now?[334] He is in the Brigade Command[335], and I'm still in the troop. I'll never write again[336,337]. Who is the security officer in the General Staff?[338] Where is your chain of command going to? Well, it ends up with him[339]. I don't want to suck up to anyone again. That will not even cross my mind. You have the information, so you can write it yourself. I will be your witness, if needed." He was stunned and remained confused. I invited him to the combat position. He couldn't, he was waiting for the military police to formally investigate and survey the damage last night. I issued precise instructions to the unit commanders Roksandić, Cvetić, Tepavac, Muminović and Jović. I went to scout the next combat position. Along the way, I met Dotlić at Milan and Nada's place. I told him about his task of warning the people at the combat position early.

The transition was in progress. After removing missiles from the launchers we noticed that three missiles had been damaged. Two near the blast, and one across from the station on the other launch ramp.

I arrived at the new combat position to find out the earth works were not done yet. I went back to the old combat position. The Military Police arrived. Bora Crnomarković hugged and greeted me. He took a picture of me. He

333   The Author and Crnobrnja were in a similar situation in the past in their former unit, after their former Commandant, Dragan Zagrajski, also misappropriated his position for personal gain. Being the security officer, Crnobrnja requested the Author and a few other officers to write their statements about the embezzlement, which they did.

334   As a result, the Author's former Commandant was found guilty and discharged from troop command duty. He was later transferred to the Brigade Command, to a 'better' position.

335   Instead of being punished for the embezzlement, he was effectively rewarded.

336   The Author lost faith in the military justice system: why bother reporting, when there was no punishment?

337   The Author's former state disintegrated when the great world powers rebalanced their influence in the early 1990s; bloody wars ensued largely along the ethnic lines or newly created ethnic identities and their militias. Some high ranked individuals reverted to their traditional tribal and ethnic identities. For example, the Commandant of the Air Force and Air Defense of the former SFR Yugoslavia, Anton Tus, of Croatian ethnicity, simply changed sides, deflected to the newly created independent Croatian State and availed him. The lack of trust in "others" was widespread.

338   The Author reminded Crnobrnja who was the new Director of the Military Security Agency (MSA), Geza Farkaš. Geza was appointed to this position shortly before the war began, after a group of senior Generals were retired as part of the powerplay.
Law enforcement decreases during periods of historic turmoil and wars, as the birds of the feather flock together.

339   The Author's key concern was possible "Hungarian ethnic mate ship" between Dani and Geza; and that Geza, who was at the top of Crnobrnja's chain of command of the MSA, would "protect" Dani at all costs.

told me, "How are you, commander?" I gave him my objection to read. He said to me, "Well done."

My classmate Matijević and Major Aleksić from the Brigade Command arrived in the Zastava Florida. The Military Police left, and Matijević approached me. We greeted and hugged each other. This became customary in this war. He told me that luck follows the brave ones.

Aleksić gathered a full hand of shrapnel. I asked him, though I knew, what it was. "HARM," he replied, "the usual shit." Varga found another missile in Mihaljevci. The peasants had been working on the field. When it detonated, they threw everything away and fled. So I was right after all. They fired at us at least twice. One missile flew over us and ended up somewhere far away. We just found out where exactly.

Crnobrnja said to keep an eye on his belongings while he was away. He will return on Friday. He also told me that, the other day, Noskov had a target for seven seconds; Djordjević kept pressing his finger on the launch button, but the launch did not go through. It was very misfortunate. "Why he didn't override the firing sequence and manually launch right away via the second channel?[340] "I wondered. "He didn't manage to do it. The angular speeds were high and everything happened so quickly. Speed often blocks thinking," I said to myself.

Before they left, I gave my objection to Matijević to personally deliver it to Stanković. We said our goodbyes and they left.

I went to Dotlić and he told me that he reconsidered my objection again and came to the same conclusion that I was right about everything. "Fuck the commander of the unit that was hit, he did not find it appropriate to come and personally see the impact, but to lie to superior command that he was there," Dotlić said. I did not tell him that I knew that he told Bora about our conversation.

We slowly hauled the equipment. The cogwheel on the vertical angle reducer (gear) of the target acquisition radar was broken, so we used cables to pull it into the U-shaped profile and tightened it with chains as a temporary fix so we can leave the combat position as soon as possible. They were the last who left. I agreed with Dotlić to signal me when the last vehicle with the equipment leave the combat position, by ringing three times; then to pick up the phone and come to me, so we can leave the position together. He will drive the Lada Niva, I will drive my Zastava.

I told Captain Cvetić,the commander of the SA-7 MANPAD section,that everyone will stay where they are tonight. Their assignment was to set up an ambush and try to surprise a plane or two if they return tonight. We will not be manning the new combat position tonight, instead, all the equipment will be dispersed around in pre-determined locations.

For the first time since the beginning of the war, we will spend the night

340   The pre-selected firing sequence automatically fires the second missile five seconds after successful launch of the first missile. In this case the first missile failed to launch. Under these circumstances, the operators could have disabled the pre-selection and manually fired the second missile.

on wheels, not in combat duty. Before we left, Dotlić told me, "Well, now that we go to the camp, you can have a beer with us!" "Excellent idea Bole! I will." Everything was taken away to Šimanovci, Karlovčić and Mihaljevci and dispersed. It was reported that night that Dotlić was decorated, Tiosav Janković, too. The medal had also been given to Roksandić and Matić. Out of the 12 of us, 11 were awarded. I had the feeling of rejection again. I couldn't fall asleep for a long, long time.

Word spread today that an SA-7 MANPAD from the Agricultural Cooperative in Karlovčić knocked down a Sea-Harrier. There was neither confirmation on the TV, nor from any videos. I doubted if that really occured, though some guy claimed that his major came and congratulated him. The plane allegedly crashed somewhere near the village of Dobanovci or Ugrinovci.

Wednesday, May 12

I woke up tired… again.

There was a need for a meeting, and I ordered the commanders of the basic units and all officers to attend the meeting. The first whole-battalion meeting since the beginning of the war. I exercised my right as the battalion XO and I summoned it. I updated the participants with the latest information received. Also, I congratulated everyone who had been promoted and awarded.

We analyzed yesterday's day and the day's work, including the actions with the radar emission imitator and corner reflectors. Dani arrived around 10:00 while the meeting was in progress. He supported me in everything today. Senior Sargeant Matić said at the meeting that our whole combat crew had behaved as fools. Instead of immediately evacuating the guidance station after the launch and moving away from the firing position, we sat in the station for another 10 minutes and discussed it.

Dani said that he, Dotlić and Stoimenov, will finish the job and that I can take some time off and go home.

Dani, Roksandić, Muminović and Stojanović went reconnoitering the suitable sites for the new combat position.

I left at around 12:00. On my way home I dropped to the office in Deč. There, I made a comparative analysis of the promoted and awarded officers and NCOs for the downed F-117A and F-16. Eleven officers and NCOs were awarded, out of twelve of us. Everyone except me. What an inconsistency.[341,342]

Why, how and who divided the combat shift that brought down the plane for the purpose of promotion and decoration[343,344] when all the duties are different?[345] How did the Brigade frame it?[346,347] Fuck this justice for who knows how long!

I arrived in Belgrade. Danka knew I was coming. It was a pleasant family atmosphere when I arrived. My neighbour, Savka, had brought a jar of homemade honey. She knew I love it. Lucia greeted me from her terrace as I arrived. Danka and I had a coffee and talked. Tears were pouring down my cheeks. The steel reached a melting point... I told Danka that I would

---

341   The combat shift crew works as one missile team. Each team member has a unique duty that differs from those of all other team members. There is neither redundancy nor the room for error.

Shooting down a plane is like a relay track-and-field race. No plane can be shot down if any team member fails to flawlessly complete his unique assignment and pass on the baton to the next runner.

A plane shot down demonstrates, by implication, that all team members have successfully completed their own unique assignments to the highest standard. Their performance was equally outstanding.

342   For the reasons explained in notes 2 to 4 above, all officers and NCOs should be awarded (or not) equally.

343   How could the Brigade Command propose the promotion and decoration for some (Lieutenant Janković); for some only promotion (Stojanović and Radivojević); for some only decoration (Major Dotlić); and for some a medal (Matić and Roksandić)?

344   What were the criteria the Brigade Command used and who prescribed them? One thing was sure; these criteria did not exist in the official government gazette and military rulebooks.

345   The Author considered it crucial to stress that there were no two identical roles in the combat crew, which, if existed, would have allowed comparison of the combat performance of those two members; fair assessment that one performed better than the other; and fact based objective decision to tailor their awards to suit their relative combat performance. Consequently, all combat-crew members should have been equally awarded, not differently.

346   In the Author's opinion, the Brigade Command applied the following two criteria:

a)A higher ranked officer could receive any award other than promotion to a higher rank;

b)Any high rank awarded during the war would create direct competition to the highly ranked officers in the Brigade Command, which should had been prevented from occurring by using all available means.

347   In hindsight, the Chief of Staff of the 250th Brigade, Colonel Dragan Stankovic, directly confirmedthe Author's opinion of note 9 above, *"There is a risk of an excessive number of high ranked officers, so that after the war they will not be appointed in the troop and they will lose their jobs,"* refer to the notes of 17 May 1999 here, after 11:30 hours.

fight for my truth. She had been supporting me all the time. She comforted me straightaway by saying,"Honey, don't wear off yourself excessively with this. This must pass one day. Man, you bear a lot of burden. Your heart may give up." I often wondered if I have one at all. I laid on the couch to sleep and woke up at 20:20. She prepared dinner while I was sleeping. I opened up to her. I told her how we had been shot at, all my observations and all my thoughts. I'll call the Generals and personally take my objection to each of them. No one answered at General Veličković's place, a daughter answered at General Karanović's place, and, at General Biga'splace, his wife answered. I left messages that Aničić had called and that I have a message for them. There was nothing else I could do.

I went to sleep around 00:15. Danka fell asleep like a baby, and I was caught up again in the unrest. "Oh my God, it hurts," I thought and I got up. This night I smoked a lot of cigarettes. I managed to fall asleep sometime around 03:00 or 03:30.

Thursday, May 13

I went to Krnješevci to meet with Lieutenant Colonel Zlatko Šobot. He wanted back the gearbox that he had given me yesterday for relocation. They tried to lower their target acquisition radar without it, but they couldn't. It was too damaged. After that, I went to Deč. The relocation of the equipment was completed this morning. It was put into operation around 14:30. For the first time we set up the combat position in the county of Soko Salaš. Djević's battalion had been here before. Their arrangement of the combat position was quite new for us. Everything was dug in, but the protection was pretty weak. The earthworks were covered by railroad ties (sleepers) that were not ideally laid. I prefered our way of work and protection. In Deč, everything was ready to move the logistical support out of the school. We packed my, Bora's and Dotlić's belongings into my business car. Dani could take his own things himself. He informed me that our next two combat positions will be the area of the villages of Bečmen and Ašanja. He went scouting and I talked to Pero Belokapić about suitable locations to accomodate our logistical support units there. Pero came back very quickly and we resolved the accommodation issue. My team and I went to the new firing position. Our shift tonight is from 16:00 to 24:00 . Just before we departed, one plane had flown very low over Deč. After that, a thick plume of smoke came from the direction of the village of Šimanovci. The detonation shook the school. Around 17:00 Danka called me on my pager. She asked if I was alive? She said,"They attacked Karlovčić and, some say, Mihaljevci too". She also said that they used cluster bombs. Who knows what types of bombs they used, but they bombed us for sure.

Around 18:00 Blagojević, the alcoholic, called from the Operations Center and asked if I established the communication lines. I said I did. "Well, why are you not working?" "How can I work without electricity in the dark. You know what this is all about," I replied. He thougt for a moment and then said," Okay, if you have to, then turn on the small AD-30 diesel generator." I heard his familiar voice and felt contempt. Muminović read my objection again. He told me that he was very interested in what they reply with, "You'll let me read it?"

Mika Stojanović, the commander of the signals platoon, became a smoker the other day, from the day he placed his mother in the hospital. He also read my complaintlettere and told me that my tone was sharp, concluding with, "Everything must be rotten to the core in the department of defence, if this is happening."

Last night I talked to Dušan about the car. He promised to fix everything. Boško Andjelković rushed to see me last night. He was with me from 21:30 to 23:00. An old buddy who had always cared about me.

I weighed myself last night. I had lost 10 kg in less than two months. I took on a tremendous workload, which contributed to this.

From 17:55, we are in the Readiness No.1. Our station is hot like an oven, and we had body armor on. It is a miracle what a man can endure. Mika was on shift with me. He won't go with Dani. I read the war issue of the Army magazine. There was another article about our unit, this time about the downed F-16.

"The medicines we got for my mother mean a lot to me. You know I couldn't even get them in Vršac in Hemofarm[348]," Mika told me, "it would be good if we could get another few boxes."

Two tires on the emergency response group's TAM 150 vehicle were flat, and no one did anything about it. The hook of the trailer for transport of the target acquisiton radar antennas was distorted and deformed. It hadn't just cracked, it was nearly broken. I called Žugić and a workshop in Šimanovci. He brought tires for the TAM 150, but he couldn't fix the hook. He said, "No way." Dani knows everything, but did nothing. He told me that he had been told that the damage was small. "What small damage are you talking about, when it's useless for relocation?" I asked him. "How come I always see and find out what's faulty and missing and you never notice anything?"

The officers were dissatisfied. Only three missile batteries remained operational. Why we are not not reinforced by those people whose missile systems had been destroyed or damaged, so we could rest a little too? The heat was unbearable. I drenched in sweat. The war had been prolonged and this tactic made no sense anymore. The defence of Belgrade did not exist any more and they can get through anywhere they want. Then why those idiots from the defense corps are tiring us off like this?

Our combat manual stipulated that a role was to manually plot the airspace situation on the transparent board. That role was not needed at all, just one more potentially dead person in the case they hit guidance station. In reality, all assessments are made by the shift commander who is also fire control commander, and who makes decisions without looking at the plotting board.

Matić said that he will help me after the war to publish my diary through his godfather.

---

348   Hemofarm was a Serbian manufacturer of pharmaceutical goods.

We were in Readiness No. 1 until the end of our shift. We listened to the radio amateur network reporting the overhead flights around Belgrade, Surčin, Batajnica, etc. Who would need us and our work, if we are not using our radars, and not directly observing the airspace at all? We will not be launching tonight, for sure. We are just unnecessarily consuming the equipment, fuel and manpower.

Dani came around 00:00 to replace me. He told me that he went to Šimanovci to visit Lieutenant Colonel Podovac. "They dropped two bombs on his equipment in the middle of the day." "I heard the plane and the detonations today," I told him. "One destroyed the power supply van and the other the radar. Fortunately, no one was in the power van or on the radar at that moment. The radar operator was at his power supply van, and all others from the crew shift were in the bunker. A steel fragment went through a 10-meter long pipe and damaged one of the trucks. " Fuck the Brigade and their assessment. This is previously known firing position. Identified before the war, and, for sure, marked as a target; the earthworks were completed in peace time. We fired from that location. It looked to me as if they had just been waiting for someone to return to the combat position and then destroyed the equipment. They did it very thoroughly and professionally.

The rest of Dani's shift was 40 minutes late. They came at 00:40.

Friday May 14

The bus transported my shift from Soko Salaš farmhouse to Deč. There was no traffic on the highway. Not a single vehicle or human soul. It felt surreal. Everything was empty. All the lights were off. It was cloudy and the driver had to turn on the lights. Were we visible from space or, I wondered, did we become paranoid?

We arrived at the camp. Logistics relocated us today. No one knew where his personal stuff was or where he was supposed to sleep. I was feeling sticky with sweat, as if my shirt was glued to my back. Savić, one of the re-servists, took me to a sink where I could wash myself. I didn't know where my personal hygiene items and accessories are. The water dried on my face.

For the first time, I was nervous about all the crap that got us. Everyone seemed to not give a shit, as they were waging war from shelters and bunkers, safe and clean. I was sick of the dirt. The Officer, indeed, is not respected in any field. We had not received our daily field allowance for April yet. We only received an advanced payment of 100 dinars. The Corps got it, and the troops didn't. Shameful. The common man, soldier, is really treated like a dog. The Government needs him to wage war and vote. All others are parasites. Especially, those in power.

Matković was wounded. He lost his eye. He'll be a hero after the war. And we, the warriors, are still nameless martyrs.

Last night, Captain Senad Muminović raised the issue of our excessive shift workload with Dani, and possibilities to get some help from people from other battalions whose equipment was destroyed or rendered inoperable. Dani replied that he would not like other people to mess around with our equipment. The question was how long we could endure it.

There was a problem with the equipment. The main shaft was twisted due to stress and fatigue and required a repair. Fatigue is taking a toll not only on equipment but on us as well.

This morning at 07:45, I called Dani from Deč and told him that we will not move to the new combat position today. The next shift should come normally. We were 40 minutes late, like they had been late last night. No one objected.

I tested our internal communication lines. After that, I tried to get in touch with the shift on the surveillance radar, the radar imitator, and the signals centre. Connection seem to work but the problem is that I could hear them, but they couldn't hear me. The combination switch on the handset cable was faulty. How did the previous shift communicate before my shift took over??? This was a matter of serious concern.[349]

This morning, I asked Dani about Stanković and the objection[350]. He said that he didn't know that I sent a complaint. "How do you not know when you signed it? Someone's crazy here," I replied in astonishment, "Yes, of course I sent it," I told him briefly.

"You have disappointed me," Dani replied.

"Have I? Well, that's my right. Are you trying to convince me that I was out of the shift and did not do my job? You forget everything very quickly."

I ordered Stojanović, our signals officer, to send one of his signal guys in every shift from now on. I didn't care who is that person, but I needed one for every shift. If we can sit here where the shooting happens, a signals officer could be in the guidance station or in a signal's vehicle as well. He could sit or sleep there, I didn't care, but he must be here.

Lieutenant Tiosavljević went home yesterday. Upon returning, he said he felt the safest in the guidance station. The city was spooky. There were no lights, everything was dark. The air-raid sirens were loud and horrible. When the lights went out, he couldn't get around in his own apartment.

There was a 40th day memorial service[351] for Captain Tepavac today. "God, has it been that long?" I wondered and asked the shift. Matijević, my classmate, went to the memorial.

Lieutenant Colonel Samardzić reported that we can take the fuel filter cover of the AD-10 or the entire AD-10 diesel generator set from Podovac. I conveyed this to Tomović at the camp, so he can pass it on to Ljubenković,

---

349   He could not even call the signals platoon to repair the fault.

350   On 11 May 1999, the Author gave his objection to Matijević to personally hand it over to Stanković and was curious to find out if Stanković mentioned it to Dani or asked anything about it.

351   The 40th day after death is a traditional memorial service, family gathering, ceremonies and rituals.

Dani or Senad Muminović. I reported back to Samardzić after I had conveyed his message to them for action, as the military rules require.

The Command of the Jakovo Infantry Brigade had been housed in Soko Salaš farmhouse since the beginning of the war, where our equipment was housed. Officers with no combat experience. Good accommodation, food, asphalt roads, close to Belgrade. They have not moved since the beginning of the war. They had been warring surrounded by Pragas and Bofforses. That was really enjoyable! They objected when we arrived, complaining that we might unmask their position. These gentlemen may have to move, maybe to some shithole and they didn't want to change their luxury and move their assess.

Major Djordjević from the Brigade has been chasing Dotlić for fuel consumption reports all morning. I told him I was not expecting Dotlić to come here. I gave him two phone numbers in Deč, at Sedlak's place and at the factory near Tomović. I guessed that they would find him somewhere.

Stojanović remained at base camp. He had been avoiding being near the equipment in all possible ways and whenever he could. I understood him. He was a signals officer, not a missileer. He was scared a lot of the time and hHis major objective in this war was to survive, like all of us. Last night, he was repairing a toy handgun for his son Djole.

Yesterday, I left a car full of stuff with Sedlak to get our gear and stuff out and to make our beds with the clean linens. Nothing was done right. Kosta told me that he hadn't seen him anywhere around and that he had no instructions.

At about 10:30, Dr. Djukić arrived at the guidance station with a doctor from the Infantry Brigade. Sergeant Radivojević told him that we have a catalogue of NATO aircraft affixed on the wall and that he can place an order for the one he wanted to be shot down. Everyone laughed in the station. We discussed the downed plane from a few days ago. The doc told us the airplane crashed into the Danube River; and a friend of his, who was in the special-forces group, told him that that they had caught two pilots somewhere behind the Avala Mountain. I didn't know from which plane the pilots were, but it turned out that the two aircraft were shot down the very same day they had shot at us in Karlovčić.

Sandwiches and hamburgers were 6 dinars here. Dr. Djukić made a big order to be delivered to the combat position. They brought three packs. In one was meat, in another sunny side up eggs, and in the third was salad. And a bag full of sliced freshly baked bread. It was our first meal since 16:00 yesterday. To their credit, they were fed well and at a decent price. God willing it will be like that after the war, that we too have some privileges and benefits. We deserved to exploit this anguish and toil.

At 11:25, I called home. Nataša answered the phone. Danka was at the hairdresser. I told Nataša that everything is fine.

At about 12:00, combat activities began at the south of the country.

At about 13:50, Samardzić reported that our team was with Podovac and that neither his AD-10 genset nor its parts were suitable for our use. They were not the same make and model as ours.

I told Bora that we had been in Readiness No. 1 since the morning and that the station overheated. "I know, dude, but there are activities down south. Everyone is in Readiness No. 1. I have just ordered them. Hold on a little longer bro!" he told me.

At around 15:00, Dani told me that they had bombed our decoy position in Prhovo, set by Djević. So, they had been recording everything and seeing everything! At least our decoys served their purpose. Only three battalions are working now. For this reason, Bora Samardzić did not even dare to order the surveillance radar emission today, although he had informed me about a target near me, 17 km away. We searched for it by using our television camera but did not find it.

At 15:30, we were ordered to go into Readiness No. 2.

At 16:00, our replacement shift came. Major Stoimenov brought in a spare shaft for the SNR-125 fire control radar trailer and they mounted it. It was taken from the Djević's battalion.

We went to the camp. In the evening, at around 18:00, hail of the size of hazelnuts fell for about 25-30 minutes. Dani came to his shift at 23:00, and he supposed to be there at 16.00. Who knows where he had been until 23:00. He acted and did what he wanted. He paid no attention to anyone, not even to us or to the Brigade Command.

I called Captain Cvetić, the commander of the SA-7 MANPAD battery; to come to the battalion HQ so we can go together to the Golić's unit. He was the one who fired a SA-7 at the Tomahawk cruise missile yesterday. I wanted someone to come on behalf of the Brigade Command and pay tribute to the man, regardless of the result. Captain Cvetić agreed. Golić welcomed us very pleasantly. He explained that, at 16:05, he saw a Tomahawk cruise missile very clearly, and had it in sight and immediately launched the missile. After some time, he observed an explosion and falling trail behind the missile. A few peasants also confirmed his account. I instructed Cvetić to hand over the damaged missile and used power sources to Barvalac. People were extremely fond of this type of touring.[352] It was an official visit after all.[353]

Just before we left, rain with lighting began, which I had not seen for a long time. The thunder was very loud. Cvetić and I drove carefully. We arrived at camp around 23:00.

Dotlić with his team goes on shift tonight. I woke them up.

At around 23:30, Dani called to say that people should stay where they were, because the combat position was flooded, and the equipment was in the mud and water. We must wear rubber boots in the morning. Only now we saw the disadvantage of this position. It was dug in. The missile guidance

---

352   People on the front line felt acknowledged and respected. Their morale boosted.

353   The command, on the other hand, had an opportunity to hear the firsthand account, impressions and learn something that could be later shared with others as collective knowledge and experience.

station was poorly protected from above and was located at the base of the fire control radar. A stream of water flooded the trench where the station was located. It was highly humid yesterday. Dani and his guys will stay on the equipment until 08:00. Practically, he will work one shift and his people two shifts. I halted the bus with the new shift right on time, just before they left for the firing position. That was a good deed, as there was no need for them to go to the position.

After that I went to sleep.

Saturday, May 15

Sedlak woke me up around 02:30 hours. Colonel Milojica Vukadinović from the Operations Center was on the phone. My sleep was broken. Dani did not have a telephone line and was unable to call me directly. He requested that Dotlić and his people put on rubber boots for their morning shift and bring along a submersible pump to pump out water that was under the van and target acquisition radar, as the water level was higher than everyone's standard issue boots. They had to go barefoot tonight to check the diesel generator.

I woke up at 07:30.

My son Vlada left a message to call him back.

Kosta and I went to Šimanovci to the CBRN unit. I needed to take them to Bečmen to add camouflage on the built combat position before manning it. I explained in detail to Miškov, the unit commander, what and how I wanted it. The works started at 12:00 and they worked until 19:30, when I told them to stop, so that we can return to the camp by 20:00, when darkness falls. The position was done in a landfill. Water floats between the ramparts. We'll mask them. There is about a one kilometer straight line distance to the old firing position, which we occupied earlier. It would be good to place a radar radiation imitator there and try to lure them from our real position. Along the way we picked up Tepavac, who was returning from home. I stopped by Milan and Nada. They were overjoyed to see me. Milan had been in Karlovčić asking the army units about me. They told him I am alive. We had a coffee. The grass is freshly mowed and it looked beautiful. You could smell the cut grass.

I called Danka from the camp. No one picked up. I called her on her mobile and she told me that she was just entering the house, that her car was repaired and parked in front of the house. "Okay, I'll talk to you later."

At 16:00 we came to the shift. At 16:40 we went into Readiness No. 2. Boris Stoimenov repaired the cable for centralized switching.

I called Danka at home from the van. Nataša answered and said that she had gone to take my statement of complaint to one of the Generals. She will tell me later tonight who she talked to and what the reaction was. I called Vlada. I have to give him a few dinars as soon as possible. He must have ran out of money. I believe he made a wrong choice to live with his mother and wondered if he will ever realize it.

This morning, before he left for a meeting with Luki, Dani (he did not return until 16:00) told me that Pera Bačvanski from Prhovo had sent me cooked fish and that he would like to be a volunteer with us. He was demobilized 4-5 years ago. He had a logistical support background and lots of experience. The fish was cooked well and Sedlak, Dotlić, Stojanović, Tomović and I ate it. It was nice to fight in the background...

At 16:00 Dotlić told me that they had been searching for a low flying target for five seconds. They did not find it, but they saw black smoke on the camera, which was going towards the ground. Luka Trgovčević from the Operations Center told him that light anti-aircraft artillery of the Army Air Defence was active tonight and that someone knocked something down. What a pleasure, and a lesson not to fly during the day.

I read in the newspapers, and I couldn't believe, that a NATO pilot was paid between $8,000 and $15,000 per flight, depending on the plane he was flying and the task. I didn't believe that information. The press like to exaggerate...

Senad Muminović was annoyed at reading an article by a well-known military commentator, journalist Lazanski, who said that the F-117A was detected by the radar of another unit, and that their merit was greater than that of the missile battery that shot it down. "When the war ends, I will write to him to tell him how incompetent he is and that he has no understanding about the topic he was writing about!"

Today, Aca, the driver of SA-7 unit, bogged his TAM 110 truck on the wet grass in the ditch by the road, when he arrived for food in the camp. It was pulled out by TAM 150 truck.

Captain Tomović was correct not to allow mass movement of the reservists inside the camp, as that could unmask the camp.

Private Djordjević was afraid to fill in the plotting board operator role. We must prevent such a situation of losing a man due to fear, and from spreading it like a plague to other soldiers ... I had an informal chat with him. I told him he had been serving his military conscription service in an elite unit, and that he will have something to tell to his relatives and friends when the war is over; about how two planes were shot down. I sent him and the guards to fix the corner reflectors that had fallen down from the storm.

There was liquid mud under the cabin. I don't know when it will dry. This morning, the Operations Center did not allow us to relocatethe equipment that was not stuck in the mud into the expected area.

Yesterday, we visited Golić and found out that the communication line to his position did not work. Today, I sent the commander of the signals unit, Stojanović, to fix it. He solved it successfully. In case of a launch ban, no one would be able to communicate that order to him. That was potentiallya great danger due to the risk of an unwanted downing. People were certainly satisfied when their problems were resolved immediately after they had been reported. It meant that enough attention had been paid to them, and they knew how to appreciate that.

Tepavac and Kosta read my complaint today. They were stunned. Milan said: "Well done. Do not worry. You have something to live on. It is not a measure of value. You have proved yourself before your friends and the people."

At 21:30, we went into Readiness No.1. The overflights and attacks had began. I listened to radio amateurs. They announced planes at very high altitudes and in all directions. These were reconnesance and distractors who go to certain places, circle, interfere and observe. In any case, this was a standard formation for the commencement of an attack. Luka Trgovčević was at the Operations Center. He asked me about the information I received from my air surveillance units via our direct link. I couldn't hear them. I was located about one kilometer away from the field switchboard and all the cabling was in water and mud. The reception was very weak, indistinct, and it was useless for me to hear from them and see the situation on the plotting board[354], when I did not see them on the radar. Their data was a few minutes late anyway. Luka wasn't independent in his work. He had been constantly consulting with someone, and only then telling us what to do.

Our surveillance radar was not radiating yet. I received information from our visual observers about the target at a azimuth 0, 15 km away, and in the outgoing direction.We turned on the radiation on the surveillance radar and observed the airspace.I didn't have it on my remote VIKO radar screen. Tiosavljević and Stoimenov were watching with me too, as well as Ljubenković who was on the surveilance radar; as my witnesses in case Blagojević, the alcoholic, repeated his malicious comment, "Are you working at all", he had already asked me. What a slander and "put down" person. Were you involved at all in this war? As if you were sitting in front of the screen that wasn't even turned on. How nice it would be for all those fagots to come here and show us what they know.

During the overflight, he ordered us to monitor the sector between azimuths 330-90. The frequencies were stable. There was no indication of interference, and the targets were not visible. After consulting with someone, Luka told me to radiate and monitor the full circle. There were no nearby targets in any direction. I ordered Ljubenković to try all radar modes, and again nothing. They had hindered us very successfully, it was more than obvious.

Luka Trgovčević told me to no longer keep people in the voltage distribution cabin. He said people should leave the cabin, as soon as the missiles were put into preparation mode and armed. We should establish a dedicated telephone line to their reserve position, so they can return to the cabin if needed. We had two people on duty. I ordered Maletić to send the soldier to the emergency intervention group, and he to come to our van, because we didn't have any other alternative at the moment.

It drizzled through the night.

I talked to Danka before the overflight, around 20:00 while we were in Readiness No.2. She told me that she had delivered my complaint to General

354   The oral communication and manual plotting delays, compounded by fast flying planes rendered it useless

Veličković's place. A woman received the letter. The apartment was in chaos, because they were moving and packing. "Where were they going, who knows?" I wondered.

At General Slavko Biga's place, his son took the letter. As soon as she returned home, Biga called her. Danka wondered how he knew what her phone was. "How did he know?", I asked myself and then told her, "I left it the other day, when I called him and talked to his wife. And he could have found it out anyway."

Biga politely introduced himself to her. His voice was similar to that of her godfather. Danka said, "Where are you, godfather?" Biga was confused at first. He obviously didn't know he had been her godfather. I think it was wrong that she discussed the content with him. She should not have. She should have just said that it was a message for him. That would have interested him, and then the letter would be delivered to him very quickly. Now, when he was familiar with the content, the question is when he will read it. Due to the nature of his job, it may not be urgent for him but it was to me. I felt enormous personal and moral satisfaction, equal to that due to my combat work I do in the unit. Danka was not a soldier. She didn't think like one. In any case, I thanked her very much for her care and what she had done. My complaint had arrived into the right hands. All that remained was to wait and see the reaction of those responsible.

Her car had been repaired, but she said the gearbox was going a little harder. She paid 50 DEM (German Mark) to the mechanic.

At 00:10, the new shift came to replace us. We radiated twice with the Imitator, as it had been ordered by the Operations Centre, at the azimuth 190 and 0 degrees, and for 10 seconds each time.

Sunday, May 16

Mud is all around us… It is a sea of mud.

I have rubber boots on my feet. The bus took us through the grain field, mud, and darkness. Sometimes someone flashes a flashlight. It's a dark night… Rain falls… We walked 45 minutes to the nearest asphalt road to catch the bus. A true disaster. People commented that it would be better to be on the equipment for 16 hours than venture through the mud.

Senad fell. He cursed heavily.

The highway is empty. Lukić drives with his high beams turned on. If we were in Kosovo and Metohija, we wouldn't be driving this way. They could target us here too. This is a great danger and possibility. Fate should not be provoked. Deč fire station and camp are 22 km away. We arrived at the camp around 01:20.

We brushed our boots on the grass. The mud stuck and was hard to re-move. Tomović, Sedlak and Dani were awake. Dani was reading the mail. Now, at this time! Weird. He came yesterday around 17:00, slept until 23:00, and now he's reading mail... We discussed relocation of the equipment. Mijović's battalion around Pančevo was hit today with a bomb. No injuries, fortunately, but the equipment was destroyed. The number of active missile battalions are decreasing, with no possibility of engaging new forces. It became a disaster.

Djević or Šobot, it really didn't matter who, prepared a very difficult position at the Soko Salaš farmhouse. We manned it. Did they think about rain, a sloping site and wet soil? The guidance station was placed next to the fire control radar itself.[355] It rained heavily, and the equipment was flooded, sitting now in the water and mud.[356]

Mud and water - one of the hardship that we had to go through while managing the missile guidance station.

The combat position is located in the middle of an arable field, and the footings were not compacted nor the surrounding soil in the embankment stabilized. If a bomb is to hit us, everything would be forced into the guidance station, as it was "dug in" up to the roof and its protection was very weak. I now see how incredibly creative we had been. How many more things we had thought about... The nearest asphalt road was located about a kilometre and a half to two kilometres away from the combat position, along an dirt road. Insanity! Djević and Šobot should be brought back in to get the equipment out of here; both of them, or just the person who decided to locate the combat position here and ordered them to do it.

Yesterday, Dani asked the Brigade HQ to allow us to move away from

355   On the opposite side of the head of the Pi-shaped embankment.

356   The run-off water accumulated in the Pi-shaped embankment, turning it into a gigantic scoop or dam, as its open end faced uphill. No drainage and the roof-high embankment aggravated the flooding.

here. They didn't approve it. This illustrates their awareness of the situation in the field... How we can fight a war like this???

Dani told me that he had been expecting us to be hit the whole day yesterday. Was this the true reason for his less frequent duties on the equipment? Anyway, I had been writing earlier on my observations about this matter.

I decided to no longer tell him any of my ideas, proposals, or solutions[357] when we are alone. So I told him in front of others that: a) when we move to the next firing position, it should be obligatory to put four to five rows of logs between the guidance station to the fire control radar,[358,359] park the station, and only then put the log protection around it,[360] b) the launch ramps, which are now in Karlovčić, should have already been relocated to the new firing position, and only then the guidance station should be placed; at the very end.

Dani asked, "What is the benefit?" I replied, "With these measures implemented, we simply reduce the concentration of people and equipment on the combat position by two KRAZ trucks, four ZIL trucks, one TAM 150 truck, and about 35 people at the position. That's a big deal! We make a smaller footprint. Then, at the very end, we bring in the missile guidance station."

After a sigh of approval, I continued about our ultimate objective, "Note that each position must be well camouflaged in advance. The situation is very serious, and the devil is in details. One must be extremely careful and conspiratorial. The war was reduced to guerrilla tactics and ambushes. American like to call that 'a snake in the grass'. Let's be that snake."

Flipping through the mail, Dani saw that Ljubenković was promoted to the rank of Senior Sergeant. It was a regular, service promotion. He said that a proposal for Ljubenković's extraordinary promotion would now go on.

Dani's words stung me as I immediately realised the hypocrisy. "Now, it is absolutely irrelevant that Sergeant Ljubenković did not spend 2/3 of his time in one rank in order to be promoted. And you told me that I had not spent 2/3 of my time in the rank of lieutenant colonel, so that was a hindrance to my promotion. You are acting in two different ways to different people concerning the same matter. You are caught double-dealing," I said to myself and then grasped, "He is, in fact, the creator of my misfortune, and this is more than clear to me now - competition and elimination." And even before I could think of what I was going to do, a vivid resolution flashed

---

357   If the precision munitions (bombs) were accurate as their manufacturer publicly stated it, then the fire control radar would be hit. If so, then the existing embankment levy made up of non-compacted earth would not be a sufficiently strong barrier to protect the nearby missile guidance station.

358   The reinforced barrier should absorb and deflect the bomb blast energy away from the missile guidance station.

359   The logs should be laid on the missile guidance station side slope of the earth embankment, one end on the ground.

360   The log protection around the station–has the primary purpose to protect against HARM missile shrapnel. Its secondary purpose would be protection against stray debris caused by the explosion of a bomb.

through my mind, "I will 'suffocate' him and his lies with the truth and my hard work."

After all, there are two options for my life after the war: One is to somehow exploit all these adversities, and the other is to hang my uniform on a pin. No one could blackmail me with my livelihood. I will fight for the truth, by using all available means and go to the highest institutions if necessary. I will fight through the system. I wanted an answer to a simple question, "Why?"

At 07:30, Dani left with the shift to the combat position. Where he had slept, I did not know, but it was certain that he was not in the camp. The phones didn't work last night. He left the unit tonight around 02:00, allegedly to find a phone, report to the Operations Centre and request relocation of the unit. At that time?! Funny! Who was his whore for tonight? Sedlak, Tomović and I looked at each other thinking of this question...

At about 08:30, an empty bus returned from the combat position[361] for soldiers needed for the relocation. Dani had come to the real phone just this morning at the guidance station and spoke to the Operations Center. They immediately approved the requested relocation. "Would they be able to pull everything out or just partially, we'll see?" I wondered...

I stayed at the camp to wait for his instructions on what to do. That was the deal.

Medic Dropulić brought me medicines for Milan and Nada.

I discussed with Tomović our situation. He told me that, in depravity and perfidy, Dani reminded him of his former missile battery commander. "Dani is so much worse." I replied, "Just look at how much time he spends in the combat shifts and in the unit. He is absent all the time for various reasons, as he likes to say 'I have some urgent work'. He constantly completes some important tasks that no one sees. These jobs are of private nature and at the expense of the unit and the society. I cannot resist the impression that he can't wait for us to be hit and the equipment damaged or destroyed; to relieve him and pave his way to promotion into the rank of general and achieve his lifetime dream. Tomović was dissatisfied. He didn't like him.

Dentist Matić and I went to the Medical Centre. He has the key. I have had the medication in my tooth for two months. Today, he replaced it with a new one. He told me that a few of his colleagues knew that the Number Five tooth has two roots. In my case, one nerve was dead and the other was not.

The relocation to the new position was underway. These were Tantalus's torments. Eventually, I hired a special tractor from the farmhouse to pull out the equipment. The tractor was as big as a John Deere one. We moved during the day. We took the combat position near the village of Bečmen.

Slush again. I was muddy to my knees.

The embankment was too close to the hedge. Due to the slippery and muddy terrain we could not position the guidance station into the Pi-shaped

---

361   The shift stayed on the position to help transition the equipment from combat into marching configuration.

embankment. We had to pull it with cables over the head of the embankment, from the fire control radar side. I had told that to Dani and he didn't believe me. It was a bad design idea to begin with. This proved to be the case in practice. The sidewalls must be as simple as possible. The position should be quickly manned and then immediately camouflaged. Alternatively, earlier camouflaging may be possible, but everything should be temporary. My idea, however, was the best; the simplest and most operational.

Cvetić[362] had not been notified about the new combat position in time. I gave him new locations: Dobanovci, Bečmen, Petrovčić and Boljevci.[363,364]

The drivers of the missile battery torn off the surveillance radar cable with their ZIL trucks. Dani, on his way to the site, found a 100-metre-long cable. I got angry when I saw how poorly the logs were installed (that was CBRN platoon's responsibility), because they had left gaps that were too big. My next shift is from 00:00 to 08:00.

Accidental or not, there were too many coincidences. The radar imitator had not been positioned at the previous position, and that was good. Dani agreed. The log protection must be much simpler and quicker to install.

The command was housed in Zoran Nedeljković's house. He worked in the federal security service. The great look of his house and how it was maintained was impressive. Crnobrnja came to tell Dani, Dotlić and me that Colonel Vita Andjelković would come with some Russian guy tomorrow. They wanted to hear about our combat experiences, see us firsthand in combat and "pick-at our brains".

Today, Armuš told me that he saw when that guy from Karlovčić hit the plane with a SA-18 missile. He told me that he saw the missile going towards the plane and explosion in the air. The plane seemed to halve. The pilot did not eject, as there was no parachute. He was hit and did not return to the base. A win-win outcome: one mosquito less for us to kill, and one item off their maintenance list. I asked him then how come there was no wreck anywhere. He just shrugged with his shoulders. I have to report this shooting to Commander Opsenica.[365]

While we were at Soko Salaš farmhouse, I found out that a Lieutenant Colonel has a video clip of the F-16 being shot down. After the war, we have to get that clip. He was from the infantry brigade.

---

362   Cvetić– Reserve Capitain Cvetić was the SA-7 (Strela 2M) MANPAD Battery Commander.

363   The Strela 2M MANPAD Battery - was divided into four Sections that were arranged on four sides around the firing position, 10-15km away; therefore creating the outer (air) defence ringthat guarded the firing position.

364   In this particular case, the firing position was in Deč and the Author told Reserve Capitain Cvetić four locations around Deč that should be occupied by his men.

365   Opsenica – Captain Opsenica was the SA-18 Igla MANPAD Battery Commander. A soldier from his battery fired a missile from the farm in the village of Karlovčić and hit the plane. The Author personally knew Opsenica and wanted to convey to him Armuš's account of the shooting.

Tonight, on my way to the shift, I saw a huge rat on the rubbish tip. We can hear them all around us. We were masked with rubbish that made our position a large-scale still life[366] piece of art.

This morning, Dotlić brought some sponge chair cushions and back supports for chairs in the guidance station. A little bit of luxury after so many days of war!

Monday, May 17

Stojanović connected telephone lines to the guard post and the surveillance radar after the last vehicle left the firing position. Last night he made a mistake by discussing locations of the SA-7 MANPAD systems in front of a stranger. Before that, he hadn't made any of this mistakes. This was his first mistake, probably caused by fatigue. People were nervous. We barely got out of the mud earlier today and here we were in it again. At 17:00, we went into Readiness No. 1.

Setting up logs to form palisades had been taking us a lot of time. I told Dani that Varga must bring fuel and it should be delivered to the combat position either early in the morning or before the evening.

Bacetić was at the Brigade Operations Center. Instead of reinforcing the field combat units, they were reinforcing the Operations Centre.

Radar operators are still repairing the cable, which was broken last night.

We were as dirty as pigs. At 17:30, Bacetić asked me a hypothetical question: if I received the "Sun" signal, would I know what it means. "Of course I know," I replied to him, while I thought to myself, "cessation of danger".

All missile operators should learn how to orient the equipment by using wooden pickets[367].

We didn't need a bus here because we could walk from one position to another. Nothing needed to be unmasked.

The new angle reflectors should be installed 250 to 300 metres away from the equipment. The other day, five more reflectors arrived with the mail, much larger in size than the old ones, and with stands.

I told Dani that it would be very good to have a SA-18 Igla MANPAD. We had had 18 launchers and over 100 missiles just before the war commenced. When it broke out we were ordered to hand them over to the troops deployed

---

366   In this case, the man-made objects also included discarded takeaway food packages, debris, litter, trash and rubbish.

367   Orientation by pickets - is a method for orienteering the missile launch ramp. It is infrequently used as it is considered to be less accurate and reliable than the method of orientation by mutual aiming of the launch ramp and the target acquisition radar.

in Kosovo and Metohija provinces of Serbia[368]. Tepavac would be happy to have an Igla, which we nicknamed "Awl" due to its distintctive features[369].

It was an extremely cold all night. Our wet clothes were drying off on us whilst we were on duty. My rubber boots were cold from the mud. I took off my socks and walked barefoot in my boots. It felt weird. My shift was in a deep sleep. I smoked too much and got nauseous.

At 06:00 we went into Readiness No. 2.

We all dozed off. At 07:30, Ljubenković managed to solder the broken cable. The radar was operational. I reported that to the Operations Center. I ordered the soldiers from my shift to start disguising their positions, as well as those in the emergency intervention group. The movement of the vehicles had unmasked the combat position and everything needed to be covered and camouflaged again. I ordered Aleksić to bring pitchforks, axes and scythes.

The workshop team came to repair other faulty cables. The blue and white cables from the launch pad were damaged in Karlovčić when they shot at us. These were replaced by spare ones. Volf drove away in the Kraz crane truck last night and returned to the shift on foot. We have to find his replacement for work on the crane.

Colonel Stanković called and told me that Andjelković was coming with a Russian from 20:30 to 21:00. He instructed me to tell him everything that might interest him, "He is a confidential man, who can be fully trusted with our ways of doing things."

I laid down to rest. Dani woke me up at 11:30. Cvetić had not called him yet, and our guests had come: Vita Andjelković, Viktor (the Russian) and Pera Djordjević. The Russian was dressed in our uniform. Colonel by rank. He was sent by his army, and in our country he had to sign that he was a volunteer; in case something happened to him, it would look like he hadn't even existed. It was his decision. He was a little nervous and his masseter muscles were twitching. Dani was pestering us with his trivial jokes. General Karanović was in Russia. "He went to the negotiations," Vita said. In order not to listen to Dani's blabbering, I went to Deč.

In Deč, I organised the camp and ordered accomodation for the combat shifts to be in houses near the combat position. I gave them the list of empty

368   The General Staff expected land invasion of Serbia by NATO forces to commence from the South (FYR Macedonia) and South-West (Albania) directions, hence it ordered the troops stationed there, and defending these borders, to be armed with the most modern SA-18 (9K38 Igla) MANPAD systems. Consequently, older versions of SA-7 (Strela 2M) MANPAD systems were deployed across the reminder of the country.

369   An Awl is a pointed instrument for piercing small holes in leather, wood, etc. It is a Serbian nickname for the 9K38 Igla (SA-18) MANPAD. It stems from the Igla's terminal maneuver to hit the fuselage rather than jet nozzle, which improves Igla's lethality on target. Given that Igla rotates at about 900 -1200 revolutions per second, a feature called the rolling frame missile, not only that it pierces the fuselage, it screws itself into the fuselage, before the additional charge ignites any remaining rocket fuel. The nickname Awl is derived from these features.

houses and who sleeps where. I brought along my field office, includinga box with permits to go home. After that I went back.

While I was in Deč, I heard the planes. One was leaving black smoke and losing height. It was clear that it had been hit. Probably by an SA-7 MANPAD. I was overjoyed. After 1 - 2 minutes another one came. I saw the launch of either an SA-7 or SA-18 Igla MANPAD. Black smoke behind the second plane as it plunged into the abyss. No parachutes. Later, I found out that Tepavac fired from his SA-7 Strela MANPAD. The other pilot probably saw his colleague being knocked down and forgot to be careful. He did not activate his heat baits and the SA-7 hit him. A moment of inattention, and he lost his life. Maybe it was seconds. The same as with us.

I went back to Bečmen. The Russian and Andjelković were in the missile guidance van. There was an overflight.

Colonel Dragan Stanković also came. He was sitting on the terrace at a table with Crnobrnja. An ideal opportunity to talk. I asked Stanković when will I talk to the Corps Commander. I told him that I worked honestly and that I did not fight this war for a decoration, but out of conviction. In fact, I was recounting what I had already written. Crnobrnja supported me. Stanković said there were mistakes. "Why don't you correct the mistake if there is one?" There was no answer. "Why do you need alcoholics at the Operations Center, who are deciding about our lives." Stanković replied that everyone's participation must be analyzed. I agreed, but when? "If everyone in the combat service was promoted to a higher rank, why would I be an exception?" He asked me if I had sent a letter to the General Staff. "I did, including to Biga, and I will send it to everyone. If I receive no reply, I will demobilize and you will be left without one honest man," I said. "There is a risk of an excessive number of high ranked officers, so that after the war they will not be appointed in the troop and they will lose their jobs," he told me. "Come-on, Dragan, don't bother me with your conscienceness and worries about what will happen after the war. Why do you care about that? I demand equality and I will not give up on that. Remember that." "We in Belgrade have nothing against you," he replied. "I doubt it," I said,"here in the combat units is the place where people die and get ranks, not in Belgrade. If there are those who envy us, send them here into the guidance station to fight and get ranks."

Crnobrnja asked if there was a legal basis for my promotion. "It doesn't matter, Bora. This is war, and the "Official Military Gazette", No. 3 of 1995 covers this matter." I saw that a lot of dust had risen. Everyone thought the dust was subsiding. They screwed up. And they screwed up big time.

The host came and interrupted our conversation. We didn't discuss it anymore in front of the host, as per the Officers'Code of Ethics and Conduct. Bora and Stanković went to the combat position, and I went to greet and congratulate Tepavac for the plane. That was yet another proof that justified the existence of our emergency intervention group, which was my brain child.

Dani invited me for lunch, as if he was the host.

I was glad that I told Dragan everything that bothered me, and that my complaint had reached the top brass in the Air Force & Air Defence Corps, as well as that by the order of the General Staff. Lieutenant Nikolić was immediately decorated and promoted. Dani, a few days later. I fought and won for the other people in the shift. I now fight for myself. Dani opposed my proposal to award the whole crew, by saying, "The Brigade will resolve it." It did not occur to them. It was obvious to me that those in the brigade command had their own agenda. A huge burden fell on me. The truth about the injustice was set in motion. I owed a lot to my girl Danka. I will never forget what she did for me.

Viktor, the Russian, Vita Andjelković, Pera Đorđević, Dani, the host and I were present at the lunch. The appetizer was cheese and ham with spring onions and radishes. After that we had sour soup and roastwith salad. Excellent.

Vita said that the Russian and he saw the downing of the third plane today. A missile went after him. He doubted that they will fly again tonight, and the Russian wanted to record everything on the tape. He watched me with interest.

Colonel Andjelković told us how he had seen the launch of missiles and destruction of the target, that had not been officially recognized yet as our hit. We launched from Petrovčić. They were watching from the Preka Kaldrma[370] intersection near Deč. General Karanović, Colonel Andjelković, Ivković and another Major saw the shooting down of an airplane. Stanković was taking notes. I thought to myself, "Then it is officially our third target, and Tepavac's hit today was our fourth downing."

I dictated to Stanković our needs in manpower and equipment. It also included remotely control the surveillance radar from the van and to send someone to fix the moving target selection block[371], which had not been working for a long time. He wrote it all down.

Last time, about 40-50 documents came with the mail but there is no enough time for everything: to do my regular shift work, paper works and to manage the whole unit. Dani did nothing, as usual. He was profiteering while I was dying at work. We were brought a brand new cable for the power supply van. Somehow we inadvertently left our Findor[372] tool set at the school in Karlovčić.

I said goodbye to Stanković after lunch and went to my shift. Vita and the Russian will come tonight to observe our combat work. Muminović was ordered not to allow Ljubenković to man the surveilance radar during Readiness No. 1. The error in the orientation of the launch pad was 90° degrees. We have to check who did the orientation, Petrović or Jaćić. The camera didn't work this morning either, because the cable was not connected to the

370   Preka Kaldrma is name of the intersection of roads connecting four villages: Petrovčić, Karlovčić, Ašanja and Deč.
371   The block for selection of moving targets is a device used during combat work to filter out reflections from stationary objects (such as hills, mountains, forests, power lines, clouds, etc.) from the radar screens, so operators could easier focus on useful reflections coming from the moving objects and real targets.
372   Findor is the brand that manufactured the tool set.

van.

Crnobrnja brought me a photo earlier today. Crnomarković took a photo of me in Karlovčić upon my return from reconnaissance, at the combat position where they missed us by 30-40 meters.

"If Kočo knocked down the plane, I would like to see Maletić's face," said Muminović. We all laughed loudly at his joke[373].

Upon arriving at the firing position we set up corner reflectors. We found out that 15 panels of profiled sheet metal were missing. Aleksić helped us with his emergency interventions group. They went out in the field to search the terrain for the panels.

For a long time, until dark, I walked around the embankments and thought about human destiny and trickery. I took great comfort in realising that the injustice towards me must be corrected. An individual against an organization. Can this battle be won?

As darkness engulfed me I entered the van and put on my bulletproof vest. At 21:45, we were ordered to go into Readiness No. 1. I was informing everyone that we have a problem with the command transmitter and reported it to the Operations Center. The frequency was stuck. I adjusted it quickly by moving the lever left and right. This took me about 5-10 minutes. After the final check, I reported that we are fine now. This made us and them happy.

Vita told us to call them when we go to Readiness No. 1, in order for the Russian to watch our combat work. They came after 45 minutes and took their seats in the guidance station. Andjelković, Pera Djordjević, Viktor and Dani came. Dani was as drunk as an alcoholic. He sat for a while at my feet and then went outside around 23:00. He did not return to the station until the end of the shift. Who knows where he regained his greed and his misfortune. A sad man. I didn't meet him along the way.

Dotlić replaced me with his shift at 00:00. Dani was not in the camp. I asked Kosta if he had seen him coming. "I did not," Kosta replied. I called Dotlić in the guidance station and told him that Dani was not in the camp and that he should send a soldier to check outside and see that he had not fallen somewhere. It was cold and there were a lot of puddles. If he fell drunk into one, he might freeze. Dotlić replied: "You should't give a rats ass. Enjoy the camp." I went to take a shower and after 15 minutes I heard the phone ringing and Kosta's loud laughter. He received a coded message from Dotlić and repeated to me: "The Eagle has Landed." I asked him what was that. He

373   In order to understand this joke, one needs to know its following background. Djordje Maletić gave nickname "Kočo" to Senior Sergeant Zoran Tepavac, after a famous general Konstantin "Kočo" Popović who was a Serbian politician and communist volunteer in the Spanish Civil War and the Commander of the First Proletarian Division of the Yugoslav Partisans during WW2). According to that analogy Tepavac will become a general. Tepavac was a very responsible member of the emergency response unit that was guarding the firing position from sudden enemy attacks and helicopter landing. His great desire was to shoot down a plane and he saved our lives few times by firing from his SA-7 MANPAD, including today, 17 May 1999.

said that the soldier found Dani who fell somewhere, drunk as a skunk" and I laughed too.

Freshly showered and tired, I immediately fell asleep. Crnobrnja slept, on a bed made of mats and pads next to mine.

Tuesday, May 18

Dani woke me up at 07:30 to go to the shift.[374] He said that he would go reconnoitring for the new combat positions.

I refused, "I've had enough of your reconnaissance. Get the engineers to do their job."

Dani instantly became repulsive. He was angry because he was still hungover from last night.

I explained to him why he was wrong; "We replaced you yesterday because we had guests. Today, you want to go to reconnoiter. When will you go on duty in the missile guidance station? You keep making things up. Fuck that. You go reconnaissance and you're away all day. I have to wage war, tie up the units, do mail and solve all the problems in the battalion while you're nowhere to be found."

Crnobrinja was very quiet. He knew that I am right.

I continued on, "What does that matter that Stoimenov is up there in the station as a shift commander? How many times has he replaced you so far? Did we say anything to the Brigade on how you behave? Now suddenly Stoimenov can't be a shift commander anymore?[375] I'm not interested in what you are doing, but you must be on duty just like us."

He realised that he screwed up... He asked who had hit our car, Zastava 101, in the bumper? "I have no idea," I told him." "Find out who that was," he said. "I have no intention. I didn't give it to everyone, like you did. I'm not a cop, nor do I have the time for that bullshit," I replied.

Boško arrived from the shift and wanted to go to Deč to sleep. Dani didn't let him go. He told him to stay and sleep here and have time off until tomorrow. Dani will now go to the shift until 16:00. My shift is from 16:00 to midnight, and then Dani again, from 00:00 to 08:00. He looked totally calm. His hangover nervousness seemed to be over. Boško went to sleep, and Dani and I stayed. Bora went to visit Tepavac. Quite calmly, as if nothing had happened, we discussed what to do today and how best to proceed.

---

374   Dani did not show up for the shift duty earlier that morning because he was drunk, so Major Stoimenov took the shift to the firing position. Dani woke up the Author to go to the combat position, instead of him, and be in charge (as the fire control officer).

375   Central to the Author's anger was Dani's sudden whim, to the effect of, that Stoimenov cannot be the shift commander. It was absurd that Stoimenov sometimes can be and sometimes cannot be the shift commander.

Stoimenov reported that the Operations Centre called, requesting us to send them a list of our personnel reinforcement needs. We quickly agreed that we needed:

- two officers for the surveillance radar,

- one missile guidance officer,

- two manual tracking operators,

- one fire control radar commander,

- one platoon commander in the missile battery.

After that, Dani went on duty.

Slobodan Kilibarda - Kiki, one of the officers who had previously left the Army, called. He wanted to join the unit as a volunteer. He asked if we could sort out the paperwork for his involvement through the Military District. If we bring him in, then we wouldn't need two manual tracking operators, only one. Kiki was also good in the target selection system. After years off the military, who knows if anything was left of that knowledge?

We arranged for Varga to return all 90 blankets that we had taken from Žika Bosić in Ogar. The CBRN section needed to take all material and equipment designated to them by the wartime formation schedule from our base in Jakovo.

Armuš remodeled the corner reflector mounts according to my idea and design. We have to try to find the Findor tool set, which remained in the school in Karlovčić. The masking and camouflage of the firing position needed to be improved. Sedlak should come and pay out allowances for conscripts and reservists. Salaries too. We had not yet received our daily allowance for March, and it was already May. I wondered if NATO would wage war if their allowances are late two months... Other tasks: prepare documentation for the 250th Brigade; Write a request letter for Mijalković: explaining the need of the unit to allow him to stay with us, no matter the fact that we had been ordered to dismiss him; Prepare a list of civilian vehicles that are with us and send it to the Brigade; Prepare a vehicle request letter outlining our needs for the vehicles from the units that were not operational; Go to Šimanovci and inspect the AD-10 diesel genset unit that we've received from Podovac. I have to go to Karlovčić, Šimanovci, Deč and Prhovo... Many obligations to do in between two shifts.

Dani asked me again about Pera Bačvanski from Prhovo and asked to visit him. Pera wanted to join as a volunteer too.

I left with Ljubenković. We stopped for a quick coffee with Milan and Nada. While we had coffee, Milan was curious, as always, asking many questions. Soon we were on the road again. We bumped into the police patrol. I stopped them and we went to the school together. If we don't find the toolbox set, they can immediately commence an investigation on who could have stolen it. One of the teachers was there. We were relieved to find the Findor tool set box. After we loaded the box in the car, we left for Šimanovci via Prhovo.

In Prhovo we stopped by the Pera's place. He was not there, his mother told us he was at work. We didn't stay and went to Armuš in Šimanovci. He was kind as always. I gave him my sketch of the corner reflectors and explained how I wanted him to make them. They treated us with strawberries. The first harvest of strawberries this spring! He washed my windscreen with something that prevents sticking and checked the oil level and topped up. From his place, we went to Deč via Šimanovci.

In Šimanovci we stopped to visit Žugić, Commander of the Technical Workshop, to tell him our issue that some wire wrapped around[376] the wheels of the antenna post trailer[377]; that the screws on the trailer wheels cannot be tightened[378]; and to come to fix it.

The drivers should be more careful not to tear off our cables, as they did it during the last equipment relocation. It is useless if they do their job and during that they tear the cables and the battalion was neither ready nor functional. Teamwork within the unit was essential. Barvalac gave us a carton of milk and some sweets for the unit, and two packs of cigarettes each. I called Opsenica to tell him that one of his soldiers had shot down the plane. We stopped by the farm to inspect the AD-10 generator set received from the Smederevo battalion. They had already been taken away to the Brigade workshop. I reported it to Colonel Stanković.

In Deč, Tomović complained that the reserve soldiers were disobedient. Savić was all talk.[379]

Somewhere in the Fruška Gora Mountain, a friend of Jeremić was killed. Jeremić's eyes were full of tears. He said the deceased had two children. I ordered Tomović to let Jeremić go to the funeral in the afternoon. They were good friends. I explained Tomović what documents Jeremić needed for the trip and how to prepare them.

Slavko came to distribute the salaries.

We arrived in Bečmen at 15:00. Along the way I received a pager message from Danka. I contacted her to see why she was upset and what was giving her the blues. I comforted her…. Who will comfort me?

Kosta served lunch. A green pea dish and spring onion salad.

---

376   The driver could not completely remove the steel wire that was wrapped around the wheel of the trailer.

377   The Antenna Post Trailer–the fire control radar was transported in two trailers that are towed by two URAL trucks. The antenna post is transported in this trailer. The Antenna Head Trailer – was used to transport all three fire control antennas and their receivers.

378   The wheel of the trailer had a lot of screws and the driver managed to unscrew some of them and remove the wire but could not tighten them because he did not have the trailer tire change key.

379   Savić – Private Savić was an undisciplined soldier from the reserve. He would argue with his superiors about orders. He would find some stupid reason and justification to discuss the orders and avoid carrying them out, because that order didn›t make sense to him. He liked to decide what he would and would not do.

At 15:40, I headed towards the combat position. My shift started at 16:00.

When I arrived, the shift was in Readiness No. 1, with the missiles in preparation. They looked powerful and spooky. Stoimenov was the shift commander and fire control officer, as Dani was not there. I asked him if Dani had been coming? He replied, "No". "Dani, really, is not a normal person," I thought to myself in endless disbelief of what I had just heard. Well, he said he was going "up" when I saw him earlier today, when Ljubenković and I went on the tour to Prhovo, Šimanovci, Deč and Bečmen.

There was commotion at the Operations Center. They saw targets around us, but I didn't have them on my radar. Bačetić worked with me. The overflight was fierce. Matić called from Belgrade. Today was his day off and he asked about his friends. We were all well.

At 17:30, we went into Readiness No. 2.

I told Barvalac today to try to get railway sleepers. We also needed some spare trucks: KRAZ, ZIL, a vehicle for transport and loading of missiles, TAM 150 and TAM 110.

The Russian was delighted with our work. He did not expect such a skinny air-defence. He had been used to working in the environment where the engagement zones of individual missile systems overlap in depth and width. The Russians decommissioned their Neva air-defence systems a long time ago.

He simultaneously watched the radar screen, multiple targets all around us, and observed our way of working together. He had imagined our work differently; that we have multiple missile units, of different ranges covering all altitudes, arranged on one side of the front line, and facing the attack of the enemy's aviation from the opposite side.

At around 18:00, I called my lucky girl. She asked me if there will be an end to all this. She had also bought spring potatoes. She was waiting for me for lunch. "Oh my dear, eat them now, before they turn green by the time I come," I told her. I was really sleepy.

At around 19:00, Varga brought fuel to the firing position. I told him that, in the future, he must do it at night. He concurred.

Conscript Živković came to the cabin to telephone home. The man, whom I had found curled up in the front door frame of the school in Mihaljevci on the first night after his arrival. I can't forget the frightened expression on his face and the words addressed to me: "Djole, get me out of here!" Now he's another man. He understands the situation. "I guess it will be over soon," he said over the phone. On the other end at his house, everyone cried whilst saying that it was good that he had called. His sons just finished school. One son had excellent marks in his report, and the other son had very good marks. Some good news at least. Only now had I really started to understand the fuss in civilian life. I understand Danka. She will be strong by the end.

At around 19:45, Crnobrnja told me that a team from Zastava Film are coming to take pictures of us during combat work.

Ivica Marjanović informed me that the radar crane[380] had arrived, and the spare oil cap and fuel filter for the AD-10 genset unit[381] had been delivered. I told Žugić to organize with Barvalac and to talk to Tomić, and he immediately went to carry out the assignment. We need the oil cap and fuel filter for our spare AD-10 genset, just in case the AD-10 that was in operation fails.

Around 19:50 we had dinner. Sliced salami, hard dough bread and a sausage. It was good to have anything to eat. No one commented. At 19:55 they ordered us to go to Readiness No. 1. That was the full combat duty mode of work. Ljubenković had voltage problems. He must turn the high voltage off before he makes a second attempt. I called those higher up to get permission. In 5-6 minutes, the radar was turned on again. Everything was OK now. From 20:05 to 20:15 Crnobrnja brought a cameraman and a lighting technician. He did not enter the cabin. The two of them finished filming the fictitious combat work, start and launch twice. We imitated the real situation. Everyone laughed at how quickly they had left. In fact, who knows, they are just ordinary people someone sent to a combat position. This was not just our war. I often have the feeling that it was… Dani and his men came to replace us at midnight.

Wednesday May 19

Dotlić was on duty with his shiftcrew until 16:00. Dani went on reconnaissance with the battery commanders. He brought along the engineers to immediately arrange the combat position. I sent Armuš to Soko Salaš to pick up sleepers and the rest of the logs. These were needed to reinforce the protection of the missile guidance station van and the people in it. Mića Mijalković brought Kilibarda, nicknamed Kiki. He volunteered and came directly to us. Lieutenant Colonel Martin, a Personnel Officer from the Brigade, advised us to send a request to the Brigade, and that Slavko would go to the Military Personnel Department tomorrow to expel someone and insert Kiki instead. The arrival of Stanković was announced. Dani returned from reconnaissance very quickly this time. He planned to go home today. He was accompanied by Bugarin, Stoimenov, Muminović and Aca.

Lieutenant Colonel Milenković came with the Praga vehicle on which a missile from the MIG-29 was placed. It wasin genius to replace a twin 30 mm anti aircraft gun with a MIG-29 missile. We talked for a long time about the tactical and technical characteristics and the ways to use it. We toured around and chose a location for it. Sergeant Cvija stayed with us on the Praga. He was a good man. This was a big deal. Practically, it was as if we have an SA-7 or Igla with a range of about 20 km. The MIG-29 missile did not radiate, it worked in passive mode.

---

380   The radar crane–is a special-purpose piece of equipment used to manually detach the antenna head of the fire control radar from its post and put it into the UV-600 trailer for transport.

381   The oil cap of the AD-10 genset cracked - causing the engine oil to leak through the crack under the pressure.

I ordered the repair of the corner reflectors. Everything around us was in the function of protection. I wasn't so sure that everything was perfectly done. In any case, it gave us some kind of piece of mind.

The locals of the village roasted a pig, about 50 kilograms, with a certificate of meat inspection. They brought it and distributed it to the soldiers. Captain Cvetić helped them with the distribution. A long time ago, I ordered the logistical support unit to inspect and certify all meat, in order to prevent possible infection with trichinosis, and that health safety measure has been strictly implemented.

Mika Stojanović was at home. Last night, Dani signed him a permit to go home while he was so drunk. Early this morning, Dani called him and asked who had let him go home? Mika was embarrassed. He showed him the permit with the Dani's signature on. Dani was not ashamed. Bora and Mića Mijalković went to look for parts of the plane and confirmation that Tepavac had shot it down.

I ordered Žugić to go to Jakovo to set up a decoy firing position with his team, and that Kilibarda and Jaćić go to Karlovčić with a crane and load the decoy misssile launch ramps, and set up another decoy combat position there at the exact location where they had shot at us.

At 18:00, while I was on shift, Jaćić personally informed me about the work done. Kiki started well.

At around 13:05 Colonel Stanković arrived. The medals and decorations award ceremony for our people will be held tomorrow from 08:00 to 10:00 in Bečmen elementary school classroom. I assigned Dotlić to organise fresh haircuts and new uniforms for everyone at the ceremony. Stanković will provide replacement for those scheduled to be in the combat shift during the ceremony, namely the fire control officer, missile guidance officer and manual tracking operators, as well as the missile battery commander. "You'll get more people than you asked for," he said. And I told him that he will receive our request for additional vehicles, which we needed as spares in case of a failure.

I also told Colonel Stanković that we Serbs are fools. Other nations ran politics, and we wage war. The computer from the unit was at Dani's house, and we are knocking on doors throughout Belgrade to borrow another one. I also told him about the planned use of the diesel generator set, about posing, and about not being on duty in his shift. I told him that I want to talk to General Petrović tomorrow.

Stanković looked at me with a glassy stare that turned into the look of disbelief as I continued talking "Talk to Dotlić and Bora,"he briefly replied, while looking at me palely, as if he had seen a ghost. "Was he able to believe me?" I thought to myself, before saying, "I'm telling you this as a friend. We have known each other for a long time. After all, if what I am telling you is not true, then you can ask yourself why have I been your, and the Brigade's, first point of contact for business with our unit?"

Around 18:30, Jović completed installation of a telephone line to Sergeant Cvija.

We now have his armoured self-propelled six-wheeler Praga armed with a MIG-29 missile fully integrated into the emergency response unit that was guarding our firing position. I sent him food and water. I'll order him to go into Readiness No. 1 when needed. He need one and a half to two minutes preparations to become combat ready and can work continuously for 4-6 hours. His working time should be taken into consideration when decision making.

I warned Dotlić and Tiosav Janković not to make mistakes.

Mika told us the latest joke, that a "drone" was a new jargon word for the wife of a mobilized soldier.

Stanković gave me contact details of a person who managed requests for additional supply of Igla MANPADs, who would let him know, and that we should just go and pick them up.

We received a manual pump with the hose and fuel filter lid for the AD-10 generator set.

I was on shift from 16:00 to 24:00. Nothing special happened.

Chernomyrdin, the Prime Minister of Russia, left around 22:30. His plane was escorted by NATO fighters. The sky suddenly became clear. I called Danka and told her that it is possible that the peace deal had been signed and that she could comfortably undress[382] and go to bed. Her neighbours, Lucija and Savka, happened to be at her place.

At 23:00, I took off my flak jacket to catch a breath as the heat was unbearable. I put my tunic on and fastened my gun to my belt.

At 22:50, we are ordered into Readiness No.2. We commented that we did not remember the last time when we had been in ReadinessNo.2 at this time of the night. It was amazing.

Suddenly, at 23:00, an order came to go to Readiness No.1. We are ready for combat work.I turned the radiation on the surveillance radaron and saw a lot of targets on the screen. They were were located 10 km to 12 km away from us. They were coming at us from five directions. Our target acquisition radar was not ready yet.

I decided to let go of the first wave and engage the second one, which was 25 km away from us.

I called Cvija and gave him the target at an azimuth of 100 degrees moving towards 120 degrees. We agreed that if I am in a a good situation and have a clear target, I will launch at it first, and that he would remain ready to ambush as soon as they attacked me, he would shootat them without any radiation. I knew that we have to surprise them.

We directed the antenna at azimuth of 180. The distance to the target was 17-18 km. I ordered to lift the high voltage on the target acquisition radar, <u>and, when the target</u> was 15 km to 16 km away, to start antenna radiation.

382   Due to the air raids, many spent nights in the air-raid shelters or went to bed half-dressed or in tracksuits (not in comfortable pajamas), ready to instantly go to the air-raid shelter at the first sound of the siren.

Very quickly, in a few seconds, the missile guidance officer Janković found the target. A small turn of the wheels for the azimuth and elevation angles and the target was brought into the crosshair. The target went into an evasive maneuver. They knew that we have them in our scope. The wheels clicked and Janković pushed them away. The target was handed over for manual tracking. The officers of manual tracking accepted the target, and after two or three seconds of stabilizing the tracking systems, I ordered: "Destroy the target with two missiles, three points guidance method!" I ordered warhead activation method, missile consumption, launch method. A deafenning noise. Ignition of the booster motor and the first missile left the ramp, after five seconds another left.

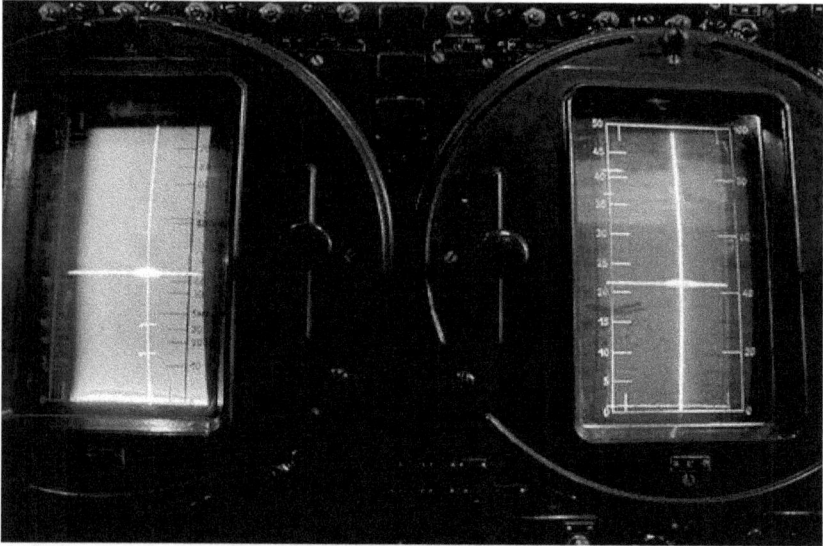

B-2 shape at the missile guidance station officer screens – UK-31. The picture is very different in comparison with the ordinary airplanes.

The missile guidance officer reported the parameter, height, speed, the first missile tracking, the second missile tracking, guidance was normal. Distance 14 km. Tiosavljević commented, "Fuck, what is this?" The reflection from the target was huge on his tracking operator's pointer. The first missile explosion in the target area, the second explosion, distance 13 km, azimuth 180 degrees. I ordered the high voltage down and equivalent[383]. It was just like a classroom training on the simulator.

The other shift came on time. They knocked on the door. The combat work was underway. I told them to wait in front of the station. Now there was a great danger, two shifts and two crews were on the combat position. We couldn't get out to swap the places because of the ongoing wave of attack.

383   High voltage down and equivalent are commands for the target acquisition radar. The first command stops the antenna from radiating, making it 'invisible' to the anti-radiation missiles. The purpose of the second command is to maintain ability of the radar to instantaneously re-commence radiation and start searching for the new target without any delay.

Dotlić was a little late and stood for two to three minutes at the voltage distribution cabin and watched the launch. He saw everything visually. The brigade Operation Centre issued a warning that helicopters are coming from Obrenovac direction. Sergeant Cvija also fired with the Praga, about a minute after us.

He informed me that he had no missiles left and that he was moving away. I agreed with him.

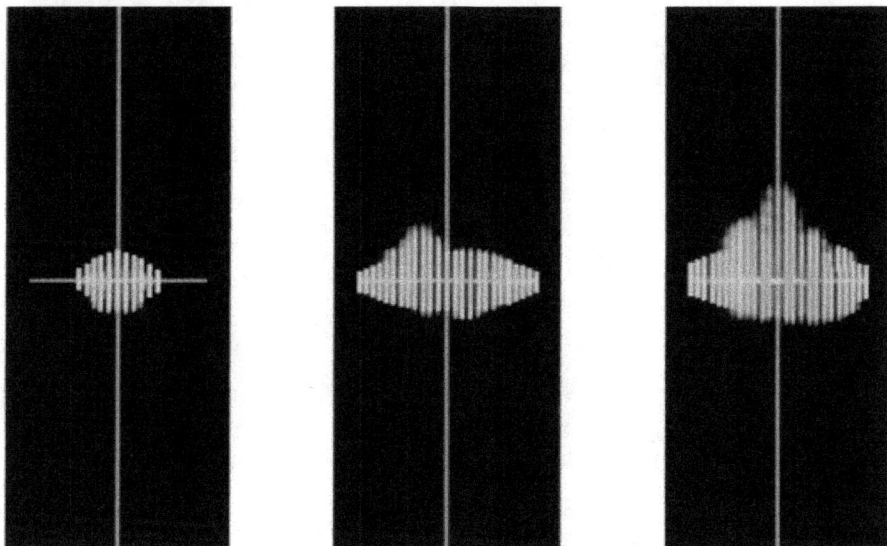

B-2 look in the manual tracking operator F1 screen in the moment of missile hit.

Dotlić entered the van and stopped in the narrow space between the missile guidance officer and operator of manual tracking by F1 and F2.

The following crew members did the shooting:

- Shift commander, Fire control officer - Đorđe Aničić,
- Deputy shift commander - Mika Stojanović,
- Missile guidance officer - Tiosav Janković,
- Manual tracking operator on F1 - Dejan Tiosavljević,
- Manual tracking operator F2 - Dragan Matić,
- Battery commander - Milorad Roksandić,
- Shift clerk – private Đorđević,
- Surveillance radar - Vladimir Ljubenković,
- Radar emission imitator - Željko Jaćić.

The waves of planes were flying over us from three directions.

The crew which launched two missiles against B-2.

Right: Lieutenant Mika Stojanović (deputy shift commander) and Lieutenant Colonel Aničić.

After the launch, we lost indication of the correct operation of the launch ramp from which it was fired. Something had happened to it. As if they knew about it, countless planes stirred the skies above us. A full-scale air raid, the strongest since the beginning of the war when I was on duty, was coming at us. From the azimuth of 205 –235 degrees, as if they knew that it was my no-go zone (impossible to launch, because our own equipment would be damaged). From the azimuth 300 – 330 degrees and 150 – 180 degrees.

A 'million' planes were in the air above us. I commanded to the deputy commander engagement azimuths for radar imitator. So many planes were buzzing around that it felt like we were in a hive. Stojanović counted down the working time for the imitator - the duration of its radiation. His commands were not short and sharp. We will have to analyze that. We were literally just jumping from one target to another and radiating for five seconds at each. Because of so many planes in the air, there was no time for longer radiation on individual ones.

From the target acquisition radar, located next to the missile guidance station van, we radiated at one group, and from the imitator to the group coming from the azimuth of my no-go zone. The third group of planes in the air was uncovered...

I again ordered the search for a target, but which one? There was a pair flying in the outgoing direction at the respective distances of 14 km and 18 km. On the other hand, a target entered the zone behind us and was located 15 km away. We didn't have time to shoot on those on the way out of our engagement zone, so we went after this one flying towards us. As soon as we radiated at him, passive disturbances appeared on our screens that covered the target, and the missile guidance officer reported that he did not see it. I ordered the high voltage down. For the reminder of the air-raid, until 01:30,we encountered the full-scale air-raid with the single imitator. The aircrafts were coming to the end limit of our engagement zone, but did not enter it[384].

Luka Trgovčević was at the Operations Center of the Brigade and he told me: "Work if you can, but be careful not to get fucked up." I told him to let me do my work and not to call me often, because it was a big commotion here. "I see it," he said, "I just want to help you, how do I know if you can see everything."

After the shooting, Stanković called and asked what the manifestation was like on the screens. I gave him the missile guidance officer Janković to explain first hand what he saw. For the first time, we managed to bring the second missile to the target. Until now, it had not entered the expecting volume of space and it had flown like a cannonball, along a parabolic trajectory. We had finally correctly tuned the second missile guidance channel at the guidance station van. I heard Stanković reporting on the action from the Operations Center to the Corps.

There were targets in the air at about 30 kilometers away from us. I ordered a quick change of the crews. Roksandić, Janković and Matić remained in the van, staying on for a second consecutive shift. They were on the 24:00 hours duty, since their replacements had gone home.

Now the number of people on the combat position had been significantly reduced. I didn't want to leave the post in the middle of the air-rad, as

384   In other words, they were provoking from a safe distance away.

that would not be fair to Dotlić. He had reconfirmed it to me by telling, "You started, work to the end." We endured... My shift did its job very professionally.

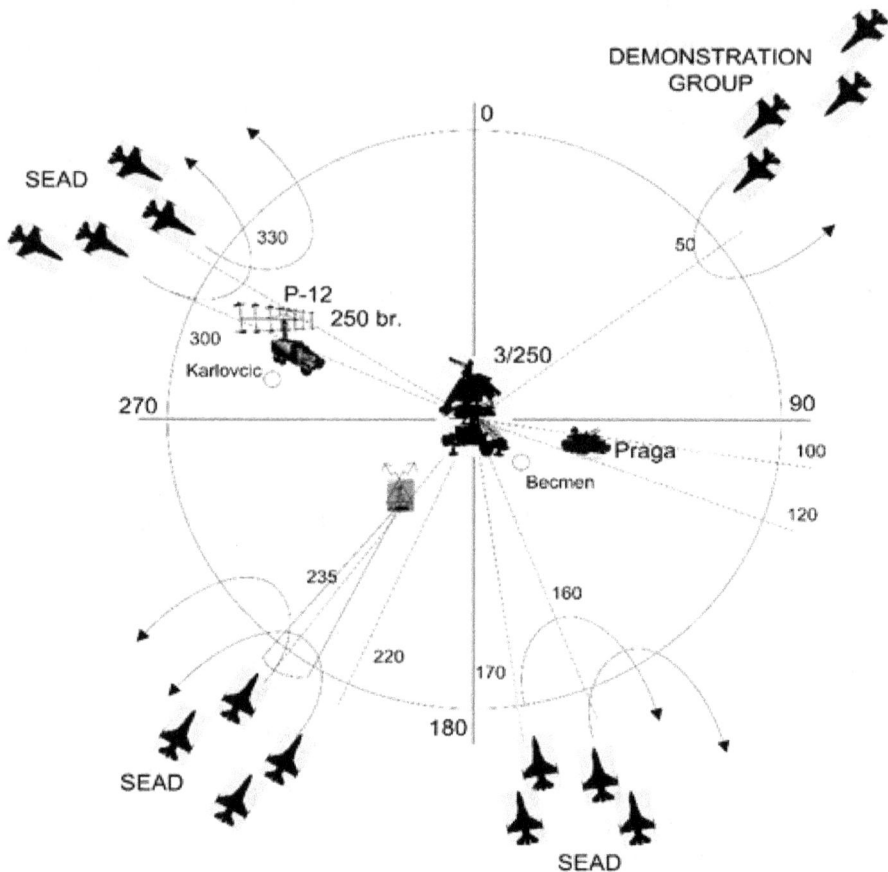

Schematics showing SEAD group attack on the battalion immediately after the launching at the large target. Three SEAD group simultaneously approaching from the different azimuths and one demonstration group from the North-East directions.

Something important had happened in the air, as soon as they were stirred like that. Matić told me: "Djole, great work, you were so cool-headed", and Dotlić greeted and hugged me saying, "Well done for the work with the imitator, so professional and enjoyable to watch. It was a textbook work." The air-raid ended around 01:30 and I left the shift.

I walked alone through the rubbish dump towards the village. Surrounded by gloom and darkness all around. I wondered why they didn't launch an anti-radar missile at us. We worked very briefly on the antennas. From the moment the target was detected to its destruction, the plane flew only four kilometers. Maybe that was the reason. We didn't give them time. We were much faster than them.

COMBAT ENGAGEMENT PARAMETERS ANALYSIS   AD-01

1999-19-05

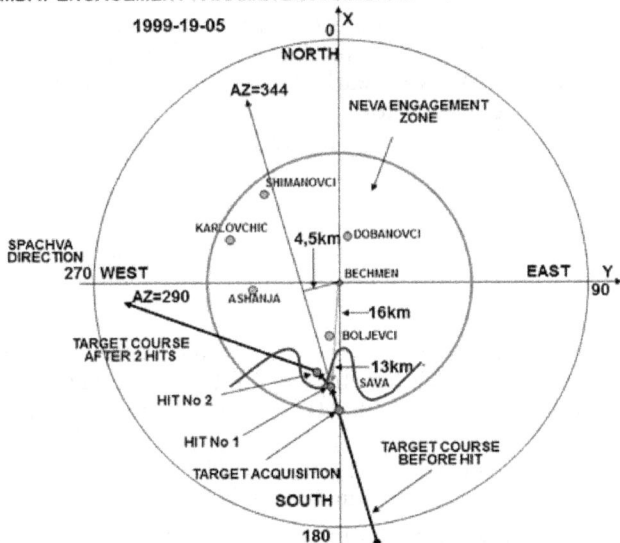

Combat engagement analysis.
(Source: Vladimir Nesković)

COMBAT ENGAGEMENT
PARAMETERS CALCULATIONS
FOR 1999-19-05   AD-02

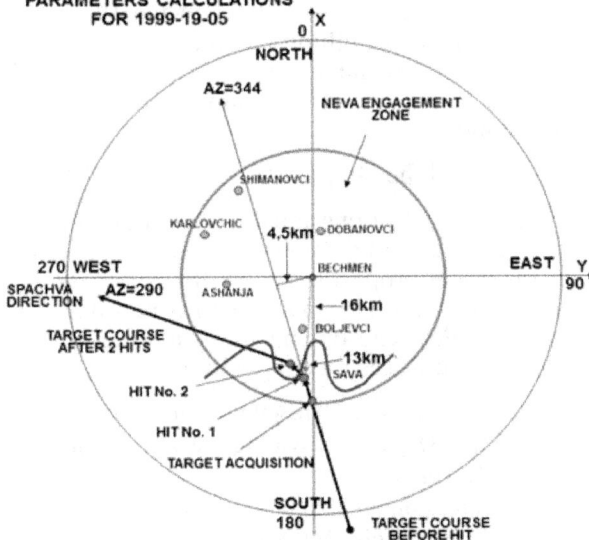

TARGET ACQUIZITION
-AZIMUTH: 180°   DISTANCE: 16km
-SPEED 200m/s   PARAMETER 4,5km

COURSE ANGLE
U=arcsin(4,5/16)=16,33
COURSE AZIMUTH Azp=320-U=344°

DISTANCE FROM ACQUIZITION UNTIL PARAMETER
$L_{zpa} = (16^2 - 4,5^2)^{1/2} = 15,4lm$

HIT
ALTITUDE: 7km ; DISTANCE: 13km

DISTANCE FROM THE HIT UNTIL PARAMETRE:
$L_{ppa} = (13^2 - 4,5^2)^{1/2} = 12,2lm$

DISTANCE FROM ACQUIZITION UNTIL HIT:
$L_{zp} = 15,4 - 12,2 = 3,2km$

TIME FROM ACQUIZITION UNTIL THE HIT:
$T_{zp} = 3,2/0,2 = 16s$

MISSILE SPEED
$V_{rak} = 13/16 = 813m/s$

HIT No 1 EXACT AZIMUTH
$AZ_{pp} = 184°$

Combat engagement calculation.
(Source: Vladimir Nesković)

279

Tepavac and his people were on guard near the first houses at the entrance to the village. I briefly stayed with them. Everyone hugged and congratulated me. The enormous psychological burden and physical fatigue was slowly waning. In the morning we will relocate to another position. That was more than certain. I went to bed around 02.30 after smoking numerous cigarettes. I just fell asleep when Stanković called me to tell me that in addition to the officers, whom he had listed earlier for the lineup, Radivojević and Ljubenković must also be present today. "Dragan, should I get them uniforms now?" "Don't worry, I'll bring them along in the morning when I come." "Good,". I hung up.

Thursday, May 20

Dani returned from home very early today. Around 06:30. He wasn't here again when the big events in the unit happened. He hugged and congratulated me. General Petrović arrived around 07:00. Stanković, Petrović, Dani and I were called for an ad hoc meeting. I had just woken up and hadn't even had time to wash my face. I put on my old shirt with rolled up sleeves, slippers on my feet and went to the meeting unshaven. No one even noticed that.

Petrović said that the Brigade could have become famous last night and that only we had shot, no one else. He wanted to dismiss Noskov and Djokić. "What Brigade?" I said to myself, "Out of all Brigade, only three battalions are still operational: Noskov's, Djokić's and ours." In his opinion, last night we shot and downed an F-15 but he still has had no material evidence. We shot right above the Sava River where it meanders near Obrenovac. He said that he must order a take-off to our MIG-21 fighters. He knew that the people - pilots would be sacrificed, but there was nothing he could do about that. The MIG-21 couldn't do anything against the superior NATO fighters. He knew that too. I told him that I had requested an official meeting with him. "Let it go the regular way," he replied.

Last night NATO scumbags targeted the Dragiša Mišović hospital.[385],[386]

Out of the 11 people who received promotions and decorations, eight were from our unit; the remaining three were from the units from Kosovo and Metohija. That was a success of historical proportions. Our slingshots worked well. "Well, my general, you have no idea how much heart is required. You are a pilot and you simply don't understand our business and our state of mind," I thought to myself. He said the Corps meeting will be at 15:00 at the

385   Dragiša Mišović Hospital - University Hospital Center Dr Dragiša Mišovićis a teaching hospital in Dedinje, Belgrade, providing specialist health care. It is colloquially referred to as "Dragiša Mišović."
386   In the air raid of the NATO forces on civilian targets, on 20 May 1999, at 00:50 hours, at least one cruise missile hit Dragiša Mišović hospital killing eleven people (seven guardsmen, three patients and a hospital security officer). The Neurology Building was destroyed and the buildings of the Childrens', Gynecology and Obstetrics Clinic and the premises of the hospital's legal and accounting services were damaged.

usual place and that Stanković and Dani should come.

After praising us for our work, he gave us four boxes of LM cigarettes and left. Colonel Stanković is a wise man. He was not talking too much. You could see that he was furious, "Someone will pay for all this shit after the war. Only the air defence is waging war. You have no idea what has been going on. They require us to use our radars more often and for longer in order to down more airplanes! What would be the purpose of that if we lose people and equipment?" he said. The pressures from the useless brass and politicians must be huge.

You could clearly see how much he was upset and pissed off.

The house owner came and congratulated me. We started the transition of the equipment a bit later, around 11:00. The awarding ceremony had to be completed first. We let the vehicles leave the combat position one at a time. There should be no accumulation of trucks on the road. Our close protection lockouts were on guard. The SA-7 MANPAD group was in the positions and on high alert. Dani went scouting and surveying the new positions. I saw him again at 22:00.

We found the reason for the malfunction of the second ramp: tonight, we launched from the third and fourth ramp beams, and the missile from the second beam dropped from the ramp due to the blast at a high launch angle. The launch crater behind the ramp was huge. During the blast off, the 13-ton launch ramp moved about 20 centimeters from its base position. We reported it to the Operations Center, to Lieutenant Colonel Samardzić. He couldn't initially understand what it was all about. Judging by his voice, it seemed to me that Lieutenant Colonel Samardzić was a bit tipsy. He told me that he would send us Lieutenant Colonel Dubajić at around 21:00, to pick up the missile and see if he can fix it.

5V27D fell from the launcher during the launch.

I left two soldiers from the intervention group as security at the last house in the village, and we all moved to the village of Ašanja, to a new combat position. We would transfer the launch ramp from Bačmen tomorrow during the day when the guys from the technical unit pick up the missile.

Blaževski - the host of the house where the signals section was located, said that a street in Bečman will be called "Tepavac Street", and the small hill will be called "Aničić Hill". Dotlić and I were the last ones who left Bečman. Kosta's courier packed up our things and stuffed them into the Zastava 101.

I left for Ašanja and came across a Lada Niva all terrain vehicle that was full of officers. They were on the way to Dr. Djukić's for a beer. Zoran from Bečman, the host of the house where the command was located, sent us grilled meat and we all, about ten of us, had a lunch in the medical centre. The other officers had beer.

At around 17:00 the transition of our equipment into the combat configuration began. The missile guidance station and the logs should be positioned first, then all other equipment. We had to work quickly and to do everything, or as much as possible, while it was still visible. We released the trucks with the equipment to the combat position one by one. The CBRN section installed the corner reflectors. The small corner reflectors will be set up tomorrow, as Armuš had to remake them. They progressed well. Miškov was their commander.

I am at the combat position with people setting up our equipment. Dotlić went to the village to provide accommodation for the people. He returned at around 21:00. The equipment was not ready yet. We agreed for him to stay and be in charge until midnight, and Dani would take over after 00:00.

After this I left for the camp. I drove without lights and about halfway met Dani with his driver Aca in the battalion's Opel Ascona. I told him what Dotlić and I had agreed on.

There had been an order from the Brigade Command for the Battalion Commanders to be on the guidance station in combat shifts from 22:00 to 04:00. Dani had been routinely avoiding that night shift duty, hence had been breaking the order by the Brigade Command.

Dani returned to the camp and an altercation broke out between us. We argued over minor things. He asked me again who had hit the Zastava 101 on the bumper. I told him that I had no idea who did it and pushed back, "You have been loaning my car to others, with and without my knowledge. It wasn't me who hit the bumper, and you can go and find out who did that." Dani then raised the issue of the flashlight that Armuš gave me, because Senad Muminović had been convinced that Armuš had sent that flashlight to him and that I kept it for myself. "Not a problem," I replied, "We will ask Armuš, with Muminović present, to whom he sent that flashlight."

We laid down to sleep. He will go on shift tonight.

I went to Deč in the morning. Once there, I handled the mail for superior command. While there I reprimanded Slavko Sedlak for not doing as I had told him. He is safe in his accommodation; He does not participate in combat operations and sleeps peacefully; He lives carefree and yet he hadn't done it properly; He did not go to the Military Department and did not do everything as I had ordered. His assignment was to resolve the issues of Kilibarda and Armuš.

Mića Mijalković arrived and I ordered him to go straight away to Jakovo and bring a uniform for Kilibarda. He told me that he had sent me a M-93 uniform via Dotlić: a shirt, pants and a jacket.

Tomović wanted to go home tomorrow. I told him to ask Dani for permission.

The next task was to organise meeting with Jaraković, from the Institute: The plan is to wait for him at 12:00 in the centre of Deč and also bring along 15 liters of D2 diesel fuel needed to test the radar imitator because the fuel was in short supply and he didn't have any. The motor on the imitator stand was in a critical condition and needed to be replaced. He also wanted to upgrade it to remote operation and control from the missile guidance station van. That would certainly help us a lot. There would be no need for people to work on the imitator during combat work. That would also eliminate the possibility of human error. Work with the imitator and its correct operation is extremely important for our combat work.

I went to Armuš to check if he had brought the railway sleepers from Soko Salaš. He told me he had not. Someone completely siphoned oil and fuel out the Ural truck that was parked across from his house. I think it was the Ural truck for spare parts for the surveillance radar. The stainless steel cables on the winders and on the body of the vehicle did not seem to have been touched. I alerted Major Stoimenov about the theft.

In conversation with Armuš I told him that there was a big misunderstanding about the flashlight and that Senad complained to Dani that I took the flashlight that was given to him[387]. Armuš immediately interrupted me, "It's nonsense and it's not true," and then explained, "I asked Senad for the

387   The lack of handheld flashlights was a serious problem during the war because of frequent transition of the equipment from combat into transport configuration and vice versa. The transitioning and relocation to new firing positions had to be done overnight because the firing positions were camouflaged, and the enemy had full control of the airspace above.
The confusion was caused by an unfortunate sequence of events, which started when Armuš gave the Author one large flashlight to keep and lent him another small flashlight, on the condition of returning it upon completing the transition that night. The Author gave the small flashlight to Senad Muminović to use that night, as he hadn't had any. Senad did not look after the flashlight and someone took it away. When Armuš asked the Author to return the small flashlight, he replied that he had given it to Senad who subsequently lost it. Unbeknown to the Author, Armuš also

small flashlight you gave him when they had been transitioning the target acquisition radar. That's why I thought it was with Muminović, and not that I sent it to him personally to keep." Then Armuš said in a much more serious voice,"I don't like the rift starting between your guys. You are very good as a unit." I replied, "I wouldn't lose face for one flashlight. What nonsense."

Around 15:30 hours I went to Deč. Dani had not been in the unit for days. I was tired and took a quick shower and had a big lunch. I felt calm in the serene atmosphere atthe logistical support unit in Deč. This was in stark contrast to the aggitated atmosphere and much more dangerous work on the combat position and in the missile guidance station van. I slept until 19:00 hours, and after that I had dinner and left. It was still daytime by the time I arrived around 20:30. Officers from other units came to help us:

Missile guidance officer, Capetain Ivan Ukić,

Manual tracking operators:

- Senior Sergeant Slobodan Stojanović,

- Senior Sergeant Slobodan Kilibarda, volunteer,

- Sergeant Zoran Vasiljević,

- Warrant Officers Miodrag Danilović and Zoran Ratković came to the missile battery,

- Warrant Officer Radenko Ratković and Sergeant Corporal Zoran Mitrović came to the surveillance radar.

I had a conversation with them. We exchanged our experiences. Around 22:00 I went to bed but couldn't fall sleep until 23:00. Aca, Dani's driver, was here and I told him to tell Kosta to wake me up at 23:40, to go to my shift. Courier Kosta delivered dinner. Aca didn't seem to tell him and Kosta didn't wake me. Dani came out of the shift around 00:10 and asked me why I didn't come to the station to replace him? I explained to him that Kosta had called the camp to tell them to wake the officers. Dotlić answered and told him that he was going on shift. That was probably why no one woke me up. "I'm not you," I thought, "to evade my obligations."

Saturday, May 22

My shift was from 00:00 to 08:00. "Shitshow" over Obrenovac. The raid lasted almost all night. We used radar emission imitator and pull them on us. They come as "flies for sweet". SEAD groups…on free hunt…They are looking for missile batteries around. The problem is that they are implementing and applying something new and we are not sure if there is the real fighter above

---

asked Senad where the small flashlight was, that the Author had given to him. This led Senad to conclude that the Author stole the small flashlight that was intended for him. Consequently, Senad complained to Dani that Armuš had sent him a flashlight to use, which the Author, as the intermediary, usurped and then leant him to use as if it was the Author's.

us or something else. The radar cross section of the target is kind a larger but that does not mean necessarily it is the real airplane. It's something new. They most likely used towed decoys. The plane is most likely going slightly below, and the image on the radar screen stays above him, something like a decoy is masking him. I left the shift at 08:00 and went home.

I'm calling Lieutenant Colonel Janjus about the tractor trailer with the logs. They picked them up. We don't have a single log for our guidance station protection. Barvalac has not yet found out where they are. Sedlak should send me questionnaires for the officers who came to help. They need to fill it. Dani and I are discussing how to involve newly arrived officers into the combat shifts. It would be better if we can make one additional team. People will have more time to rest, recuperate and go home for a short leave. The shift commander shall be one of us. We all do the same. Dani wants to mix the other officers with ours. Our guys doesn't want to do that.

This morning, around 06:30, Lieutenant Colonel Bajić called me. Dani was due to pick him up at 05:00 in Šimanovci. He neither waited for him nor told anyone that Bajić is coming. I have to send a vehicle to pick him up. Bajić comes with a team to install thermal imaging camera on the fire control radar. We are all looking forward to exploit that new addition. We will be able to shoot without radiation, thus further hiding our location, and completely surprise them. After the installation, I told Dani that it would be good if Bajić and his team train guidance officers and manual tracking operators to work with her.

I'm still under the impression of our shooting, from the other night. What surprises me is that there are no results and confirmation reports from the field. The guidance officer Tiosavljevic has drew me what he saw on his screens, as well as both manual tracking operators. That's what they saw.

The Operations Center reports that the Noskov's battalion has been hit. He was targeted with three anti-radiation missiles and five bombs last night, around 00:30. Airplanes first illuminated the site with a light bomb then sequentially bombed it.

We will also get a Kub (SA-6) mobile missile system. In a centralised command, they are under the command of the 250th Brigade, but in practice that centralised command really doesn't exists anymore, and in decentralised organization we will command them.

Mika told me that he was called by a Warrant Officer Cvijo from the "Praga", anti aircraft artillery battery, who said that "He is not going to work with anyone else except Lieutenant Colonel Aničić." Mika was delighted. Around 11:00ish I left for home. I'm free until 08:00 tomorrow morning, when I need to get back to the shift.

There is no electricity in the apartment. Danka told me she spoke with my sister Ljubica. Can she send me a few box of cigarettes from abroad. She knows it's war and I'm a smoker. Is there any cigarettes or tobacco in our country to buy in free sale.

I slept like a drunk all day. It's amazing how a man can be tired without even feeling that exhaustion. A neighbor, nicknamed Pop, came in to install the clamps on the cabinet door. Danka called him and scheduled before. I was with him for a while and then fell back into sleep again. I don't even know when he left... Shameful...

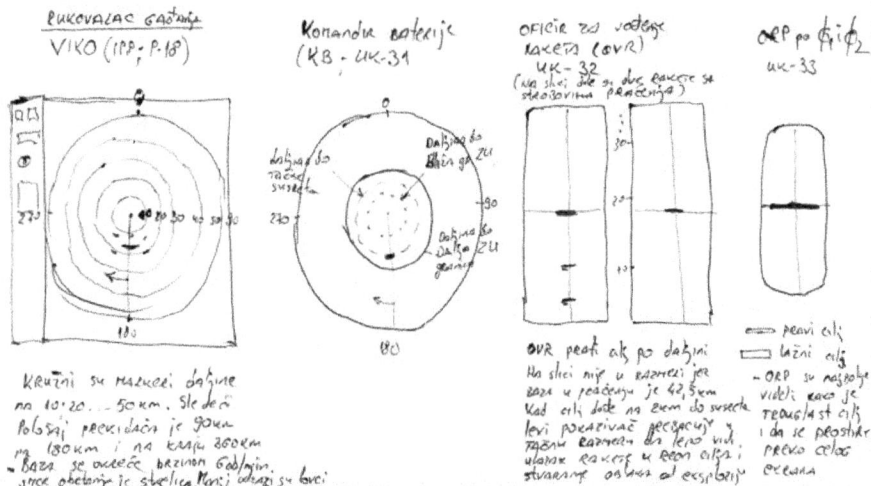

A handmade sketch of the operators' screens: from left to right - VIKO (P-18 surveillance and radar tracking screen); battery commander UK-31 screen; missile guidance UK-32 2-screens and manual tracking operators F1 and F2 UK-33 screens.

Reservist Mikica, from the Noskovs' unit was at home and he called me. He told me they were hit. He went to our unit to bring us their radar emission imitator. It is much better than ours. Their equipment no longer exists. Fortunately, an anti-radiation missile broke the cables, so they left the missile guidance station. After that, an illumination bomb exploded, which illuminated the whole fire position and then they were bombed systematically, equipment by equipment. The shift ran away into the ditch 100 m away from the combat position and during that run they had to hit the ground at least ten times. It looks like thet they were pinpointed, maybe during the aerial surveillance or somebody tipped them off.

It annoyed me to come home and just sleep. This is the second time since the beginning of the war that I spent time off in my apartment. I wake up at 06:00. We drank a coffee and than I'm off go again into uncertainty, into a war which I did not cause. Why the war at all? What is the failure of the policy and which one?

Mine is not for sure.

Sunday May 23

Upon arriving at the unit, Dani told me that three combat shifts had been

286

formed[388]. "He adopted my suggestion," I thought.

At the office in Ašanja, I found Viktor, the Russian, Lieutenant Colonel Zagrajski and Colonel Vito Andjelković.

Dotlić was on shift and I had to replace him shortly. He will go home later today[389].

I thought to myself, "Each shift will be only six hours. If so, then if I were in the shift from 6:00 to 12:00 and from 18:00 to 24:00, Dani would fill in the other two timeslots, including that from midnight until morning[390]."

"Since just the two of us could command the shift, it's best that we go for 8 hours each,"Dani said to me[391].

"And you would avoid the post-midnight shift again," I thought to myself, "I will beon from 08:00 to 16:00, and he will be on from 16:00 to 24:00. I will re-enter from 00:00 to 08:00."

After ariving in the missile guidance station van, I realised that the radar emission imitator, which was obtained from Noskov's unit, had not been put in combat operation yet. Immediately I phoned Dani and asked why. He replied that he will resolve this issue. "So, here we are again," I thought to myself, "I do all the work, for which he gets all the credit." When he goes to superior command, he can say whatever he wants about anyone of us, and we wouldn't have a clue about it at all. By not knowing what was said about you, you cannot defend yourself. This is wrong as it opens the room for manipulation[392]. A procedure should be put in place for subordinate officers to evaluate performance of their superiors. Among other things, the performance evaluation should include the professional expertise, attitude towards subordinates, respect for legal norms and a sense of working with people. Whoever did not receive passing grades, should not be on command duty. It was not right that someone, because he was a commander, be

388   The 3rd combat crew was formed from the officers that came from other missile battalions that had been hit and taken out of service. This enabled combat work to be shared among three combat crews.

The three combat crew commanders (Dani, Blagojević and the Author) and their respective crews rotated after 6 hours in four daily shifts: 0-6, 6-12, 12-18, 18-24 hours. Consequently, over a 24 hour period one combat shift (comprised of the commander and his crew) would spend a total of 12 hours on the equipment (that was located on the combat position), the other two would spend six hours each.

389   If any of the three combat crew commanders went home on a 24-hour leave, then the unit was left with two commanders and three combat crews (as that role required prior completion of the role-specific training).

390   The post-midnight shift was the most critical for us because we we if did not sleep during the day, then one could not sleep at night too. Our exhaustion created an additional combat risk of making an error during combat, because one's body was naturally shutting down due to the internal process that regulate the sleep-wake cycle known as the circadian rhythm.

391   Dani cunningly changed the duration of the shift rotations so that he would not be on duty in the post-midnight shift. It was obvious to all.

392   The conscious and deliberate manipulation was of concern.

allowed to do everything that he would not allow any of his subordinates to do[393]? By doing so, one would have been effectively exploiting others, whereas all the accolades would have been attributed personally to him. That was sad. I recalled the story of the officers who served under Blagojević, an alcoholic, as their commander. The officers in the unit were effectively ranked according to how many crates of beer they had drunk during the period of seven consecutive days on combat duty. How appreciated were other officers who weren't in that circle[394]?

We were supposed to relocate today, but the Brigade Operations Center did not allow it. We stayed where we were. Kilibarda was my deputy. Ukić was the missile guidance officer. We talked and exchanged experiences. They familiarized me with the practice in their units and how they were hit.

At 12:00 hours, the new shift, comprised of the officers who were helping us, came to the combat position.

Blagojević called me to tell that we should take over from Warrant Officer Corporal Brmbota and Lieutenant Sekulić from the Noskov's unit by 17:00 tomorrow. I called Dani, and then he unsuccessfully tried to get to the Operations Center.

My flack jacket is heavy. I was soaked to the bone. The pressure from my elbows was hurting my knees. I couldn't sit normally anymore. I sat like a mummy, and I was drenched in sweat that just flowed. It was Kilibarda's son's birthday today, and he was here. His wife was making a "F-117A" birthday cake for the child. "I didn't know that such a cake existed. Invisible? Definitely not," I thought to myself[395]. She complained that she couldn't finish it because there was no electricity. What made him come to this fucking van voluntarily, after so many days of war? He left voluntarily three years ago. He could no longer stand the military organization. Now he was here with us again. What would my "little one" say if I wanted to do the

393   The commanders should lead by example and not by "do as I say, not as I do".
394   Were they valued "zero" and marked accordingly?
395   The Author imagined an F-117 shaped kid's birthday cake on a tray, and his mind subconsciously floated above it for a moment, trying to cling onto the past: the video-clip of the F-117 on the radar screen was unwinding in front of his eyes like a bolt of lightning that compressed 23 seconds of the action into a flash (one bright dash nailed to the crosshair, another bright dash approaching it from below, then a small blurred cloud real-time image of the explosion as the two dashes merged on his radar screen, that vanished as both objects disintegrated into pieces and quickly fell out of the narrow beam of radiation of the target acquisition radar).
Then the Author's mind tore away from the image of the cake on a plate, after the dominant left side of his brain identified a logical inconsistency in the concept of the invisible F-117 shaped cake on a tray (F-117 planes became a synonym for the invisible due to good marketing). If the F-117 were really invisible, then the tray would appear empty to the kid, who will then cry because he didn't get his birthday cake. Otherwise the F-117 was not invisible.
The logical consistency was restored after the Author said to himself, "The F-117 is as invisible, as Titanic was unsinkable".

same? There would be fierce quarrels.

The life of an air-defense missile operator is patience.

I called the camp. Dani was not there (déjà vu). He had some "important" work to do again.

Sloki shaved. He came to us with a beard, which, I was sure, had not been shaved since the beginning of the war. Seem to me that I totally failed in choosing my profession…

Mika told Dani again that he would not be on duty with him in the cabin. "It's not my job," he told him.

Time had been passing so slowly, as if it was crawling. I stretched many times and had a sandwich, which Danka had prepared for me. Kiki and I drank a litre of milk. I liked it.

Mika was delighted with the Kub air defense system. It was easy to disguise it, set up and shoot. It was an extremely mobile system, it took just 5-6 minutes to transition from combat to marching configuration and vice versa. The Russians stopped using the Neva (SA-3) air defence system as it was obsolete for them. We use it as our basic weapon – the backbone of our air defence. Tonight, the equipment for Djević was supposed to be repaired and ready.

Again, three missile battalions were defending Belgrade tonight. A drop of water in the ocean. This was madness, caused by the mistake by the Army leadership and political establishment.

It was raining all morning. The clouds seemed to be clearing up in the afternoon. Everyone in the guidance station was reading newspapers and magazines. I was writing my personal diary, as I had been doing each time after combat work or during a break. Kilibarda was in a thoughtful mood. He stared through the open door, with his back turned towards me. He was napping occasionally.

As of this morning, we were at Readiness No. 1. Djokić's battalion was not combat ready. We covered them.

Raindrops were dripping from the logs. The weather was terrible. Who made the six of us spend hours upon hours together? We had been sharing a similar destiny even everyone had their own. I was tired and my eyes were closing. It was uncomfortable and I couldn't fall sleep. I had been stretching my legs frequently. I was thirsty. We remained in the Readiness No. 1 until 16:00, until I left the station. Dani came with his shift on time…

Monday, May 24

My shift was from 00:00 to 08:00. There was a weak overflight tonight, relative to the previous nights. Nothing came close to us. In fact, we had no longer been closing any direction. This direction of the approach to Belgrade is lightly defended. All that was coming to us were, in fact, SEAD groups and nothing else. Professionals. No doubt. Typically, 10 to 12 airplanes were assigned to attack our battalion. This put us in a very crappy situation. They could attack us from any direction they wished. I would like to know what our tacticians at the Operations Centre had come up with now. Easy sacrifice of people in the field.[396] How else could you interpret it?

Dotlić replaced me in the morning. His shift was from 08:00 to noon. Dani will be from 12:00 to 18:00, then my shift again from 18:00 to midnight, and Dotlić again from 00:00 to 06:00. Dani was avoiding the after midnight shift again. Deja poop!

I returned to the camp and we discussed how Noskov's equipment was completely obliterated. Zagrajski left Dani a schematic drawing of the attack. According to his sketch, there were 7 airplanes that they saw on the radar screen, "And how many were out that they did not see?" I said to myself. All equipment was destroyed. Everything that pilots saw was destroyed. Fortunately, no one was hurt. This was really good luck.

Laser guided bomb craters after attack on the missile guidance station.

The missile guidance station was buried in a crater made by more than one bomb. The station looked swollen from the detonations and blast wave overpressure. The people were unable to count how many bombs had fallen.

Dani, with the battery commanders, went scouting, and I went to sleep. I had been in Readiness No. 1 for two straight shifts, 8 hours each, 16 hours in total. I was tired and exhausted and woke up around 11:40. Boško Dotlić arrived at 12:10. We sat and talked about what would be here after the war. It would the same as it was in Bosnia and Herzegovina after the war ended. No one would give a shit about the war veterans. It was true. I guess we would have a few bucks, and what would become of all those countless people whose factories had been destroyed? What would they do for living? Where would young people find a job?

---

396   Similar to the famous address of the main antagonist of the 2001 animated feature film Shrek, Lord Maximus Farquaad, to his knights: "*Some of you May Die, but it's a Sacrifice I am Willing to Make.*"

I called Danka to calm her down. She knew that I was in the night shift. The mother of her wedding godfather had just passed away. She was about to leave to express condolences to his family. After 16 years of marriage, her wedding godmother still didn't know their address in Čortanovci. She didn't give a shit about him or his parents. And I went through all of that before, and all of that by myself. It seems very clear now looking from a different angle, but I could not see anything while I was in that situation.

Dani was in shift from 12:00 to 18:00. They radiated twice with the radar for five seconds each time. They searched for a target and did not find it. Tiosavljević said they had searched too high. Who knows how many times I saw them flying lower during the day. Clouds were very low today. They called Ljubenković because they thought the surveillance radar was broken. It wasn't, there was a lot of interference and noise from jamming that saturated the receiver.

We must be careful tonight. When I entered into the guidance station, they had already been in Readiness No.1. Sekulić and Brmbota didn't come to us as planned. The radar emission imitator had not been put in service yet. Boris Stoimenov and Senad Muminović located the fault. A small 1.4 A fuse blew up. The same fuse was used in the oscilloscope. If they couldn't find it in the spare parts cabin, why they didn't take it from one of the oscilloscopes?

Samardzić reported that Bajić would come at 05:00 to try again to install the thermal imaging system. They failed last time. We'll see tomorrow if it will work this time.

Muminović listened to the news at 19:00. We got our cigarettes rations. Three packs of Filter 57 brand each.

Dejan Tiosavljević thought that it would be good if the electronic blocks and radar screens for the manual tracking operators, missile guidance officer and battery commander could be relocated at least 100 m away from the station. It would be great if this can be done, as the crew could be in a trench or shelter, well protected and far away from the equipment at the combat position. How much more relaxed it would be to go to, and safer to work in shifts. Without that, we had always been playing at the sharp edge. It was interesting to realize how the exposure to an imminent danger brings new ideas for protection against it.

I need to talk to Bajić. We had an issue tonight after we had wired the communication lines. They asked us to work with the radio. Crazy!!! The enemy would have immediately found out the location of the transmitter and bomb it.[397,398]

One generator must be in the post office, as the main power often went off. Otherwise, we would not have a communication line with the Brigade field command centre as we did not have sufficient PTK cable length to run

___

397   As they did it during the 1990 Gulf war and destroyed the Iraq's air-defense batteries. In addition, the enemy could have jammed the radio-communication frequencies.

398   For these reasons, the Author's unit used the wired telephone communication lines with field handsets only.

it directly to the centre. In addition to being unsafe, the radio link would not be totally reliable. The radio-amateur stations had been jammed on a regular basis. There was a guy, nicknamed Cuckoo, who was cuckooing trying to jam our radio-amateurs. The story was that he was a Croat who had lost his legs in the war. He had a very strong radio station. It amazed me that our radio amateurs had not silenced him so far. For many, who had weaker radios, the signals did not pass, and they could not be heard.

We had rice with sauce for dinner. The shift crew will have the same dinner after midnight. I just had lunch today. Dani was not in the camp again. He only comes when it's time for his shift. No one knew where he was or what he had been doing.

The phone at the camp was busy all the time. We had been trying to get to the camp for 50 minutes.[399] If something was urgent, we wouldn't have been able to let them know on time. This must not happen again.

I reported to the Operations Center our next position with the coded signal "Bojana" and requested help with the radar emission imitator from Noskov. Sekulić and Brmbota did not come, as agreed. We did not receive the SA-18 Igla MANPAD system, which Stanković had promised.

I let the fuel supply truck on the combat position at 20:10, when the sun had started to set, so as not to unmask us. We had been in Readiness No. 1 until 22:20, when they ordered us to Readiness No. 2. I didn't understand the tactics. The raid had just begun, and they switched us into "number two"?!

Dotlić came to his shift at midnight. I returned to the camp and went to bed right away.

Tuesday, May 25

I woke up at 04:30. Dotlić called me and said that the bomb had fell near the center of the signals platoon field position and that someone should go to check if there are any injured.

Bajić arrived with the team to installa thermal imaging camera on our target acquisition radar. I had to go to the combat position. All parts of the unit were informed to commence transition of the equipment.

About twenty meters from the command post of the signals platoon, I came across a scary sight in the woods. The bomb fell and made a crater 5-6 meters deep, maybe more, and about 15-20 meters in diameter. We all crossed ourselves when we saw how big the crater was. It was most likely a GBU-15 bomb[400]. The weight of the bomb was somewhere around 1,100 kg, and that of the warhead, as far as I remember, was 910 kg; filled with nearly

---

399   The telephone line in the camp was busy all the time as the soldiers and reservists, when not on duty, used that line to call their families at home. There were no mobile phones at that time.

400   GBU-15 - The Guided Bomb Unit or GBU-15 is an unpowered controlled glide weapon used to destroy high value enemy targets.

half a tonne[401] of explosive. The blast wave butchered the forest: trees were uprooted all around. The bomb fell about 600-800 meters away from the key equipment at the combat position. They tried a classic way to destroy our unit – brute force. The visibility was poor. Two or three groups of planes flew at medium altitudes and marked our unit; after that 2 to 3 of these planes descended low and went after it. The shrapnel fragments weighed several kilograms. When we reached the crater, Boško took a shovel and buried a piece of the shrapnel in the ground and covered it with soil. He said, "That's how it should be done – you should always bury enemies where they died[402]."

Several trusses of the neraby farm irrigation system were torn apart. The field communication control& command vehicle, and TAM 110 off-road ambulance truck were parked alongside in the forrest next to the road. The bomb fell less than twenty meters away in the forest. No one was hurt[403]. This was pure luck.

Destructive power of the laser guided bomb. The sheer size of the crater is stunning.

I could not not to think what would have happened if the bomb fell on the combat position? If it exploded near the equipment, it would have, most likely, blown away the logs or the palisade would bury the station together with the people inside it. In that case, we should have pickaxe or fire axes in the cabin, so we could break the floor and get out.

401   465kg of high explosive Tritonal.

402   This comment prompted the Author's thoughts, "Boško must have learnt about that custom from his family's storytelling about past wars. It must be how his father, grandfathers, uncles and great-uncles had been burying invaders and occupying armies. In fact, the burial requires effort and it is an act of respect for the dead, a godly deed and military honor," and a philosophical conclusion, "… the unwritten code of ethics, passed through generations that sustainably reconciled spiritual and material worlds."

403   The thick forest trees provided a miraculous shield; not only was no one hurt, but also none of the vehicles were damaged.

While moving the equipment, Sergeant Bugarin landed the Kraz truck that was towing a launch ramp into a roadside ditch. We tried to get him out, but it was in vane. It was just wasting of time. Somehow, we had to make a dirt road around the Kraz, for the trucks with the logs to pass around, and then to pull out the ramp. The ramp is very heavy and we struggled as we pulled out the Kraz so the big muscle is necessary maybe a big tractor, IMT 520[404], to tow out the Kraz, in a manner that the launch ramp did not slip further into a one and a half meter deep ditch, and roll over.

Dani told me that it was rumored that the remains of a large plane with eight charred bodies had been found between Batajnica, Ugrinovci, Dobanovci and Vojka. If that was true, then it was no wonder that our air defense units had been chased so ferociously. It was me and my crew who fired from Bečmen and hit a B-52 strategic bomber. That was yet another success for the history books. I would be very happy if that was comfirmed 100 percent by finding the wreck. For now, it is only "I heard..." In war many stories popup.

In order to improve operation of the unit, I had requested a spare Kraz, Ural and TAM 110 trucks, and two TAM 150 trucks. The response from the Operations Center was that they will send us a Kraz and mobile crane for the supply and installation of missiles on the ramps. We also desparately needed the other three requested trucks.

I drew to Miškov's attention the required distance between the corner reflectors and target acquisition radar. They were placed too close at the firing position in Ašanja.

Bajić, Koman and Stančić came to retrofit a thermal imaging camera to the target acquisition radar. They will not start work until we relocate to the new firing position. Stojanović went ahead to wire the communication set-up.

At 20:00 we were granted permission to commence the march. At 21:00, the last vehicle from the missile guidance battery left. The missile battery went next. At 23:00 they ordered us to go to Readiness No. 1. They have lost track of time. As if they didn't know where we are, where we needed to go and what was needed to do to be in Readiness No. 1. That deadline was totally unrealistic. Someone's dumb mistake (one of many...).

Today, while Dani, Dotlić and me were talking about the tactics of using the two new radar emission imitators, I suggested to locate a more powerful imitator[405] 4-5 km away from us, and that the weaker one follow it. We already had another weaker imitator at our disposal. So we would literally imitate two combat units. The alternative suggested tactic was to be covered by a powerful imitator during our radiation. They both agreed that the idea is good and that we should apply the first alternative.

We needed to get 2-3 meters of 3x2.5mm^2 cable, three large clamps and

---

404   IMT -Industry of Machinery and was a Serbian company that produced tractors and agricultural machinery.
405   New imitator had a much more powerful electromagnetic radiation power output than the other.

one junction box[406]. I took it upon myself, since I already planned to go to Šimanovci with Ljubenković for cabling. I took him to see which of the existing cabling could be used from the Ural trucks. The radar cables were placed on the Ural truck that was parked across from Armuš's hardware store. The vehicle was not much damaged and it could be repaired.

Mika screwed up tonight. He did not drive the vehicle with the imitator on time. People from the unit for setting up the combat position waited for 2-3 hours until night fell. What was even worse, they didn't take their part in transitioning the missile guidance battery and missile battery equipment. It was a triple error, and yet no one could be reached by phone, as both communication lines were non-stop busy. In the afternoon, two more bombs exploded in the forest in Ašanja, but much further from us.

In the period from 17:00 to 18:30, Colonel Lazović, the Brigade Commander, and Šumarac visited us. We saw Lazović for the first time after his traffic accidentat at the beginning of the war, when Sremčica was bombed. He was still on crutches. He felt sorry that he had let down Stanković, and that Stanković bore all the burden of the Brigade's work by himself. He said he was very sorry for the people. We lost 9 men and 9 battalions are more or less damaged. Tonight, while we were transitioning the assets, Djević was hit for the third time. This time with cluster bombs. The equipment was rendered useless. Bajić said that they could make only one operational battalion from those nine damaged.

Lazović said that the Brigade had shot down 10 to 11 planes so far, with an average consumption of three missiles per plane. Tonight he will be at the command post of the Brigade. He returned to the war on crutches, with more than half of the Brigade knocked out and unable to fight. The batallion from Kraljevo launched yesterday. He said that we desparately needed to shoot down a plane now[407], and that the war, according to his estimate, will end in two or three weeks. The only question was which side would prevail.

Before the war, we had eight batallions and three reserve ones. Now, only Djokić and I were still functional and in combat. Other units no longer existed as a combat entities.

Colonel Tomić, a member of the VOJIN unit[408] from the Corps, came to visit us. His unit for the aviation intelligence, reporting, reconnaissance and guidance did not exist any more. For two months, we had been fighting with a single trained air defense radar officer and hastily trained soldiers! There was a number of trained air defense radar operators with no radars!? Why did our brigade practically lose nine combat units, wheres the Kraljevo regiment comprised of four missile battalions, still has three in combat? Well

---

406   They wanted to make an extension lead with the power board to supply power to the weaker new IRR from the diesel generator for the powerful new imitator (in order to avoid the need to run a dedicated diesel generator for the weaker imitator.

407   In order to reinforce our bargaining position for peace talks.

408   VOJIN unit - is Aviation intelligence, reporting, reconnaissance and guidance unit (Serbian: Vazduhoplovno obaveštavanje, javljanje, izviđanje i navođenje; abbr. VOJIN).

done to Veselin Pavlović, the commander of the 450th Air Defense Missile Regiment.

Tonight, when I was coming, one vehicle broke down in the village. Dani drove the Kraz truck with the generator trailer out the village and ordered Aca to stop all the oncoming vehicles. At one point there was a long column of our vehicles and assets lined up one behind the other. That created an ideal opportunity for the enemy to swoop down on the column and destroy everything in a swift attack. I urgently ordered the vehicles to move instantly and make a distance of 100 to 200 meters between them. The drivers understood the purpose of the order and moved without a word.

Dotlić was on duty until midnight, Dani will be on from the midnight to 06:00, and I from 06:00 to 12:00. Dotlić was in the after-midnight shift the night before. Dani loudly said that he will be in the after-midnight shift tonight. He was aware that the equipment at this combat position will certainly not be ready by the morning, nor that the installation of the thermal imaging camera could be completed before his after-midnight shift ended.

While I was walking with Colonel Tomić towards the combat position last night, a vehicle that was towing a launch ramp, slipped off the road into the mud. Again, Bugarin and Horšić were responsible. Kraz couldn't get the ramp out. When we arrived, I sent another Kraz truck from the missile battery to get them out of the ditch and to start manning the new combat position. They were still setting up the logs[409], while the target acquisition radar was standing unattended[410]. Time worked in Dani's favour.

Dotlić and Dani found accommodation in Mihaljevci. The commanding officers will go to Cveja Roglić's place. Dotlić said it was the most beautiful house in Mihaljevci. I agreed with him about that. I had known Cveja and his family for a long time. Cveja's father paid him to go to Belgrade every day, just so that the neighbours could see how he went and studied. He was a controversial businessman after the collapse of the state. Sergeant Dražen Petrović Pižon came to the unit to help us on the surveillance radar.

Danka called me urgently from work. She told me that Boško Andjelković called about some computer monitors. He had found second hand ones for our unit, 23-inch and 24-inch size, and a computer in good condition. He got them from the Director of the State Textbook Publishing Corporation. Barvalac called regarding the railway sleepers to protect the roof of the missile guidance station van. Someone should contact Djorđe Babić, Head of the Road Maintenance Section, by 07:30 this morning. I finally tracked down TAM 150 and TAM 110 trucks. The former was full of tents, and the brakes didn't work on the latter. The logistics support and their management... eh... We desparately needed the vehicle, and they hadn't unload it. "They safeguarded the tents," I said sarcastically to myself[411].

---

409   The logs were placed around the missile guidance station and the power supply vans.

410   As officers and soldiers from the Missile Guidance Battery were still busy doing other things, transition of the target acquisition radar into the combat configuration had not commenced yet.

411   Officers from the Logistics Support Platoon knew that we needed the vehi-

I was at the combat position until about 13:00 and then I went to rest, because I was on shift in the morning.

Wednesday, May 26

My son's birthday is today, and I'm sitting in this shithole, filthy and wet. It's scary how humid it is today.

Last night, Koman, Bajić and Stančić remained in our Lada waiting for completion of transition of the equipment on the combat position into the combat configuration. Their assignment was to set up a thermal imaging camera on the fire control radar and train us on how to work with that new equipment. I found them there in the morning. They had slept in the car.

Last night, upon arriving at Mihaljevci at around 01:10, the guard dog didn't allow us to enter the Cveja's house yard. We turned around and thought about what to do. I remembered the local Crisis Headquarter so we went there. Under the candle lights, two local villagers played chess, and the attendant on duty had no idea where the unit staff would be located while we were at this combat position. The one who had been on the duty until midnight did not convey anything to them. At that instant in time my misery and disappointment boiled over. I reached the breaking point. Dani told them we should arrive here between seven and eight in the evening. What the fuck went wrong with the timing of our arrival?! I swore aloud and poured out all my anger and disappointment of this carelessness that I could spit out. I had stank with the all the accumulated sweat and dirt on my wrinkled uniform and these two jerks had been concentrating on chess! I couldn't concentrate on newspapers and TV, not even radio.

I calmed down relatively quickly and requested from the locals to bring homeowners here, while reassuring myself that they should be able to stay awake one night and that my request was not excessive. They should come here and wait to provide accommodation for the troops as they arrive, unit after unit. Our host Cveja came as well. We went to his house.

I had a second thought and suddenly I felt sorry for blaming these people. It was not their fault. The government had done what it had done and were now looking for victims to blame for their own inaction and stupidity. I would try my best to not fall victim to this stupid policy. I had faith that the spirits of my late parents were guarding me and that God himself was guarding me too.

I came to the shift this morning. The equipment had not yet been properly positioned and connected. Dani told me that he had planned to go home. Just like that. Out of nowhere! In a moment, he "vanished" from the position. He also forgot to meet with the engineers in Boljevci and to show them where to arrange our next position. They called me from the Operations Centre and told me that the engineers had been waiting for us. I replied that only Dani

---

cle, and instead of telling us that they could off-load the tents and give us the vehicle, they chose to say nothing.

knew the place and that it would be pure nonsense that I send a man who did not know where the new position is.

How to fix this mess? I gave Samardžić and Marjanović Dani's phone number. No one will answer that phone call anyway because Dani turned off his pager and mobile phone. He was simply not interested in what was going on and what the situation is in our unit. Dotlić and I both agreed on that. Dotlić was late to replace my shift by about an hour and ten minutes. That's how much later I'll come to replace him.

Instead of going for a rest in Mihaljevci, I went to Nada and Milan. I told them how disappointed I am in the army organization. I was thinking of Danka. And I was thinking of her very often… Milan admitted he made a lot of mistakes about her when she was a kid. The injustice hurts me. I slept for an hour and a half or maybe two and woke up around 16:10 and stay laying the bed a little bit more. Milan and one handyman mounted a new door onto the meat smoker building. They did it well. A neighbor, Dule Oljača, arrived. He discussed warfare. I was not interested in his conclusions. He was a retired military musician. Again, Danka was right. Something needed to be radically changed but it is hard to teach an old dog with new tricks...

I was not even aware of how much I am gambling with my own life. Out of many teams that had installed the equipment at the combat position, only six of us stayed here. Everyone else had left and went to different shelters. I trusted in fate.

This morning, Cvetić and I came together to the shift. At about 19:00, Koman came to install the transformer on the thermal imaging camera because the picture was unstable. He went with me to the position and finished the job in 30 minutes.

People from the surveillance radar went into a nearby ditch after the radar emission started. The crew of the power supply and distribution van did the same after the missiles and ramps were powered on. Only six officers remained in the missile guidance station cabin as the enlisted crewmember, a manual plotter operator, had been ordered not to go to the shifts. There were no more of The Magnificent Seven in the missile guidance station cabin.

The surveillance radar had never been located so close to the launch ramp on any previous combat position, as it was at this one. In addition, both were located too close to the cabin. Uncomfortably close. And yet today, Senad Muminović boasted of how well he had organised the missile guidance battery and how everything went flawlessly… Ughhh…

Tomović told me tonight that Djević battalion had been hit at 00:05, just at the time when both shifts were at the combat position. Only a few guys suffered minor injuries from shrapnel. No one died, which was the most important. It a good luck, even no casualties. This was the third time they had been hit so far.

I was in shift until midnight. Nothing interesting… Dotlić came to replace me. Dani was at home. He should be here in the morning, but I knew that he would come in the afternoon. I walked by the communication and signal centre, and then to the Nada and Milan's house to sleep there. I didn't want to go to Mihaljevci. It was too far away.

Thursday, May 27

This morning I was on shift from 06:00 to 12:00. Ljubenković, the surveillance radar operator, went home to visit the family. He brought interesting news. His neighbor worked in a bakery, whose owner worked in the State Security Service. That night, when we fired from Bečmen, around 03:00 hours, he came to the bakery and brought a liter of whiskey to share with his workers. "Tonight," he said, "a B-2 strategic bomber, an 'invisible' stealth plane, called 'Spirit' was shot down.[412,413]" The radio amateurs reported it too. The Croatian State Radio and TV Corporation reported it only once, and never again.

The telephones were not working and I was unable to call my son to wish him a happy birthday.

Today, Sekulić and Brmbota came to our unit to help. The Brigade Command was sending people to reinforce us.

At 12:00, Dotlić replaced me. I went to Nada and Milan to have a nap. At around 17:30, I went to Mihaljevci to check if Dotlić was informed that Dani had arrived. He was. Dani was on duty from 18:00 hours to midnight.

Armuš called me to meet him in Šimanovci and I went. Zoran Armuš took me home. Stana, his wife, roasted a lamb. It was delicious. Unfortunately, I ate only one piece. I had lost my appetite.

I left them and went to Nada and Milan. I had to prepare for the shift tonight from 00:00 hours.

Friday, May 28

Nada washed my uniform yesterday afternoon. She told me that the water was black. No wonder why, with so much accumulated dirt and sweat. It was a wonderful feeling to be clean again.

---

412   U.S. Air Force officially reported the B-2's combat debut was in 1999 during the first eight weeks of the war in Yugoslavia, see "B-2 Spirit Fact Sheet" (*https://www.af.mil/About-Us/Fact-Sheets/Display/Article/104482/b-2-spirit/*). (Retrieved 27 July 2020).

413   The timing and duration of this combat engagement can be interpreted as confirmation that the B-2 stealth plane was indeed shot down as reported in this diary; which then prompted U.S. Air Force to immediately cease all B-2 combat operations in order to avoid the risk of further losses, embarrassment, capture of the wreck and consequential transfer of the stealth technology to adversaries if it fell in FR Yugoslavian territory; as had already happened earlier with the F-117 stealth plane and was subsequently widely reported by the media worldwide.

I came at 00:00 to my shift to replace Dani. However, Colonel Lazović had ordered him to be in the field all night. I asked him why he hadn't told me not to come. I could have slept. He replied that he had not been able to call me. Crap again! He could have called the signals centre and they would have called Mika, who would come to tell me that. I walked in vain thorough the dark for 20 minutes to the combat position and just as much back; solely because he had not been courteous or willing to let me know that.

It was my turn to go home today. Dani didn't really like that. He asked me when the last time was that I went home. "After you," I replied, "You were home yesterday, and today I am going." He asked," If you leave, who will be on duty?" "We were on duty when you were at home, so maybe you could be on duty as well." He was not happy with my answer.

I returned to Nada and Milan around 01:15. It didn't make sense for me to go to Belgrade at that time. There was no electricity there and I couldn't get into the building without yelling from the outside and calling Danka to come downstairs and open the door. If I did that, then I would wake up the whole neighbourhood. So, I just went to sleep. I woke up around 09:00. Milan and Nada were preparing a parcel of what to bring to Belgrade.

Only Nataša was at home. Danka worked today. I phoned her and then went to the "Nicholas" to pick her up.

It was good to be at home again. I had a bath and we had lunch. There was no electricity. In the evening we discussed the war with her neighbor Lucia. Danka and Lucia had become war strategists. That is funny They analysed where and what was bombed and drew conclusions. We discussed the failed politics that had led to the war, government and people; the highly educated people that had left the country in pursuit of a better life abroad after their own country couldn't provide the basic means for existence; the Army and the rotten political system- all the negative things in the society were also reflected on the military -the autocracy and despotism. Everything was the same.

Milošević, Milutinović, Ojdanić and Stoiljković[414] were declared war criminals and the supporting documentation was sent to the Hague tribunal. Had the message been sent to the world that the sovereign country should not defend itself? That those who defend their countries would be declared war criminals??? This would abolish the right of peoples to defend their sovereignty.

The war veterans would end up like their counterparts from the war in Bosnia and Hercegovina that beg for a few coins or wash windscreens at road intersections, with no jobs or any work available for them.

This was one big incident and injustice. To allow to be cornered in a situation of war with the 19 most developed countries in the world without a single ally. Insanity!!! If they had to come, then they would have better came

---

414   Slobodan Milošević, Milan Milutinović, Dragoljub Ojdanić and Vlajko Stojiljković–respectively were the President of Federal Republic (FR) Yugoslavia, the President of Serbia, the Chief of the General Staff of the Armed Forces of FR Yugoslavia and the Minister of Internal Affairs of FR Yugoslavia.

as friends rather than enemies. We stood no chance. Russia and China had been backing us only by words and very minor help.

The women were absolutely right.

Are they going be chasing us and arresting after the war, like in Bosnia and Hercegovina? Would they or would they not hunt us in villages and towns? Will they get after the war what they didn't during the war? To march in with the troops? That would be the true face of the New World Order.

During the day, Danka and I dropped in to Vrdnik. The Fruška Gora Mountain was beautiful. My eyes clouded when I saw the high grass in the yard and the deserted place half taken over by the vegetation. My abandoned old family house.

We ate strawberries. There were plenty of them around. Clover sprouted in the other half of the garden, which Djole had sowed. In the basement, we felt the scent of the stall air because everything had been closed all the time. I felt very sad. We took candles from the house and went to the cemetery. My parents' grave was overgrown with the grass. We lit the candles. They burnt quietly, as if the father and mother were glad that we came. This is the saying when the candles burn evenly. Tomorrow is the Memorial Saturday[415] for remembrance of all dead. In my thoughts I spoke to my parents to keep me safe and to stay alive. As if they could do that. Tears came out my eyes. I wished I were here alone and could simply cry it off. Danka comforted me. She tidied up the graves. I cleared the gravestones. For my father, as usual, I lit a cigarette and laid it on the grave. God, how much I felt the need to visit their graves and thank them for keeping me safe. I wished they knew how much I had been taking care of the house.

Danka had not left Belgrade since 13 April. She enjoyed this outing. On our way back we stopped by her parents. We brought Nada what she had missed. The cactus that I had brought from Vrdnik blossomed and the yard was flawlessly tidy, in sharp contrast to my yard in Vrdnik. At around 20:00 we left for Belgrade. We talked about everything. I wished for this senseless folly to stop ASAP.

Saturday, May 29

I woke up around 09:00. We had breakfast. I didn't want to rush from home. My plane was to be in battalion around 14:00. At 15:00, I went to the missile guidance station van, and dropped by the signals Platoon's Communication Centre on my way. Dotlić was on shift. He said that he would stay until 18:00, and that Dani had been ordered to be on shift from 18:00 to 06:00 the next day. "So, he should be on duty for 12 hours, good," I thought to myself, "let him make up for the time we were on duty."

I went to Cveja in Mihaljevci. Dani was there. I told him what Dotlić

---

415   The Memorial Saturday – (Serbian: Zadušnice; " Memorial of Souls") is a day set aside for the commemoration of the dead. Saturday is a traditional day of prayer for the dead, because Christ laid dead in the Tomb on Saturday.

had just told me. When he heard, he thought that was not fair and square. He went to the upper floor of the house to call the Brigade Command Post, to hear for himself. He didn't like it and his face turned pale. Everything he had been avoiding was now coming to him. I had a clear conscience and had nothing to do with it.

Dani asked me to replace him from 18:00 to 21:00, because 12 hours would be too much for him. I agreed thinking, "I'll make small concessions for you, and I'll fuck you up with bigger things. Like you screwed me over."

Around 19:00, Lazović called me to urgently send him a 250 m long piece of cable for the immitator, to the Brigade Command Post. I unsucessfully tried to tell someone to do that. All the phones were dead since the power went out. I couldn't send anyone on foot from the combat position and didn't have a vehicle. Dani was supposed to come around 21:00 hours, and I will sort it out then. Vukica, Cveja's wife, was preparing dinner for us from the command tonight. Dough with potatoes. I loved that. I will tell Stoimenov to send the cable when I go to the dinner. So I did it.

However, around 23:00 Mika came to Cveja's place to tell me that Dani had called me and requested to call him urgently. We went to the post office in the centre of Karlovčić. I called Dani who told me that Lazović had ordered me to write a statement why he had not received the requested cable, after four hours had elapsed since he had requested it. This request pissed me off. When we request something, it takes days. My head was bursting with torment, injustice and resentment. I returned with Mika in a bad mood. It was already past midnight. Who should I take a piece of paper from and write the fucking statement? Aca, Dani's driver, was drunk and didn't know where the paper was. I wondered how intoxicated his boss was, when Aca was that drunk ?! "I'll do it in the morning," I thought, "there's no electricity anyway." I didn't feel like driving tonight because I was already exhausted and will sleep here tonight. Cveja, the host, was outside, listening to and observing the airspace.

Sunday, May 30

Sunday morning.

I woke up around 05:30.

Aca brought a piece of paper and I wrote the "famous" statement. For the first time in 19 years! I wrote it quickly. Dani told me to give my statement to Bacetić,[416] who had spent all night at the missile guidance van with him, to courier it to the Brigade commander, Colonel Lazović.

Dotlić went home yesterday after 18:00. Dani and I will cover all shifts while he is away.

---

416   Lieutenant Colonel Bacetić – was assigned to the Brigade Command, after his 7th Battalion has been hit and the equipment destroyed. He came to observe the combat work of our unit.

I had coffee and went to my shift. The weather was ok, so I decided to walk, and got there at around 07:00. Dani was about to leave with Bacetić. A Pinzgauer vehicle came for them. Dani handed the duty over to me.[417]

There was unbearable heat in the cabin with temperatures of 37 °C. I covered two shifts and stayed in the cabin all day long. Dani did not show up at the shift changeover time at 18:00. I looked again at my watch at about 19:00. He had not showed up yet. Déjà vu.

I had breakfast at around 11:30 and no lunch. and thought I would have dinner in time. My nerves were stirred to the core. I called Kosta and Aca and asked them where the heck Dani is. They told me that he had left the house[418] with Lieutenant Colonel Bacetić at around 18:30.

It was 20:00 when he finally arrived at the combat position. I was pissed off. He came, gayly smiling. That completely knocked me out.[419] I asked him if he had a watch? "Where are you so far? Do you have any honor? What do you have instead of cheeks, a shoe sole???" I told him that he was just a faggot. A fierce verbal duel followed.

We went in front of the power distribution trailer. The station was in operation, so people probably didn't hear anything that we spoke. We sent each other to mother's cunt, with yelling, cursing and bitching each other continuously. "You are the stereotype of a fool and man without morals! You sleep in people's houses, they feed you and you throw yourself at Cveja's wife. You fool! You know that he's awkward and if he find about that you won't live for more than two seconds. You're a dead man. He will rip your head off!" I told him.

"Vukica, Cveja's wife, told me last night that her husband was an oddball and crazy jealous." I was ashamed to listen to her. She also told me that Dani had told her that he was thinking of her when he was sleeping in her bed and caressing the pillow. He imagined that she was beside him. At one occasion in Vukica and Cveja's bedroom, he looked at their family photo album and told her that she was a very beautiful woman and that he will take one of her pictures for a memory. He cleaned the fish with her, cut it and cooked lunch, and went with her to the garden to pick up vegetables. She was pissed off and she told him so, "You have a wife, a wife to think and to care for, you have your Irena. If I tell my husband, knowing how crazy he is, he will make a big mess."

When I told this to Dotlić he was speechless and looked at me with his

---

417   The Author could not simply hand over his handwritten statement to Lieutenant Colonel Bacetić during the shift changeover for military procedural reasons. Namely, a general affairs officer from the camp in Deč should have come to take the handwritten statement, type it and then give the Author to sign it, in order to make it official.

418   The house – was a house in the village of Mihaljevci where the Battalion command was located.

419   The Author disliked that smile because he knew it was forced and provocative show of superiority because Dani had mates in the Brigade Command. The Author didn't want to get into submission and chose to put the things straight.

eyes widely open. I told the same story to Boro, who had yesterday joined our unit. Dani had been ashaming the army and disgracing his uniform wherever he had been appearing. I put it all in his face. I told him that he had been nowhere to be found in the unit. He had not been taking combat shift duties and so on… Bacetić was sitting on the voltage distribution trailer shaft and remained silent during our verbal fight. When the steam blew away, Bacetić said that we should calm down and be friends. "What friends, at my expense? Fuck that!" I smoked two packs of cigarettes that day and I had no more left. Bacetić had some. I took it from him, but not from Dani, who had offered it to me as well. "I don't need anything from you," I told him.

I left the firing position by saying to Dani "You saw me here now, and you could write down when you will see me again. In a day, two, fifteen days, three months. I don't know! I've had enough of this BS!" I could tell that he was upset. He told me, "Go home, take a rest for two days and then come back." "And then what?" I replied, "When I return, I will be nonstop on duty and sleep in the guidance station because you will disappear again!"

When I came to the camp and told Bora and Dotlić everything.

I took some food, no idea what it was, and then went to Milan and Nada for some rest.

The planes had been flying like crazy that day. During the 13.5 hours duration of my shift, we may have only been 1.5 hours in Readiness No. 2. The remaining 12 hours we spent in the active combat work: observing the airspace and waiting for someone to enter into our engagement zone, directing the radar towards the incoming target; we radiated, made so many attempts to locate the target and lock onto it. We played our hide-and-seek game with the radar emission imitator and fire control radar. They launched three HARM anti-radiation missiles towards us. Two exploded: one at position K1, the other at position K2. The next day, Kosta and I found a third, unexploded, one in K2, about 500 m away from our position. It was stabbed like a pillar in the middle of a green sea of the clasping wheat field. The body of the missile protruded about a meter and a half above the ground.

I went to bed around 22:30 but couldn't fall asleep. Colonel Lazović told me tonight that he had forgotten about my statement, so it stays with me and may never see the "official circles". "Djole, it would be good if they launch missiles tonight in standby mode." Lazarević told me. I felt something like that would happen and the shift would work tonight. It didn't matter to me at the time, because Dani was very late. He went tonight to investigate the exploded "Harms". A classic avoidance of the missile guidance station and shift duty. I fired everything right into his face. To make myself calm, I told all this to Milan and Nada. They are outraged and asked me to take care of myself and go on sick leave. "Son, you can't wage a war on your own," Nada told me.

Monday, May 31

I couldn't fall asleep for a long time. The last time I looked at my watch was around 00:50. Around 04:10 I was startled by the start of a missile; five seconds later the second missils started. Milan and I ran outside. We could not see the missiles. After a long time we heard two muffled detonations about five seconds apart, like the bursting of soap bubbles. I knew they had missed and went back to bed. We will have to move the assets early in the morning.

I woke up around 08:30. We had a coffee. Nada prepared breakfast. The equipment on the firing position were no longer visible; they had already been transitioned and extracted. No one called nor informed me. For the first time, I felt absolutely indifferent and uninterested. Bora was passing by and he dropped in for a coffee.

I went to Mihaljevci to pick up Kosta and my stuff. Yesterday, a tire on my Zastava punctured. The guys from the signals platoon were nearby and changed the tire for me. I should go to a tyre repair shop today. On the way to the new position, I stopped at Obrad's house to see him. We greeted and hugged each other. Tepavac and his people were located there. Obrad showed me a picture he had painted for me, with the Serbian Cross on it. He also explained his new wording for the motto depicted by thefour "fire striker" shapes on the cross;"Only Sremac knocks down the Nighthawk[420]." His eyes were full of tears as I was leaving, saying, "I can hardly wait for the war to end, so that everyone can come to my place."

Cveja was in Pećinci. I called Vlada, my son. I hadn't seen him since 13 April. My former father-in-law Mile said he is in Belgrade. Kosta and Cveja's eldest son went to take a photo of the "HARM" missile that fell in the wheat field. They didn't find it. Kosta was unfamiliar with the rural fields and dirt roads. There was no electricity in Pećinci.

I didn't repair the punctured car tyre and went back with unfinished business.

Mika gave me the amateur radio report for 20:05. He found an article about the downed B-2 plane in the Ilustrovana Politika magazine of 29 May 1999. Only our unit had fired that night. If it was true, then we all know who had shot it down. It was the most expensive plane in the world.

I found Bora in Deč. He told me to go to Ašanja in order to meet Lazović there. As requested, I went there. After an hour or an hour and a half, Šumarac and Lazović arrived, accompanied by Bora. We sat in the office. Colonel Lazović said he had only been in the war for nine days. He came on crutches. Bora did what he had promised. Laza told me, "Djole, let me hear what the problem is, how can I help you?" I told him everything about Dani's tricks,

---

420   Only Sremac knocks down the Nighthawk- Is the new motto *Samo Sremac Skida Sokola*, where "Sremac" is a resident of the Srem region in Serbia.

nonsense, avoiding shifts, his negative impact on the unit[421,422,423], about the computer he had taken home, the womanizing, dishonourable conduct, etc[424]. "He has not been doing anything. I can't take it anymore. I'm tired. I'm too honest and it hurts me."All three of them listened to me without a word.

Eventually Dani came. He was scared. When asked to present his side of the argument, he only repeated the bare words of the arguments from our past dialogues, without stating the context and reasons why they were said. I agreed with his recollection of what was said and that the words sounded rude and unprovoked. I acknowledged it was true that I had told him everything he mentioned, but that he had also told me off. He had simply become a careerist, who stopped thinking about our war unit, that people were not supportive of him and his conduct, and that profiteering had begun. He started calling me "Mr. Lieutenant Colonel[425]."

Lazović asked us if this could somehow be resolved. That we had been waging the war by ourselves, largely isolated from the others and all that impacted our outcomes. That we had been together for 70 days so far and that it would be best if we forget what we said in anger. "How can I explain to the Corps Command now that you two will no longer fight together?" Before that, he asked me how well I worked with Roksandić, my classmate. He probably wanted to replace Dani, and to appoint my classmate as my deputy. I only realized that later. Dani replied that I am an extremely smart, hardworking and quality man, and that he would like to continue working with me if I wanted to. The main problem was that, as he said, I no longer trusted him. He had no idea how right he was. "How can I trust you when you do everything just for yourself," I thought briefly before I answered to Laza (Lazović), "One of us will have to leave and it will be the end of someone's career. To go to another unit, where you don't know the quality of the shift and the people, would be nonsense." I replied to Laza that I

421   Impact on the unit–is the Author's shorthand diary entry for explaining Dani's conduct on 11 May 1999 (on the 3rd firing position in Karlovčić – Karlovčić 3) after the unit was hit with a HARM missile that exploded about 30 – 35 meters away from the missile guidance station van and the combat crew under the command of the Author. This explosion damaged cabling and the fins on four missiles. Dani was at home at the time of explosion.

422   When the Brigade Command telephoned Dani, he replied that he would immediately return to the unit. However, he did not return to the unit, but called the Author to tell him that he was at home and if anyone from the Brigade Command asked for him to tell them that he was around somewhere. While the Author would be supposedly looking around for him to let him know, and he would call the Brigade Command from home, as if he wason the firing position with the unit. That would be his master lie.

423   Dani's request that the Author takes part in that big lie became all-consuming and unforgettable.

424   Dani did not do his work as the commander. The complete wartime operation workload of the unit fell upon the Author, who was struggling to keep up with the pace due to physical exhaustion. There was a real risk of the unit imploding and all the successes to come to an end.

425   The Author considered that expression to be demeaning.

could continue to work with him, provided that these jokes and put downs stopped, that he really return back to the war unit and its core business, and away from posturing and mischief. He extended his hand to me and I accepted it. I talked to Laza, Šumarac and Bora for about two hours. After that, I went outside and Dani stayed. They talked with him for about half an hour. I never found out what they were talked about, nor was I interested in it. After that, Laza left. He said goodbye to everyone. During that time, I coordinated the sequence of actions with the commanders of the basic units. The equipment started moving again. This time through Kupinovo – Progar corridor, towards its destinationin Boljevci. In Progar, Maletić, who was driving the Kraz truck and towing a generator, let me go in front of him. At the exit from the village, around 22:00, three Tomahawk cruise missles flew over Kosta and me. These were flying to Belgrade. The two missiles flew first, and then, after about a minute or two, a third one. They were definitely not more than 100 metres high. Whistling, creepy sound, no light was coming from the engine. Just sound and nothing more. It was now clear to me why the SA-7 could not intercept them. There was nothing to latch on to. Simply darkness and a traveling messanger of death. They came through the valley of the Sava River, as I said a long time ago, at the beginning of the war. I remained at the combat position until 02:30 hours.

June 1999

Koman was in the guidance station. He had installed the video feed, monitor screen and a camera that records the screen of the missile guidance officer.

Last night Dani's shift launched a missile in the passive regime,[426] by using a thermal imaging camera.[427] The launch was on the wide beam and when the missiles appeared on the screen they didn't switch onto the narrow beam, the target went into the clouds and the operator lost it. That was the reason for the miss. Dani didn't learn the lesson from Djević[428] from the beginning of the war.[429] They made the same mistake.[430]

On the positive side, there was something good in all that: the airplanes immediately ran away and had not returned the whole night. Probably because it was a complete surprise and they didn't know what we had at our disposal. There had been no radar emissions to warn them, but missiles were launched out of nowhere. There was no radar emission, and there was no visibility for the optical system but still someone shot at them. They suddenly became risk averse.

Last night, when we moved the equipment to the new position, there were some activities but further south. In the Belgrade area, only cruise missiles.

There was a malfunction of the motor that rises and lowers the fire control radar antennas, so Ljubenković and his boys had to do that manually. The cables to the station had not been laid in parallel on the ground, which further increased the time needed to collect them. Ljubenković needed more men. The CBRN section put more corner reflectors in the battalion's combat formation. Miškov made a lot of mistakes with his guys. Dimitrov didn't put the big radar emission imitator because he couldn't find a good spot. The locals were pretty much indifferent. Most of them were of the Slovak ethnic

---

426 Passive mode – is the operation without radar radiation in the space.
An optical video camera is used by day, and a thermal imaging camera by night.
427 At the beginning of the war, the 250th Missile Air Defense Brigade had only two thermal imaging cameras. These were mounted in the 1st Battalion, in Batajnica, and the 8th Battalion, in Obrenovac.
428 Lieutenant Colonel Steva Djević– was the Commander of the 1st Battalion.
429 At the beginning of the war, Djević's combat crew fired in the passive mode (read thermal vision), without radar radiation into the space.
430 In both cases, the operators, Djević and Dani, did not timely switch the camera / thermal imaging field of view to the narrow beam when the missile appeared on the screen; so in the first case they lost it due to dust clouds during the day, and in the second case due to the missiles entering the clouds at night.

background.

Last night, Lazović brought Sekulić to the Noskov's battalion, as his equipment had been repaired. The day before Sloki had a breakdown and ended up in the psychiatry medical unit.

This new position was well prepared. There were trenches and dugouts. Dani was engaged in the preparation. One trench intended for the evacuation of the crew from the guidance station was 25 m long, 3 m deep but straight. This was not good. The shrapnel flies in the straight line. I told this to Dani and he replied that I was 100% right and he hadn't thought about it. He came into the shift between 00:30 and 01:00 and stayed there until 06:00 hours.

From now on, Dotlić and I will cover two daytime shifts, of 15 hours aggregate duration. Dani, as ordered by Colonel Lazarević, will be on the night shifts, from 21:00 until 06:00. Dotlić took over the first day shift from Dani and stayed until 13:30. I took over from Dotlić and stayed until 21:00.

Our camp was at the Seka's house in Boljevci. She was the kindergarten principal. Was this just a coincidence or not?[431]

I spoke with Danka around 23:30 last night. She was very worried but was holding tight and brave.

So far, I had been seeing enemy airplanes only on the radar screens and once when SA-7 acted but yesterday, in Ašanja, I saw one high above, in the clouds. It looked white and was moving very fast. It was not alone for sure. I was sorry that it was infesting our sky. The sounds of explosions and the jet noise differed here from those in the guidance station. It was frightening, especially for people who had no military experience.

Habits are weird.

After we woke up, and had our morning coffee, Dani, Aca and I went to recce our new combat position. We arrived to Deč when the spring downpour started. We couldn't do anything until the rain stopped and torrents receded. We cannot drive across on dirt field roads with our Opel Askona sedan. We had sent our four ZIL trucks from the edge of the Progar forest to Ašanja… The boys didn't get their breakfast. They will eat at the Varga's place.

It was time for my shift. I gave orders to Kosta what needed to be repaired on our Zastava car. While we had been reconnoitring the new positions, the radio played a song by Djordje Balašević[432] and his words hit me…so much feelings. The message of his lyrics touched me deeply. Something in me suddenly changed as if I could start crying at any moment. Was that a flow of emotions or had I become too sensitive? One usually cries out of hope-lessness.

Yesterday, everyone read an article in the Ilustrovana Politika magazine about the B-2 bomber we had hit. Dani, as usual, when I was not present spoke that we had most likely fired upon a decoy. "That was so pedagogical and encouraging of him to say towards his subordinate officers," I sarcasti-

431   Dani decided to accommodate the command there.
432   Djordje Balašević- was a famous singer and author of popular ballads and cantatas in the former Yugoslavia.

cally concluded to myself.

I wondered what kind of logic and psychology he had studied? What decoy could fly at the speed of 200 m/s and simultaneously performs maneuvers??? Maletić told me yesterday: "Buddy, congratulations to you," and tapped his hat, "you told him everything as it should be!"

On my way to the combat position, from about 50 m away, I saw a rabbit. Wild animals became our friends since the war started. I instinctively thought for a moment about the handgun, but I stopped and looked at him and thinking of how free and cautious he was. He left though the wheat field along some path known only to him.

When I arrived at the station, Dotlić told me that he had heard from Sergeant Matić that General Ljubiša Veličković was killed last night in one of missile unit near Pančevo. Matić heard that from his neighbour yesterday, when he was on leave. The general was not in any of our units. He must had been in one of SA-6 Kub units. I felt sorry for the guy if this was true. I'm sorry for every person. Death is not a punishment. There should be some other punishments too. He was one of the few generals who had been in the station during combat operations. He was often with us, as well.

During my shift from 13:00 to 21:00, Readiness No. 1 lasted for an hour only. All other time we spent in Readiness No. 2. Dani came on time.

I went to the camp in the Askona. Zoki, the host of the house we were accommodated in, was there together with driver Lukić, Captain Muminović, Dejan Tiosavljević, Kosta Ćurčić, a courier, Dani's driver Aca, Boris Stoimenov and Boško Dotlić.

At around 21:40 we heard a loud noise high above us – maybe 4-5 airplanes a few minutes apart. We saw a flash in the air and after about 10 seconds the tremendous explosions could be heard. They were bombing the Obrenovac garrison. There were about 4-5 explosions. Why were our guys were not working, we asked ourselves.

Mika and I took the Pinzgauer and went to the communication centre at around 23:00. I spoke with the boys and I was happy with their work. They were proud that someone from the command came to speak with them. They had been resolving ongoing things on the go. I welcomed their initiative. They were glad that I was spontaneous.

After that, I went to visit Dimitrov who was manning the radar emission imitator. Things were not good there. I will have to deal separately with that unit and solve the problems. The problem was relations between soldiers. Dimitrov is too gentle and hesitant. For that reason, Boris had emerged as a leader, but was not accepted by the troops. They don't have the travel record sheets for the aggregate on the imitator.

At around 01:30, we returned to the camp and went to sleep.

Dani worked with an imitator and radiated tonight. They did not acquire the target and therefore did not shoot.

There was no electricity in the village. I needed to shave and bathe. I stank. It was disgusting.

313

I really slept well last night and woke up at 08:00. Other than last night's actions, nothing else had happened in the airspace. Dotlić replaced Dani this morning and will stay until 13:30. I will go again from 13:30 to 21:00.

We had coffee. I ordered Žugić and Barvalac to hand over their respective TAM 150 and TAM 110 trucks to Dimitrov's CBRN unit for his people. They did that but didn't leave a designated driver for the radar emission imitator...ugh... I need to have a meeting with all basic units' commanders. They have to coordinate their work. Dani went scouting for a new combat position.

At 13:30 Dotlić and I changed over shifts.

Janković and Tiosavljević, together with others from our shift, discussed that, instead of representing the unit's interests, Dani had been the first one to doubt our scores. By doing that, he was belittling people and combat crews.

This morning, Dani took the Ilustrovana Politika magazine I had been reading and said that he would look for eyewitnesses. "The journalist, Slobodan Milošević (the same name as the President)," Dani said, "should also be found."

Ljubenković gave me the phone numbers of the bakery store, owned by a man from the State Security Service, who bought drinks for everyone that night, on 20 May, when we fired from Bečmen, and who said he had seen a B-2 bomber being hit twice. The man's name is Petar Paušek. I'll give his phone number to Mika to find him and reconfirm. Matić said that then we would be able to tell Dani: "Here's your eyewitness!"

Crnobrnja called from Deč, from the logistics unit, and said that we have to organize ourselves much better regarding the logistics work, as "There are," he said, "plenty of problems." I replied, "Okay. We will meet and sort it out. What is Tomović doing?"

The Russian envoy, Victor Chernomyrdin is coming to Belgrade today to negotiate with President Milošević.

I called Danka. She told me that she had bought the latest Ilustrovana Politika magazine and read an article about the invisible "Spirit". Only 20 B-2 airplanes had been produced so far.

Žugić and Armuš came to repair Ljubenković›s Ural truck that had overheated. Dani was not at Armuš›s place although he had told me that he would go there. I explained to Armuš that the guidance station cabin must be covered first with the longest logs and then the shorter ones should be put on top of them. The cover they had made earlier today was not good. Not only the cabin could be damaged, but also it could not be pulled out quickly; only after all the logs were removed first. That would slow down the work and relocation.

I ordered Ljubenković to write a statement on why he drove the Ural truck without the engine cooling fluid and why he had overheated it? For the imitator I assigned Boris to assess the radar emission imitator aggregate condition at the combat position, and to speak with the guys from the Brigade to resolve any problems.

I told Milojica that the drivers of Ural and TAM 110 trucks were not in the unit, which was not what had been ordered. He told me that the Kraz truck would be returned from Noskov to our Battalion tomorrow. The vehicle for the missiles transport and loading will stay with us, but its driver will return to Noskov.

Roksandić should take back the repaired TAM 150 from from Žugić and bring Brković from Jakovo and Kokanović from Ašanja to the radar emission imitator. Bugarin performed this task. The TAM 150 had an issue with the brakes. They had locked in a position.

Žugić said it would be best to bring the Zastava 101 to Šimanovci, where they could do some body work.

Stojanović sent a list of the consumables he needed for the uninterrupted operation. It should be dispatched by regular mail tomorrow.

It was unbearable in the station, 35°C. Sweat was just pouring from us.

I sent Boris to Ljubenković to repair the motor for lowering and raising the antennas of the surveillance radar.

Today, Roćko from the emergency response group came for a photo shoot next to the missiles. He'll print pictures for all of us - Tiosav Janković, Dejan Tiosavljević, Roćko and I. He's a taxi driver by profession and adores me.

I have to check with Stanković about a military conscript, Aleksić. He is looking for a permanent job in the military police after the war.

I had been thinking today. If we really knocked down five planes with 11 missiles that we had launched so far, it would have been be an unprecedented success: F117-A, F-16, See-Harrier and B-2. We do not know yet what the fifth airplane was. We are all living legends. To the best of our knowledge, that one unknown was most likely another F-117A. This is for the history books.

Dani came around 21:00 to replace me.

Stoimenov with Ljubenković repaired the motor for raising and lowering the antenna.

Upon arriving at the camp, I had coffee, lunch and dinner, all at the same, and Aca took me to Mika. Once there, I assigned Mika the task to find out everything about the downed B-2 via the State Security. Dani told me that a guy with the family name Todorčević, as far as I can remember, Dragan was his name, the president of the Deč municipality, saw the missile hit and then the aircraft starting to mumble. The hit was for sure. Some of the engines were damaged.

The crew of the radar emission imitator had behaved irresponsibly. I ordered Mika to call the signals guys to check on them every half-hour. Their wires had been broken and disconnected from the phone handsets too often.

The night we visited them, their commander Miloš was at home, but so was his deputy. They had one on sick leave. So, three of nine of them were absent. Too many!

Mika showed me the article about the 20 May night's downing of a B-2 that had been posted on the internet yesterday. I have to find that site. Dani had finally begun to believe in our shooting results. His opinion didn't even matter to us anymore.

Thursday, June 03

Boško was in his shift from 06:00 hours to 13:30 hours. I was so tired and sleepy when I got up. I passed by Dani, Kosta, Aca, host Zoki and his wife Seka. Dani told me that he had something to tell me when I got back from the toilet. Something nice.

Last night, when he was in his shift, he spoke to Dragan. He introduced himself as Lasta (the swallow), because that's what we were because we had been moving all the time and asked him if he knew anything about the B-2. "Yes, of course!" Dragan replied him, "I have a recorded conversation between the pilots and AWACS. The plane fell into the forests of Spačva near Županja, just across the border in Croatia." This was great news. We agreed to meet Dragan between 10:00 and 11:00 at the church in Boljevci.

A meeting with the commanders of the basic units was held in the orchard by the equipment, from 18:30 to 21:00. The agenda included the following items:

- Actions dynamics - expecting areas, reconnaissance of fire position.

- Vehicle drivers.

- Food distribution.

- Radar emission imitators and their importance in combat work.

- The decoy combat position.

- Home leave absences from the unit and the maximum allowable percentage of people who could be absent.

- Sick leave absences from the unit for treatment and home care.

- Use of the SA-7 and how this weapon shall be used.[433]

- The role of the rapid intervention platoon – to safeguard the temporary resting place during transition, be the first team to arrive at the new combat position and examine the terrain.

- Accommodation for the basic units to be provided by the basic unit commanders; for the command by Major Dotlić.

433   The need for this additional training arose after one uncareful SA-7 operator unintentionally launched the missile, so it hit a peasant's cow and killed its calf in the region of the village of Deč.

- Military IDs <u>must</u> be carried all the times.
- Travel worksheets <u>must</u> be filled-in and submitted.
- Fuel at the combat position <u>must</u> be delivered <u>after dark</u>.
- Commander of the logistic unit – an officer from the 250th Brigade Command.
- Analyses of information received since the last meeting.[434]
- Tepavac and Cvetić need to hand over to me the return slips from the Military Tribunal Rulings, so these could be formally returned to the Brigade Command.[435]
- Proposals for promotions and awards for soldiers and officers to come from their basic units.

I discussed a lot at the meeting in order to facilitate the best possible outcomes. Everyone listened to me carefully. This was the first meeting of its kind since the war broke out. "Eh my battalion commander…" I thought to myself.

By the time the meeting ended my shift had just finished. Dani took over the next shift.

I went to the camp and, for the third consecutive day, had lunch and dinner at the same time.

After that, Mika and I went to arrange a decoy combat position. There were problems to be resolved on the go, while trying my best to properly set up that unit. I resolved their problem with the vehicle; Dotlić and logistics guys were assigned to find a driver for their unit. I explained to them what my expectations were and told them what to do.

After busy day, I returned from the meeting at around midnight and went to sleep and fell asleep quickly.

Friday, April 04

Dani woke me up at 05:30 hours. Dotlić had replaced him on the shift. We had coffee. He seemed polite this morning. He told me that he was not my enemy and that he was not that kind of man. Should I try to trust him?

---

434   The 250th Air Defense Brigade Command briefing about the wartime enlargement and new composition of the units was shared with the commanders and discussed.
There was no need for the basic unit commanders to familiarize with other briefings that did not impact their units.
435   Tepavac and Cvetić were commanders of the basic units and envelopes from the Military Tribunal arrived for some of their soldiers as registered mail. These had to be signed by the addressee and the return slip returned to the relevant military department along the chain of command.

We went to Kupinovo to inspect the site for our new combat position before the engineers would arrange it later today, so that the missile guidance station and the power distribution would be dug in and camouflaged. For the first time, the surveillance radar will also have dirt flank protection without being dug in. The power supply generators will be located 60-70 metres away, and these would also be protected by compacted dirt berms.

Dani asked me about the best way to shoot: "What is the best combination of radar emission and thermal imaging." I explained to him all the variants and recommended the most reliable combination. In any case, we would much less rely on the radar emissions, which would make our work much safer.

I met with Captain Rade Končar, an engineering officer. He will do the job with two machines.

After that, we went to Deč, to inspect our second next combat position. The position will be located in an orchard, among the apple-tree crawlers. Drive-through or dig-in type?[436,437,438] It would depend on the depth of groundwater table.[439] Končar had some good ideas. I connected him with Tomović, who had already drafted sketches for the protection made of scaffolding and logs.

I briefly went to Barvalac in the logistics center for a box of cigarettes and ordered to return the Kraz truck to Noskov.[440] Marjanović called to confirm his understanding of the number and type of radar emission imitators we have. That should be conveyed to Stoimenov tomorrow, as he went home today with Dani. I was in a hurry to get to the combat position to replace Dotlić, who was at shift.

I arrived there at 13:00, straightaway into the Readiness No. 1. We had been in Readiness No. 1 until 16:00 when Luka, from the Operations Centre, ordered me to turn on the surveillance radars. As soon as I had done that and reported back the airspace situation, we were ordered to go into Readiness

---

436   Drive-through and dig-in – are typical types of battlefield earthworks (embankments, fortifications) used to protect equipment, for example, the missile guidance station.

437   Drive-through embankment– has one entry point, one exit point, and the protected equipment is located in the midpoint between them, where the height of the embankment is the highest, typically up to the roof of the protected piece of equipment. One could think of it being made by an excavator that starts digging, say at the entry, then deeper and deeper into the soil as it moves forward. Once the required depth is reached, the excavator gradually reduces the depth of digging as it further moves forward towards the exit point, which is leveled with the surrounding soil.

438   Dig-in embankment– has a common entry and exit point, it is Pi-shaped and protected equipment is located at the opposite end, where depth of the excavation is the highest.

439   Dig-in embankment– is more suitable for shallow groundwater table areas; typically in the vicinity of large bodies of water and seasonally flooding plains.

440   The KRAZ 255B truck- belonged to the 5th Battalion, under the command of Lieutenant Colonel Miroslav Noskov.

No. 2. I couldn't believe my ears, so I had to check it. Luka confirmed. Indeed, we had been ordered to go to Readiness No. 2. What a mess... I switched off the equipment and went to the radar for a coffee break.

Dani called me from home while I was on the command post. The Brigade had called him to submit the list of our proposals for the awards[441] by 15:00 sharp. All proposals must be at the Brigade HQ tomorrow by 10:00 hours. The percentages[442] shall be as follows: officers 15%, 8% for NCO's and 3% for the enlisted staff.

He didn't know what the awards would be, and he sent the list of the following men:

(1) Officers:

Lieutenant Colonel Djordje Aničić, Major Boris Stoimenov;

(2) NCOs: Senior Sergeant Djordje Maletić, Senior Sergeant Vladimir Ljubenković, Sergeant 1st Class Zoran Tepavac, Sergeant Saša Bugarin, Sergeant Zdenko Volf;

(3) Enlisted men: private Davor Bložić, missile guidance battery, private Selko Radovanović, missile guidance battery, private Slaviša Pavlović, missile guidance battery, private Miroslav Aleksić, SA-7 battery, private Sead Ljajić, missile guidance battery, private Sladjan Dragašević, missile battery.

The basic unit commanders wrote the letters of support for their people, and I wrote for Stoimenov and Tepavac.

It was Sergeant Matić's birthday today. My Classmate Roksandić, Mika and I went to the café in the village, where Matić had been expecting us to come. The intervention platoon was there. The whole off-duty shift was there. They were real rascals.

They said that they had booked the "Stenka" restaurant for after the war and two pairs of military field induction phones: one for the bar and the other for the music, so they don't need to get up. Only the selected guys will be invited. They said that it would be the men's party, without girlfriends and spouses. Let's all "kill ourselves" with alcohol!

They nicknamed me "the spirit". The one can feel that they were proud to be in this unit. At about 21:30 hours my classmate Mika and I left. I tried to sleep, though even I didn't believe that I could and I was right. As I couldn't sleep at all, I went to the shift tired.

Tonight, I will be on duty from midnight to 06:00.

---

441   The type of the awards was not known at the time. These could be medals, monetary awards, awards in the form of leave of absence, etc.

442   The percentages—were based on the head count in the unit by the category. For example, if there were 15 officers in the unit and if the unit could propose 15 percent (of them) for the award, then only 2 names could be put forward.

I came to the shift. The guidance officer reported to me that the 2nd missile guidance channel was faulty. It could not grip the target. We only had a clutter grip.[443] Volf and Panić tried to adjust the control system. They couldn't fix it until 01:30. Bora Samardžić was at the Operations Center. I told him that he can count on us if he finds a target near us[444,445]and to send Miša Ivanović in the morning.

Tiosav Janković, Volf, Matić and I discussed about doubting Thomases. They had been saying we had shot at a decoy. Dani was the first one to say that. In Ogar, when his shift fired, the target launched decoys and instead of the target at the crosshair they only had a clutter or decoy. The missile went through that cloud and did not activate.

In contrast, both our missiles activated. Zoki, Seka's husband, and many others personally saw it and confirmed the explosions. After the missiles exploded, the intermittent jet engine operation was heard. Dani told me this afternoon that he considered that the target had been shot down.

The proposal for my decoration was separate to that concerning the downing of a F-117A, for which only the trooper and I received no award, promotion or decoration... not even citation. The decoration would have been an acknowledgment of my work so far. Terrible!

According to the engagement rules, we did hit the target. Both missiles exploded on the target and created a cloud of debris that scattered electromagnetic waves. It was a classical hit. We did not see a sudden change of the parameters of the target[446] because, for safety reasons and immediately after the explosion of the second missile, we shut off the antenna and high voltage. All we need, in lieu, is Dragan to bring us the transcript of communication between the pilot and the AWACS, as recorded by our Military Intelligence.[447] This is the prima-facie evidence of the successful hit.[448]

---

443   The clutter grip – is a jargon term for the fault situation when the ground station strobes do not receive radio beacon response signal from the launched missile. This manifests on the radar screen as a drift of the missile away from the vertical crosshairs. In other words, the 2nd missile couldn't be guided by the signal received from its beacon.

444   The 1[st]missile guidance channel was operational.

445   The crew would have shot with one missile and then the probability of destruction would be lower and about 75%, while with two missiles it would be about 95%.

446   Parameters of the target –refer to its location and trajectory as seen on the radar screens in the guidance station.

447   In 1999, the FRY's Military Intelligence listened to the unencrypted comunication between the NATO planes and their control center in the AWACS plane, the code name for which was "Mother".

448   Prima facie is a legal claim having enough evidence to proceed to trial or judgment.

In the yesterday's mail, a letter from the Brigade came; they requested the opinion of Battalion commander, Dani, in relation to my complaint letter.

WO Dragan Matić and Tanja missile. The first one which hit B-2.

Naming missile with female names became a practice - Natalija i Živadinka cartoon.

I was at shift until 06:00. Matić told me that the missiles we had launched on the B-2 plane bear the names Tanja and Ivana.[449]

449   The noun "missile" is of the feminine gender in the Serbian language, so

On my way to Zoki's house, I met Mika at the bus station in Boljevci. He waited for the bus to go home.

I slept till 10:00 hours. The nightshift made me so tired.

Dani arrived from home. He asked me if the proposal for awards had been typed. "Not yet," I replied, "The commanders wrote an opinion for their people and I wrote for Tepavac and Stoimenov. I wrote nothing for myself. I cannot write it for myself. You have to do it for me."

Dani wrote justification for his proposal for my award. In addition, and as requested by the Brigade, he wrote his explanation of why I had written to the commander and sought an official interview with the commander of the Air Defense Corps. He wrote everything about me in superlatives; regarding my complaint, he wrote that it was true that I participated in the work when the F-117A was shot down and that I should have been awarded as the others were. "He couldn't have written anything else," I thought for myself, "This is further proof of what the system has been trying to hide, as if the Brigade Command doesn't already have a list of the crewmembers that shot down the F-117A. That night, I had personally read and dictated the composition of the combat crew to the Chief of Staff, Colonel Stanković."

Around 10:30 Miša Ivanović arrived, as the much-needed help, which I requested from Samardžić last night.

I left for Deč so Slavko and Tomović could type the proposal for awards and take it to the Brigade Command.

The other night, Dani called Stanković during his shift and told him he had irrefutable evidence that we had not shot the decoy but the real B-2 stealth bomber. I was overjoyed! The airplane that my shift downed is one of the strategic bombers. It carries 90 tonnes of fuel and 34 tonnes of explosives; its wingspan is 53-57 metres, its length is about 24 metres and its height is about 5,18 meters. These airplanes were named after the states. 20 pieces were produced, and the one that we downed was called "The Spirit of Missouri." The first missile that hit it was named Tanja.

I spoke to Danka. I was in a hurry to meet her after work. Along the way, I bought cucumbers, tomatoes, baby potatoes and hot peppers. I arrived home at around 13:15.

Nataša was at home. Danka criticized me for paying too little attention to her in my diary. Hmmmm....

We took Nataša and her two girlfriends to the Uroš's birthday party.

On our way back we passed the General Staff and the Government of Serbia buildings. The pile of broken concrete looked terrible. The collapsed building, broken glass, and many gaping holes where the windows once were looked cataclysmic. Only shell of the Government of Serbia building remained. A dark silver curtain slipped through the broken window and fluttered eerily in the wind from outside the building.

---

the crewmembers usually named them after their loved ones, usually wives, girlfriends, daughters, mothers, aunts, sisters, grandmothers or, rarely, pets.

We stopped by my apartment. I got a message on the pager to contact Branislava, my ex-wife. I called her. She sought money. I told her that we are working for the same employer, and that she knew our paycheques had not arrived yet. She asked for 400 DEM and told me that this was the amount she had borrowed for the apartment.

She asked me if I knew that I have a child.

I had called him many times so far, but he was never at home.

"You didn't think that Vlada needed a father when you divorced me. Who are you to remind me that I have a child!" I hung up.

This conversation upset Danka even more than me. She told me to get away from women like that. My ex didn't care if I was alive or not. Money is all that matter. The good mood was lost. We went home. We had coffee and ate cherries. Nataša arrived relatively early. There was no air raid alert in the city. I fell asleep sometime at around 23:00.

Sunday, June 06

I must get to Boljevci by noon today, so I left Belgrade at around 11:00 hours. When I got there, only Kosta and Gugleta were in the camp. Kosta was packing stuff. The equipment was already transferred, and people went into a waiting area, which was supposed to be in the Bojčinska forest. We couldn't find anyone there, so I thought jokingly, "I know where they should be and I can't find them, so how would the enemy find us?"

Our Zastava car lost its rear muffler in the woods. Bane and Kosta tied the exhaust pipe with wire and then went to Deč.

The expecting area was Ašanja. I came to Tomović and Sedlak. In Deč, I found Mika, Cvetić and the emergency response team. They were located near the combat position. I took Mika to the combat position to show him a spot for the radar emission imitator. The CBRN unit did set up angular reflectors. There should be no mistakes this time. Last time, they placed angular reflectors between launch ramps and surveillance radars. The radar was dug in for the first time, additionally protecting the people there.

The next stop is Šimanovci to visit Dimitrov and his men, to see for my-self how the other radar imitator was set up, what the quality was of the trench and to inspect the tent for accommodation of the off-duty people.

I saw Stoimenov and Boško Dotlić in the center of Šimanovci. Dotlić had drunk a few beers and was tipsy. Pera and Bora Crnobrnja were also there. Pera owned "Medikola", a factory that produced surgical threads.

Bora wanted to talk to me. He told me he saw a list of people proposed for awards. His name was not on the list and asked me why I hadn't "scratched" his back by putting his name on the list. I couldn't believe he asked me that question. And why he chose to ask me. He had spent the whole war off shifts. Not a single time was his life was in danger. "Boro, I proposed your name, but we were constrained by the percentages." "I don't give a shit!" he replied, "I'll be Captain in a few years anyway, but I still expected there would be some award for me, as well." "This was Dani's list," I told him, "but I have been very actively involved with Dani in making that decision. We made it together. People on the equipment endured the burden of war. It is hard to have or define a criterion for the awards." Bora said that he would go to Ašanja in order to taste freshly made ham a guy named Zdravko had made. I left them there…

Log protection for missile guidance station.

It was time to move the equipment. It was scheduled to sequentially transport the equipment in batches from here to Ašanja. In the meantime, I went to visit Milan and Nada and have coffee with them. They are over 70 years old and sick.

My classmate Roksandić told me that Dani had a conversation with General Petrović last night, during the shift, and told him that we have reliable information about downing of the B-2 stealth bomber and that he had already marked it as a hit. We had audio record, from the State Security Service, of the conversation between the pilots and AWACS, where they reported to have been hit and sought permission to leave the plane. They were ordered not to leave the plane, but to continue flight and cross the border. They had to prevent us from having any evidence of the plane crash. The pilots did not seem to have been able to save themselves. The plane crashed into the forests of Spačva in Croatia, just across the border. This created utter chaos there.

I was on the equipment until 01:00 hours. Everything was finished on time and of a high quality. Maletić's exhaust pipe burnt Mika's communication cable. Other than that, everything went well. Our meeting with the basic unit commanders the other day and the agreed actions gave the result. My idea was executed to a tee. Mika was pissed off because of the cable. Dani came to the equipment. He shook my hand and told me that I must take a short leave. Aca driver was waiting for me. Finally, a human gesture from Dani; I realised that he was trying to fight for me. He did hurt me a lot. As the old proverb says: "The jug goes to the well until it breaks." After that it's never the same again. I am that jug?

Monday, June 07

It was amazing how much attention and respect Dani treated me with today! Another handshake, when we finished, quite manly with strong grip. I left combat position to get some rest. When I got our Zastava car, I remembered to send Aca to get Kosta to come along. We went to Šimanovci to our accommodation. Not bad, although the house was empty. It looked like no one lived there. As if the owner was a Gastarbeiter.[450]

I woke up in the morning and had to go to Deč. Dani returned from his shift and had breakfast. He invited me to join him. I declined because I was still tired. I went back to bed and slept until 10:00 hours.

When I woke up for the second time, Aca made a coffee. We had breakfast. In Kumanovo, talks continued between representatives of the Yugoslav Army and the UN (probably NATO) on the technical side of the withdrawal of the Army from Kosovo and Metohija.

At about 11:30, I received a message from my son on my pager. We quickly agreed to meet at noon in Pećinci, in the village centre. I hadn't seen my son for almost two months. When I left, Dani was still in bed.

The encounter with my son was touching, as usual. I didn't feel a shiver this time. He came with Milja, a little girl, the daughter of my ex-wife's first cousin. She wrapped herself around my neck. She hadn't seen me for almost three years. She told me that she would go to school this summer. So cute little girl. I adore small kids. I took them for ice cream.

Cveja Roglić arrived with a van and told me that he was going to Ruma. He saw me and came to say hi. He loves me like a brother. I told him about confirmation that the plane, indeed, crash-landed. He was overjoyed. While we spoke, Bane Šuca with his wife and children suddenly popped up. Everyone greeted me. I looked at those familiar faces from my former life. We went to a cafe for a drink. Milja and I had a mushy pear juice, and Vlada took a Coke. I told him that his mom had called me and asked him where she lives now. He replied, "In Rušanj, at her girlfriend's house." He was there only once and decided not to go anymore. He lives now in Pećinci. Today at 14:30 he will go to Belgrade. Tomorrow, he has six exams in grade two of the veterinary high school. I wished him luck and success.

---

450   Gastarbeiter – (German compound word, meaning "Guest worker") is a person with temporary work permit in Germany. It became a generic word for anyone who works in another country. Many think that Gastarbeiters were the foundation of the German post WW2 economic miracle.

Danka was right. My ex-wife only asked for money. She didn't give a shit about my life. Not a single time she had ever asked or been interested in how I was or whether I needed anything.

Everything would settle one day. This war must stop one day as well...

I left for Deč because I needed to replace Dotlić at 13:30 in the shift. My shift will end at 21:00.

Maletić told me that he had seen Dotlić and another guy having a beer at a pub in Boljevci. Dani must have given them some money. We all laughed. I stated that Dani paid Dotlić and the guy to go and watch a movie. That was fun and everyone laughed. I felt a shiver of apprehension for all those scams, the crisis of morality and the meanness and felt sorry for all those who were scammed.

I tried to fall asleep but couldn't. Dotlić went home. I heard the bus pull off the shift around 23:30. Aca opened all windows to ventilate the house and left a "million" mosquitoes inside. They bit my feet. I had a shower before went to bed, but I either did not have any clean laundry or Kosta could not find it in the car. Suddenly, at about 00:00, I heard the start of the first missile, then, after five seconds, that of the second missile. Dani fired!! I ran out. Aca and Kosta were already there. We watched the missiles in the distance, their trailing exhaust plumes looked like two flying fluorescent lamps.

Tuesday, June 08

The target was detected by thermal vision at a distance of about 25 km. The surveillance radar was switched on and measured 18 km distance to the target. Thermal vision again, then raising the high voltage on the fire control radar; locking onto the target and, at 12 km away, launching the missiles. The target altitude was seven kilometers, the azimuth was somewhere around 0 degrees. The skies were clear, without a single cloud.

As soon as the target was illuminated, it started with electronic counter measures - jamming our radar. Our manual tracking operators were unable to completely filter out the electronic jamming. Otherwise, we could have launched in pure thermal imaging mode.

The pilot avoided the first missile by a sharp manoeuvre towards the ground, at an angle of about 90 degrees, initiated just before the missile reached the interception point. The evasive manoeuvre generally works, if undertaken in the time interval between 1-3 seconds before the missile reaches the target; otherwise the manoeuvre does not make any difference. The second missile, which was launched five seconds after the first one, caught the manoeuvre and followed the plane in dive. It was a surprising downward manoeuvre. Initially, it had been falling like a rock, then, at an altitude of about 500 meters, it straightened, flying for a while parallel to the ground, and then abruptly climbed up and went to safety. The pilot was a real professional.

The anti aircraft artillery cannons started firing, but it was too late. They

326

had an ideal opportunity to knock him down. There were also a few SA-7 MANPAD missiles launched. The airplane applied heat decoys and one of the missiles activated on a heat decoy. The pilot launched three heat decoys in the form of a fireball.

At around 01:30 hours, Dani called me to prepare everything for the move. We left at around 03:30. I called everyone, ordered their scheduled departure time, and went back to bed. It will be a very busy day for me today.

Kosta was ordered to prepare things for departure, and I went to the equipment. Among other things, I had to provide accommodation for people, because Dotlić was at home.

A large radar emission imitator was deployed at the end of the village of Pećinci, at the local entrepreneur, Boća's place. The Battalion command officers will be accommodated at the home of the Sibač local community's Mayor, Djordje Čikić. The other officers will go to the municipality office, and the troops across the street, where the tavern used to be. The signals centre, the emergency response group and doctor were all concentrated in one place.

The weather was unbearable: high humidity and sweltering heat. We were soaked in sweat.

Around 14:30, the first neighbor of my former father-in-law, Bane Vladin, arrived with Lada car to take me out for lunch. I told him that I couldn't because I was so busy, but he persisted. "I will leave and you and my ex father in law will continue to live side by side. I don't want you to have any problems," I explained. I felt sorry for him. He spent his fuel[451] to find and honour me. In the end, I left with him. Everyone was thrilled to see me. In Pećinci and Sibač, I was considered to be a good and principled man. No one mentioned the past. I was grateful to them for that. Novica, a neighbor across the street, came to see me too. It didn't matter to anyone that they would have been seen with me in public, neither what my ex father in law and their first neighbors would think and say about it.

The equipment had been relocated by daytime. That was not very smart. It was all over by 21:15 hours, and really quickly this time. Dani told Dotlić not to report to the Brigade Command that we are combat ready until 22:00 hours. This saved him at least one hour on combat duty.

At around 21:40, I went to the camp and woke up Dani. He was in a deep sleep. Woke up was repeated twice. He got up with difficulty, and in a bad mood. I told him that my classmate Matijević called and that the mail must arrive at the old place tomorrow by 15:00. The Brigade Command had also requested our proposal for awards for the reserve squad officers: regular and extraordinary promotions, commendations, leave of absences and cash prizes. We would think about it tomorrow. Dani left, and I stayed with the host, Mika, Dotlić, Kosta and Aca.

I went to bed around 23:30 hours. The breeze began to blow. It felt pleasant relative to that oppressively hot and humid daytime weather in the flat

---

451   It was wartime and fuel were scarce and very costly to buy on the black market. It was sold in bottles.

lands.

Wednesday, June 09

When I woke up at around 07:30 hours, Bora was already in the backyard, waiting for me to get up. Dani was still sleeping. Dotlić was on duty from 06:00 to 13:30. Bora asked me how Dani and I were doing now? I told him that our relationship was OK now and that Dani regularly goes to his scheduled shifts. He told me that Dani had wanted to take away my car and mobile phone. "Well, if he does that our unit will suffer the most. It would fail very quickly," I replied. "I know that," said Bora, "I will go the Brigade Command today. I know that no one can stand him, neither the officers nor the soldiers. He doesn't know how to work with people."

We had coffee. Bora had a flat tire on his car. So did I. Kosta and Gugleta took both the cars to Sava's tire service.

I noted that Bora had been in a bad mood since the day that we had spoken about the awards. "Well, my friend, imagine what it's like for me, who has been directly involved in everything, and in the end I received nothing," I thought for myself, "did it cross your mind how much it may hurt me?"

My girlfriend was right. The most important thing is to stay alive. That is my only preoccupation now.

Bora left and Dani woke up. We had breakfast. He told me that he had been fishing with General Bane Petrović and had had lunch with Rančić, manager of the Živača fish farm. I immediately recalled a small road sign for the farm on the road between Boljevac and Progar; and thought for myself, "You went fishing with him several times during the war, and that's why you eliminated me." Dani told him everything he knew in relation to the B-2. We have reliable data.

"You weren't fair to me and other people. How many times you tried to make fools of us? You were the one who launched that stupid decoy story? You or that alcoholic Colonel Blagojević?" I told him. I also told him that he had already seen twice what a radar decoy looked like on the radar screen;[452] the decoys didn't activate the missiles.[453,454,455,456,457] Many times, the truth is

452   The two shooting events occurred on 29 April 1999 (Ogar) and 8 June 1999 (Deč).
453   The combat crew always aims at the target (airplane) and the missile flies towards it.
454   If the airplane launches decoys in front of it, then the operators of manual tracking could transfer tracking to the "closer" target, which is a decoy; because it is physically closer to the missile guidance station and, as such, has a relatively larger radar cross section (than the airplane far behind).
455   At that instant, the missile captures the decoy and flies towards it.
456   In the meantime, the airplane goes into an evasive maneuver and, in practice, avoids the missile.
457   The missile does not activate its warhead when it reaches close proximity

328

a bitter one.

On behalf of the Battalion, we strongly supported the proposal for re-wards, all proposed names, the Commander of the Rapid Intervention Unit, Devrnja, had put forward. We had already sent our proposal for regular and extraordinary promotions of reserve officers[458] and non-commissioned offi-cers. We are not interested in verbal praise and commendations. For mon-etary awards, we proposed Crnobrnja, Golubović, Žugić and Panić. These were all my suggestions.

The day before yesterday, Golubović reported they had returned from Russia. He would come to work on Monday.

It was agreed that Stoimenov would replace me in the shift at 13:30, so that Dotlić could get some time off. I would go to Deč, in order to sort out the mail with Tomović and Sedlak.

When we met, Sedlak told me that the son of Major Lešić, who lived close to the Bežanija Sports and Recreation Centre, knew about the downed B-2. Some of his men went to the forests of Spačva[459,460,461,462] and brought back to the decoy; because of its small physical dimensions (relative to those of the air-plane) the decoy does not reflect back sufficiently strong signal required to activate the warhead.

At the radar screen in the missile guidance station, this is clearly seen as the missile flying through the crosshairs and not exploding.

458　　As the XO, the Author had a list of reserve officers and soldiers that would join his unit in case of war. Their personal information included specialty skills, awards, the date of any past promotion and scheduled date for the next promotion.

459　　The Spačva (40.000 ha) and Bosut oak forests (16.000 ha)- form a contin-uum of forest swampland in Croatia and Serbia respectively. It is a part of the Srem region of the southern Pannonian Plain, which lies between the Danube and Sava rivers.

460　　Bosut - is a river in eastern Croatia and northwestern Serbia, a 186 km long left tributary of the Sava River. In its lower course Bosut slowly flows and meanders through swamps and oak forests of Spačva and Bosut.

461　　Studva - is a 37 km-long right tributary to the Bosut River, which flows entirely within the Syrmiaregion of both Croatia and Serbia. It is a slow, meandering river and spills over into several marshes. The border between the two countries par-tially runs along the Studva River, including its most Western local point, between the villages of Soljani and Morović.

462　　They were likely guided by the local Serbian men who knew the terrain well, and who had been ethnically cleansed after the Spačva region had fallen under the Croatian control on conclusion of the civil war in 1995.

Namely, immediately after Croatia unlawfully declared its independence from SFR Yugoslavia in 1991, the local Serbs self-proclaimed in one-part western Srem an autonomous region called the "Serbian Autonomous Region of Eastern Slavonia, Baranja and Western Srem". They declared their independence from Croatia.

That region was one of the two Serbian autonomous regions that formed the self-de-clared and unrecognized Republic of Serbian Krajina. Both regions were ethnically cleansed of its Serb and some other non-Croat population leading to some of the

329

parts of the downed B-2.[463] He said that the pilots did not survived. Poor guys. Soldiers like me. They died because of someone's order that the plane shall not crash on the Serbian territory. Lives lost in order to hide the proof. It was a sheer madness by the NATO politicians and generals. Recklessness has no borders and nationality.

Missile at a higher elevation with SNR-125 Low Blow radar in the background.

Mića Mijalković told me that he had been driving a Lieutenant Colonel to work that day (most likely Orlović) and that he had told him that B-2 had been shot down last night. I didn't know from where that officer had got that information.

One reservist (Kosta has his details) said that 4-5 days ago, the media reported that the unit that had shot down the F-117A had also shot down the B-2. I had never said, in front of anyone, that it was my airplane. It was the entire combat shift's airplane, not just mine, regardless if I was the shift commander. I really think, and I will always think, that it was the teamwork. The fears and work are the same for all shift crew members. Our lives are equally important.

It is a fact that I was the only officer who had been in a deputy and com-

---

most serious violations of human rights and human lives.

463   The B-2A strategic stealth bomber fell in the Spačva forest just 15 km inside the Croation territory, across the heavily forested border from the Serbian village of Morović. The damaged plane, with all lights on and roaring engines with no power, rattling like a lawn mower, flew low above the village in the middle of the night and crashed in a ball of fire that lit the skies; when many had already been watching the night fireworks in the distance played by the air-defense tracer bullets and large explosions. The plane came from the direction of the fireworks.

mand roles, and who had participated in shooting down both stealth air-planes.

I returned from Deč around 16:00 with Kosta and a reservist who went to see Dr. Đukić. Dotlić and Stoimenov were together at shift. Dani had not informed Dotlić that Stoimenov will come instead of me.

I called my shift crew for a meeting to share the latest information re-ceived. This included official confirmation on passing of General Veličkov-ić. He died at a combat position near Omoljica on the "Kub" missile system in the 7th second of radiation. This proved how dangerous it is to stay on missile equipment and how unjustified the requests were to extend the ra-diation time. The general had been the most senior ranked victim of NATO aggression. This was an additional proof of importance of shortening the firing cycle time that I had introduced during downing of the F-117A plane.

I spoke with my sweetheart. She was in a good mood. She asked when I would come home. The news was that she had bought a new Panasonic cell phone. Her number was unchanged.

Dani asked me today if I had brought a cell phone. I did. But I had no SIM card and the battery was bad. He told me that he has both. "To hell with you and your phone," I thought to myself, "fuck you and your cell phone. I don't need anything from you".

At about 18:50, the command ordered us to go to Readiness No. 1. We are the Battalion on duty, and probably the only one. What a bureaucratic way of thinking…

I still didn't know what was new on the political scene.

So far, we have launched 13 missiles, plus the one that fell from the ramp when we engaged the B-2.

Will our politics derive any benefit from all of this? We had invested our lives to guarantee political concessions. I wondered if the politics would be a bitch again. All this time we, and similar units, had been buying time for our politicians.

Sergeant Bugarin signed a contract today to extend his army service for another three years. Too small a satisfaction for what he had invested. Gam-bling is a strange thing…

Danka heard from my sister today. She told me that she was depressed, that she worked a lot and that they plan to come in the summer. Viktor, my brother-in-law had been drinking more and more. I got rid of my unsuc-cessful marriage and misery. She was still an addict of her marriage. It was probably the price of a struggle for existence. He had never equaled to her in anything, especially in terms of culture.

Thanks to my parents and God for looking after me. My sister and I had been very good children. Thanks to our parents for everything, for our up-bringing, our honesty and for teaching us life. It was hard, but it paid off. We had become honest and good people. I should put my mother's picture[464] on

_____

464   A photo of the deceased is made on an oval-shaped porcelain plate and

her gravestone.

I should also ask them for forgiveness and understanding. We are only humans, and every human being sometimes commits a sinful act. We had probably sinned. You too reader... Our life is intrinsically episodic, the period between birth and death. One should master the art of living it. In many respects, I probably hadn't mastered that art. If it hadn't been for our parents and our obligation towards them,[465] I would have immediately suggested to my sister that we sell the house. I would tell her to get rid of her failed marriage. I hate meanness. You only live once.

And my sweetheart was right.[466] "For whom we wage war?" I reassured myself.[467] She told me again today, "When it's all over, I'll make you take sedatives and then I will tell you everything." "I have known about all this for a long time, my little one.[468] I just need time to admit it to myself."[469]

At 21:00, Dani came to replace me in the shift. I walked to the camp. At around 22:00, Novica came to pick me up to go to dinner. Mika was sitting with me. He would go too. At the Novica's place, Pera Banga and his brother Jova had already arrived. We sat, talked and laughed. Pera wanted to come to our unit. Vesna was cutting hams, sausage, fried eggs, tomatoes and hot peppers.

At that moment, we heard the announcement of the armistice. All surrounding villages exploded in celebration, as 20/3 mm AAA tracer bullets lit the sky. If this armistice would end the war, its misery and carnage, then it had been worth fighting for.

Dani told me last night that we will keep on the right-hand side of the road Petrovčić - Karlovčić, and Noskov will be responsible for the left-hand side, as seen from Belgrade.

    There were five new combat positions to be prepared, in the region of the then cemented on the gravestone to complement the personal data (name, dates and places of birth and death, etc.) of the person buried there.

465   There is an unwritten moral obligation not to do anything your parents would not have approved had they been alive, in this particular case to sell the old family house. It stems from the traditional Serbian code of ethics, in which the greatest heroism is chivalry, which is that victory when you save others from yourself.

466   Danka was upset with collapse of the public moral and cultural values and rising inequalities in the society. The ordinary people and citizens had been sidelined, yet they bore all consequences of the failed policies. Those in power did not feel any consequences of sanctions, misery and humiliation.

467   The Author had been replying Danka that politicians just come and go; the state and people should be defended.

468   The Author fully understood her critique of all shortcomings in the society, including inappropriate attitude towards the army, but his conviction (emanating from his upbringing and education) that the country must be defended outweighed her undisputed arguments.

469   The Author knew that it would take time for Danka's arguments to fully sink in into his head, before he will even consider change of his mindset and commence to advocate much less for defense of the country.

villages of Prhovo, Subotište and Brestač. I knew their approximate locations.

The equipment was located in the area of the village of Sibač, two and a half to three kilometers away from the village of Budjanovci. The village of Budjanovci was clearly visible. Was this meant to be our destiny, the game of life, or just toss of a coin? There, at the beginning of the war, the first plane was shot down and, here, we ended the war.

I left Dani to inform the night shift. I'd go again in the shift in the morning. Boško Dotlić should have been administering the leave requests and reporting it.

Thursday, June 10

I couldn't fell asleep for a long time. Dotlić, Stoimenov, Kosta and Aca were sleeping. I was sitting at the front porch of our host's house. I felt as if I was on the guard duty. The night was pleasant. I went to bed again at around 03:00.

My morning shift was from 06:00 to 13:30. Kosta made coffee. He became a coffee maker…

Stoimenov and I walked to the combat position. As soon as we got into the guidance station, we were ordered into Readiness No. 1 - combat duty regime. We remained in this full combat duty regime until 12:00. We didn't spend a lot of fuel, about 200 liters of diesel D2. The ceasefire was signed, together with the Kumanovo agreement. Is this really peace?!

Warrant Officer Danilović, who came to our battalion the other day, told us his 1991 war time stories about relocation of the equipment[470] from Croatia to Manjača[471] near Banja Luka.

Both the Battalion Commander and his Deputy Commander had fled the unit.[472] Dani was the most senior officer who remained in the unit and, along with other officers who came to his aid, they pulled the unit out of the encirclement[473] in Croatia and relocated it to Manjača.

470   The equipment – was the complete missile air-defense system Neva-125 (the same as that of the Author's unit).
471   Manjača - was a large tank military range, located 22 km south of the city Banja Luka (the capital of the Republika Srpska entity of Bosnia and Herzegovina; the other entity was the Muslim-Croat Federation, the capital Sarajevo) on the slopes of the mountain of the same name.
472   They deserted the unit, probably in order to either simply run away from danger or to join the self-proclaimed independent Croat state.
473   The strategy used by secessionists in Croatia (probably masterminded by their foreign sponsors) - was to encircle the army barracks in SFR Yugoslavia, cut access roads, supplies, electricity and water and then force them to surrender, with or without use of the arms previously smuggled from abroad.
That strategy was not always successful, particularly where traitors in the army were

Once they reached the safety of the Serbian territory, they went to a local tavern in Manjača. Dani had a few drinks and started throwing himself at a waitress. The problem was that there were other drunken soldiers around, who probably went through a similar or much worse combat ordeal while breaking through the Croatian encirclement. One of them took a handgun and fired it at Dani from a distance of about two or three meters away. The hit was straight into his heart. Fortunately, Dani had a thick wallet in his left pocket. Everything was punched through, but the bullet stopped after hitting the key, which was in his wallet. Dani fell down from the force of the impact but was not wounded otherwise (except probably for the bruise). Later, this "wounding" was presented as if it had been inflicted upon the equipment evacuation from Croatia. I'm not sure if was this true or just an "urban legend", but I have no reason not to believe it either. I wasn't there anyway.

Soldiers from the emergency response unit arrived. They wanted us to take pictures next to the equipment. I asked them if the pictures were intended for "The Hague Tribunal"[474] and they all laughed.[475,476] They replied that they will pretend not to know me when they see me in the news. Who knows what could happen after the war... Bad experiences already exist.[477]

Dotlić replaced me at the shift at 13:30. I asked him for his information on the downed B-2 and what was his source. We knew its price, dimensions, and payload. We also knew how many had been manufactured. We downed the "Spirit of Missouri" (AV-8-88-0329). Dragan Antonić had told Dotlić, and he conveyed that information to Dani. Dani was silent, of course. He didn't tell me that he had found out the serial number and the name of the plane we had hit.

Everyone liked to take photos next to the missile launcher ramp. They were riding them and taking photos in various poses. Missiles are ordinary rifles. The brain is in the missile guidance station. Everything is concentrated there, both the wit and speed, and launch and joy and sadness.

According to the old custom, missiles were baptized with female names.

cowards who just fled away.

474   The Hague Tribunal referred to jokingly – was The International Criminal Tribunal for the former Yugoslavia (ICTY).

475   Many considered the ICTY to be a "kangaroo court," established to punish Serbs for their sin of daring to oppose the will of the sole superpower at the time (from 1989 to 2008), by standing for their constitutional rights for self-rule and self-determination, in their capacity of a Constitutional Entity according to the Constitution of the SFRY at the time.

476   The weak and flexible "rules of evidence" made it a kangaroo court in the eyes of many, because these were strongly biased against the accused. ague Tribunal had it adopted the same rules of evidence for criminal offences as those that exist in any respectable jurisdiction, for example those that apply in the UK, Australia or Canada.

477   The Author had in mind persecution of the Bosnian Serb leaders at the Hague Tribunal, including of those who refused to implement what the foreigners had requested them to do without prior approval of the Parliament of Republika Srpska, as well as the quite recent, 1999, persecution of the FRY Serb leaders.

The officers of the missile battery and the rest of the crew choose their names. In one of the stories, Matić asked me what my wife's name was. I told him Danka. Later, while walking across the combat position and watching our beauties – missiles – I noticed Danka's name written on one. It was standing on the first shaft of the second launch ramp. If we launched from that ramp, it would be the first one to blast off. Danka is too beautiful name for such a cruel killing assignment. Danka shouldn't be someone's fate. My preference is that it remains in its place.

If the war continues, Danka will find an uninvited adventurer, break his wings and bring him down to where he belongs. My fragile super-girl is defending the state. She'd be proud when I tell her this.

The day passed as usual. The second day since the war ended. It is a miracle how everything looks wonderfully calm and safe now. No more war tensions and danger.

Friday, June 11

I woke up early. Dani was sitting with privates Kosta and Aca. They discussed something. The other day he was supposed to meet with General Petrović. They were supposed to go together to Rančić, the Director of the Živača fish farm.

The 16 June - the Day of the Yugoslav Army - was approaching.

We had to secure and strengthen our combat positions.

Dani wanted a meeting with the emergency intervention unit at 12:00. Yesterday, or the day before yesterday, they fired several bullets into the air celebrating the cessation of hostilities. He was mad at them. Dani did not show up, as he went to meet Petrović; a working meeting, as politicians would say, and they would be fishing while they talked.

Personal business was more important than the unit's business. This had been the case throughout the war.

My assignment for today was to find suitable site for a new combat position, then to go to Šimanovci to take the engineers and their earth moving equipment to that site to make a new dugout and a new ambush position. Then I would go to the Medicus company in Deč.

I quickly found a suitable site, next to the canal on the dike for the flood defense. Donji Srem was intersected by drainage channels, not the irrigation channels. The scope of earth works included deepening the dike and cutting one descending ramp. Arrange the logs on top - and by God's grace it would be good position. We would be blended into the environment – like chameleons. An ideal masking that would not disturb the appearance of the environment. We had been doing this since the beginning of the war. After that I'll go home.

Tomović downloaded data on the downing of the B-2 from the Internet.

He made a copy for the unit and he also brought the 29 May 1999 issue of the Ilustrovana Politika magazine that had extensively covered the event. He was proud that he had comprehensively collated all that information.

I finished everything at around 13:00 and was at home in Belgrade by 13:30.

Danka had a sore leg and had asked the best man for her wedding to take her to the doctor before I come. He came shortly after I arrived. Of course, I would take Danka to the doctor. I thanked him and we went our separate ways.

Along the way, Danka told me about his bad fortune. We got to the doctor. I stayed in the car and I fell asleep like a baby while waiting for her. She woke me up by knocking on the door window.

We went home. Shower first, then lunch. She seemed relaxed and the pain in her leg eased. As soon as I was at home, she was fine. She told me that her neighbors would tease her about it. In the evening, her daughter Nataša went to her friend Daniela's birthday party. The two of us were left alone, aware that the war was over and that I was alive.

I talked to my sister. She had a hard time in Italy and started crying uncontrollably. If need be, I told her, send everything to hell, come home and, if necessary, sell everything and live your own life. You only live once. The kids will go their own way anyway. She interrupted me, because she had bust into tears and couldn't talk anymore. She said that in Italy, shit is eaten with a spoon. Our parents knew that and that is why they advised us not to go anywhere abroad, "You will be eternal foreigners there." They were right.

I arranged with Dani to come to the unit by 18:00 hours.

Saturday, June 12

We woke up at 05:30. Danka made her usual morning coffee. She told me that I had slept badly and had been grinding my teeth. "That was my subconscious relaxation of the psyche and nerves," I commented. Her balcony was beautiful. All in colourful flowers, the flower oasis brought up with great love and care.

I arrived in Sibač at 06:30, and Dani had already left at around 06:20. He didn't even wait for me. He also took a mobile phone that he had given me, which was on the table. He even rummaged through my bag to find an adapter. "As far as I'm concerned, he could permanently retire..." I thought to myself.

Crnobrnja also came – a man in charge of our unit's security and compliance with the "positive legal norms". The only thing he had learnt well was to keep quiet and report everyone.

After Sibač, I left for Deč to personally see how the works on the new combat position had been progressing. I gave them advice and instructions for anything that was unclear and then I went to Karlovčić for lunch. Danka should come to visit her parents too.

Nataša and Mara also came. Nataša's skin was as white as cheese. As if she hadn't been outside for the past two and a half months.

Milan and Nada had not received their pensions yet. Zdenka, a lady who was usually bringing them pensions from across the border from Croatia,[478,479,480] told them that the custom officials had confiscated the money at the border. The woman nicely told them that these were the pensions of the elderly couple who had fled Croatia, but it was in vain. Around 600 German marks, in total. Fuck the money and everything else. Health and nerves should be more important. There would be plenty of everything if the health and nerves were in order.

Before the lunch, I took Nataša, Danka and Milan to the K2 combat position location to see the anti-radar missile that had been launched on us.

Obrad, a 'naive tyle" artist, brought his painting to show it to Tepavac and me. "Be a buddy" were his crutch words, mostly without any true meaning, that gave him more time to think about what to say next. He loved the military. "After the war, every year you have to come to me, at a certain time, to hang out," he said. I promised him.

During the lunch, my pager rang, and I received an invitation for lunch at the Bačvanski's place in Prhovo. They were roasting a pig.

At around 18:30 I left Milan and Nada's place and made a courtesy stop by the Pera's place. His brother Jova was a bit tipsy. The CEO of Lifam was at lunch there too. I had a juice and went to Sibač. Bora was waiting for me.

Vida, the wife of our host Čikić, was preparing dinner: fish soup and stew. I ate fish soup but could not taste the stew.

At the village outskirt, the locals had been roasting a bull in our honor. We stayed out of respect for them. Gedža and another host organized the event. The music band from the motorized brigade was there. They announced me as a man worth two billion dollars and then sang their favourite songs. Strange but true... It seemed that everyone there wanted to greet and be around me, as if to rub off on some greatness and glory. The locals knew me. They were proud that an elite unit was in their village and that they have an opportunity to host us. I acted tired and humble, as if it was all about someone else.

I left with Mika at about 22:00. It is my shift tonight. Mika wanted to come with me, though he didn't have to. "Djole, I have to tell you some-

---

478   Cash money courier - due to the economic sanctions against FR Yugoslavia regular electronic bank transfers were cut off, which, as usually, most adversely affected the weakest in the society – pensioners.

479   Many international money transfer businesses sprung off filling in the void in this grey area of the economy, however they all charged a fee.

480   The cheapest way was to authorize someone to collate the pensions and find someone who is crossing the border anyway and ask them for a favor to courier the money (usually a friend, an acquaintance or a friend of a friend).

thing… If I had learnt anything in the military, I learnt it from you," he told me. I looked at him and patted his shoulder. We both realized the closeness that was bonding us.

It started to rain, rather heavily, and those gathered around the bonfire had to disperse. People had not been drinking or partying during the previous few months. I did not know most of them nor their personalities, which made it difficult to control how they would be releasing their accumulated internal pressure. One of the army guys took my rank insignia from my vest as memorabilia. "He shot down that plane in Karlovčić when they had been targeting us," I recalled his face. Everyone loved me as if I was someone important. That guy said that he personally knew the Odjila gipsy band, and many other bands, and that we would have a great party and feast after the war. He asked for my phone.

Mika was in charge of the technical stuff. Accompanied by the rain, we arrived at midnight in our shift. Vladica, a guy from the village, invited me to be a guest for lunch at his house tomorrow. I couldn't promise anything.

Sunday, June 13

My shift is from 00:00 to 06:00. The guidance station looks cramped, dark, and surreal, as if it hadn't been my friend and ally for the last three months. My chair is uncomfortable and itching me and I feel sleepy. God, will I ever fall asleep and rest from all this fatigue, night vigil and rush. My eyes are closing and feel like they're burning.

The tension was easing - that was more than obvious. At 01:50 an order came to go to Readiness No. 1. The Battalion on duty! On what duty and for whom?

The Russians entered Kosovo and Metohija the day before yesterday. NATO explained that that was a mistake. Russians had started charging NATO the interest for underestimating them. They took control of the military airport in Priština, the underground one. They repainted their vehicles and marked them with KFOR signs. The West had been watching in awe ever since.

Yesterday, Slavko took away the documents related to the peacetime position and the barracks. A return to peaceful way of life is expected soon. I trust that that will be another beginning. At least I hope so.

Our hosts prepared lunch for us, for the whole team.

Dani returned from home between 21:00 and 22:00. Dotlić went home. I will be on duty again from 14:00 to 22:00.

Danka is with Slavica. Nataša is at home. Since Nataša's birthday, she has been going to Daniela for a sleepover whenever I come home. That gives Danka and me some privacy.

It's been drizzling all day, an ideal time for sleep and rest. And I'm back

338

at work…

At the beginning of the war, the locals were seriously scared. Their rationale was, "They will shoot at you, and thus on us as well!"

Since then, they had been watching us, how seriously and quickly we had been working. Their attitude had changed. "Congratulations," frequent comments were heard. As the time passed, they raced over which one of them would leave a stronger impression on us; that is for now, and after the war all that will surely fall into oblivion. Past problems would be forgotten. And we would fall into oblivion too, and only sometimes we would be the topic of conversation among a few…

I found it annoying to be in the spotlight and have no desire to talk about everything that had happened. Let the dust settle on all this and let my soul find its desired peace.

I'm thinking of how some people behave and of part of the public that has been condemning the Yugoslav Army, and therefore me as an officer. In the future, if someone ever slanders something in a conversation, then I would take my girlfriend and leave.

Dani came to replace me at 22:00. I went to the camp. Stoimenov was waiting for me and said that the host, Boća, where the platoon for the decoy position was located, had invited us to dinner. And Djordje, my host, told me that he had been waiting for me to have dinner together. I explained to him that Boris and I would go to Boća to Pećinci, a few kilometers away and hoped he would not take it personally. I was not hungry. I absolutely didn't feel like eating roasted pork at this time. We went there just for courtesy.

Dimitrov and his guys no longer wanted to be on duty at the radar imitator. Private Joksa was the loudest of them. I had a feeling he was the only one talking. I made them aware not to relax and that this was the most sensitive period. "As long as the missile guidance station crew is on duty, you will be on duty as well," I told him.

Miloš Vladović told me that I've been born to be a politician. "It's just amazing how much power and authority you wield over people. You will be a General one day," he told me.

Everyone listened carefully to my presentation. I deliberately included a slight dose of open-ended criticism, "So what if we are still on duty? There is probably a reason for that."

We walked away from them. I couldn't eat. I had a fruit juice.

I couldn't fall sleep for a long time. Next to me, Boris was breathing evenly in a deep sleep.

Monday, June 14

I woke up at around 08:00.

Bora came by car and brought along Slaviša Golubović, the Commander of the Missile Battery and Darko Nikolić. They returned from training in Russia. We hugged each other as brothers. We had been talking about them while they were away, discussing and guessing the type of the air-defence system they had been training on for six weeks.

The Russians received them nicely. The Russian officers were poorly paid, as our officers, somewhere around 1,500 Rubles per month. The Russian currency was weaker than ours. They did not like Yeltsin. Younger Russian officers knew nothing about the Neva system. The older generations remembered it very well. Their military discarded its use many years ago, replacing it with few successive generations of more modern air-defence systems.[481]

Stoimenov will be in the shift from 06:00 to 12:00. I'll be from 12:00 to 18:00.

We scheduled a meeting between the command and commanders of the subordinate units for 17:00. We agreed for me to chair a separate meeting with the emergency response unit at the combat position, at the beginning of my shift. They didn't want to talk with Dani, and they were not alone in that respect. It seemed like they didn't like him at all.

All base unit commanders were notified of a meeting at 17:00 while on their equipment. We had to work hard and with dignity to the end.

Bora, Dani and I discussed on how to celebrate the Army Day, 16 June, and to whom to award the gratitude plaques. We made a list. Dani went out to make a phone call, and Bora told me that one way or another Dani will have to return the computer and all the equipment he had taken home. HIs children had played for long enough. The Sugar Factory sought back their Opel Askona car Dani had been driving, because, for them, the war is over. I told him to return it when we get back to the barracks.

Dotlić returned from home around 10:00. Dani came to the combat position. He had a haircut. He was prepared for the Army Day. I assume that he expected to receive some award, maybe a decoration.

I held a meeting with the emergency response unit and gave Tepavac guidelines for further work.

Yesterday, an F-16 engine was brought in from the village of Nakučani, located on the slopes of the Cer Mountain.

The whole unit was ordered to line up in Deč at 10:00, with no belts and weapons for the officers, and soldiers with the belts. Troops to bring their portions and cutlery. Bašić to bring the accordion, Zeka would sing. One beer per person was the allowance.

Celebration of the end of the war would be held at 16:00 on Saturday, at the restaurant Palma in Pećinci. All officers, local municipality members, local community members, village mayors, school representatives and individuals would be present.

---

481   In other words, one should go to a Russian military museum in order to see a NEVA S-125 air-defense system.

The list of awards for soldiers:

Commendations: Vlada Vasković, Zoran Zec, Rade Antić, Aleksandar Vještica, Milutin Obradović, Zoran Rajić, Nenad Danilović, Corporal Zoran Koren, Predrag Manić, Branislav Vojvodić, Ivan Kolišin, Predrag Janković, Momir Ninković, Dejan Jovanović, Željko Obradović, Zoran Katnić, Nenad Kostov, Dušan Ilić, Aleksandar Kostin, Mladen Lončar, Veljko Djikanović.

Award Leave of Absence: Dragan and Vladan Notev, Ivan Golubov, Mirko Ljubojević, Vladimir Milić, Nenad Milić, Dragan Branković, Goran Mirković, Branislav Djordjević, Igor Jevtić, Ratko Maljković, Nenad Dropulić, Aleksandar Knezević, Vladimir Joković.

The list of awards for officers and NCO's:

Commendations:

Senior Sergeant Slobodan Kilibarda; Senior Sergeant Radomir Petrović; Lieutenant Dragan Jović; Master Mechanic Milenko Golubović: driver Ranislav Lukić; Milan Barvalac, Devrnja, Miškov, Dimitrov, Cvetić, Tomović;

Award Leave of Absence:

Milan Panić and Slavko Varga.

In my opinion, the commanders of the reserve units should also be awarded.

Two TAM 150 trucks and a ZIL special truck were out of order.

Stoimenov to order Varga to recall all short barrels (guns and revolvers) and ammunition, bombs, etc. and report back.

At around 19:30, the villagers of Sibač brought a roasted pig to the combat position.

After the meeting, I remained in the office and spoke with Dotlić, Roksandić and Golubović. Golubović told us his impressions about the training course in Russia, challenges, and difficulties. They were trained for the TOR system and the guys from the mobile KUB systems were trained for the BUK system. They had left, he said, a good impression on the Russians.

When I left the position at around 21:00, Golubović followed me and told me that he was very glad that I had downed the B-2 and that he personally felt proud of it. His battery buddies must have already told him what had happened here while he was away for the past six weeks. He was also proud of Tiosav Janković, a guidance officer, whom he highly valued as a young man and a san officer. He also told me that he did not understand why Dani was treating people like that and that he had not expected that from him. I looked at him and shrugged.

Danka called me at the command post. Dani gave her the phone number after she called him on his mobile phone. I didn't like her interacting with him.

I was with our host Djordje and Boris Stoimenov until 00:30. We discussed situation in the society.

Dotlić should have ended his shift before midnight. Dani came in at around midnight and went straight to bed. He didn't go to the night shift. Dotlić would remain until 04:00. Boris should replace him from 04:00 to 11:00.

Tuesday, June 15

I woke up at around 08:30. Dotlić was still sleeping. Who knows when they finished eating the roasted pig last night. Dani left and told Kosta to tell us to organize everything, because he had a meeting at 11:00 at the Brigade Command and he didn't know when he will return. Today will be yet another day he skips his duty. I will go in the shift from 11:00 to 18:00. Dotlić will go from 18:00 to midnight, Boris after him.

Boris will go to Deč to process the mail. I will do the same tomorrow – to write an order for awards. Yesterday, after the meeting with the commanders of the basic units, Mića Mijalković and Slavko Sedlak came to talk to me. They brought mail and some order lists concerning 16 June. The financial award proposals for the officers were approved, so Slaviša Golubović will receive 2,100 dinars, Bora Crnobrnja 1,900, and Milan Panić 1,400 dinars.

I told them to go get ready and buy us a drink for the good news. The Command seems to have smoothly approved all our proposals.

Yesterday, Cvetić was ordered to withdraw all individual Strele SA-7 teams to Deč, with complete equipment. For them, at least for now, the war is over. Today, I ordered him, Jović and his driver to also move to Deč and to be with their unit and to prepare for discharge. Students should be discharged by 18 June (they served as reserve troops).

I talked to Danka. She was at work and in a bad mood. She was upset that the war found me near the place where my ex-wife lived. I had nothing to do with it, nor did it mattered, but it was hard for her to understand that it was completely irrelevant. I knew from before that she could fall over herself after some nonsense ideas, but I hate that she was not capable of rising above that primitivism I had once been surrounded by. I am sorry that I lost 16.5 years of my life in vain. But she doesn't seem to know it or doesn't want to know it. She should have been perfectly calm about it. If I wanted reconciliation, no one could have stopped me. And she knows it very well, and yet, for no reason, she is upset. I really can't help her there, even though I wish I can. The only way out of her nightmare is for her to trust me, as much as she trusts herself.

Crnobrnja said that we will have to return the cars[482] very soon and that he will go around the area and drive while he still could. My military academy classmate Roksandić came together with Bugarian to see me. He said he should visit some relatives in Ogar and take some things to them. Crnobrnja's statement instantly triggered an uncontrollable flash of thoughts in

---

482   Under the war legislation, civilian vehicles could be appropriated for the army defense purposes.

my mind: Dani went who knows where. He had gotten too close to General Bane Petrović, and maybe he took him to the ceremonial event in the Sava Center tonight, on Yugoslav Army Day.

On our way to Ogar, there was a typical Srem house with three small children, two little girls and a two-year-old son. The father has long hair, he doesn't work anywhere, he plays music in the local pubs. Everyone in the house, big and small, call my classmate Roksandić "an uncle." The house was dirty; the yard was littered, untidy and muddy. They made dinner, sliced ham and fried potatoes. We had a little bit.

After that, we left the village, which welcomed us in the best way possible since the war started. On the way back, we made a quick stop in Pećici to have a drink with Dragan, nicknamed "Tiganj" (Serbian word for skillet), before the celebration of the end of the war in the restaurant "Palma" begins.

There were some troops inside by the time we arrived. A Gipsy band played folk music. Gedža was there and he didn't allow anybody to pay for a round of drinks. However, all three of us were anti-alcoholics. He told us about his wartime experiences, what he had been doing and what he had seen during the war; how he manages in life. He finished only two grades of an elementary school. Tiganj was a typical businessman of this new time, and the stereotype for "New Money" (people who've built their wealth in the current generation). He wears thick gold necklaces and massive golden rings that show off his status. The ambience was beautiful for rural conditions. It felt so warm and intimate. At the tables next to us were a dozen reservists from the motorized brigade. They were already drunk. They enjoyed the music. They were requesting songs from the band and decorating the accordion.[483]

Wednesday, June 16

Today is the Yugoslav Army Day. It used to be on 22 December, in happier times when the Socialist Federative Republic of Yugoslavia (SFRY) existed. At around 09:00 a bus with troops and officers left for Deč.

I was in my shift from 06:00 to 09:00. Dotlić arrived to replace me because Dani had ordered it.

Neither Dotlić, Stoimenov nor I wanted to go to Deč for a celebration. As deputy commander, I had to go because it was my duty. Stoimenov and I left.

483   Decorating the accordion–is a local live band entertainment party custom. The band (that includes an accordion) leaves the stage and mingles with the seated guests who are ordering songs for the band to play "to their ears". The guests are tipping the band for the song by inserting a note (or notes) in the squeezebox of the accordion (which the accordionist skillfully opens and closes to hold the note). This coordinated action of the guest and accordionist creates an exhilarating audio-visual effect, in which all could see the note, hence the amount of the tip, and flapping of the note(s) as the bellows move forth and back. The band then moves to the next table and plays the favorite song of the guest(s) sitting there. Along the way, the amount of decoration of the accordion increases with time.

There was a festive atmosphere when we arrived. Dani gave me the list of awarded names. I had to correct a few things. I was faced again with the mistakes the Brigade HQ had made. We had recommended Dragašević, Aleksić, Slaviša Pavlović and Sead Ljajić, enlisted soldiers, and they were the only ones who did not pass "the Brigade triage" and will not be awarded. I rehearsed the ceremonial guard of honour with the troops to pay tribute to the fallen comrades and to welcome the commander.

I delivered the report to Dani so indifferently. For the first time since the war began, the troops were lined up. The officers, NCOs and soldiers were in line. Many were absent because they were on a regular daily duty. By the decree of the President of the State, Milošević, I was decorated with a war decoration. Dani read my name loudly. I read all other orders. After my name was announced, a thunderous applause from the line erupted. The line of those who were praised, awarded, and honored was enormous.

The unit participated in the competition for the best unit of the Yugoslav Armed Forces. Only the battalion that participated in the fighting in Kosovo and Metohija was ahead of us. That was fair, because their situation and conditions were probably more difficult, though each job has its own weight.

The list of awards we received from the Brigade was not done by the stipulated percentage: 15% for officers, 8% for NCOs and 3% for enlisted. Not even Tepavac was awarded. This was a great shame and injustice. I will write a complaint… unfortunately, I can only do it for soldiers, not officers. Our guests included the Mayor of the Municipality of Pećinci and Chief of Police in Pećinci, Lazarević.

We have been in Readiness No.2 for days. It was good that we had not been preparing for combat work. The army has been withdrawing from Kosovo and Metohija. We were not updated, as we have not been following the news. Dani appeared with Milošević at the reception, together with Lieutenant Sekulić. He didn't tell us anything about that. No one even asked him about it. In fact, it was the result of his attitude towards people. He deserved it for his behavior.

Thursday, June 17

After sorting the unit's mail, writing the letter of objection, and requesting the review of the awards that had just been awarded, I went home at around 13:30.

The paperwork to end Senior Sergeant   Dragan Ranković's secondment to our unit was completed and he was ready to return to his base unit[484] in Mladenovac. He will leave tomorrow. He had helped my classmate Roksandić. His personal characteristics should be written and included in his discharge documentation.

---

484   The 5th Battalion, 250th Missile Air-Defense Brigade, under the command of Lt. Col. Miroslav Noskov.
After their equipment was destroyed, he was seconded to the Author's 3rd Battalion.

Parade rank - war unit at the commander's inspection.

They had also requested us to send them an analysis of the use of SA-7. Dani and I did it very studiously. Dani took a copy because he will go fishing with Lazović and Bane Petrović and wanted to personally hand it over to them.

Dani no longer attended his shift duty, as if the battalion was not his anymore. Dotlić told me that General Bane Petrović was looking for an officer from Lazović, and Lazović offered him Dani. Bane told Lazović, "You can keep him for yourself... fuck it, I don't need him." Dani seemed to have become a disposable commodity. He screwed up a lot. He took off too high. Time will show. I asked Dotlić where he had got that info. He didn't tell me because someone interrupted us in the middle of the conversation. I did not insist on the information afterwards, nor was I really interested in it.

I had a nice time at home. Nataša was glad to see me, what a lovely child. Danka and I enjoyed a coffee for two on the balcony. It rained all night. I parked Danka's car at a better location. We talked a lot. As always, we exchanged opinions and experiences. In the morning, after coffee, I went back to the battalion. There was no more anxiety, at least not until the time interval provided for the withdrawal from Kosovo and Metohija expired. I hoped that everything would go well and that we would return to some normal peacetime living conditions.

These days, many have been coming to take pictures with the missiles and with us. The legends and characters of this war will fade out quickly. We will discharge tomorrow the Conscript Class of March 1998 soldiers (their 12 months term was extended). The conscription commenced after high school; so those who enrolled in university spend a gap year in the compulsory military service. Their farewell would be a solemn act for them, and for us. The pride or part of the pride of these people and the war unit would go on a well-deserved vacation tomorrow.

345

Danka treated us with lunch. It was a community barbecue on the lawn in front of the building complex. Ingenious butchers made a practical decision to donate to the public. There was no electricity in the city.[485] Many had lost everything in their deep freezers, especially those whose apartments were on the west side.

I can't help but to think of the sentence that Golubović said to me the other day as I was leaving the combat position: "I'm glad for the downed plane, the B-2, and that you did it." I was deeply touched by the sincerity of that man, the leader, not just the commander of the missile battery, and an honourable man. I felt comfortable. I knew that this single sentence contained all his respect for me, as a man and an officer.

Friday, June 18

I was in my shift tonight from 23:00 to 06:00. Our equipment was off. We dozed off, so the hours went by.

After a morning coffee in the camp, I went to Deč to sort out mail that had arrived. I farewelled my comrades-in-arms who were released from the war unit today. I went to a car body shop for a quote to repair scratches and dents on my Zastava 101. I will not seek another quote. The war is over and return to a peaceful way of life is approaching. I should call him on Sunday, so he can fix it in a day. The car registration expired earlier this month.

I called Danka at work and told her to buy herself everything new for tomorrow's celebration - from underwear to shoes. I wanted to spoil the woman who had been caring about my life throughout the war and, at the same time, to show everyone at tomorrow's celebration how nice and beautiful she is. What I want is to give her the status she deserves, both in society and in my life. She was overjoyed about it. The women's business... I love her a lot. She has been the voice of my conscience on many issues and will be my companion in times to come. I hope that we will be together for a long time.

What is worrying me is her pathological jealousy...

I called Milojica and said that I was looking for officers from other battalions to come to us and fully cover one shift tomorrow night, from 18:00 to 06:00 the next day, so that the complete war unit could be present at the celebration. Let none of us be in that shift.

I suggested to Dani that our wives and girlfriends come to the celebration too, as they took care of the children and cared for us during the war. We will organize transportation from the Sava Center to Sibač and back.

Thank you letters of appreciation and gratitude are to be written for all those who had helped us in our past. A special statue to be awarded to Ar-

---

485   The NATO aviation bombed key power infrastructure supplying the capital of Belgrade, causing widespread blackouts. This included targeted destruction of key transmission lines, transformer stations and switch-yards that caused long-term outages.

muš. He told me that many things he had done would not have come to his mind had I not requested him to do them, and that my ideas and solutions were ingenious. "The unit fought 80% thanks to your ideas," he told me. I took it all very calmly. He gave me a 10-packet box of the best brand of cigarettes, "Just in case," he said.

Stoimenov was on duty all day. I'll be up all night.

Tomović called me from Deč and said: "Hello, Colonel!" Nikola Marinović, a journalist from the Politika newspaper, called him and said that he had reliable data that, on 20 May at 00:23 hours, a B-2 fell near Županja, in the forests of Spačva, after it had been hit by our missiles named Tanja and Ivana. Parts of the hull and engine were found. There was irrefutable material evidence. He wanted to be the first one to convey us the good news.

All of them, from Dani onwards, can now only hate my shift crew and me. We had shot down a strategic bomber and that was completely certain. I was the only officer who was in both crews that shot down the F-117A and the B-2, so were non-commissioned officers Matić and Tiosavljević. NATO's dream had been shattered. I am overjoyed!

Fuck all the radar lures and other nonsenses they were convincing us that we had been shooting at. Justice has already been served in this case, and there will be more to come. We will obtain all the evidence and then request all the crew members to be awarded according to the law. I remembered Dani's words, "Bring the plane down and you will get the rank." What a wretch...

My son came. I gave him 100 dinars, as much as I had. Young adults always need money. He had really grown up.

Vida, the wife of our host Djordje, told me that my ex-mother-in-law Radmila was at the post office, where she worked, to ask her if it was true that we were staying with her. Vida and my ex-wife were schoolmates from primary school.

Saturday, June 19

The day of celebration in the privately owned restaurant Palma in Pećinci had arrived.

I lost the middle section from the exhaust on my Zastava 101. Mića, nicknamed Pipca, welded it for me for free, as if to a brother. No one talked about money.

Yesterday, my son Vlada told me that Vidovdan[486] was approaching and that he would like to go, with another friend, to my house in Vrdnik to celebrate our Slava. He requested the keys. I was surprised. I didn't answer anything. Who knows, maybe I would be able to go too, if the war was really

---

486   Vidovdan is a Serbian national and religious holiday, a *slava* (feast day) celebrated on 28 June (Gregorian calendar), or 15 June according to the Julian calendar.

over. Danka didn't mind. I doubted that I would give him the keys, because he didn't even know where the main water supply valve is located and how to open it, or where the electricity meter box keys were located and how to turn on the main switch I am yet to resolve this dilemma.

I arrived in Karlovčić to pick up Danka at around 15:30. She came about ten minutes before me. I took a shower and laid down to rest, but I couldn't sleep. I felt early common cold symptoms: lack of warmth and chills.

After getting ready and dressed, we arrived in Pećinci. The restaurant was full. Almost everyone was there when we arrived. I introduced Danka to guys and their wives. It was enjoyable to be Djordje Aničić with his better half last night. Everyone greeted us and came to meet Danka.

At the very beginning, Dani tried to spoil the mood. A table was reserved for the VIP guests: General Petrović; Lazarević, the chief of the local police; Bora Noskov the president of the Municipal Assembly of Pećinci; Irena-Dani's wife, and for me and Danka, and we had already agreed on the seating arrangement. Dani and I were supposed to sit with the VIP guests. When Danka and I approached the table, Dani told me that there was no room for us.

I swallowed a huge dumpling, gave him the cold shoulder and pulled up my smile in order that Danka wouldn't notice; and then we smoothly proceeded to the next table and set into a much more relaxed atmosphere with Dotlić and his wife, Stoimenov and his wife, Djole and Vida, our hosts from Sibač, Professor Milićević and another unknown couple. It quickly became apparent that the atmosphere at our table was more relaxed and natural. We laughed ourselves to tears.

According to a habit of addressing the guests and unit, Dani took the microphone and briefly informed us about what everyone already knew. For this occasion, a cake was made in the shape of an F-117A plane. Dani announced its arrival.

At that instant in time, I came up with an idea, quickly ran to the kitchen and asked soldier Kosta for an empty tray. I quickly took it with both my hands; turned around slowly and while carrying it carefully I came to Dani. He looked at me with a surprised expression on his face, then asked me with his eyes, and then loudly: "Djole, where is the cake?" I pointed to the empty tray. And then everyone started laughing themselves to tears. Yes! The cake was invisible (stealth), as was the plane we had smashed to pieces.

Dani publicly said that the Brigade Command had recognized us with three planes shot down, and that the B-2 was our hit. "That was done by my deputy, XO and his shift!" he said. The big applause cheers and whistles, and shouts of approval followed his announcement.

I met a journalist and our witness for the downed B-2. The journalist already had information about me. He took my home phone number. Cvetić cried when he hugged me. He was very emotional and in tears. He told me that I was a man worth 2.1 to 2.3 billion dollars. "Whenever I see you, I cry," he told me. Everyone wanted to take a picture with me.

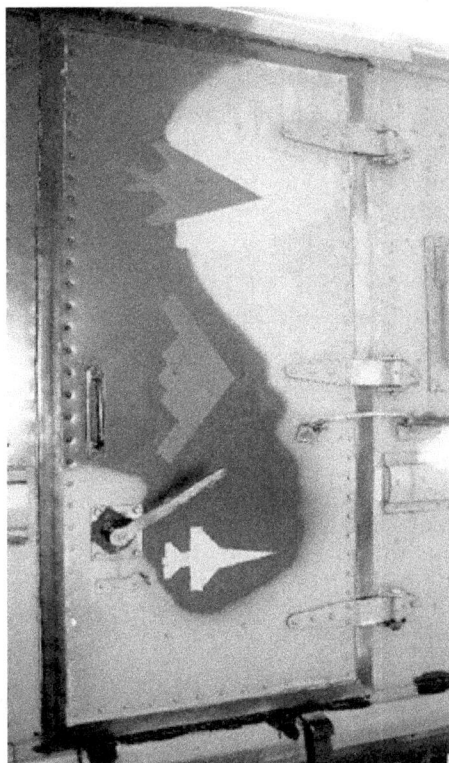
Kill marks on the missile guidance station door.

When the band played the song "My friends are fierce guys,"[487] we spontaneously started jumping with joy. We were carried away with our emotions and emerged in the lyrics in the totally relaxed atmosphere.

Srećko Morić told me: "Congratulations!"

Lazović and Stanković came a little later. Laza no longer had crutches.

I talked to General Petrović. He asked me if I was satisfied now. He referred to my decoration by the President. I told him that I was not happy. I also told him that I am glad for the B-2, and then (before I could finish the sentence) he told me: "The time was 00:23 hours when it fell near Županja,"and then explained that if he had that information earlier on, then we (my combat shift crew and I) would have been national heroes. I quickly replied to him that it was never too late for heroes.

He then commented that we could have done more. "If we could - we would," I replied.

I analysed his words thinking to myself: "I still live in the war; my sleep pattern is shattered, and I live in the pain of the system's injustice. And he told me that if he had known about the B-2 earlier on, then …. No, his words

---

487   The year 1994 song "My friends" by Bajaga (see: https://www.youtube.com/watch?v=oAEKtxAJnuY)
Momčilo Bajagić "Bajaga" is a famous Serbian rock musician.

make no sense, as after the Second World War many combatants became National Heroes; and it took up to 7-8 years after the war ended to decide on their awards. What else did I have to do to be recognized?

I challenged Lazović and Stanković with the same arguments. I saw that they had also known details of the fall of the B-2 for a while. And yet, they had all been pretending to be so sceptical and had literally made fools of the six people (my crew and me). The truth must win, no question about it, at least in my case.

Laza asked me if I had married Danka. "I didn't." "Get married, man!" Later, I found that he spoke with Danka and advised her to marry me. He was trying to set us up for marriage.

Noskov invited me to come fishing at their pond. He danced all the time next to me.

Danka often danced with a bald Colonel, a security officer from the Air Force and Air Defense command - Todor Petković. He lived in Zagreb before the Croatian breakup and danced well. Danka is a good dancer too, but I've got two left feet and cannot dance gracefully.[488]

It was an electrifying atmosphere that words cannot describe; one had to be present there in order to see, feel and experience it.

At around 01:30, we went to Karlovčić. When we were leaving the hall, everyone stood up and farewelled Danka and me with a big and long applause. It was a great token of appreciation for everything I had done for the unit and each individual.

During the celebration we did not have a shift on duty because the Brigade had not sent us the requested replacement officers for one shift. So, we had no choice but to inform them that we would be "defective" until we "fix the equipment breakdowns," our estimated completion time was 02:00.

After the celebration, Dotlić went on duty with his shift and informed the Brigade that we were operational again.

Dani loaded the leftover food and drinks in his Opel Askona and took them home.

We didn't have anything to eat for breakfast in the morning. The comments varied... Aca, his driver, said that Dani's car was a mobile warehouse...

Sunday, June 20

It was a wonderful night in Karlovčić. After a shower, we went to sleep. For the first time since being together Danka and I slept in Karlovčić, in her parents' house. Mosquito bites ruined our peaceful sleep.

488   The Serbian proverb (the Author used) for someone who dances badly is "Like Milenko in the cornfield." It means that the person's feet, body and arms work resemble that of a person manually harvesting the corn and slowly moving from one stalk to another.

We woke up at around 09:30. We had strong black coffee and then breakfast. Nada and Milan slaughtered a pig yesterday. Their neighbour Sima was helping by melting čvarci[489] in a large pot. We tried those he had just made; they were still warm, beautiful, and tasty. We also had roasted liver and meat, too.

I left around 11:30 and went directly to the equipment to replace Dotlić. Tomović was there with his wife. We took pictures next to the missile guidance station. His son was very young, about two years old, and a cute and inquisitive little toddler.

At about 17:00, Crnobrnja brought a promotion order for Captain Golubović, who is now an official Major, as well as the tracksuits for children, which Professor Milićević had promised us.

The other day, Golubović said that he had a lot of work to do and that he had to level up the terrain for a new combat position in Jakovo.[490,491,492] I met the engineer, Captain Rade Končar, who, when asked directly, told me that he had procured everything without Dani even showing up.[493] Shameful... After all, I knew from a long time ago that Dani was lying. This was not the first time... nor the last...

The other day, we had pulled back a small radar emission imitator to our equipment, and today we pulled back a big radar imitator that was paired with another small one.

Dimitrov was very worried because he was stuck in court. He had not responded in a timely manner to the mobilization call.[494,495]

489   Čvarci are a variant of pork «crisps», jokingly called "lollies" in butcher shops; made by cooking small pieces of lard until they brown-up; most of the fat melted away and was extracted in this process.

490   Which was the same as the unit's base combat position from the begining of the war.

491   In case one forgot, on the first day of the war on 24[th]March 1999, shortly after the unit had left its base combat position in Jakovo and left imitation equipment in its place, the decoy UNV fire control radar was destroyed. A bomb hit it and made a large crater in its place.

492   The real UNV fire control radar must be placed there, so it was necessary to bring the stone to fill-in the crater and level the surface.

493   Dani was supposed to do that the other day. As the commander of the unit, he was supposed to provide the stone that the engineers needed to fix the combat position in Jakovo. This included to purchase, pay and transport it to the site.

494   Dimitrov reported to the unit after the mobilization deadline, because couriers from the military department had not been able to personally deliver him the mobilization letter.

495   Later in the court, it turned out that he had not been avoiding military service and mobilization, but one of the couriers falsely informed the military department that he was not at his home address and that he was in hiding. His neighbors testified in his defense at the court. The Author didn't know exactly how many days Dimitrov was late to report for duty in the unit, but he was a very responsible man, an educator and the Principal of a high school for mechanical engineering.

The emergency response group was around us.[496] All others had been pulled back to the locations in Šimanovci and Deč.[497] Bora asked me: "Has Dani been attending his shift duty?" I told him that he hadn't been showing up on the equipment for the past 7-8 days.

It was officially announced that the bombing had stopped and that the war was over. The return of the equipment, the dismissal of people from the combat units and the return of the dispersed mobile property to the barracks were purely logistics issues.

And now, the unit will return to peacetime operation. The 3ʳᵈ Battalion relocated 22 times, engineered 11 combat positions, traveled over 100,000 km, without an accident, shot down 3 officially recognized and two still un-recognized aircraft, and preserved manpower and equipment.

The unit that had never been hit by anyone, and which had been waging the war alone for 15-20 days (all other battalions were hit and incapacitated for combat).

The unit, which knocked down two stealth aircraft:[498,499] the F-117A and the B-2.

The unit, which was targeted at least 23 times by HARM anti-radiation missiles but was never hit.

The unit, which deserve to be placed in legend (and become well known to a lot of people).

We returned to our barracks in early July.[500,501]

---

496   The unit has been located near the village of Sibač since 8 June.
497   All parts of the war unit were withdrawn to those two locations - Šimanovci and Deč. Prior to this grouping, these had been scattered over 10 locations.
498   In his view, the unit had shot three stealth aircraft, not two.
Namely, the latest confirmation that another stealth F-117 plane was hit on 30 April 1999 was published on 1ˢᵗ December 2020, on The-War-Zone page of the popular Thedrive.com website by Thomas Nedwick, *Yes, Serbian Air Defenses Did Hit Another F-117 During Operation Allied Force In 1999.*
The article referred to (the latest at the time, 24ᵗʰ November 2020) The Afterburn podcast, in which *"retired Air Force Lieutenant Colonel Charlie "Tuna" Hainline, a former F-117 pilot, confirms what had, for many years, been a rumour: that a second stealth jet was hit by the Serbians, but managed to return to base."*
Note that Thedrive.com concluded that the incident occurred on 30 April 1999, though pilot did not mention the exact date explaining the event was still classified. (See https://www.thedrive.com/the-war-zone/37894/yes-serbian-air-defenses-did-hit-another-f-117-during-operation-allied-force-in-1999?s=08)
499   Two other independent confirmations that another stealth F-117 plane was hit are described in the 30ᵗʰ April section of this diary, see the footnotes.
500   To be exact, on 4 July 1999.
501   The unit had repaired their old base combat position but did not return to it. A few days later, the 250ᵗʰ Air Defense Brigade Command ordered them to occupy

That morning, I returned from home very early. In spite of that, I found out that the unit had already gone. This time, I was not at the back of the column; as I had been each time during the war, correcting all omissions, fixing glitches, and resolving problems as they arouse.

This unexpected realisation filled me with emotions and memories, while staring at the empty lots the equipment had been parked. I was disappointed that Dani had left with the battalion without me. While there was a war and while there was a need to address and resolve all the problems, he needed me, and now that it no longer mattered if a vehicle broke down, or it stopped for some other reason, it obviously didn't matter to him anymore and he didn't need me. It was a continuation of his strategy to eliminate and remove me as the deputy commander and XO. It was not humanly just for him to leave without me. He could have called me to come from home early, but he didn't. So, I sarcastically said to myself, "In this way, Dani acknowledged me for all that I had done for him personally and the unit." I turned around and went towards Jakovo.

I arrived alone in Jakovo, 12 kg (24 lb) lighter after 78 days of war.

And just one phone call would have sufficed to bring the battalion back in the same way we went to the war. Was I right that I didn't trust him???

The plains around us looked so tranquil. Budjanovci could be seen in the distance. And what about me: was I at the beginning or at the end?

. . . .

Yes, that was the end. The end of the war and the beginning of my struggle to find such a simple answer to the simple question: "Why was I, out of all members of the combat crew that was the first one in the history of warfare to bring down a plane of immense stealth technology, the only one not to get any recognition?"

I was left to fight on another front, where the stakes would not be life itself, in an elementary sense. It will be a fight through the system, against the system and all those negative things that had transferred from society into the Armed Forces.

I was aware that my fight would surely cost me a lot, emotionally and professionally. The fight against the common belief that the Law of the Army of Yugoslavia is unidirectional and that it always applies in the direction of the subordinate. The command and superiors do not make mistakes, nor are they willing to admit their mistakes. What level of awareness would be needed to change this in practice?...

My second fight just started...

_____

the fortified base combat position previously held by the 5th Battalion that was located in the barracks in Jakovo.

Appendix

Missile Complex S-125 'Neva'/SA-3 Goa

The S-125 Neva/Pechora/SA-3 Goa Surface to Air Missile system was developed to supplement the proven S-75 Dvina/SA-2 Guideline in Soviet and Warsaw Pact service. The S-75 Dvina/SA-2 Guideline was designed to provide medium-to-high altitude air defence coverage primarily against bomber aircraft. As such, it was not well suited to the engagement of low flying targets, especially fighter aircraft and cruise missiles. The design aim of the S-125 Neva/Pechora/SA-3 Goa was to produce a system with a low-to-medium-altitude engagement envelope, providing protected airspace overlapping air defence coverage for all altitudes. Specifically, targets traveling at speeds of up to 1,500 km/h, at altitudes of 100 to 5,000 metres, at ranges of up to 12 km were to be engaged and destroyed. Such performance is today characteristic of a point defence weapon, but during the 1950s it was more typical of area defence weapons.

The Soviets sought to build on the experience gained with the S-75 Dvina/SA-2 Guideline using command link guidance and a proximity fused warhead, but recognized from the outset that a fundamentally new engagement radar design was required with much better clutter rejection performance than the workhorse RSNA/SNR-75/Fan Song series. The requirement for narrower antenna mainlobes drove the designers into the 9 GHz frequency band, well above the ~6 GHz operating range of the earlier RSNA/SNR-75/Fan Song series.

Development was initiated in 1956. The resulting weapon was more compact than the previous S-75 Dvina/SA-2 Guideline, permitting two rail launchers and use of a solid propellant sustainer, the first in air defence missile design. Canard controls were also employed. Like its predecessor, the missile used a solid rocket first-stage booster. Numerous development problems were encountered throughout the system, especially with the performance of the radio proximity fuse and command link guidance at very low altitudes. Trials of the V-600P missile and a new radar demonstrated the capability to engage targets at speeds of up to 2,000 km/h, at altitudes between 200 and 10,000 m, with the target pulling up to 4G at 5,000 to 7,000 m and up to 9 G below 1,000 m at transonic speeds. Estimated single shot hit probability was 0.82-0.99%, deteriorating to 0.49-0.88% if chaff was deployed.

Missile guidance station (left) and SNR-125 Low Blow radar.

5V27 missile on 5P73 launcher.

While the new system met the needs of air defence branch, its stow and deploy times were similar to those of the SA-2 Guideline and thus too great for the army air defence units, who rejected the design, resulting in the development of the high mobility 2K12 Kub/SA-6 Gainful system. The S-125 Neva/SA-3A Goa achieved military acceptance in 1961 and was first deployed as part of the Moscow region SAM belt.

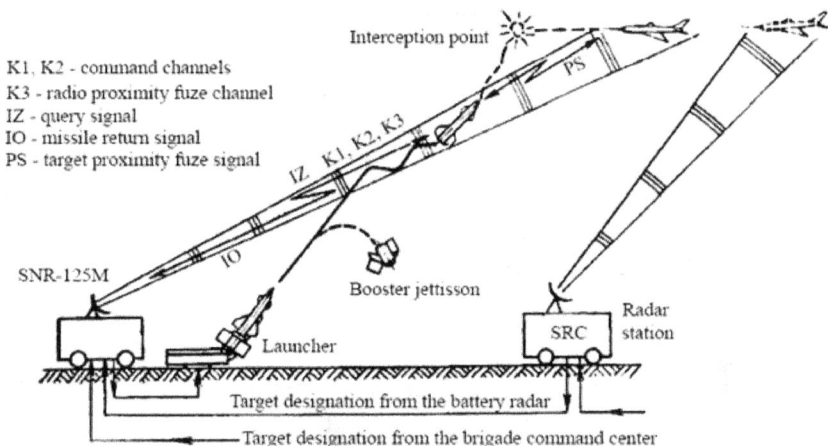

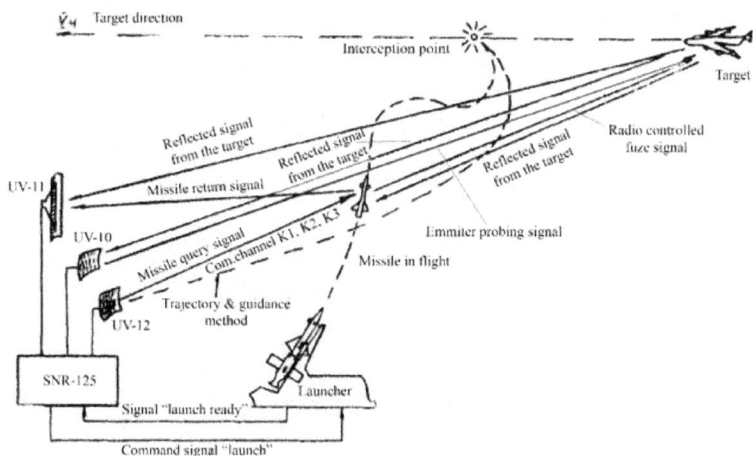

K1, K2 - command channels
K3 - radio proximity fuze channel
IZ - query signal
IO - missile return signal
PS - target proximity fuze signal

S-125 system diagram (top) and SNR-125 guidance diagram (top).

Complex SA-3 is a single-channel by target and two-channel by missile air defence missile system. The composition of its equipment allows engaging the targets in conditions of the enemy's extensive passive and active countermeasures. The complex is designed to engage strategic, tactical and naval aircraft, as well as air-based missiles in a wide range of conditions and use.

As in the previous SA-2, in the complexes of the SA-3 family, several types of target tracking methods are used:

- 'manual' by all coordinates

- 'automatic by angular coordinates and hand-by-range

- 'automatic' (by all coordinates)

In the case of electronic countermeasures and jamming, the 'manual' mode by angular coordinates applies (with the guiding to the 'center' of the source) with the setting of a distance mark on the far edge of the affected area. The missile radar guidance is conducted by signal of onboard radio transmitter only in automatic mode on all coordinates.

All equipment is mounted on trailers, semi-trailers and on towed wheeled chassis, which made it possible to deploy to full combat readiness in virtually any conditions. A typical deployment area for battalion level might be 200 x 200 m2 with low-rise protection berms around.

The basic tactical unit is a battalion; in the Soviet classification, 'divizion'. Missile components are assigned to the 'battery'. Typical battery composition is a single SNR-125 Low Blow series engagement radar, four dual rail 5P71 or four dual rail 5P73 launchers, and multiple PR-14 series dual round transporter/loader trucks carrying reserve missiles. Most SA-3 operators deploy the system at fixed sites, with revetments using concreted pads and bays, and/or earthwork berms, for protection. The basic SA-3 Goa qualifies as semi-mobile system, requiring several hours to deploy. A prepared peacetime position for the SNR-125 missile guidance station (Stanitsa Navedenya Raket) is a semi-buried reinforced concrete structure or fully underground bunker with an additional dirt cover. This type of building provides additional facilities for the battalion command post, as well as a room for on-duty combat crew, and a classroom which can also be used as a shelter for communication and power supply unit staff. The premises is equipped with a filter and ventilation system. Protection against chemical attack and gas is provided too.

Missile launchers at the prepared positions are located in semi-ring embankments, usually with the concrete slabs facing the battalion's designated responsibility sector. The launchers may be covered with camouflage nets. Field conditions require solid ground beneath the launchers and gravel is often used

N7 reinforced concrete structures were built to store 8-16 missiles, which included working space for the personnel of the preparation unit. On the structure roof, a visual observation post (PVN as per Russian abbreviation)

was usually built, where anti-aircraft machine guns or shoulder launched missile systems were located. In special conditions, for example in the absence of building materials or suitable sites, it was allowed to store a set of missiles in N1 packs in an open position.

UNK (fire control center) equipment is installed in the cabin, mounted on the semi-trailer OAZAZ-828 equipped with a filtration unit. To ensure acceptable conditions for combat operations and carrying out combat duty on the unprepared position, a van may be equipped with an air conditioning unit and electric space heaters.

It is important to say that the potential opponent in most cases is aware of the prepared position and in war these prepared positions are the first to be attacked.

SNR-125 'Low Blow' Fire Control and Engagement Radar

The main purpose of the S-125 air defence system – engagement of low and medium altitude targets – determined the construction requirements of the radar antenna system and the configuration of the antenna post UNV.

UV-10 antenna is used to search and illuminate the targets. During target acquisition, pencil radar beams (3 cm wavelength narrow radar beam) scan the space in the sector 1-1.5 degrees by azimuth and 10 degrees by angle vertically. The antenna emits a bundle of probing electromagnetic pulses from the transmitter, and reflected signals from the aerial target are received for processing. The transmitter/receiver switch provides protection for the receiver from the powerful signal of the transmitter during its operation. The antenna is controlled from the UNK cabin and can scan by azimuth without restriction and by elevation from -5 to +79 degrees. It is possible to search for targets in almost the entire upper hemisphere.

When conducting autonomous combat operations, automatic aerial target searching mode is provided:

- Radial survey (Krugovoi Obzor) – rotation of the antenna post 360 degrees in 20 seconds

- Small sector search (Malii Sektornii Poisk) – scan sector 5-7 degrees by azimuth with change in manual mode, position of antennas in elevation angle

- large sector search (Bolshoi Sektornii Poisk) – scan sector 20 degrees by azimuth with the possibility of adjusting the amplitude of the azimuth change to the small sector search mode.

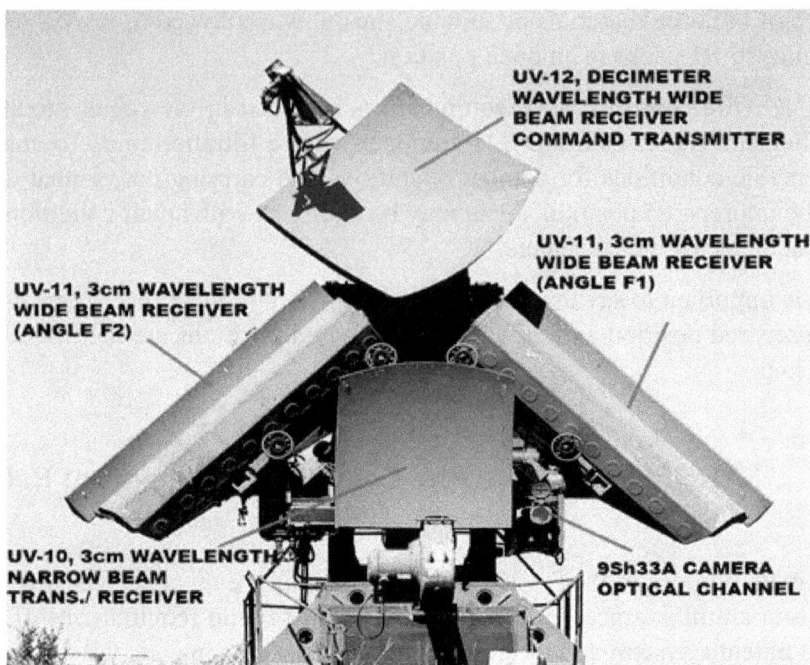

SNR-125 Low Blow antennas with frequencies bands.

5V24 and 5V27 Surface-to-Air Guided Missiles

The 5V24 (V-600P) missile is a two-stage solid fuel guided rocket (Figure 4-6 top). The first stage of the rocket is a booster with a solid propellant engine, PRD-36 (military designation 5S45), developed in KB-2 of plant N81 under the leadership of II. Kartukov. The PRD-36 is equipped with fourteen single-channel cylindrical gunpowder pens, type NMF-3K, with a diameter of 134 mm and a length of 1,180 mm. The total mass of the engine charge, which received the index 5B84, is 280-281 kg. The maximum operating time for the booster is four seconds. The booster is equipped with an igniter 5B94. The nozzle of the starting engine is equipped with a 'pear', which enabled regulating the critical section depending on the ambient temperature. Each console of the rectangular fin stabilizer is fixed with a hinge on the front frame of the tail section. During ground operation, the longer side of the stabilizer adjoins the cylindrical surface of the starting motor housing.

During blast off the screed which secures the stabilizer arms is cut with a special knife under the action of inertial forces and the fins turn more than 90 degrees, joining the outer surface of the tail section of the booster in the form of a cone. The slowdown of the stabilizer's console before contact with the surface of the tail section is provided by the use of a brake piston device, as well as a collapsible pin fixed to the stabilizer console. The extreme rear flight position of the consoles provided a high degree of static stability of the spent launch vehicle after separation from the marching stage, which led to an undesirable expansion of the danger zone of the fall of the starting stage. In subsequent versions of the missile, measures were taken to eliminate this shortcoming.

Missile in the transport container.

In the 1960s and 1970s a few derivatives of the 5V24 SAM were developed, including the 5V27, 5V270, etc, which were much more effective than the basic version. The 5V24 and 5V27 SAMs are two-stage rockets featuring canard configuration. The missile is fired from an inclined position. Its launcher is aimed in azimuth and elevation. In flight, the missile is controlled and guided towards the target via radio commands sent by a ground-based (shipborne) guidance station. The warhead is activated at a certain distance from the target by a command generated by the electronic fuse or sent by the ground-based guidance station. The first stage of the 5V24 SAM is essentially a solid-fuel booster fitted with four stabilizing fins which unfold after the missile is launched, and two braking surfaces (fitted to later models) designed to shorten the booster flight path after separation. The sustainer stages of the 5V24 and 5V27 SAMs consist of compartments containing the electronic fuse, control surface actuators, an HE fragmentation warhead, airborne equipment, a solid-propellant rocket motor and the control command receivers.

The SAM's flight control system elements include four aerodynamic control surfaces located in the tail section of the sustainers and the ailerons fitted to the sustainers' wings. The ailerons are used in the launch phase.

The response time of the missile self-destruction device is set to 26 seconds after the launch, after which the missile is destroyed if it has not already detonated. The length of the V-600P missile is 6.09 m, the starting mass 912 kg. The diameter of the hull of the flight stage is 0.375 m, the diameter of the booster is 0.55 m.

The S-125 surveillance radar stations P-12 (P-12NM) or P-15 Trail (Flat Face according to NATO codification) are equipped with autonomous diesel power stations for the installation of antennas on the automobile chassis. To increase the range of targets detection at low altitudes the P-15 station is equipped with an additional antenna on the mast device 'Unzha' (P-15 with antenna placement on the mast device (Squat Eye)).

The complex uses ground-based radio friend/foe checker 'Silicon-2M' and 'Password-1'. Usually in combat positions at the prepared locations, the hardware vans and diesel-electric power stations of the surveillance radar stations are located in concrete engineered structures.

5V27D blasting off from the launching platform.

For the purposes of training the operators, as well as the guidance officers, combat simulator 'Accord' is assigned to the S-75 and S-125 systems, typically one set for four battalions. The combat simulator is placed in the semi-trailer OdAZ-828.

"With regard to President Clinton's third objective — deflating Serb military capabilities — Milosevic's forces, particularly the land forces that are the bedrock of his military strength, remain intact. NATO's operational and tactical defeat."

Dr. E.Tilford[502]

The Yugoslav Air Defence System survived the NATO air campaign to force the removal of Serbian forces from Kosovo, which ran from 24 March to 9 June 1999 and at its height involved over 1,000 aircraft. Survival of the IADS was achieved by employing three different methods to negate NATO's air power. The NATO decision not to use ground forces certainly made Serb defensive measures much easier. By deliberately not employing all their defence assets at once, known as the strategy of withholding military force, the Yugoslavs could move their mobile surface-to-air missiles about to ensure they could not be targeted.

A defending ground force needs to be forced to expose itself, thus allowing it to be attacked by air power. A major lesson NATO learned was that an opposing force must be driven out from cover. One option is to stage an attack that is designed to compel a defending force to react. To enable air power to hunt down and destroy targets requires robust Intelligence, Surveillance and Reconnaissance (ISR) systems and Precision Guided Munitions (PGM). Terrain masking and deception measures by small forces in complex terrain, such as hilly and/or jungle terrain, as occurred in Kosovo and in the various conflicts in South East Asia, often negate the use of ISR systems, presenting difficulties in locating and positively identifying targets.

The aim of Operation Allied Force was 'to stop Serbian forces attacking' ethnic Albanians and eject them from Kosovo through the application of air power alone. This was to reduce casualties on the NATO side, but it made life for the Serbian forces in Kosovo easier as there were no ground troops to worry about, except KLA separatists and a few NATO special forces either fighting with the KLA or independently. By withholding military force the Serbs avoided having their air defence and field units being destroyed in the first days of the air campaign. They had absorbed the lessons of Operation Desert Storm and preserved their assets for the long haul. This was a successful strategy: Serb forces were still firing surface-to-air missiles on the last day of Operation Allied Force. Employing passive systems such as elec-

---

502   Operation Allied Force and the Role of Air Power.
https://press.armywarcollege.edu/parameters/vol29/iss4/10/

tro-optical tracking equipment further enhanced the survivability of IADS components, by not creating an emission signature that NATO defence suppression aircraft could lock on to.

Bad weather and the 'rigid' insistence on avoiding collateral damage and casualties to the attack force dogged NATO planners. It led to an over-reliance on Precision Guided Munitions (PGMs). In the first three weeks of Allied Force there were only seven days of favourable weather for air operations and ten days on which fifty per cent of the strikes had to be canceled for fear of collateral damage.

Ninety per cent of the ordnance dropped was PGMs which had their own problems. GPS-aided munitions, the only affordable all-weather munitions, can be inaccurate due to the cumulative effect of numerous errors, as well as small inaccuracies in the targeting aircraft, maps and the munition itself. This is called the 'sensor-to-shooter error budget' in US parlance. Further, the amount of cloud over Kosovo caused many laser-guided bombs (LGBs) to 'lose lock' and 'go rogue' often landing kilometres away from their intended target or hitting civilian targets.

The reliance on GPS guided bombs caused a shortage that became so acute in late April that the GPS guided Joint Direct Attack Munitions (JDAM) were available for only the B-2A Spirit bomber. By late April the ratio of PGMs to unguided munitions used had dropped to 69 per cent. Many of the targets struck by PGMs in Kosovo were not judged to be worth the cost of US$12,000 per Paveway II bomb kit (the price tag at the time), and could have been hit safely by unguided ordnance. The fire control avionics fitted to most NATO aircraft enabled very accurate bombing using 'dumb' bombs, albeit with a necessary reduction in bombing altitude.

Serbian ground forces were hard to locate due to their small unit size and movement, generally being company-sized units of 80 to 150 personnel and around six armoured vehicles, operating autonomously or semi-autonomously of each other. Using the woods and mountains, and by not being a large target or moving in a set direction, prevented the building up of an intelligence picture and thus made these forces difficult to locate from the air.

The air campaign over Kosovo severely affected the readiness rates of the USAF's Air Combat Command during that period. Units in the United States were the most badly affected, as they were stripped of their personnel and spare parts to support ACC (Air Combat Command) and AMC (Air Mobility Command) units involved in Operation Allied Force. The Commander of the USAF's Air Combat Command, General Richard Hawley, outlined this in a speech to reporters on 29 April 1999. Further, aircraft would have to be replaced earlier than previously planned, PGM inventories would need to be restocked, and the war-stock of AGM-86C Conventional Air-Launched Cruise Missiles dropped to 100 rounds or fewer. Of the more than 25,000 bombs and missiles expended, nearly 8,500 were PGMs, with the replacement cost estimated at $US1.3 billion.

Thus the USAF suffered from virtual attrition of its air force without having scored a large number of kills in theatre. Even if the US's best estimates of Serbian casualties are used, the Serbians left Kosovo with a large part of their armoured forces intact.

Successful Deception Measures

Sun Tzu wrote that all warfare is based on deception. Serbian deception measures were very successful. Decoys were a real problem for strike aircraft, as loitering over an area at low altitude made them targets for MAN-PADS, infrared guided point defence SAMs such as the SA-9 Gaskin and SA-13 Gopher, and SPAAGs such as the BOV-3/30 series and the Praga M53/59. Hundreds of decoys were hit that were thought to be real targets. Some decoys were hit multiple times. Pilots would not loiter over them trying to discriminate between them and real targets. Air forces have not always invested sufficiently in sensors to counter deception and camouflage techniques, and the Serbs exploited this quite successfully; this was noted in the post-Allied Force after-action study.

NATO flew approximately 30,000 sorties during the war, and just under 2,000 of these saw ordnance expended. These sorties were claimed at the time to have destroyed 93 tanks and 153 armoured personnel carriers (APCs) out of the approximately 350 tanks and 440 APCs believed to have been in Kosovo. NATO also claimed to have hit 339 military vehicles and 389 artillery pieces and mortars. These figures were wide of the mark, as General Clark, the Operation Allied Force commander, agreed, conceding that not all targets hit were destroyed, and that only twenty-six vehicles could be confirmed as kills.

In a *New York Times* article, there was an interesting view immediately after the war[503]:

> *Towards the end of the Balkans air war, rarely a day passed when NATO did not triumphantly declare that allied warplanes had destroyed several more Yugoslav tanks or artil-*

503   Eric Schmidt, 'The World; Bombs Are Smart, People Are Smarter', *New York Times*, 4 July 1999.

lery pieces with precision-guided bombs or missiles.

Now it turns out that a significant fraction of those weapons that looked fearsome from 15,000 feet up may have been nothing more than artfully designed decoys meant to fool allied pilots. Indeed, the Serb military, outgunned by a technologically superior foe, proved to be a master of camouflage, concealment and deception. Yugoslav commanders built 'tanks 'of wood and plastic sheeting, sometimes draping them with camouflage netting. To trick thermal sensors, they put metal tape or plates on some decoys and even set trays of water inside them that heated up in the sun, just like a real tank would.

Some suspected artillery revetments turned out to be disguised pits, empty but for a long tube protruding towards the sky. And to the dismay of the NATO air commanders, several Yugoslav MIG-21 fighter jets emerged from hidden caves once the war was over.

Of course, the air campaign's overall results were still devastating and no doubt instrumental in forcing the Yugoslav President Slobodan Milosevic to cry uncle and withdraw his forces from Kosovo.

But the phony targets have become a sore point with NATO's military commander, General Wesley K. Clark, who now says the alliance destroyed only 110 of the roughly 300 tanks that Yugoslavia poured into Kosovo, not the 150 tanks NATO initially thought it blasted into scrap.

'For the most part, our pilots recognized those decoys,' General Clark bristled last week. 'There is a concerted disinformation campaign underway by the Government of Yugoslavia to protect the reputation of its armed forces and to diminish the reputation of NATO's air power campaign.'

Yet one of the emerging lessons from the air war is that low-technology countermeasures can still fool high-technology weaponry and sensors enough of the time to make a difference. 'The history of warfare suggests there are always countermeasures, and human ingenuity will find its way,' said Eliot A. Cohen, a professor at Johns Hopkins who directed the Air Force's definitive study of the 1991 Persian Gulf war.

'One of the big surprises was the extent to which the Yugoslav military was able to use ground decoys to cause us to strike targets that weren't real,' said one senior Defense Department official.

Serbian techniques included constructing false bridges, fake artillery pieces made of long telephone poles painted black with old truck wheels, anti-aircraft missile launchers constructed of old milk cartons, wooden mock-ups of MIG-29 aircraft, self-propelled artillery vehicles constructed on old vehicle shells and chassis from the scrapyards, radar reflectors and special camouflage nets (developed by one of the authors) around the real military equipment, extensive use of field camouflage, to name but a few. Some of the ingenious deceptions included cow manure in combination with metal plates to attract NATO thermal guided missiles. Manure naturally radiates heat similar to the heat radiation signature of a tank engine. Real tank engines were often covered with mattresses soaked with water to lower the thermal radiation. One of the authors designed thermal sleeves for artillery and tank cannons to prevent thermal emission detection after firing. To quote a NATO officer who performed field assessments after the war: 'Our guys in Kosovo have found hundreds of imitation tanks, trucks, artillery pieces, missiles and missile launchers, roads and even bridges that NATO aircraft and cruise missiles had "destroyed". From up close they look like junk, but from three miles up, they'd look like the real thing.'

Missiles made from sheet metal used as a decoy on the fake combat position. Hitting these fake targets, NATO considered that as a successful mission.

In particular, radar imitators played a crucial role in the survival of the missile battalions, and in cooperation with fire control radar emission successfully defended the missile battalion when under attack. In today's air defence, radar imitators are standard issue for every missile battalion. Russian battalions may use six or more imitators per unit.

20/3 anti-aircraft artillery (front) and radar (in the background) decoys.

Fire control radar imitator - Anti-radiation missile decoy system - very effective way to "confuse" the anti-radiation missile guidance system.

Fixed Air Defenses Damaged but Mobile Air Defenses Survived

NATO air planners were certainly concerned that not as many Serbian SAM batteries were destroyed as they would have liked, with the then commander of the USAF in Europe acknowledging the success of Serbian SAM battery shoot-and-scoot operational tactics.

Mobile systems suffered few casualties, but the fixed defences were badly damaged. Two of Serbia's three static S-75 Dvina/SA-2 Guideline SAM battalions and seventy per cent of their static S-125 Neva/SA-3 Goa SAM sites were hit and most taken out of action. Some of the systems were damaged but repaired after. Only three mobile 9M9 Kvadrat/SA-6 Gainful SAM systems were hit and damaged.

Serbia certainly left Kosovo and suffered a tremendous amount of damage to its infrastructure in Serbia, but Serbian combat power remained substantially intact. Even if the Milosevic regime did not achieve its political objectives Serbia retained its ground combat strength in the face of overwhelming air power, and the Kosovo Liberation Army was 'disarmed' as part of the political settlement.

Opponents

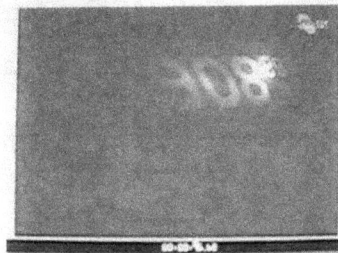

Lieutenant Colonel Dale Zelko, pilot of the downed F-117A

Lieutenant Colonel Todd Flesch. his F-117A was damaged and scrapped.

Lieutenant Colonel (later General) David Goldfein. Pilot of the downed F-16CG.

Alleged "big target" that crashed in Croatia "Spirit of Missouri". USAF still didn't confirm any loss.
It took 20 years to confirm the loss of second F-117A...

Sea harrier allegedly damaged but managed to get to the carrier but the pilot was force to eject...

F-117A wing on the permanent exhibition in the Belgrade Aeronautical Museum

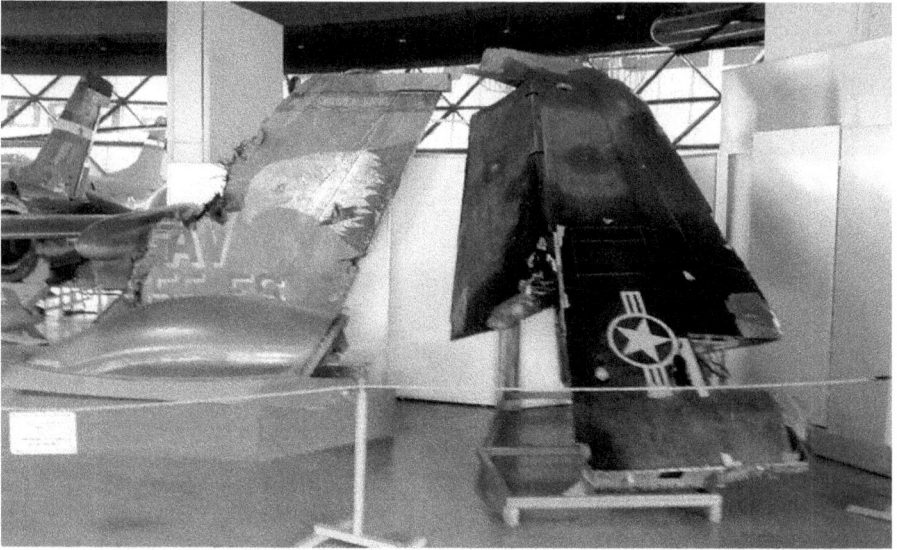

Belgrade Aeronautical Museum exhibition – F-16CG and F-117A parts.

www.ingramcontent.com/pod-product-compliance
Lightning Source LLC
Chambersburg PA
CBHW060451090426
42735CB00011B/1966